RUPERT MURDOCH

RUPERT MURDOCH

The Untold Story of
the World's Greatest Media Wizard

NEIL CHENOWETH

CROWN
BUSINESS
NEW YORK

Published by Crown Business, New York, New York.
Member of the Crown Publishing Group, a division of Random House, Inc.
www.randomhouse.com

Originally published in Great Britain as *Virtual Murdoch* by Secker & Warburg, London, in 2001.

CROWN BUSINESS is a trademark and the Rising Sun colophon is a registered trademark of Random House, Inc.

Printed in the United States of America

Design by Leonard Henderson

Library of Congress Cataloging-in-Publication Data
Chenoweth, Neil.
    Rupert Murdoch : the untold story of the world's greatest media wizard / Neil Chenoweth.— 1st ed.
    1. Murdoch, Rupert, 1931–   2. Mass media—Australia—Biography.   I. Title.
P92.5.M87 C48   2002
070'.092—dc21
  [B]   2002019397

ISBN 0-609-61038-4

10 9 8 7 6 5 4 3 2 1

First American Edition

For Joe . . . slayer of dragons, part-time visionary,
fairest of traveling companions

CONTENTS

Author's Note   ix

Introduction   xi

PART I — MANHATTAN STINGER 1

1   A BUSINESS OF FERRETS 3

The mayor's pest problem distracts, as a dynasty derails in Detroit.

2   A MUDDLE OF MOGULS 14

General Motors remains entirely motionless.

PART II — ATLANTIC CROSSING 31

3   VOLTAIRE'S UNDERGRADUATE 33

Young Rupert Murdoch considers the consolations of philosophy, while his party goes swimmingly.

4   THE DRUNKEN SAILOR 48

Ted Turner, Rupert Murdoch, and the intercontinental consequences of riotous success.

5   THE PARTY LINE 70

In which Rupert Murdoch finds salvation at a New York soirée.

6   THE FUGITIVE 87

The man who keeps News Corporation's secrets has to run.

7   THE PRETENDERS 106

Anna Murdoch muses on sex and the summer while the family talks money.

PART III — AMERICAN JIHAD 117

8   LOST IN SPACE 119

Rupert Murdoch and John Malone hurtle round each other.

9   HERB ALLEN'S PORCH 132

The Masters of the Universe do brunch, and Ron Perelman thinks he is the clever one.

10 THE APPLE FUMBLE 153

How Gerry Levin and Ted Turner foiled the Second Coming.

11 WIRED 172

The High Court learns that someone has been listening on the telephone.

12 THE POKER PLAYER 183

Rupert Murdoch declares war on everybody.

13 DIVIDED ROYALTIES 199

Newt Gingrich discovers that friendship has no price.

14 THE TESTING OF PAT 223

Televangelists, diamond mining in Zaire, and the perfect children's program.

15 MAN FOR ALL SEASONS 242

Midnight mishaps by footballers, baseball clubs, and a large polo player.

16 THE MOUSE WARS 259

Michael Eisner sets a trap.

PART IV — MURDOCH'S ARCHIPELAGO 279

17 THE TROUBLE WITH TONY 281

The prime minister regrets picking up the telephone.

18 RUPERT'S ROCKET 304

The Murdochs take some collateral damage but reach escape velocity.

19 THE MANHATTAN WINDOW 330

In which a global media baron discovers he has a second chance.

Postscript: The Other Side of Tuesday   343
Chronology   360
Notes   366
Bibliography   386
Acknowledgments   389
Index   390

AUTHOR'S NOTE

THIS BOOK WAS TRIGGERED by a telephone call I received in February 1997. The caller was brief and anonymous. He said that if I was interested in following Rupert Murdoch's media empire, the News Corporation, I should look up a court judgment days earlier in the High Court in London. The case was about an American-Israeli financier who once ran the most secret arm of News Corporation. The remarkable thing was that he was on the run while he did it, ducking an outstanding arrest warrant on fraud charges in New York while he flitted around the world on Murdoch's business. Now Murdoch's private security agents were pursuing him. The judge in London was talking about wiretapping.

Where was this going? I had been covering the News Corporation for almost a decade. Deciphering Murdoch, I knew, was like doing a cryptic crossword puzzle. In such a pursuit one thing is clear: You need to put your own personal history clearly on the table.

I almost worked for Rupert Murdoch. For ten minutes I regarded myself as virtually on the staff. Ten minutes isn't a long time if you're running a worldwide media empire, but it does tend to drag a bit when you're waiting to get a job. In February 1988, after returning to Australia impoverished from the Middle East, I went looking for a job at my old paper, the Brisbane *Telegraph*. If the *Telegraph* editors had a life ambition, it was to wrap a higher-quality piece of seafood. But I was broke. And they had promised they would always have a job for me. Newspapers always say that. They can't help themselves.

It would be wrong to say that they laughed when I arrived to make my little pitch. My former colleagues held their heaving sides and actually rolled on the floor, howling all the while. You may not have seen a large number of journalists beside themselves with mirth. It's not picturesque. Every few minutes one of them would muster enough strength to stop laughing for a moment and try to tell me why my job request was so intensely amusing. But then a new spasm of mirth would convulse them, and the contortions and gargling would resume. Ten minutes later the editor entered the newsroom to announce formally what they had been trying to tell me: that the new owner, Rupert Murdoch, was closing the *Telegraph* that day. He wished us luck finding another position.

Rupert Murdoch had saved me from the fish-wrappers, and as I wandered off into the wilds of television and magazines, I was mildly grateful. My journalistic pursuit of his empire has not been animated by rancor. Actually my interest in Murdoch began with a really bad career decision. I blame the whole catastrophe on Martin Peers.

Peers is a media writer with the *Wall Street Journal.* At least he is today, but in 1990 he worked in Sydney for the *Australian Financial Review.* The first time I came across him, he managed to spoil an entirely drinkable cup of coffee. By then I was Brisbane correspondent for a magazine called *Australian Business.* In my experience, working as a correspondent fosters—actually, it requires—a natural tendency to indolence and a vast feeling of self-satisfaction. So it was really very annoying, one morning in April 1990 as I sat back to drink a cup of coffee and scan the morning papers, to read a disgracefully good story that Peers had written about a mysterious stock deal by Rupert Murdoch's family company. The deal involved the company that published the Brisbane *Telegraph.*

It was outrageous. I was the local correspondent, the living authority on the northeastern quarter of Australia. And Peers, a big-shot out-of-town journalist, had sniffed out this fascinating story without even leaving Sydney. It was almost too much to bear. Not the least of my complaints was that in the course of reading this story, my revolting instant coffee had grown first tepid, then cold.

Twelve months later my attempts to follow up Peers's story had triggered an inquiry by the Australian Securities Commission (ASC) into the Murdoch family companies. The ASC was talking about reversing a secret 1987 stock deal and sending Murdoch into bankruptcy. For me, this spelled professional calamity. In a country where Rupert Murdoch owns 70 percent of all the newspapers, starting something like this is so dumb, it goes off the scale. You have to consider whole new classifications of Stupid. Of course, by then there was not a lot left to lose. I became a Murdoch watcher because Rupert Murdoch was always the best story in town.

Martin Peers owes me another cup of coffee.

INTRODUCTION

S TRONG MEN and hedge fund managers don't cry. So when the stock market fell apart in the summer of 2001, there were no public displays of grief. Western civilization might have been tottering, but that was no reason for clamor in the streets. The market had been falling apart for eighteen months now, a slow, remorseless slide to disaster, so they were starting to get used to it. The philosophers on Wall Street were not without resources. One of the comforts of life in the twenty-first century is that you need never be surprised when calamity overtakes you. That's why God made Hollywood. Filmmakers have always shown us that no matter how grim and nasty the present may seem, the future can always get worse. Tell me how the world ends, and three West Coast screenwriters have already shopped the film outline. So in August 2001, when stock prices fell into another sickening death spiral that threatened the end of life as we know it, it was only natural to look to Hollywood to understand just what had happened.

Hollywood doesn't explain calamity to us—it just shows us how we feel about it. One of the Hollywood's most vivid images is the purge scene from the *Alien* movies, the series of science fiction films that have made so much money for Rupert Murdoch's 20th Century–Fox. The scene is so compelling that three of these films, whether the director is Ridley Scott or James Cameron or Jean-Pierre Jeunet, all return to it as their final climax. After ninety minutes of celluloid horrors, Sigourney Weaver as Warrant Officer Ripley is out of options. She is trapped in a spacecraft (again), losing the battle against the nasty green monster. With a last desperate effort, she opens the airlock door. The camera shot dissolves in a storm of flying debris. Everything in the spacecraft that is not tied down is being sucked toward the hole. Weaver, the alien, and anyone else who is still alive cling desperately to handholds, fighting the force that is drawing them remorselessly toward the void. Oblivion beckons. Slowly their handholds start to slip . . .

It's a simple moral: Survivors rule. In the fall of 2001 American investors were experiencing their own Sigourney Weaver moment. There was no oxygen. The collapse of the technology stock bubble had caused a massive implosion on financial markets. In eighteen months $4.3 trillion had hemorrhaged out of the system, a disaster in stock valuations that would affect, directly or indirectly, the jobs and the retirement plans of every American. It wasn't just that the world's great love affair with tech stocks was over. In its place, as the economy slowed, an ugly antitechnology sentiment was stalking Wall Street and the community at large. Investors looked at the wreckage of the tech giants, shook their heads, and asked, "What were we thinking?" A generation of new-media and technology start-up companies had already been consigned to the void, and still the evacuation continued. The survivors—mostly old-media and telecom companies—faced the worst advertising conditions in a decade. They had put their ambitious growth plans on hold for the next year. This was a time to sit tight and hang on. If there was a symbol for technology stocks and media companies in August 2001, it was a row of white knuckles.

This was the bitter legacy of the technological revolution. If the last two decades have shown anything, it is that technology regularly delivers exactly the reverse of what it promises. In the 1980s it promised the paperless office—and the forests are still being denuded to supply it. It promised us five hundred channels of television—and there is nothing to watch. Technology applied to stock trading gave us derivatives, the rocket-science trading instruments that were supposed to take the risk out of the marketplace—and in practice they magnified market risk a thousand times. In the military, technology promised the West security and bloodless victory—and it gave us body bags. But most of all, with the Internet and the information revolution, technology promised us media diversity, a profusion of voices, and endless freedom of choice. Instead there will be fewer media players, even fewer voices. When the airlock door closed again, the world would belong to the survivors, to the old-media giants who had managed to transform their iron grip on our past into a monopoly on our future.

Rupert Murdoch was there holding on desperately with the rest of them, as the financial decompression continued through July and August 2001. After three decades living in the United States, he had lost much of his accent, though under pressure he still showed the Australian habit of packing an extra five vowels into every second word. After half a century of wagering the News Corporation against impossible odds, Murdoch's empire was now more vulnerable than ever. Which placed him closer to the airlock door than most of the other media moguls stretched out beside him. It's the same Ridley Scott scene: a group of survivors holding grimly on, the only sound the swirl of air still escaping through the hole in the spacecraft, as the fingers of one of the figures is slowly slipping . . . No, they're not slipping. Rupert Murdoch has let go with one hand, so that he can look at his watch. He's looking around, then he's pulling out his cell phone. In the middle of a disaster movie, Murdoch is negotiating the biggest deal of his life. He is intent on a gamble that will give him control of the second-largest media empire in the world, one that will change the way that most of the world communicates. It's not that he isn't worried about the market meltdown that's threatening the great media companies. It's the nature of the man. He's a survivor. He is focused on what happens next. He's seventy years old, and he's been holding on all of his life.

*   *   *

The really awkward thing about Rupert Murdoch is that everybody in the media has their own story about him. They met him in a lobby once, or in the elevator, or at a dinner. Or they know someone else who has. He's so out of the frame, so unlike what you would expect. He's the most powerful media mogul in the world, and he's talking about vitamins—*vitamins*—and his calorie intake. He's walking down the corridor flanked by his senior executives, and he's the one who stops to ask the guy washing the floor what he's doing with the mop and bucket. And he's fidgeting. He's listening to you, but you know he's having at least a dozen mental conversations of his own at the same time. You're talking to a butterfly mind that still manages a bewildering command of detail. The humor, which shows when he's sneaking up on you, is deadpan and terrifyingly funny. Or just plain terrifying. The man is interested in everything and nothing. He makes you feel like he's your best friend. He's a monster that News Corporation execs have nightmares about. He remembers personal details about people forever. He will never forget to ask about the report that you promised in a ten-second conversation three months ago. What was your name again? He goes back to South Australia every year to have a cup of tea with his oldest shareholders. He uses people, then dumps them. He sacked News Corp's chairman, Richard Searby, his friend for forty years, by letter. He is endlessly persuasive. He never stops moving forward. He's a social disaster—the man has no damn small talk. He finds your emotional button and pushes it. He wore Puma trainers to his daughter's wedding. He has rotten taste in socks.

It's an anonymity by ubiquity. Rupert Murdoch's fingerprints are all over the culture. He's in your face with the Fox network and Fox News; he has what looks like a permanent franchise on worldwide sports. If you look at the some of biggest movies of the last decade—*Titanic,* or *Independence Day,* or George Lucas's *Star Wars*—that would be Rupert Murdoch. Or programming like *The Simpsons, The*

X-Files, The Practice, Ally McBeal, Temptation Island, tabloid news shows, the whole reality television thing—Murdoch again. But the direct product is just a fraction of the wider impact Murdoch has on his peers. Murdoch has stalked and infuriated and cajoled and threatened and spooked the American media industry for a quarter of a century. Media executives spend their lives looking over their shoulders, trying to work out what Murdoch will do next. "That's not the question!" NBC president Bob Wright interjected in 1996 in a Sun Valley debate about the future of communication. "The question is, 'Where's Rupert?' "

Murdoch is one of the most intensively scrutinized and chronicled people in the world. But when I began researching him more than a decade ago, I found a growing chasm between the Murdoch history recounted by his biographers, by his executives, and by himself, on the one hand; and the quite different picture that emerged from the documentary evidence. The discrepancies are not minor. Murdoch's biographers, and the Murdoch legend that they helped create, were wrong—profoundly wrong—about almost every part of his life: his childhood, his excruciating family relationships, his personal finances, his time at Oxford, how he gained control of the empire, and the nature of his great gambles that have transformed the world's media industry. Even the best-known story about Murdoch—his harrowing debt crisis in December 1990, when a little bank in Pittsburgh almost left him broke over a A$10 million loan—covered a far murkier tale.

How do you make sense of Rupert Murdoch? Here is a player who loses most of the battles he fights. But what a survivor he turns out to be. His spectacular and humiliating defeat in the space wars of 1997 helped trigger the $4 trillion tech stock boom that followed on Wall Street; and four years later he climbed back into the bear pit to refight the same battle. He has done more than almost anyone else in the world to shape the technological revolution in media, but he actually hates technology. His unfortunate friendship cost Newt Gringrich his career. He spooked Michael Eisner and crippled Disney's earnings. He feuded with Ted Turner for nearly two decades over a boat race and stalked Gerry Levin and Time Warner for even longer. And his problems with the troubled conscience of Pat Robertson, the world's best-known televangelist–turned–diamond miner, cost his shareholders $1.5 billion.

Murdoch has always said that News Corp, the worldwide media empire that he built out of a small newspaper company in South Australia, is a reflection of "my personality, my values." If we are to understand him, he says, we must look at what he has built. Unfortunately News Corp suffers from the corporate version of multiple personality disorder. This is the man who revolutionized the economy of sports, of animated films, children's programming, broadcast news, and television networks. Who led television's trend to get down and dirty. And who has ended up in a race to win absolute control of a media empire that will be second in size only to AOL Time Warner. This is a media group that keeps its secrets so tightly that even when it almost goes broke, its senior executives don't hear about it; a business culture that allows its accountants to embellish their earnings reports in ways that can only be regarded as bizarre; that exists, in a financial sense, stateless somewhere among the tax havens of the world; yet that is powerless when a U.S. fugitive whom it has inadvertently helped escape justice uses the tax archipelago against News to engineer a huge fraud.

When Michael Wolff, the media critic for *New York* magazine, met Murdoch for the first time in a hotel foyer in 2001, he reported that "suddenly, helplessly, I had a surge of fond feeling for him." Wolff gave us a new vision of the media mogul: Murdoch the Marvelous Old Geezer. *He's old. He's really old.* And he's talking about his seventieth birthday! "This is a lion in winter," Wolff intoned straight-faced. It's probably as kind a reading of Murdoch as you will find, the sort of charitable prescience that only a $750,000 book advance from Murdoch's HarperCollins properly illuminates. But it's double-edged. It has the same spiky quality as Murdoch's description of his ex-wife Anna's new husband, William Mann. "He's a nice old guy," Murdoch said of Mann, the day the news of their marriage was announced in October 1999, three months after Murdoch's own marriage to Wendi Deng. Wolff's description of Murdoch invites the same easy dismissal. But Murdoch isn't a nice old guy. Dismissing him like that is a bit like saying, "Here, Rover," and offering a doggie biscuit to a hammerhead shark. The question is not whether he will bite you but how much of your arm the microsurgeons will be able to reattach later.

With Murdoch, it doesn't work to start with an anecdote. He doesn't allow a conventional biography. We take this cameo, this telling little insight, and magnify it monstrously into a larger-than-life figure that looks . . . well, sort of monstrous. Everyone begins with a different story, so we end up in a room crowded with giant figures, all of them claiming to be Rupert Murdoch. Each of them wants to take over the world's media business. The ones near the door wearing the Dodgers caps want to buy the American satellite broadcast industry. In the back some Rupert Murdochs with British accents are shuffling newspaper photographs of topless women. And kowtowing modestly over there beside the door is Chinese Rupert.

Rupert Murdoch has a corporate personality. He is that big. To understand him, you need to put your preconceptions aside and find another way of looking at him. He is probably the most influential and powerful media figure in the world. His empire triggers effects directly and indirectly across the globe far beyond the size of his company. He wields this power unfettered by other shareholders or bankers or independent directors or even by national governments. He hasn't achieved this power by accident. While he is a great media man, he is first of all a great businessman. In Murdoch's world, the money does the talking. It is impossible to understand what Murdoch has achieved and how he has gained his power without following the tortuous deals that have produced them. Murdoch is a product of his finances. He is a creature of the cash trails that wind through the tax havens of the world before heading back to the United States, Europe, and Australia. This book is about those cash trails and about the way that one person's financial legerdemain has produced a devastating series of consequences around the world. It concentrates on Murdoch through his three great campaigns—in the 1980s, when his determination to launch an American television network overturned the media industries of three countries; in 1997, when Murdoch took on every broadcasting group in the United States; and finally his desperate struggle to set up a global satellite network based on DirecTV.

The consequences of being Rupert Murdoch have been so wide, his influence so pervasive, that somewhere along the line this book became a larger picture of the changes that have reshaped our world in the last fifteen years, triggered by technology and information flows. It is easy to forget just how shocking the changes ushered in by the rise of technology have been. What is at stake is how we understand them. Many of the ideas and the preoccupations and the politics of the last decade have represented a continuing battle to come to terms with the rolling crisis triggered by technological advance, where the world's new addiction to change means that many of society's ground lines are on the move, where appearance is everything, and where nothing is as it appears.

Today the issues that will shape our media future turn on distribution and media reach; copyright, encryption, and the keeping of secrets; the struggle to control the agenda of the news media; the effects of media translated endlessly across international and cultural borders—the dubbing down of America; the ideologies that determine how we regulate media; and the battle for programming. From Napster to cross-media laws, from CNN to *Survivor,* from AOL to *The Power Rangers,* the issue is always about information: who gets it, how they get it, and what they do with it. These are the issues that absorb Murdoch.

At the turn of the twenty-first century, reality—the scale and measure of the everyday—has become a very strange thing. In a society marked by impermanence, where the form of things is more significant than the substance, Murdoch is a shape-shifter, a conjurer of realities. In New York, in Los Angeles, in London, Beijing, or Jerusalem—on each stage Murdoch is the compelling player when he appears, the figure around whom so much else turns. Yet he is also the least substantial figure, the most elusive and inexplicable player to track through a dozen costume changes. His appearance varies depending upon whom he is standing next to. Where are the hard edges to define this character? Murdoch is arguably the most secretive figure in world media. Where in his privileged childhood, in a business career conducted over three continents and half a century, and in the frenzy of deals he initiated at the turn of the millennium, do we find the keys to understanding this opaque figure? In half a century, the only constant in Rupert Murdoch's life has been the dazed expression on the faces of those he leaves behind. Faced with the succession of images thrown up by this master reality shaper, which is the real one?

PART I

MANHATTAN STINGER

1

A BUSINESS OF FERRETS

Avenue of the Americas

WHEN THE STORM BROKE in the newsroom of the *New York Post* in midtown, the staff broke into the defensive huddles that mark a newspaper where the editor has just proven mortal. There had been no warning of what was coming. On Monday, April 23, 2001, just before five P.M., as the paper was gearing up for the serious business of getting an edition out for the next day, the publisher, Ken Chandler, called the staff around him. Xana Antunes, their Scottish-Portuguese editor, was with him, sucking the pink lollipop that was her trademark since she quit smoking. It came out whenever she was under stress. Two days later the *Post* would announce a 10 percent rise in its circulation. A cut in the cover price had given the paper the biggest sales hike in its history. But it wasn't enough to save Antunes's job.[1] Chandler announced briefly that Antunes was stepping down immediately to pursue personal interests. She said she had a book project. The new editor was an unknown Australian, Col Allan, currently the editor of Rupert Murdoch's *Daily Telegraph* in Sydney. In the stunned silence that Chandler's announcement produced, the *Post* staff struggled to understand what this news meant. Any power realignment in the Murdoch firmament raised a thousand imponderables. But in the hour of crisis, the most immediate question was: Where would they go to talk about it?

Only journalists can love old newspaper buildings. They have an anachronistic charm that may be detected only by the very nostalgic and people on prescription medication. Newspaper offices absorb part of the histories that flow through them. With the accretions of the years, the atmosphere in their newsrooms comes to reflect the individual styles and practices of the paper. They become comfortable, familiar, down-at-heel, redolent with tradition. They smell. A newspaper has its own odor. This is due not so much to the natural aroma associated with large numbers of journalists in a confined space as to the nocturnal manufacturing

3

process, the muscular, messy business of applying ink to several acres of newsprint each night, then cutting the end product up into little bits and putting it into large trucks.

A blind man could navigate his way around Rupert Murdoch's newspapers by his nose. The *New York Post*'s old pressroom on the waterfront on South Street mixed the residues of truck fumes, newsprint, and decades of grime with other, more exotic traces. The fanciful could imagine a whiff of the drug deals that at various times in its august history went down in the paper's loading bays, along-side the rats in the parking lot. Murdoch's Fleet Street newspaper offices in London are a shadow of their old selves, based now in an anonymous industrial plant in Wapping. In Australia the pervasive aroma at Queensland Newspapers, the Brisbane chain that became the Murdoch family's lost birthright, is a product of industrial-strength disinfectants, the soap factory next door, and the cattle stalls in the showgrounds nearby. When News Corporation's Australian editors met for a conference in the building in early 1999, toilet seats had to be replaced and the more aromatic sections sealed off, to make the effect less overpowering. Before Lachlan Murdoch's renovations, News Corp's headquarters in Sydney had a distinctive bouquet of old beer and perspiration, an unhappy combination that in large quantities acquires the aroma of urine. Advertiser Newspapers in Adelaide hosts a more pungent smell when waste trucks pump raw sewage from the building's septic tank.

There is something about the newspaper business that is never far from the down-at-heel and scruffy. Grunge is a part of newspaper ethos. This is one measure of how lethal the march of technology has been for traditional newspapers—because the first by-product of the information revolution is *hygiene*. It's an insidious thing. Almost every office has endured its own little technological revolution in the last two decades, a modest mirror of the wider changes buffeting the culture. There is no such thing as introducing a little technology. What you're really buying is an ecosystem. Computers are no good without the network: the laser printers, scanners, and servers, the graphics workstations. That means new furniture to stick them on, no question. Why be coy about it? It's a new office architecture. And the ducting. You have to have a new floor for the ducted Category 5 UTP cabling that is obligatory everywhere for the networks. Add in a new ceiling for the no-glare lighting. You've already beefed up the air conditioning to protect the servers. Total climate control is a phrase that rolls around your mouth. Firewalls. Offsite backups. And then senior management works out how much all this has cost, with so little to show the board of directors, and it all hits the fan. That's when you get the new paint job. Just like that, you've got a squeaky-clean, hermetic environment. There goes the neighborhood.

Newspaper offices have been no more immune than other businesses to the revolution in the workplace. Renovations have changed their floor plans, social interactions, and management structure. Often the whole newspaper has moved. In the mid-1990s the *New York Post*'s newsroom weighed anchor and shifted from its longtime moorings in South Street in lower Manhattan, to settle on the tenth floor of News Corp's headquarters at 1211 Sixth Avenue. The result of all this techno-hygiene has been a strange dislocation in traditional newspapers. The craft of journalism itself is caught halfway through an uneasy transition from the reporter's traditional role as cynical ambulance chaser to the new role as cynical media savant. Such dislocation is most apparent when the world goes wrong. For the shocked *Post* veterans on April 23, their emotional home was still back in the paper's old haunts downtown on South Street, where all their history lay. The information revolution had left them stranded in midtown, fifty blocks north of their comfort zone. Where were they going to go? Under pressure, the fourth estate headed for the closest friendly harbor. Which turned out to be around the corner and down West Forty-seventh Street at Langan's Bar and Restaurant.

Rupert Murdoch has always had something special going with the *New York Post*. When asked what he thinks about the world, he tells the questioner to read the *Post*'s op-ed pages. Now that he was back in New York, the *Post* was back to being a star in his heaven. The *Post* is America's oldest newspaper, with a history of continuous publication since 1801, when it was founded by Alexander Hamilton. The paper is part of the fabric of the city, albeit a rather jaded and grubby part of that fabric. Since Rupert Murdoch bought the *Post* in 1977, it has been best known for headlines like "Headless Body in Topless Bar," "Teen Gulps Gas, Explodes," and "Pulitzer Sex Trial Shocker: I Slept with a Trumpet." And for its vehement support of any incumbent politician favored by Murdoch.

"Outsiders, even some insiders, don't understand the differences between the *New York Post* and the New York *Daily News*," says Murdoch. "They have absolutely different audiences. New York is a strange tribal city."[2]

New York Times columnist Andrew Sullivan drew the distinctions a little differently: "Australian and British journalism is based on far lower principles than American journalism; it is an opinionated, coarse and alcohol-driven exercise, rather than a selfless and objective pursuit of the public good. But even here,

Americans can take solace from the fact that the central attempt to import it wholesale—*The New York Post*—was a commercial failure."[3] Sullivan, it goes without saying, is British.

After Chandler's announcement on April 23, the *Post* journalists observed a decent interval of quiet sympathy for their fallen leader. Two minutes later they raided the office of the *Daily Telegraph*'s New York bureau several floors away, to grab back copies of the Sydney paper. They wanted a look at their new editor's handiwork. Then they hit the phones and the Internet. They hit paydirt with an Australian website, Crikey.com.au, where a former *Daily Telegraph* chief of staff, Stephen Mayne, had compiled an extensive dossier on the man he called Col Pot. Col Allan was the man whom Australian politicians feared most, a hard-drinking, pugnacious editor of the old school. He could take a three-line wire story about a rise in births outside of marriage and create a front-page screamer, "Nation of Bastards." He had a photographer shadow the Sydney mayor around until he caught him jaywalking. Allan ran the picture on page one under the head-line "Lord Muck." Allan once called the paper's New York correspondent at four A.M. to tell him to fly to Washington, obtain a sheep, and tie it to the White House fence, to protest U.S. lamb import quotas. When Allan worked in New York in the 1980s, his nickname had been Canvas Back, a comment on his perfor-mance in barroom brawls. But the story that everyone came back to was Col's Closet.

In Sydney Allan had a washbasin in a closet in his office. As a shock tactic with new staff, he would urinate in it during their first news conference, without a break in his conversation. The *Post* had its share of wild boys, but Antunes, a for-mer business editor, had maneuvered the *Post* upmarket with sophisticated media and business coverage while retaining much of its raucousness. Allan sounded like a return to the bad old days of the late 1970s. What was Rupert Murdoch *think-ing*, the bemused *Post* journalists asked from their field headquarters at Langan's. In fact, where was Murdoch?

They went home with no answers. There was another story involving Murdoch that day, but it was covered by the business desk of the New York papers. It was another megadeal. The axing at the *Post* ran in the Metro sections. Not until much later did anyone suggest the two stories were connected. The following Monday an elegant pedestal washbasin wrapped in a red ribbon was on the editor's desk when a still jet-lagged Allan made his appearance at the *Post*. He wasn't overly amused, and no one admitted to the prank. New York meanwhile settled down to watch Allan fall on his face.

Many Americans are confused by English tabloid newspapers, which is the thing that the *New York Post* most resembles. In particular they don't understand the tabloid maneuver known as the reverse ferret. English tabloids are news-driven creatures, built upon a hard core of self-righteous cruelty and inexhaustible moral indignation, which may be leavened to a greater or lesser extent by an audacious sense of humor. When the humor works, the tabloid can be very funny, or at least roguish. The newspaper—and this is important—is never wrong. Kelvin McKenzie, probably the world's greatest tabloid editor (certainly the most obnoxious), used to stalk the newsroom urging his reporters generally to annoy the powers that be, to "put a ferret up their trousers." He would do this until the moment it became clear that in the course of making up stories, inventing quotes, invading people's privacy, and stepping on toes, the *Sun* had committed some truly hideous solecism—like running the wrong lottery numbers—when he would rush back to the newsroom shouting, "Reverse ferret!"[4] This is the survival moment, when a tabloid changes course in a blink without any reduction in speed, volume, or moral outrage. In the midst of a disaster of its own making, it pulls a ferret out of a hat and sails on. It's an equal combination of miraculous escape, misdirection, and a new start. It's no accident that McKenzie perfected this at the *Sun*, because Rupert Murdoch's entire business style may be characterized as a reverse ferret. Time and again when his plans have gone awry and he has found himself facing calamity, his superb survival skills have saved him. Just before he hits the wall, he does a little dummy, he feints this way and that, and then he sets off with undiminished speed in a new direction. This is Murdoch's genius: not that he gets into a jam, but that he is able to walk away afterward, an implausible winner.

So there was Col Allan in May 2001, under pressure to perform, deciding his only hope was to do something ferretlike. And it was just coincidence that the person on whom he would perform this maneuver was, in real life, New York City's number-one ferret-hater. One of the more spirited battles of Rudolph Giuliani's term as mayor had been over his insistence on banning ferrets and iguanas from the city. Giuliani hated them; he couldn't understand what pet owners saw in them. "This excessive concern for little weasels is a sickness," Giuliani told one radio caller.[5]

Allan's biggest problem when he arrived in New York was that the *Post* had become too close to Mayor Giuliani, whom it had supported slavishly for years. "The *Post* [is] so locked into Giuliani that they could call it the *City Hall Post*," Charles Rangel, Democratic congressman from Harlem, told the *New York Observer.*[6] In return Giuliani had been just as valiant on behalf of Rupert Murdoch's interests, most notably through tax concessions and his support for Fox News in its fight with Time Warner in 1996. The gossip-hungry *Post* had been unusually reticent when it came to stories about Giuliani's love life. Early one morning the previous year a *Post* photographer had caught Giuliani coming out of the house of his mistress, Judith Nathan, but had sat on the photos for weeks until the *Daily News* broke the story. By May 2001 Giuliani was in the last months of his tenure as mayor, recovering from aggressive radiation therapy for prostate cancer, when his wife, Donna Hanover, sought a court order to bar Nathan from Gracie Mansion. Even by New York standards, what followed was a spectacularly spiteful public slanging match. But the *Post*'s editorial line on Giuliani was set in concrete. The mayor was right, no matter what. Allan was boxed in. How was the *Post* going to cover the story?

New Yorkers woke up to the answer on May 13. Purely because the *Post* was the mayor's greatest friend, the *Post* was forced to share details about Rudy Giuliani's sperm count. In a page-one story titled "Judy Stands By Her Ailing Man," Andrea Peyser painted Judith Nathan as a hero tending to the mayor's woes after the radiation treatment. This was in contrast to the lack of support from the mayor's heartless wife, whom Allan would later banner as "Cruella deHanover." Under the guise of sympathy and support, the *Post* was free to nuke Giuliani as no one ever had, quoting affidavits from the "hilariously titled" court case. The mayor, poor fellow, was impotent. Not just impotent, he was vomiting up to eight times a night. Even when he wasn't hunched over the pedestal, the poor lug couldn't sleep because he would be awakened by his wife's exercise equipment. The macho mayor was a testosterone-free zone, the *Post* zestfully reported. In fact he *didn't have a trace of male hormone in his entire body.*

A newspaper less wholly committed to the mayor's cause might have regarded some of this as too much detail. It was no trouble for the *Post*. The mayor didn't have any comment about Col Allan, his new best friend, or about the *Post*'s adroit change of course. He was spending his time at City Hall, where, as fortune would have it, he was busy using the mayoral veto that very day on yet another real-life attempt by lesser legislators and pet owners to re-legalize the little weasels. It was only after September 11 that the *Post* realized the magnitude of its error. It thought it had been having some fun at the expense of a desperately ill politician at the end of his political career. Instead it had trashed a man who was about to become a national icon. Not that it would admit this, of course. The *Post* would deftly change course again and sail on as if its support for the mayor had never wavered. Even before the mayor's display of staunch heroism after the attacks on the

World Trade Center, the *Post*'s coverage of him and his wife was clearly mean, self-serving, and vindictive. But then, tabloid journalism usually is.

New York was awash with irony that summer. Not the least of it was that these merry japes were unfolding at the *Post*, a grubby tabloid that represented the oldest of old media, just at a time when the new-media businesses that had trumpeted themselves as the face of the future were themselves becoming history. The tech bust continued like a lethal landslide in slow motion, grinding stock prices remorselessly lower. As grand visions of Internet dominance faded, old-media companies had gone back to their knitting. Consumers did not really want to surf the Net all day, they concluded. The thing that American households did best was watch television. Any technological progress would be based upon the television, and it would be incremental—beginning with interactive television and video on demand. The future belonged to the pay-television operators: to cable companies and satellite broadcasters. And there would be fewer of them. Within three years it was likely that the American media would be dominated by three pay-television groups: AOL Time Warner, the AT&T Broadband business, and General Motors' satellite broadcaster, DirecTV. The last two were up for sale. As each of these three groups headed toward 20 million subscribers, the balance of power would shift dramatically from the media groups that provided programming and content toward those that controlled distribution.

This was where Rupert Murdoch came up against a second piece of irony that summer, because after half a century of battling media rivals on all continents, Murdoch's future would be determined by a car company. For a year as the market had continued to spiral down, Murdoch had been negotiating with GM chairman Jack Smith to merge Murdoch's satellite group, Sky Global Networks, with GM's Hughes Electronics. In twelve years Murdoch had built a worldwide satellite empire that began with BSkyB in Britain, stretched across Germany and Italy through the Middle East, India, Southeast Asia, Japan, covertly in China, down through Australia and New Zealand, through South America, and up to Mexico. North America was the only hole in the network, which was where Hughes Electronics, with its DirecTV satellite operation, came in. Winning DirecTV would give Murdoch an unbroken world highway that could reach three-quarters of the world's population. And he would control what ran on that highway, with a global voice and power that no one in history had ever had.

"We're just minnows," Murdoch said to critics like Senator John McCain, who worried about the power that this deal would give him. But News Corp is a company that is larger on the inside than it is on the outside. Its stock was worth

$40 billion, which put it only in the third rank of major media players. But in media the important measure is not size but power. Murdoch's global highway was based on a string of companies in which News Corp held management control, though only a minority shareholding. If you added in these companies, Murdoch controlled a $70 billion conglomerate. With the Hughes deal Murdoch would head a $100 billion media empire. It would be the second-largest media group in the world, and AOL Time Warner's only serious rival for global media dominance.

This was the prize that Murdoch had been inching toward all of his life. After five decades of striving, it was finally within reach. In a matter of weeks—even days—it could be his. But first Murdoch had to convince General Motors to commit to this deal. If there is a modern vision of purgatory, it must be spending eternity negotiating a media deal with an American carmaker. When Murdoch turned seventy on March 11, he told journalists that he had another seventy thousand hours of working life left in him: "I hope not too many of them will be spent negotiating with General Motors." The final hurdles had seemed to be resolved in February, when the GM board gave the green light to begin due diligence talks with News Corp to finalize the deal. But the talks broke down again two weeks later. By April the process had been going on for thirteen months. The market was still in free fall, and it had become clear to Murdoch that he was facing a brutal choice. This brought him to the other, more personal crisis facing him that summer.

After decades as the perfect family man, Rupert Murdoch's personal life almost overnight had come to resemble the soap operas that his newspapers and television programmers so enjoyed exposing. On Thursday, May 10, a News Corp spokesman confirmed newspaper reports that Rupert Murdoch and his new wife, Wendi Deng, thirty-seven years his junior, were expecting a baby. Murdoch, who had had radiation therapy for his own prostate cancer at the same time as Mayor Giuliani, gallantly declined to inflict his own personal details on the populace of New York when the *Post* nuked Giuliani on May 13. This was just as well, because medical opinion was that this was probably an *in vitro* conception, achieved within days of Murdoch's seventieth birthday, using sperm stored before the cancer treatments began in May 2000.[7]

In 1989 Doris Lessing wrote a novel called *The Fifth Child*, which explored how a happy, well-adjusted family with four children disintegrates under the pressure of another birth. Wendi Deng's baby, with the uncertainties it created for succession in the Murdoch empire, carried similar disruptive potential. Within two weeks of the public announcement of the pregnancy, Murdoch's estranged daughter, Elisabeth, had reconciled with her former lover, English public relations consultant Matthew Freud, the great-grandson of Sigmund Freud and a man whom Rupert Murdoch loathed. While the announcement of the engagement had nothing to do with Wendi's pregnancy, Freud promptly arranged a profile for himself in *Vanity Fair* in which he was able to get a few things off his chest about his prospective father-in-law, in particular his chauvinism against daughters. Meanwhile Anna Murdoch, Rupert's second wife and Elisabeth's mother, was arranging her first interview since the acrimonious divorce. Anna told Australian journalist David Leser that, despite her former husband's claims to the contrary, their marriage had ended because Rupert refused to end his affair with Deng.

Murdoch had a daughter from his first marriage, Patricia Booker, but while her husband worked for News Corp, she herself had no role. For a man as focused on family as Murdoch, who has tended to see family as a natural extension of business, his sons were two of the only bright spots on his horizon: James running Star TV in China, and Lachlan, the elder son whom Murdoch had been grooming for years to succeed him, in New York. This was the heart of the brutal choice that now faced Murdoch. If he did this deal, the Murdochs would still control News Corp, but the engine room of the empire, the satellite platforms, would be in Sky Global. General Motors, Bill Gates at Microsoft, and the wily John Malone of Liberty Media would be shareholders in the new company. Under the deal that Murdoch had negotiated with GM in February, News would end up with 35 percent of Sky Global, and Murdoch would control it. But the deal had broken down, and Murdoch knew that to get the talks restarted, he would have to make concessions. The biggest concession that Jack Smith at General Motors was demanding was that Murdoch cut his stake to 30 percent. This was a critical change for Murdoch, because although he would still control Sky Global, it wasn't a big enough stake to ensure that he could pass control to his children, to a young and untried Lachlan. The personal cost to Murdoch of winning DirecTV was that he would probably have to jettison the succession—to accept that his children would inherit the wealth without the power.

"Lachlan is in a very difficult situation," said a former News director in March 2001. "Rupert is going to go on working forever. Lachlan could find himself forty-five years of age, then suddenly miss the opportunity to run News."

The children would still be fabulously wealthy, influential and connected, but running News Corp would amount to little more than overseeing a media investment holding company, with a few newspapers on the side. The engine rooms of the empire, Sky Global and Fox Entertainment, would be in other hands. The

General Motors subcommittee handling the sale of Hughes had called a final meeting for April 23. It was time to put up or shut up. That was why the *New York Post* journalists could not find Murdoch when they went looking. That evening when Ken Chandler announced that Xana Antunes was stepping down, when the *Post* staff regrouped across the street at Langan's, Murdoch was in Detroit, facing a choice between dynasty and destiny. Should he walk away from this deal, limiting his prospects for the sake of his children, or should he seize the day? Of course, Murdoch had already made his choice. He wouldn't have been in Detroit otherwise.

That was where the real irony about the sad little scene at the *Post* that day lay. The previous December Rupert had appointed Lachlan deputy chief operating officer of News Corp. The move was aimed at quashing widespread speculation in the market that John Malone, who had just taken what would become an 18 percent nonvoting stake in News Corp, was the most likely successor to Murdoch at the head of News. The appointment put Lachlan third in line in the News hierarchy, behind his father and the chief operating officer, Peter Chernin. But Lachlan, who had been elevated to New York in late 1999 after five years in the Australian operations, in practice controlled only a tiny part of the empire. His biggest move had been a $280 million investment in an Australian and British telephone company called One.Tel where he sat on the four-man board. (In April 2001 Lachlan had no idea that One.Tel was days away from going into liquidation. He was too focused on events in New York.)

In America Lachlan ran the U.S. publishing interests, the coupon inserts business, and odd bits and pieces. His most high-profile responsibility was the *Post.* What was obvious to anyone who knew Lachlan's history was that the only person who could have chosen Col Allan to replace Antunes was Lachlan. He had worked with him for years. Just six months before, Lachlan had appointed Allan's close friend and amiable drinking companion John Hartigan as chief executive for News in Australia. By appointing Allan to the *Post,* Lachlan was asserting his authority and independence: He was making a big call in the small part of the empire that he controlled. This little gesture of autonomy came on the very day that his father was in Detroit offering a deal that would limit the aspirations of his heirs.

The cruelest thing was that no one would believe that the *Post* decision was Lachlan's. Story after story would note Lachlan's growing involvement with the paper and his regular attendance at *Post* meetings with and without his father; but any decision at News Corp had only ever been seen to be Rupert's. And the *Post* was one of the things closest to his heart.

Some fathers throw their sons the car keys. Others can offer larger toys. In the turmoil that Antunes's sacking triggered that summer, with the string of journalists that left the *Post* or were fired in her wake, in the trail of tabloid victims that marked the *Post* under Allan, the paper would be called many things. It was everything from a "triple espresso" to start the day, as columnist Steve Dunleavy put it, to "like being battered in a boxing match," as Governor Mario Cuomo once described its political coverage. For the nearly half a million people who bought it every day, it was just part of life. In two hundred years of publication, what no one had ever called the *Post* was a consolation prize.

2

A MUDDLE OF MOGULS

Manhattan, October 27, 2001

IT WAS STILL EARLY on Saturday morning, October 27, when Lachlan Murdoch slipped out of his loft apartment on Lafayette Street to make the trip a few blocks across SoHo to TriBeCa. Seven weeks after September 11 the streets of lower Manhattan had a curious dead echo, a zone of unfamiliarity that extended north from the barricades around the World Trade Center site. Lachlan was heading to his father's triplex penthouse on Prince Street. If this was the most important day of Rupert Murdoch's life, he was going to spend it with his elder son. Win or lose, he wanted Murdoch blood and kin around him. So this day, which would do so much to shape the future of the world's media industry, would be played out in domestic surrounds: Rupert Murdoch in casual attire, at home with his heavily pregnant wife Wendi Deng, with Lachlan, and with several battalions of lawyers and advisers.

Barry Diller, the man who founded Fox Network for Murdoch, once said of his former boss, "Rupert Murdoch at his best is probably when he is cornered or when he does have great adversity going against him." Diller paused, then added, "And maybe it's his moment of greatest pleasure."[1] The rider is such a Diller thing to say, the transformation of a quality of character into something like a secret weakness. As if in the media business virtue and vice came wrapped up in the same sandwich. But in half a century of empire building, Murdoch had learned a lot about facing a crisis. The first rule is that these things generally take a while, so you might as well make yourself comfortable. Ever since his empire had almost been crunched by the banks eleven years before and he had spent three months scurrying from banker to banker in city after city, Murdoch had taken care to handle his crises at a distance, by telephone, preferably from his yacht. Let the other side sweat the numbers, catch the red-eye flights. Murdoch knew how to fight smart. The best gamblers do.

In the last weekend of October 2001 the board of General Motors was about to buckle down to resolve the sticky problem of whether to sell Hughes Electronics Corporation to Rupert Murdoch. By the standards of the automobile industry, actually deciding to make a decision was something of a bold step. A lesser corporation might have regarded the eighteen months spent to date in negotiations as wholly inadequate and recommended another six months to mull over the finer details, to seek another tax opinion, and to check the spelling. But General Motors was not that sort of automobile company. In fact, General Motors wasn't really an automobile company at all. True, for decades GM had made and sold more cars than anyone else in North America. But it had achieved this principally because it was really a finance company that helped people to buy cars. The business of making automobiles accounted for only one-fifth of its balance sheet. In September 2001 the biggest item in the GM accounts was its $145 billion of bank debt.

The debt made GM intensely vulnerable to the credit ratings that determined how much interest it paid to its bankers. Unfortunately, several years before, Standard & Poor's and Moody's had decided GM wasn't a finance company either. The credit rating agencies concluded that General Motors was really a giant retirement scheme. It had $37 billion in unfunded pension schemes and postretirement medical plans for its huge workforce, sitting like a big black hole on its balance sheet. The emergence of that black hole had at one stroke destabilized the GM balance sheet and transformed its workers into potential megacreditors. By 2001 it had had two consequences: GM management looked perilously close to losing control of its destiny to its workforce at any moment; and unless GM could make some major asset sales in a hurry, its credit rating would take another hit, compounding its woes. GM's only option was to sell its satellite production and broadcasting subsidiary, Hughes Electronics.

In 1985 GM had paid $5.2 billion to buy Hughes. The company Howard Hughes had founded in 1923 as Hughes Aircraft Company was now a defense and aerospace contractor and a leading manufacturer of satellites. In 1990 Hughes had been in talks with Rupert Murdoch, NBC, and Chuck Dolan's Cablevision cable group to launch an American satellite operation, Sky Cable, but the venture fell apart—as had another Murdoch satellite attempt in 1983. Instead in March 1994 Hughes had launched DirecTV on its own. It was one of the most successful product launches in history. Michael Armstrong, the Hughes CEO and chairman, then moved to head AT&T, where he paid $105 billion to build AT&T Broadband into the largest cable operation in America. In 1998 Jack Smith, who was then the General Motors CEO, appointed his brother, Michael, as Armstrong's replacement.

By the summer of 2001 DirecTV had 10.3 million subscribers, and the service had become too successful for GM executives' peace of mind. At the height of the technology boom in early 2000, even after selling off the defense and aerospace arms for $13.25 billion, Hughes was still worth considerably more than General Motors itself. In June 2000, as a defensive move to placate stockholders and to deter takeover threats, GM spun off Hughes as a tracking stock to its stockholders. Under this arrangement GM still owned all the physical assets, but the holders of the tracking stock were entitled to the income earned from the Hughes assets. GM also transferred 35 percent of the tracking stock to its pension funds, as a way to make up the payout shortfall without paying any tax. This seemed like a clever idea at the time. But as the price of the Hughes stock fell, the shares transferred to the pension funds were worth less, and the pension shortfall grew again. Now GM was stuck with selling a company where it owned all the assets but only 30 percent of the tracking stock, with a lot of unhappy minority shareholders who would jump up and down if they didn't like the buyer.

By mid-2001 GM had been trying to sell Hughes for fifteen months, and it was running out of time. It had become a running joke: How do you buy a small satellite broadcaster? You try to buy a large one from General Motors. When Rupert Murdoch first approached GM in March 2000, at the height of the tech stock boom, Hughes was worth $62 billion. Murdoch wasn't the only interested suitor. But GM needed to sell Hughes in a way that didn't trigger a huge capital gains tax liability. This proved such a complex proposition to set up that months stretched past. By September 2000, when Hughes's market value had dropped to $50 billion, the original sixteen interested buyers had narrowed down to four groups talking seriously. Three of them dropped out, leaving only News Corporation ready to meet GM's sale conditions and price. "It's a dream," Murdoch said in November 2000 when asked about the Hughes deal. "And you can read into that what you will." By then Hughes's share price had slumped to $32.30, pushing the value of the company down to $43 billion.

On February 6, 2001, the GM board gave the green light to begin due diligence on a deal to spin off Hughes and merge it with News Corp's global satellite business, Sky Global Networks. By then Hughes stock was under $28. Two weeks later GM and Hughes executives decided News was getting too good a deal with a 35 percent stake in the merged business, and the talks broke down. When negotiations resumed in May, Hughes stock was down to $23. And still the talks dragged on. By late September Hughes had dipped to $12. A company that had been worth $62 billion when the sale began was now worth only $16 billion.

GM executives looked like deer in the headlights. Their obsession with avoiding tax liability and not being taken for a ride by Rupert Murdoch had cost their stockholders a fortune. The more they stalled, the farther the price fell. But if they did the deal and the price then recovered, they would look even worse. Meanwhile the credit rating agencies were getting impatient for GM to sell its amazing disappearing satellite company. GM was a forced seller with only one buyer. Whichever way it turned, Rupert Murdoch held all the cards. Murdoch's mastery in this situation is the key to understanding what happened next: how in late 2001 the perfect business deal turned into the saga of the tortoise and the hare.

Murdoch's efforts in Detroit on April 23, the day Xana Antunes was dumped from the *New York Post,* did not go unrewarded. A week after he agreed to all the concessions that General Motors was demanding, the GM board graciously gave the green light to its lawyers to restart the due diligence procedures to sell Hughes Electronics to Murdoch. More than a year of corporate intrigue and serpentine negotiations had finally reached a resolution. To the marriage of true souls, let there be no impediment, was the general gist of the announcement. Murdoch now faced an awkward situation: He needed to finalize a $30 billion deal with the chairman of General Motors after engineering the departure of his brother.

The initial deal Murdoch had agreed to with General Motors on February 6 busted up just two weeks later, when Hughes chairman Michael Smith walked out of a News Corp presentation. The day before, Smith had flown to Denver to speak with Charlie Ergen, who ran DirecTV's major competitor, EchoStar Communications, about an alternative bid for Hughes. Smith bad-mouthed News at an analysts' conference in March and made it clear how little he regarded the overseas satellite operations that Murdoch wanted to merge into Hughes. Through March and April Smith tried to secure an alternative offer for Hughes, and then when that failed, to fund a management buyout or stock market spin-off for Hughes. Finally the GM board called time. Smith was forced to go back to dealing with Murdoch. The awkwardness in this situation was not just that Michael Smith would have to swallow his words about Murdoch; it was also that his elder brother, Jack Smith, the chairman of General Motors, was telling him he had to do this.

The News Corp spin doctors had no doubt about how to understand Michael Smith's actions: They were obscene. This was a naked grab for power by a man who didn't want to lose his job. But that wasn't the only reading that could be made from this sorry saga. The alternative viewpoint was that News Corp management had gone into a feeding frenzy.

"This is the drawback to the management style at News, those guys tend to play the man and not the ball," said a former News director. "It's a problem. That's what killed the deal with Charlie Ergen in 1997. Murdoch has always underestimated Ergen."

The problem was so avoidable. After the GM board gave the green light in February, Murdoch and the News Corp executives just needed to sit tight, focus on the due diligence procedures, and keep massaging their opposite numbers at General Motors and Hughes. Most of all they needed to show what swell partners they were all going to be. This is where the deal began to unravel. News Corp has one of the most aggressive corporate cultures in the world. For five decades Murdoch had run News as a one-man show. In that time he had never had a successful partnership. Where would he begin now? The News execs had been bad-mouthing their opposite numbers at Hughes for weeks, about how undermanaged Hughes was and how much better they would run the company. Hughes expected a partnership. What it got was a boarding party. There was nothing personal, it was just the News style. Unhappily it spooked Hughes management.

So in May a history of bad blood hung over both parties, as News Corp group counsel Arthur Siskind and the team from Skadden Arps Slate Meagher & Flom started putting back together the pieces of an extraordinarily complicated deal. The plan was to spin off Hughes as a separate company that would merge with Murdoch's Sky Global Networks. John Malone at Liberty Media would kick in up to $1 billion in cash, and Bill Gates at Microsoft would invest another $4 billion for a small stake. At the end of the day GM would walk away with a large pile of money, and Murdoch would control the new company with what was now reduced to 27 percent of its stock. This was a global merger, with complicated tax, antitrust, and cross-media laws to consider in country after country around the world. Murdoch's lawyers were also renegotiating the deal. After agreeing to all of General Motors' concessions to get back to the table, Arthur Siskind was out to claw back a lot of that lost ground.

Charlie Ergen at EchoStar hadn't given up on Hughes. But he needed a war chest. On May 21 J. P. Morgan and UBS Warburg announced a $1 billion convertible note issue for EchoStar, then fell into a fierce quarrel over the pricing. With Ergen there was always a fight about money. He was unbelievably frugal. He insisted his senior executives share hotel rooms and travel with cheap fares on late-night flights. On one occasion they were forced to beg for lifts from executives of rival companies in their rental cars, just to get to their hotel. In 1997 Ergen sued Murdoch for $5 billion. The case settled, but Ergen was still fighting his old legal team in Texas, which claimed EchoStar owed them $112 million. The case would go to mediation in October just as the Hughes negotiations were at their peak. "When it comes to spending money I have a memory lapse," Ergen said later.[2]

By Thursday, May 24, EchoStar's bankers had untangled themselves, and the $1 billion was safely raised. EchoStar's counsel David Moskowitz now filed an 8-K notice that said General Motors was willing to establish a dialogue with EchoStar to talk about Hughes. The news made headlines in Friday's newspapers. Hours later Michael Smith resigned as chairman of Hughes. While no reason was cited, there seemed little doubt that News Corp had pushed him out. The discovery that Smith was covertly encouraging another run by EchoStar had prompted outrage from News. Whether or not that was the actual reason for Smith's sudden departure—analysts attributed it to frustration by the GM board—the News camp was overjoyed at the removal of the man who was "the biggest thorn in our side." Smith was replaced by Harry Pearce, the GM vice chairman who oversaw Hughes, and who had been secretly talking to Murdoch for months. "These changes were the result of intense and comprehensive discussions among the Hughes-GM management board and Mike," Pearce said in a conference call after the announcement. "Mike Smith elected to retire, and it was his decision and the Hughes board agreed."[3] Pearce had to resign from the GM board to take up the position, so GM lost both Michael Smith and Pearce. News was now locked into a negotiating process that had cost the brother of the chairman of General Motors his career.

Talks inched forward through June and July, now focusing on the delicate antitrust concerns in Latin America, where the merger of DirecTV and Murdoch's Sky Latin would remove any satellite competition. Despite reports that EchoStar was on the verge of raising another $3 billion to fund its bid for Hughes, Ergen could find no partners. Rick Wagoner, who had suceeded Smith as General Motors CEO in 2000 when Smith became chairman, said that while talks with News were progressing, "We've got to keep our eyes open to something better coming up." Ergen spoke to Hughes management, but the talks went nowhere. Wagoner and other senior GM staff refused to meet with him. EchoStar's half-year report on July 19 said Hughes had recently informed it that GM was "unwilling to further consider EchoStar's proposal." Ergen was out of the picture. A final deal to approve the sale was due to be put to the GM board on August 7.

Media moguls should never go on vacation. Strange things happen when their minds disengage from the daily pressures of running an empire. In the last week of July Ergen went back to his hometown in Tennessee with his family. The first his senior executives knew that something had happened was when Ergen called them on Saturday, August 4. "Charlie called me and said to catch a plane to New York," EchoStar director of communications Judianne Atencio said later. "He said he was going to make a bid for Hughes."

The following day in New York Ergen announced a $30 billion bid to buy Hughes in exchange for EchoStar shares. Ergen said it was a spur-of-the-moment decision. One morning he climbed out of bed on the other side and made up his mind. UBS Warburg's version was that it had been pressing him for weeks to make an unsolicited bid, known as a bear hug. There was a little disagreement about fees with EchoStar's public relations firm, and then with UBS Warburg also, after Ergen was reluctant to sign the customary indemnity clause or to guarantee the $20 million UBS fee. These disagreements raised some skepticism about the bid, but Ergen insisted he was in earnest: "I don't come out and spend time in New York and I don't put a suit on unless I'm serious."

Murdoch said later, "At the last minute Charlie gave them what they call a bear hug, and a lot of shareholders rang up and said, 'Hey, they're going to make more money out of this.' "[4]

Ergen had made a gambler's bid, one that he knew was unacceptable. He had offered stock when he knew General Motors would sell only for cash. But by going public, Ergen ensured that General Motors had to talk to him, to at least give the appearance of listening to him, before accepting Murdoch's bid. That's when Ergen would make his real offer, which would include cash. Ergen just wanted an audience.

"If the decks are a bit stacked against you, spread the deck on the table and let everybody look at the cards, and then they can see if it's stacked or not," he said.[5]

The following Sunday, when Ergen met with GM's chief financial officer, John Devine, he called in David Boies, the antitrust lawyer who ran the Justice Department's case against Microsoft. Boies gave a presentation to GM executives at the New York offices of their attorneys, Weil Gotshal & Manges, to argue persuasively that a merger of America's two major satellite broadcasters would pass antitrust scrutiny. Talks ground slowly on. Ergen had another meeting planned with GM execs in New York for the afternoon of September 11.

Everything changed when the two planes slammed into the World Trade Center. Murdoch was stranded in Washington by commitments to three heads of state. The previous Saturday, September 8, Lachlan Murdoch had celebrated his thirtieth birthday. That weekend the Australian embassy in Washington contacted Murdoch to ask if he would meet the Australian prime minister, John Howard, when he arrived in New York on Wednesday, September 12. Howard was desperate for Murdoch's support in the looming Australian election. But Murdoch had a speaking engagement in London on Thursday and was reported to be planning to speak to British prime minister Tony Blair about investing in ITV, the British television broadcaster. Caught between two anxious prime ministers, Murdoch agreed to fly to Washington to have dinner with Howard on Monday evening, after Howard finished his meeting with President Bush. On Tuesday morning Murdoch was preparing for a round of hand-shaking on Capitol Hill when the third hijacked plane flew into the Pentagon. With the News Corp jet grounded, Murdoch drove back to New York. TriBeCa had been evacuated and Manhattan was sealed off, so Murdoch spent the night at the New Jersey home of the chairman of Fox News, Roger Ailes, before taking a ferry to Manhattan to be reunited with his heavily pregnant wife, Wendi.

Murdoch didn't know it, but that column of smoke rising from the World Trade Center had determined his future. September 11 was a watershed for the American media industry. It wasn't just the rediscovery of hard news that it triggered, accompanied by the collapse of the advertising market. The tragedy had taken a personal toll on the executives at the top of the world's biggest media companies. John Malone of Liberty Media, Murdoch's partner in the Hughes bid, was a couple of blocks away when the first plane crashed into the north tower. Jean-Marie Messier of Vivendi, who had moved his family from Paris to New York eight days before, was having a business meeting over breakfast in a private dining room. He watched the second plane hit the south tower from the Seagram building. Gerry Levin was so affected by the tragedy that he resigned as CEO of AOL Time Warner two months later—the same day Messier's deputy, Edgar Bronfman Jr., bailed out of Vivendi. Rick Wagoner, CEO of General Motors, was at an auto show in Berlin on September 11 and was trapped by the air embargo until Friday on the wrong side of the Atlantic.

Ergen was in Denver, about to fly to New York for his meeting with General

Motors. GM suggested a telephone linkup, but instead the meeting was post-poned to the following Sunday, September 16. This meant Wagoner was available to attend, which meant EchoStar was finally talking to the senior ranks at GM. So it turned out all right for Charlie Ergen. It turned out well for George Bush too, transforming his presidency, while it completed Bill Clinton's slide into oblivion. Clinton was in Australia, being flown around by a slick Assyrian businessman, the son of an Iraqi squadron leader who flew MIG-17s. Clinton's host had just raised $65 million in an apparent Ponzi scheme that promised investors in Australia and the United States 200 percent returns from an investment collecting shopping carts.

If there is a single figure that represents the angst and uncertainty of life in postindustrial society, an icon for the terrible, conflicted process of being alive and doing business in the early twenty-first century, it is the modern automobile ex-ecutive. To live in Detroit and be part of senior management in the big three is to live in a state of anxiety, to wrestle with existential doubt, to be on a perpetual quest for identity, defined by a continually changing mission statement. Detroit had been built on an engineering culture that survived the oil shock of the 1970s, the end of the gas guzzler, the inroads of the Japanese, the return of the gas guz-zler, European emission standards, Lee Iacocca, several major corporate failures, and the rise of the SUV. An environment of constant threat had built a manage-ment structure that was deeply involved with itself: cautious, defensive, a strong believer in the careful management plan. So who would believe, when faced with the consumer crisis that followed September 11, that General Motors would tear up the rulebook and embark on its most aggressive marketing drive in a genera-tion?

Three days after the attack on the World Trade Center, as car sales dried up and gloom and dismay swept the country, Ford cut its production quota. But General Motors' agreements with its workforce meant that cutting back produc-tion and closing plants was not an option. Instead, on September 17 Robert Lutz, the former Chrysler president who only weeks before had been appointed GM's vice chairman and head of product, committed GM to a national campaign offer-ing buyers zero percent financing. It turned the car market around and forced Ford and Chrysler to follow it down a ruinously expensive sales path. Overnight GM was suddenly winning back market share, reversing the decline of two decades. But the cost of this bold move showed up in GM's credit position. On Monday, October 15, Standard & Poor's downgraded its credit ratings for Ford and General Motors by two notches to the third-lowest investment grade, with a negative outlook. Two days later Hughes CEO Jack Shaw had just told an analysts' briefing, "I believe we are nearing the home stretch [in the Hughes sale talks], and we're hoping that we'll reach some kind of conclusion in the very near future," when UBS Warburg announced on the business wire that it had raised $5.5 billion to fund an EchoStar bid for Hughes. Shaw was clearly taken by surprise. General Motors had found an unlikely savior.

"We were told they were under a short, tight time fuse," EchoStar counsel David Moskowitz said later of the intense meetings with GM that followed. "We were negotiating literally twenty-four hours a day. People would go home, take a shower, get a bite to eat, then return."

General Motors decided on its zero percent financing plan on September 17. In a spectacular piece of bad timing, that was the day Murdoch told GM that in view of the disastrous fall in the Hughes stock price, he was taking $1 billion in cash from his bid off the table. This was doubly unfortunate because the day before Ergen had been pressing his higher cash offer in Los Angeles. The S&P downgrade meant that GM had to sell Hughes quickly. GM was about to issue $6 billion in bonds. It was also talking about raising $2 billion for PanAmSat, the Hughes satellite-maker. EchoStar's money suddenly looked very attractive.

Charlie Ergen has always been Rupert Murdoch's blind spot. Murdoch had believed that Ergen's opportunistic bid was only a delaying tactic. Now sudden doubts assailed him. Arthur Siskind, the News Corporation counsel, and the forty-odd lawyers in the News legal team who had been sweating for an eternity on the deal always believed that Ergen didn't have the money for the deal and he had little prospect of obtaining antitrust approval to merge the two biggest U.S. satellite broadcasters. Yet intense signals were now coming from GM that management wanted the board to give the nod to Ergen.

The clearest signal for outsiders was Ergen's demeanor on Tuesday, October 23, during an analysts' telephone hookup to discuss EchoStar's September results. Ergen was subdued, distracted, unwilling to talk anything up. Listening to his restrained delivery, it was a shock to realize that the only reason that Ergen had dropped his usual upbeat promotion must be because he was so focused on Hughes. He really thought that he could win this. "I don't know how he was able to hold it together for that briefing, there was so much going on with General Motors," EchoStar communications director Judianne Atencio said later.

News Corp's lobbyists had hit the phones in Washington to make it clear how problematic any merger of EchoStar and DirecTV would be. Murdoch imposed a final deadline: GM had until the following Saturday, October 27, to decide on the

News Corp offer. After that Murdoch would walk. And then on Thursday, right on schedule, Ergen ran out of money.

Late on Thursday afternoon, October 25, two days before GM made its final decision, the two banks that were providing Ergen with $5.5 billion in cash for his bid, UBS Warburg and Deutsche Bank, were bickering over fees again. UBS also was stalling over an exit clause to its half of the funding. General Motors CFO John Devine wanted the clause tightened up. He was taking a $6 billion bond raising to the market the next day, and GM was about to extend its zero percent financing promotion, so this wasn't a time to take chances. Moskowitz, who had been working around the clock for a week, felt the earth shift under him suddenly. GM had been saying the deal was EchoStar's to lose. But as the talks continued all through Thursday night and then through Friday, the differences with UBS became intractable, and the exchanges grew acrimonious.

"David Moskowitz is scary smart," said Antencio later. "Charlie always says David is the kind of guy who can go without sleep for nights and still pull together really complex contracts. He can hold it together."

By Friday evening UBS had walked away from the deal. Ergen was hours away from the final General Motors board meeting, and his bid was $2.75 billion short. Devine slipped across to the News Corp offices on Sixth Avenue to tell Murdoch that the deal was his. Ergen had until eleven A.M. the next morning to find some more money, or the GM board would drop his bid. Devine also told Murdoch that GM's internal legal advice was that the EchoStar deal had only a 30 percent chance of passing the antitrust review. The smart choice had to be going with Murdoch. So on Friday night Murdoch was nervous, but he knew he had the numbers.

That evening Ergen flew back to Denver for an EchoStar board meeting early Saturday. Moskowitz continued going through the motions with the GM lawyers, then caught a plane to Denver in the early hours of Saturday to be there for the EchoStar board meeting, which would begin at six A.M. It was eight A.M. New York time. At ten-thirty A.M. Devine called Murdoch again. Murdoch told Charlie Rose later, "About ten minutes before their board meeting started on the Saturday, they rang us, and said, 'He has not got the money. We're all going in now. Four banks were going to recommend you. We, the executives, are going to recommend you. And we'll let you know how the board goes at the end of the afternoon.' "6

While Murdoch was talking to Devine, the EchoStar board meeting was breaking up. Ergen had already been talking to General Motors, as he pitched his last-ditch offer. He would personally guarantee the $2.75 billion funding shortfall with some of his own shares in EchoStar, which he would put into a separate trust. "I was personally very surprised," Moskowitz said. "From the view of Charlie's friend and adviser, I was concerned that he would be willing to put his personal wealth at such great risk for the transaction."

This was a feel-good offer that meant very little. When a company has trouble paying its debts, its stock price dives into a hole. So if at the end of the day EchoStar was in such desperate straits that it couldn't find the money it needed to pay for a half-completed deal, then the EchoStar stock Ergen was offering General Motors as security would probably be worth much less. Ergen's offer was still unfunded, with the balance of GM's internal legal advice saying it was unlikely to be approved. But the response from GM was to encourage Ergen to put the proposal in writing. When the General Motors board meeting began at eleven o'clock, discussions proceeded directly to the News Corp bid for Hughes. Directors apparently had not been told of the offer letter that Ergen was now drafting.

A modern board meeting is a sprawling, multimedia affair. Rick Wagoner, the General Motors CEO, was across town in the Weil Gotshal & Manges offices on Fifth Avenue, on phone hookup. In addition to the official discussion, the quiet asides, and the regular telephone calls from the EchoStar and News Corp camps, the merchant bankers and lawyers advising the board kept up their own private interaction with text comments exchanged via their Blueberry personal assistant devices. The first two hours of the discussion were focused on the News Corp proposal for Hughes and the complex financial, tax, and antitrust issues involved. While News Corp was the choice of GM management, the chairman, Jack Smith, had gone on record the week before referring to the uncertainty of the News Corp bid. Wagoner underscored the "sticky tax implications" of the deal. Directors raised concerns about the concessions negotiated with Microsoft in order to win its support. As the imponderables about the News Corp offer mounted, the mood of the meeting changed. The consensus moved from a readiness to rubber-stamp an agreement hammered out over eighteen months, to unease and a desire for an alternative.

Just before midday in Denver, Ergen faxed in his offer of part of his own holding in EchoStar as security. In New York, where it was two P.M., the letter produced an immediate impression. The feeling was that this was a significant gesture by Ergen that should be considered carefully. Wagoner asked for a break to consult with Jack Smith and senior management. Across town in his apartment in TriBeCa, Murdoch knew he was in trouble. "The chief executive of General Motors, who was on the telephone, who was not at the board meeting, said could they have time out to discuss with the General Motors representatives at the board meeting," Murdoch said later. " 'Just a few minutes,' he said. And they were gone an hour. And they came back and said, 'We recommend that we delay it for a day or two.' "

News Corp is not a show that plays well in Detroit. There is a culture gap between the line management that was Jack Smith's and Rick Wagoner's background, and News Corp's history of wheeling and dealing. But the reserve that characterized Smith and Wagoner was balanced by the more direct style of Devine, the CFO. Murdoch believed he knew where he stood with Devine and that at the end of the day Devine would support the pragmatic choice to go with the News Corp offer. He wasn't so sure about the other two.

Murdoch had lost his greatest ally when Harry Pearce took a leave of absence from the chair of Hughes to care for his sick wife. In his absence the leading role fell to Hughes CEO Jack Shaw. He had held a meeting of senior Hughes staff the week before, to review the News Corp and EchoStar offers. "At the end I asked each person in the room to tell me which opportunity they felt would provide the best value to our shareholders and the best future for our company," Shaw said when the decision was announced. "And to a person they said we should merge with EchoStar."

This decision was all the more remarkable because in an EchoStar-DirecTV merger most of those executives would probably lose their jobs. Murdoch had been selling the dream of a global satellite highway. Ergen's adroit management of GM and Hughes directors and executives had stressed the down-to-earth advantages of EchoStar. "The synergies are just—they're so clear, they're so simple," said Shaw. "You can get your arms around them."

EchoStar was offering stock valued at $25.8 billion. GM would end up with $4.2 billion in cash. The Sky Global offer was reported to be $22 to $23 billion in stock, with some $3 billion in cash delivered to General Motors. On paper EchoStar's deal looked better, but only if it passed the antitrust hurdles. The GM team was suffering from negotiation fatigue after months in close quarters with Arthur Siskind and the Skadden Arps lawyers for News Corp. "The GM guys said that being in a room day after day with Arthur and the Arps guys was just a misery," said an executive close to Hughes.

Siskind's tough negotiating style had won a lot of prizes for Murdoch, including the *New York Post* for the second time in 1993, and Star TV. But now he was pushing too hard. While public attention focused on the longstanding rivalry between Ergen and Murdoch, the strong feelings went down through the ranks. When

EchoStar sued News Corp in 1997, its process servers had been unable to gain entrance to the News Corp offices in Manhattan. Instead, David Moskowitz had gone to Siskind's home in Larchmont and served him with the $5 billion writ personally. "That wasn't very well received," he said.

Not everyone at General Motors was an EchoStar supporter. Indeed, News Corp had been presented to the board as management's preferred choice. The business of wanting to drop Ergen because of an obscure let-out clause in the UBS funding documents smacked of a split within GM management. If there was serious doubt about an EchoStar deal getting antitrust approval—as Devine had told Murdoch on Friday there was—then a money problem for Ergen made the whole decision much simpler. If a Hughes sale to EchoStar fell through on antitrust grounds, which on the balance of probabilities GM management on Friday apparently believed it would, then the failed deal would cost General Motors a lot of money. The DirecTV business would inevitably slide during the interregnum, even without considering the effects of a recession. EchoStar had agreed to buy Hughes Electronics' PanAmSat business for $5 billion regardless. At the end of the day GM would still have to sell Hughes, but it would have to pay EchoStar a $600 million breakup fee if it did find another buyer. If GM had to go back to Murdoch, he would not be forgiving.

The whole eighteen-month process had come down to this conference call between GM and Hughes executives and the GM chairman, Smith. Would they go with the News Corp deal, or would they take a risk on Charlie Ergen? Murdoch was stewing in TriBeCa debating whether he should rush across town to speak to the GM directors personally. "I nearly did that," he said later. "I was thinking of it that afternoon because I knew that Charlie had been calling in on the telephone from Denver. And I heard about this at three in the afternoon. I nearly jumped in a taxi to go in there. I thought, 'Maybe I'll be thrown out on my ear.' "

When the board meeting resumed, GM management recommended postponing any decision for forty-eight hours. The board would resolve the issue by not making a decision. It took another hour to agree to a delay that, it was clear, would deal Murdoch out of the game. Murdoch already knew the outcome when Devine called him with the news at four-thirty. Murdoch recalled, "I said, 'Well, this is about the tenth deadline that I've let pass. I'm not letting this pass. It's clearly the—somewhere in here the deck is stacked, so we'll just take a walk and get on with life.' "[7]

At least that was the gist of his comments. Accounts closer to the date suggested a more colorful exchange. Murdoch immediately released a prepared statement saying News Corp had no option but to withdraw its fully negotiated and financed offer. News Corp was "disappointed with the Board's inaction in the face of an as-yet unfinanced counter proposal. I am surprised that the board of GM did not share my vision and enthusiasm for what would have been a one-of-a-kind global multimedia company with superior growth prospects."

In Denver it was six-thirty P.M. and the EchoStar team were walking out of their headquarters, an old shopping mall that Ergen had bought for a very reasonable price. They knew about the postponement but not about the News Corp announcement. Ergen, Moskowitz, and others were in the parking lot, when Judianne Atencio's cell phone rang. It was Andrew Sorkin of the *New York Times*, asking for comment on Murdoch's withdrawal. The response was jubilation.

Murdoch called Ergen's home to leave his congratulations on the answering machine. He also called John Malone to let him know they had struck out. Malone was already into the next scenario: "Where do we go from here?" he said. Murdoch's other calls were not so cordial. Any faint possibility that remained for reconciliation that evening was snuffed out by the fiery telephone conversations between Murdoch and GM management. Murdoch believed Jack Smith had been the pivotal player in the decision, that General Motors had been stringing News Corp along for weeks to give EchoStar time to come up with an alternative proposal. News Corp executives referred to the decision as an "inside job." "The deck was stacked," Murdoch would later maintain. "I lay awake, I was pretty damn angry the first couple of nights, wondering what had gone wrong, and, you know, what have I done or what could I have done differently. . . . If I'd laid the law down earlier, I might have had a better shot."

Twenty-six hours later GM had settled a deal with EchoStar. The funding problem over the UBS escape clause was no longer a concern: GM itself would provide the $2.75 billion bridging loan, backed by Ergen's guarantee. At eight-thirty Sunday night, as the EchoStar team filed onto the Hughes jet sent to bring them to New York, they finally relaxed and broke open beers. Atencio finalized the press release with General Motors. The exhaustion in her voice was palpable as she spoke over the aircraft noise.[8]

The Hughes stock price fell on news of the deal. Elsewhere, the deal was heralded with almost universal acclaim: from Gerry Levin at AOL Time Warner, Jean-Marie Messier at Vivendi, Sumner Redstone at Viacom, Michael Eisner at Disney, Barry Diller at USA Networks, all of the major cable operators. The way much of the support was couched, the jubilation was not because Charlie Ergen had won but because Rupert Murdoch had been defeated. Within a month the next wave of megadeals triggered by the Hughes outcome would begin.

Everyone said that after September 11 the world would never be the same. But nobody understood what that really meant. The GM board meeting on October 27 would be the moment that crystallized the new direction that Big Media was taking. That direction was all rolled up in the future of one man, Rupert Murdoch. If he had won over the skeptics on the General Motors board that day, the effects would have bounced back and forth around the world. The disquieting thing about Murdoch's history, though, is not what happens when he wins. It's what happens when he loses. The repercussions for American culture and business from his defeat on October 27 would be just as overwhelming. To understand why Murdoch failed on that Saturday, or why one failed deal proved so important—why the American media industry, almost to a man or woman, schemed, demanded, and clamored for Rupert Murdoch to be shut out, to be stopped, no matter what it cost—you have to understand the wave of economic disaster that was already unfolding before September 11. This is the story of one man riding that wave—and the history that caught up with him.

PART II

ATLANTIC CROSSING

3

VOLTAIRE'S UNDERGRADUATE

Cruden Farm, Victoria 1966

> *I suppose [I am] a fairly average person, a fairly average, ex-troverted person, I think perhaps with a little bit more than the average share of ambition. Which may be attractive or unat-tractive to people, I don't know.*

RUPERT MURDOCH, 1966[1]

EVERY CHILDHOOD COMES to an end. When it does, not all families can talk about it. While for some the rites of passage hold no trauma, others are not so fortunate. If the subject surfaces at all, it is in acerbic after-dinner exchanges at Christmas or Thanksgiving. Media dynasties have the curious advantage that family members do not have to have their conversations face to face. When the Murdochs will not speak to each other directly, they communicate via the media. In the Murdoch family archive, Dame Elisabeth is the keeper of secrets. The only time she has broken her silence about her son's upbringing—and her regrets—was for a television program in the 1960s. She has been silent ever since.

The face is younger; the picture is showing signs of age. It is black and white, shot in 1966, and in the intervening years some of the grays have leached out of the sixteen-millimeter film. But the lines of the face are as strong as ever. It is Dame Elisabeth Murdoch: widow of Sir Keith Murdoch, the man credited with building Australia's largest newspaper group; mother of Rupert, the country's newest media entrepreneur; and a powerful woman in her own right, knighted in 1963 for her charity work with the Royal Children's Hospital in Melbourne. At this point Rupert Murdoch's international media empire is just a vague promise. At fifty-seven years, his mother is in her prime.

The film was shot for a forty-minute program profiling Rupert Murdoch, one of a series by the Australian Broadcasting Commission titled *Six Australians*. It is the earliest portrait of Murdoch on record, the only picture of Murdoch before he burst onto the international scene and his profile blurred into some strange transatlantic echo. In 1966 Murdoch was still an Australian phenomenon. There were grave concerns about his habit of gambling his media company on risky ventures. But he had no British newspapers yet, and despite the photograph on the wall of Murdoch with President Kennedy in 1961, any American aspirations were still only pipe dreams.

The routine for visiting film crews is well established. Earlier that day the crew entered through the ramshackle front gates of Cruden Farm, thirty miles south of Melbourne. From there they followed an avenue lined on each side with rows of lemon-scented gum trees. The driveway of crushed stone eventually sweeps around to circle in front of a house set in one of the major private gardens in Australia. Around and beyond it are glimpses of the walled garden, the picking garden, the terraces, the lake, and the little bridge. It's a television director's dream. As the camera crew plans the tracking shot down the avenue of gum trees, the on-air talent looks at the picking garden and decides to do their piece-to-camera *there*, beside the delphiniums. Faced with a feast of color, the producer wonders uneasily how much foliage and flowers they can decently run without turning the interview into a segment from *House and Garden*.

The clapboard house is half of an antebellum southern mansion. The ninety-acre farm was a gift to Dame Elisabeth from her husband, Sir Keith Murdoch, when they married in 1928. She was nineteen, on her mother's side a descendant of an upper-class English family. Her father, Rupert Greene, was an affable but wild Irish gambler. Elisabeth's new husband was forty-three, editor of the Melbourne *Herald* newspaper. The Murdochs had moved in successive generations from prosperous Edinburgh merchants, to a hellfire preacher in the Scottish fishing village of Cruden, to the head of the Congregational church in Australia, and finally to Keith Murdoch, who started out as a penny-a-line journalist. Six months after the marriage Keith Murdoch was appointed chief executive of the Herald and Weekly Times (HWT) group, the largest newspaper chain in Australia. Several months after the birth of their first child, Helen, in 1929, the Murdochs headed off on a world tour, and an architect was commissioned to remodel their weekend cottage at Cruden while they were gone. Seeing the Virginian columns on their return was the couple's first indication that the architect had a somewhat grander vision than they had anticipated. There followed an appalled silence as the Murdochs realized that, like Scarlett O'Hara, they had come back to Tara.

The living room is reached down a minor hallway from the front door. It is a large room, warm with the afternoon light that drifts through the leadlight windows. The furniture is oak, the floor is polished wood, and the heavy beams on the ceiling are hand-adzed. Armchairs are grouped around a large stone fireplace, with a grand piano in the corner and a Georgian dresser. The walls feature early Australian painters—a large canvas by Rupert Bunney, several small William Dobells, and a painting of a very young Rupert and his elder sister Helen. It is a quiet, composed room that speaks of order and permanence. It is a fitting stage for the formidable charms of Dame Elisabeth herself.

Dame Elisabeth is natural talent. The commanding presence she still has nearly four decades later shows here at its prime. She does not yet have the confidence of old age, but she has a coquettish charm. She has Princess Diana's unstudied mannerism of bowing her head in deprecatory fashion, then modestly flicking her eyes up to catch the camera. She has the cultured, rounded vowels of upper-class Melbourne matrons of the postwar period. She speaks with the assurance and resolution of her class. She is a lively conversationalist who conveys genuine warmth and affection, a talent she has passed on to her son, mixed with an appealing and steely determination. She is sitting in the heart of Murdoch country, in the front living room of Cruden Farm. And she has something she wants to say.

For all that, the interview is ordinary. It is cut to reflect an idyllic upbringing for the four Murdoch children on the farm. Helen was born in 1929. Keith Rupert Murdoch entered the world at the stroke of midnight on March 11, 1931. Anne was born four years later, in 1935, and a fourth child, Janet, in 1939. They grew up in the most expensive house in Melbourne, with eleven servants. Their weekend retreat, Cruden Farm, had four staff. Then there were two country properties that ran beef cattle. Dame Elisabeth wanders among mementos. "This picture has always been very dear to me," she says. "We had just been three months in England with three very small children. . . . Rupert at the time was like every little boy of between five and six, full of mischief. Very happy. Quite amenable. And I think that my husband had great hopes for him."

The film fades to rural rhapsodies, lingering over the sweep of lemon-scented gum trees along the drive of Cruden Farm, intercut with old pictures of earnest children fishing, cycling, and riding in the family car. Children frolic at the big townhouse, the weekend farm, the two cattle properties, with the beloved nanny, while the voice-over intones: "And in surroundings straight from A. A. Milne, four children, including son and heir Rupert, romped blissfully toward adolescence."

The break, when it comes, is unexpected. Dame Elisabeth launches into a sidetrack. She breaks off the discussion of childhood on the farm to talk about the decision to send Rupert to board for eight years at Geelong Grammar, a boarding school that specialized in educating the sons of wealthy landowners. His mother, a natural athlete, sent him there because she wanted to "toughen him up a bit" because she feared he was growing up too soft. Suddenly in this interview she is struggling. The marker for her discomfort is a class thing. Australian women of her background flag awkward or uncomfortable conversation subjects with the word *perhaps:*

> I think perhaps his home was such a happy one. And he did of course adore being with his father. I think perhaps there was a slight feeling of resentment that he'd been sent away to boarding school. Perhaps his Scottish blood was dominant in this respect. My grandparents were shocked that I was so keen on boarding school. And I'm not *certain* really that my husband was so very keen about it. And I was very young, rather determined, and perhaps I wasn't always very wise. But . . .

In the course of the speech Dame Elisabeth has progressively lost contact with the camera and the interviewer. She has lost her composure. The film cuts to bridging shots of Geelong Grammar. The moment hangs. Watching it half a lifetime later, in that moment of discomfort, the mind wanders. As Dame Elisabeth speaks on the old, grainy film shot a third of a century ago, her words conjure up in the mind a much earlier picture, circa 1940, twenty-six years before. The picture is wholly imaginary, of course. It is shot in black and white, no color at all, and moves with the stiffness and irregularity of prewar home movies, dark and bordering on the unrecognizable. The picture is of a boy who has not yet turned ten, dressed in cap and knickerbockers, walking alone into school as the camera pulls back. The film lingers there for a time, then runs out.

Dame Elisabeth is made of sterner stuff. She rallies: "But I think Rupert perhaps wasn't a conventional schoolboy, insofar as he didn't excel or wish to excel at sport. . . . But on the whole I think that he was very happy."

The editor breaks this sentence up with a sound bite from Rupert saying that he hated sports, and that he didn't know whether he was happy or not, but he didn't think so at the time. Sir Keith's death in 1952 was the keenest sorrow to her.

Dame Elisabeth longed to help Rupert prove worthy of his father, she said. And while he may have made mistakes, he had indeed justified his father's faith. Proving worthy of the father is a refrain to which the family will return again and again in interviews in the following decades. What the family does not say is that there is more than just sentiment to this movement. They see it also in the legal terms of Sir Keith's will. It is the knot that ties the family tightly together.

The Murdochs hated the film. For a family that has profited so much from exposing the frail secrets of others, it has always been remarkably reticent about baring its own. This is a family with almost no capacity for self-awareness. In 1993 each of the four children wrote a chapter about their childhood for Dame Elisabeth's biography, *Two Lives*. And what peculiar stories they told. The older sisters, Helen and Anne, would catch and skin rabbits and collect manure, which their brother Rupert would sell, pocketing the money. Dame Elisabeth allegedly had Rupert sleep in a hut outside the house, once again "to toughen him up a bit."

There is Murdoch's own story about how his mother taught him to swim on a ship back from England to Australia when he was five—in a pool that was itself moving up and down as the ship pitched: "I clearly recall my mother throwing me in the ship's pool—the deep end—and not letting anyone rescue me. I had to dog-paddle to the side, and I was screaming. That was the way to teach you to swim in those days."

And there is Helen's story of how she was so desperate to avoid competing in a diving competition at the local beach—which her mother, the golden girl who shone at all sports, always won—that she burned herself with an iron. "I suppose I wanted to shine for them, but I didn't," she said later.

The common theme in these stories, which are told affectionately, is power and denial. Dame Elisabeth looms in her children's accounts as a commanding figure, with a deep sense of duty and frugality. While the need to prove worthy of Sir Keith may be the family litany, the cult of the father is administered by their mother. Her power in the family is no less because she is a person of exceptional charm and genuine personal warmth, ready to give visitors a hug, an unexpected gift, or a donation.

By contrast, Sir Keith Murdoch was indulgent but distant, reluctant to praise, much more willing to be annoyed by his son's efforts to win his attention (a "disobedient, wild, sullen boy").[10] At work he was a fearsome political power broker, with a reputation as a great shouter. "Rupert was afraid of his father, he was always trying to please Sir Keith but to no avail," a contemporary told Thomas Kiernan, the Murdoch biographer who was closest to the family. "I don't think Rupert was born with the traits that have sullied his reputation as a grown-up. He developed them out of his desperation to encourage his father's approval."[11]

"As a boy he was rough as guts, he wasn't very subtle or gentle," said one of his schoolmates at Geelong. "He was known alternatively as Bullo Murdoch—being a bullshit artist or something—and Commo Murdoch, because he pretended to be a communist. He was rebelling against a capitalist father, I suppose." [12]

In all these exchanges, the 1966 interview is the only time Dame Elisabeth has revealed any direct concern about the decisions that shaped Rupert Murdoch's childhood. The force of that concern is in her careful understatement. The public statement is a reflection of private conversations, of wider regrets that range beyond any simple decision on schooling. All this has been frozen into an icon, a single frame, an emblem of the childhood of a man, Rupert Murdoch, whose pursuit of the future has been so relentless that it begs the question as to what he is leaving behind in his past.

The interview is notable for another feature. It lies hidden in the image that Dame Elisabeth's words have painted of the nine-year-old at the school door, standing there in that moment of realization that even the most golden childhood one day comes to an end. It is an indistinct image that only partly resolves when you ask, What is the figure doing?

In the sixity years since then, it is the only picture where Rupert Murdoch is looking back. Rosebud?

Oxford, 1950–53

> *I can't die yet. I've got to see my son established, not leave him like a lamb to be devoured and destroyed by these people, by John Williams.*
>   SIR KEITH MURDOCH, 1952[13]

In 1950 Murdoch found himself for the first time free of his family's expectations. His parents flew to Europe with him to see him settled into England before he started at Worcester College, Oxford. They stopped in Rome for an audience with the pope. "I was quite overwhelmed," says Dame Elisabeth. "Rupert said he was unimpressed, particularly with the little silver medals the Pope gave him."[14]

In between being thrown into the lake for lack of patriotism, buying a bust of Lenin to annoy his father, and being banned from politics for voting irregularities, Rupert Murdoch's lasting contribution in Oxford was to the academy. He helped to found an entirely bogus philosophical society.

Murdoch arrived at Worcester College for the start of Michaelmas term. A short, stocky figure, thickly built but not fat, he soon settled into the life of a well-upholstered leftist, achieving a level of opulence that most Oxford undergraduates only lusted after. He established himself in the Thomas de Quincey room, named after a nineteenth-century beneficiary who learned to smoke opium there. The oak-paneled rooms were among the most spacious and luxurious in the college. He owned a car, a beige Austin A-40. "It was like having a private airplane or a Rolls-Royce in terms of being noticed by your contemporaries," one of his Oxford friends, filmmaker Michael Weigall, said later.[15]

Several of Murdoch's contemporaries from Geelong Grammar were also at Oxford, including John Piper, later a senior Australian diplomat. Piper was at Brasenose College, and through him Murdoch became a regular feature of the group of undergraduates around Brasenose.

"He spent most of his time in the junior common room at Brasenose and the beer cellar," said one of the group, James Mitchell, later director of the National Consumer Council in Britain. "He was . . . a quiet individual who made very little impression at the time. All I have is a visual image of Rupert Murdoch with a group of people drinking beer and never actually saying anything."

Patrick Seale, who went on to become the London *Observer*'s Middle East correspondent and the author of controversial biographies of Syrian president Hafez Assad and Palestinian terrorist Abu Nidal, remembers Murdoch as very bluff, boisterous, and charming. Years later he said, "He had a raw animal energy. Great shrewdness but not a great intellectual, with a bulldozing approach to human relations which I suppose is something one associates with people from Australia. But it certainly cuts corners. . . . He's the sort of chap who goes straight to the point, tells you exactly what he wants, no beating about the bush. Obviously too, a strong streak of ruthlessness, but that wasn't so apparent at that time; there was more a tremendous kindliness."

Not everyone at Brasenose perceived the kindliness Seale mentioned. "He was a sick, spoiled, overbearing man—what other impression could he make?" said one former contemporary. "He was agreeable, he had a certain amount of charm, but behind it I think was the money."

"He was a bumptious, opinionated young man from the colonies who had more money than was good for him," said another fellow undergraduate. "He was overbearing in his views and aggressively self-confident on political topics."

While reactions to Murdoch were many and varied, what the group at

Brasenose agree on is that Rupert Murdoch was extraordinarily close to Robin Farquharson, an exuberant, erratic South African undergraduate whose brilliance overshadowed the group. What they could not work out was why. "It's very hard to say what the basis of that friendship was, because they were really very, very different," said James Mitchell. "Robin would talk sixty to the dozen on any subject and had wild intellectual and political fantasies that he would build up as he was talking. And Rupert never said anything about anything."

In his first year Farquharson was already being described by dons as the most brilliant undergraduate they had ever come across. "Farquharson was exceptionally brilliant, extremely intelligent, a very quick man," said Robert Shackleton, a Brasenose professor. Farquharson's doctoral thesis would win the 1961 Monograph Prize of the American Academy of Arts and Sciences in the field of social sciences. It was published in 1969 by Yale University Press as *Theory of Voting*, and it described as the mathematics of the process that politicians use to vote tactically. More simply, it was about the science of rigging a democracy.

"I am a manic-depressive," Farquharson wrote in *Drop Out!*, his memoir about his later life on the street. "When I'm up I have no judgement at all, but fantastic drive. When I'm down, I have judgement, but no drive at all. In between, I can pass for normal well enough." It had been a long-term problem. "Intermittent psychosis, mania, cyclothymia, manic highs [have] dogged my life since 1955," he wrote. That was the year when, as a promising candidate for a fellowship at All Souls in Oxford, he destroyed his chances by making a telephone call to the warden: Farquharson called him away from his High Table to tell him that he had a message for him from God. By the 1960s Farquharson's struggles with his illness had put any conventional form of occupation out of the question, and he lived in homeless shelters. He embraced the squatter movement in London, living in derelict houses, occasionally descending without notice on old friends, then disappearing back into the streets. But in 1951 at Oxford Farquharson's bipolar condition was still quiescent. He shared an apartment with American John Searle, who went on to become a professor of philosophy at Berkeley; and later with Nigel Lawson, who went on to become chancellor of the exchequer.

Murdoch spent the European summer of 1951 driving to Istanbul with another Australian student, George Masterman, and two history fellows at Worcester, Harry Pitt and Asa Briggs. Sir Keith had engaged Briggs to offer his son some extra tuition in his politics, philosophy, and history courses. Rupert's economics tutor, J. R. Sargent of Worcester, said his student had "not much interest" in the subject: "It was pretty clear he was interested in the world of politics and journal-

ism and not much else. He is said to have scraped through with Briggs' help. . . .
Under the Oxford system it's not very easy to fail. I mean, the statistical percentage of those who actually fail is very small. He did get into the lowest class."[16]

By late 1951 the group around Murdoch had become convinced that, in order
to get jobs after Oxford, they needed to spice up their curricula vitae. They
needed their own club. "The reason the Voltaire Society was founded was that it
had more officers proportionate to membership than almost any other university
society," said Michael Weigall. Positions were held for only a term and circulated
among members. As for its aims, the most that could be said was that it was a
group that, like Voltaire, was generally opposed to organized religion.

Said Weigall, "One of the most often quoted statements of Voltaire was that if
God did not exist, he would have to be invented. . . . That's how Voltaire saw it,
and the society's motto—Rupert, like me, was a founding member—was that if
Voltaire did not exist, he would have to be invented, which of course rather accu-
rately summed up the circumstances in which the club was founded. It was basically a dining club."

American alumnus John Brademas was a member; he ran unsuccessfully for
Congress two years later on the basis of his Oxford record and later became president emeritus of New York University and chairman of the President's Committee
on the Arts and Humanities. The Voltaire Society's stationery for the Trinity term
of 1952 shows eleven elected officials and only fifty regular members. The Voltaire
Society patron is listed as Bertrand Russell. The masthead notes augustly, "The
Society is affiliated to the Voltaire International," and coyly reminds members,
"The Society's Library and Iconographical Collection are available for consultation in the Secretary's rooms at 19 St John St on Sunday mornings in term."

No Voltaire International existed. The "iconographical collection" consisted of
one bust of Voltaire, under the care of the official iconographer, Colin Leys, now
a Marxist scholar of third-world development. As a job title, at least this was better than the previous term, when there had been an official iconoclast, whose job
it was to sneak around pinching busts from other societies. The society also had an
office of gardener, said Weigall, because Voltaire was rather keen on horticulture.

Accounts vary as to whether the society library, under the care of the librarian,
Michael Smart (president of the Labour Club the year before), comprised two
books or just one. In any case the library and the bust were kept in the rooms of
the society's secretary, Robin Farquharson, who was assisted by the officer without portfolio, Rupert Murdoch.

With characteristic gusto, Farquharson leaped at the idea of a bogus society and promptly cycled to Paris, where he bought a bust of Voltaire from the curiosity shop attached to the Louvre. The bust was unveiled at one of the society's meetings in a private dining room, after Weigall gave an appallingly drunken speech. He recounted later, "In the stunned silence following what everyone regarded as an inept performance quite out of keeping with the solemnity of the occasion, the only person who applauded was Rupert. He came and shook me by the hand and said it was the best speech he had ever heard."

As well as the Voltaire Society, Murdoch and Farquharson teamed up again to run the student magazine, *Cherwell*. In the Trinity term of 1952 Murdoch became publicity manager of *Cherwell*, while Farquharson took over as production manager. Like the Voltaire Society, the *Cherwell* team's aim was to take a snide shot at the world in general. References to Murdoch in the magazine described him variously as "cataclysmic chauffeur from the outback and prototype of Hollywood's peripatetic publicists" and as "turbulent, travelled and twenty-one."[17]

Murdoch's friendship with Farquharson was important for two reasons. First, Farquharson was a mathematician. Oxford in the postwar period was teeming with ideas, one of which was game theory. In 1948 John Von Neumann and Oskar Morgenstern had published their groundbreaking work on the subject, *Theory of Games and Economic Behaviour*. At Princeton in 1951 John F. Nash, at twenty-one years old, published the paper for which he would share the Nobel Prize forty-five years later. Game theory grew out of the study of poker games and chess. It challenged the classical doctrine that economic outcomes are attributed merely to impersonal forces. Instead it looked at the role of individual people, who it assumed could be mendacious, nasty, and often stupid. The tactics it studied were backstabbing, cheating, and mistrust. At one level game theory seemed to turn everything around, with its implicit suggestion that the successful player in business or politics was the one who ignored convention and social expectations, who cut corners, who broke unwritten rules, who did what no one else in the game was prepared to do. It was what Rupert Murdoch would always do so well.

Today game theory is best known for the Prisoner's Paradox, a story told about two suspects being questioned by police over a robbery. Each prisoner must decide whether to maintain his innocence, in which case he may be charged with a minor offense; or to inform on his companion in return for immunity, in which case the informant—a sophisticated game player—walks free at his companion's expense. But if they both inform, then they both receive the maximum sentence. So the question for each prisoner is, How is the other player going to act? This is the difficulty: From an individual's perspective, it is always a better prospect to make the opportunistic choice, to inform on the other players or take advantage of them in some way. But if one player does this, then the long-term result is that everybody else ends up making the same opportunistic choice—either at the start or the next time that the same situation comes up. Inevitably everyone ends up worse off.

John F. Nash, whose life story was portrayed by Russell Crowe in *A Beautiful Mind*, is known as the father of game theory. Like Farquharson, he battled for years against mental illness. While one does not have to be mad to understand game theory, being able to think outside the box seems to help. Farquharson meanwhile was developing his own version of the Prisoner's Paradox. It was a sort of Politician's Paradox that he began to develop in 1953 to explain why, when he looked at voting records in the U.S. Senate, so often the end result of legislation was a compromise that nobody liked.[18]

So at a time when Murdoch and his contemporaries were taking gibes at the Establishment, the brightest star in their intellectual universe was propounding a theory that spelled out the advantages of doing just that. Or rather, of doing it and getting away with it. It was the science of when it was safe to cut corners. Murdoch would reap a huge financial benefit in doing what no one else would accept, whether it was running topless girls on page three of the *Sun*, as he did two decades later; or taking on the entrenched British printing unions, as he did in 1986; or exploring the bounds of reality TV, as he did in America in the 1990s with shows such as *When Animals Attack*. British society has always been more regulated by the social contract, the unwritten law, than has North America. This helps explain why Murdoch, the natural game player, has been so much more successful in Britain. In Britain, as he told *The Economist* in 1996, "all you had to do is just to work hard." In America, when it came to being a tough game player, he found he had to take a number.

Farquharson went on to demonstrate that the effect of breaking down the social contract in a system, a rush to the bottom, eventually became a disaster for all parties. It is a basic feature of game theory analysis. Today game theorists talk about game strategies where everybody wins. But Farquharson's friend Rupert never got to this part of the lesson.

The other significance of the closeness between Murdoch and Farquharson was that Farquharson was gay—spectacularly, flamboyantly gay. "I was the victim, as I saw it then, of a grave and distressing homosexual condition wholly resisting treatment," he wrote in *Drop Out!*, which is peppered with sexual one-liners. "Look after the penis and the ponce will look after itself," he concluded grandilo-

quently while describing with great gusto the romance of a seventeen-year-old
boy. "I lack courage, I know, just as I lack stability and application and patience,
qualities I value, and as I also lack consistency and temperance and chastity, qualities I do not value at all."[19]

In the Oxford scene there was nothing unusual in Farquharson's sexuality.
What is interesting is that in the course of the next decade Murdoch came to re-
ject almost every aspect of the life that Oxford represented. It was not only his
politics that would become more conservative. His views on other people's sexuality would also change. It would be reflected in his newspapers' growing homophobia, and the zeal with which they would "out" public figures.

All this, however, was still a long way off. The more pressing question was, what
was Murdoch to do after Oxford? Says Michael Weigall, "Sir Keith Murdoch had
obviously been a very strong, dominating person. His father seemed to be set
there for always and was such a powerful man, Rupert said, 'It's not a world for
me.' "

Rupert retained his powerful ability to annoy his father. He had bought a bust
of Lenin that he installed on his mantelpiece and continued to refer to Lenin in
his letters home as "The Great Thinker." In 1952 his father was concerned enough
to confide in Hugh Cudlipp of the London Daily Mirror group, "I'm worried
about my son Rupert. He's at Oxford and developing the most alarming left-wing
views."[20]

An aquatic excursion of early 1952 puts to rest any doubts about Murdoch's
left-wing credentials. As one of his contemporaries tells it, Murdoch had just sent
out invitations for a cocktail party when King George VI had the bad grace to die
on February 6. The state funeral was set for the day of Murdoch's party. A less
dedicated bon vivant might have considered another date, but not Murdoch. He
got around the ban on private celebrations by sending out new invitations turning
his get-together into an interment party. This levity was regarded in some quarters
as bad form, and a group of patriotic souls, so the story goes, set out to demonstrate that no man is an island by turfing Murdoch into the lake. It was "the best
thing that could have happened to him," one of those present declared happily decades later.

By mid-1952 Murdoch was under investigation by the Labour Club at Oxford.
After he ran for the post of secretary, he was accused with others of breaking the
prohibition on direct canvassing or electioneering, a practice that was not unknown. Gerald Kaufman, the chairman of the Labour Club in the Trinity term in
1952, set up an investigation made up of former chairmen of the club—" 'the

Bloody Tribbyanal' as the irreverent K. R. Murdoch immediately dubbed it." The verdict in September went against him. "I think Murdoch felt it was hard luck that he was one of those who were caught while others were not, and I must say I had some sympathy for him," said Michael Smart.

Murdoch, however, had much more to worry about. Late on Saturday, October 4, 1952, his father died of a heart attack. By the time Rupert reached Australia a week later, his father had been cremated. The Herald and Weekly Times chairman, Harry Giddy, was coexecutor of the will with Dame Elisabeth. Sir Keith's deputy, Jack Williams, had given the eulogy. What made this particularly awkward was that on October 2, two days before he died, Sir Keith had discovered that Williams was plotting a coup to force him out of the company and apparently had the numbers on the board of directors to do so. The next day Sir Keith faced down the board and fired Williams. On October 5 Williams was back in charge, opening the safe in Sir Keith's office. Some reports say he used a jackhammer to do it.[21]

Sir Keith left the townhouse, Cruden Farm, the two cattle properties, and half shares in two newspapers operations, Queensland Newspapers in Brisbane and the smaller News Limited in Adelaide. But he owned almost no shares in the Herald and Weekly Times Group. In the family's view he should have had far more. He had built the Herald and Weekly Times, and now his former friends had jackhammered through the inheritance. It was outright theft. Jack Williams thought the same thing, but he saw a different perpetrator. He didn't see how Sir Keith had managed to build a private empire on his newspaper salary, as generous as that was. "Williams said that Murdoch had managed to divert News Limited into his own pocket, had managed to filch the property owned by the Herald while he was head of the company," Cecil King, former chairman of the London Daily Mirror group and the nephew of Lord Northcliffe, claimed years later. "Williams regarded it as disgraceful skullduggery, absolute unblushing theft."[22]

When Williams broke into Sir Keith's safe, hours after he had died, he was looking for stock transfer documents and other records. The Herald and Weekly Times had provided financial support to help Sir Keith buy a half interest in Queensland Newspapers, and Harry Giddy's board believed it had an option to buy the stake from Sir Keith's estate.[23] The half share in News Limited had once belonged to the Herald and Weekly Times, but after a slick set of transactions, the half share had ended up in the Murdoch family company, Cruden Investments, for little charge.

Sir Keith Murdoch was the most successful and powerful journalist Australia had ever seen. The sheer scale of his rise, from his start as an impoverished, penny-a-line reporter to the international stage, as a kingmaker and confidant of political leaders in Britain and Australia—all this meant that in the eyes of his family and his colleagues, he was one of a kind. For some, nothing the son achieved could ever match the brilliance of the father. Rupert could never outrun his father's shadow. Remnants of that family judgment remain today.

Not only could Rupert never match his father's accomplishments, he was forced to watch powerlessly as almost all that his father had built up was dissipated. To pay out debt and death duties, Giddy sold the country properties, convinced Dame Elisabeth to sell the half share in Queensland Newspapers to the Herald and Weekly Times group, and almost persuaded her to sell the News shares as well. Giddy's concern was to see Dame Elisabeth and her three daughters provided for. The son upon whom Sir Keith had at times poured such open scorn would be quite capable of making his own way. "I felt very bitter about the destruction of the newspaper group because a lot of hard work went into it," a close family friend later recalled. "In my opinion it was stolen. And if I felt like that and I wasn't Sir Keith's son, how do you think Rupert felt? . . . It was an absolutely appalling business."[24]

Sir Keith's will had been equivocal:

> I desire that my said son Keith Rupert Murdoch should have the great opportunity of spending a useful, altruistic and full life in newspaper and broadcasting activities and of ultimately occupying a position of high responsibilities on that field with the support of my trustees if they consider him worthy of that support.

A later codicil repeated Sir Keith's caveat: "if my trustees judge him worthy of such a place in the community." In April 1952, five months before his death, when Sir Keith was rushed to the hospital for his second prostate operation, he wrote, "It could be that Rupert's strong political views will make his career in newspapers impossible."[25]

Sir Keith's executors shared this skepticism. When Rupert convinced his mother to retain News Limited, the Herald and Weekly Times made another buyout offer, this time threatening a circulation war to drive News out of business. The Murdochs eventually emerged with a half share in News valued at around $200,000. In present-day money values this was about $3 million.

In the aftermath of his father's death, three things became clear for Rupert.

The first was that a huge gulf exists between the people who own a company and the paid staff. Second, the more the Murdochs' sense of injustice over the inheritance grew, the more need there was for Rupert to take up the cudgels for the family, to rebuild the family empire. The greater the Murdochs' grievance, the more secure Rupert's position became, though he did not as yet control the family holding company, Cruden Investments. And so the family inheritance would be locked up in the News shareholding for four decades, controlled by Rupert.

Lastly, after a childhood marked by gestures of resentment and rebellion against his father, Murdoch had a new range of patriarchal figures to challenge. The bitterness that would mark his struggles suggests that, while the Murdoch family may have wanted to restore the family honor, Rupert Murdoch had a more basic drive. He was looking for revenge.

4

THE DRUNKEN SAILOR

URDOCH WAS FIFTY-FOUR years old when he began his great adventure. Everything that led up to this point in 1985 was merely preparation. Just getting to America took him twenty years, and he did it via Britain. He spent another decade living in New York before he became a serious player. When Murdoch took over News Limited in South Australia at the end of 1953, its profits had been dropping for three years. In 1951 News earned just A£24,877 (about US$50,000). Two years after Rupert took over its net assets had doubled. He fought off a rival Sunday newspaper that was launched by his father's old newspaper chain, went into television in Adelaide, expanded to Perth in Western Australia with a Sunday newspaper, then leapfrogged the continent to Sydney in 1960 to revive the *Daily Mirror*, a faded afternoon tabloid.

The pattern was already set. For half a century Murdoch would spend the first years of each decade recovering from his latest great gamble. By the middle of the decade he would have settled the empire down, beaten back the bankers, and embarked on the next growth phase. The deals would grow dizzier and dizzier until by the end of the decade Murdoch's News empire would look impossibly stretched, his critics declaring that this time this crisis would be his last.

In 1964 Murdoch launched a national broadsheet, the *Australian,* in Canberra. The paper's first editor, Maxwell Newton, recalled Murdoch running everywhere with immense enthusiasm the first night. Later over drinks he said he had a strange feeling that Murdoch was trying to justify something. Murdoch told him: "Well I've got where I am by some pretty tough and pretty larrikin methods . . . but I've got there. And now what I want to do—I want to be able to produce a newspaper that my father would have been proud of.' "[1]

In 1956 Murdoch married a flight attendant, Patricia Booker. They had a daughter, Prudence, in 1959. But the marriage became increasingly unhappy and ended in 1966, after divorce proceedings so acrimonious that Murdoch reportedly ordered that the name of his wife's lawyer should never appear in any of the News publications.[2] The following year Murdoch remarried. His new wife was a twenty-two-year-old journalist he had been dating for almost five years called Anna Marie Torv. Anna grew up in difficult circumstances. Her father was a war refugee from Estonia who had married the daughter of a family with a dry-cleaning business in Scotland, where Anna was born on June 30, 1944. When she was ten, her parents emigrated to Australia, where they ended up running a snack bar in a Sydney trailer park. When the snack bar went bankrupt, her mother walked out, leaving Anna, as the eldest, with many of the child-rearing responsibilities for her sister and two brothers. When she was sixteen, Anna left school at the Sisters of Mercy convent and, after a succession of jobs, ended up as a cadet journalist at the Sydney *Mirror* in 1962. She was eighteen, bright, serious, and very attractive, with great hopes for a writing career, when she interviewed her boss for the in-house paper—and ended up going out with him.

It was a fitful romance. When Murdoch launched the *Australian* in 1964, Anna went to Canberra as part of the sales promotion team. Later, when Anna worked as a reporter, she moved in with Rupert in a Canberra apartment. Rupert and Anna married on April 28, 1967—two years before Murdoch's third wife, Wendi Deng, was born. Patricia had won custody of Prudence, but as Patricia went from one disastrous romantic entanglement to another, Prudence asked to live with her father. Prudence came to live with Rupert and Anna in Sydney at about the time that Anna's first child, Elisabeth, was born, in August 1968. Overnight Anna had a new baby to look after as well as a nine-year-old stepdaughter. Two months later she lost her home. Rupert telephoned her from Melbourne and told her to meet him at Sydney airport.

The Murdochs flew to London in October 1968 in answer to a plea for help from the Carr family, whose News of the World Organisation Limited was facing a hostile takeover bid from Robert Maxwell, an ambitious Czech-born media entrepreneur with a talent for corporate theft. The company's major asset was the *News of the World*, a down-market Sunday newspaper with a circulation of 6 million. Murdoch convinced the chairman, Sir William Carr, to issue voting shares to News Limited in exchange for various News subsidiaries that were earning £1.1 million a year before tax. After other cash purchases Murdoch emerged with 49 percent of the voting stock of News of the World, and six months later, despite a promise to retain Sir William, he had forced him to step down as chairman.

In November 1969 Murdoch took over a struggling British afternoon newspaper, the *Sun*, which was in such dire financial straits that the initial purchase

price was only £50,000, the first of a series of annual installments. The total payment was to be £500,000, but only if the paper survived long enough. Two years
later the *Sun* was earning this much every month. The mix of cheeky headlines,
sensational news and scandal, cash promotions, and pictures of topless women
on page three prompted *Private Eye*, the British satirical magazine, to christen
Murdoch "the Dirty Digger." The British establishment was outraged.

"There's been nothing in Rupert's papers to make you say, 'Now that's a new
idea,'" said Cecil King, the former chaiman of the London Daily Mirror Group
and the nephew of Sir Keith Murdoch's mentor, Lord Northcliffe, in 1983. "There's
never a new idea. What his papers are about is going further, being louder and
more vulgar."

Despite the criticism, sales of the *Sun* took off. At the time Murdoch took over
the paper, its circulation was 1 million. It hit 2 million in 1971 and 3 million in
1973. By then Murdoch had left Britain. In October 1973 he paid $19 million for
two Texas newspapers, the *San Antonio Express* and its afternoon stablemate, the
News. Under Murdoch the papers became more profitable as they became racier,
with headlines like "Armies of Insects Marching on SA" and "Killer Bees Move
North." The Murdochs settled in New York, but to qualify to own Australian television stations, he listed his home address as a cattle property near Canberra. Both
Murdoch sons were born in Britain—Lachlan on September 8, 1971, and James
fifteen months later on December 15, 1972—but Anna never seemed to enjoy living in England and clearly found life in New York more convivial.

The business struggles in Murdoch's early years as a media proprietor had
bleached away his loosely held political convictions from Oxford. In 1959
Murdoch's *News* in Adelaide had campaigned hard for Rupert Stuart, an Aborigi-
nal on death row, convicted of murder despite a strong alibi and evidence by linguistic experts that he could not have written his confession to police. After a
political storm in South Australia, the *News* and its editor, Rohan Rivett, were
charged with criminal libel. The trial ended in a hung jury. Facing the prospect of
another trial—and that charges might also be brought against himself—just as he
was making inroads into Sydney, Murdoch backed off the story. The *News* apologized to the government. Stuart's sentence was commuted to life imprisonment.
And Murdoch did no more campaigning for black men. He had also become ho-
mophobic. The staff at his Sydney paper in the 1960s expressed the hiring policy
as an informal mantra: "No blacks, no poofters [Australian slang for gays], no
suede shoes."

In London Murdoch turned down a request by Anthony Blond, a Brasenose alumnus who had helped Robin Farquharson publish his book *Drop Out!,* to help his old friend. "He said, 'No, no one can help him,'" Blond recalled.[3] In April 1973 Farquharson died of burns after two men who shared an abandoned house with him set a fire, forgetting that he was asleep upstairs. Death by absentmindedness. Murdoch didn't make it to the funeral—he had left Farquharson behind him long before, along with everything else from his time at Oxford, from a past that was now closed to him, a world that no longer offered any possibilities. Over half a century Murdoch's odyssey would be marked regularly by the painful moments when he jettisoned cargo: people, ideas, and places he had outgrown. His direction was always forward. Later, when explaining the latest in the long list of executives that he had dumped at News Corp, Murdoch would say, "I learned when running a public company not to grow too close to people."

In 1974 Murdoch launched the *National Star* in the United States as an unsuccessful rival to the *National Enquirer.* Two years later it was relaunched as the *Star,* a women's magazine with a circulation of three million. In November 1976 Murdoch finally established a beachhead in New York when he persuaded the longtime owner of the *New York Post,* Dorothy Schiff, to sell the loss-making paper to him for $30 million. Murdoch then moved on New York Magazine Company, founded and run by Clay Felker, who had befriended Rupert and Anna, and introduced them to New York society. Despite a spectacular fight with the outraged Felker, Murdoch bought the company for $26 million and picked up *New York* magazine and *The Village Voice. Time* magazine ran a cover showing Murdoch as King Kong standing on top of the Empire State Building, with the caption, "Extra!!! Aussie Press Lord Terrifies New York."

Murdoch behaved in New York as he did everywhere else. He became a firm friend of the incumbent mayor, Ed Koch, and each of his successors. He dragged the liberal *Post* over to the right, he wheedled favors from whichever politician was in town (Jimmy Carter was his easiest mark), he reintroduced newspaper bingo, and in the summer of 1977 with the New York blackout to agonize over and the Son of Sam on a shooting rampage, he had a fine old time. It was all very colorful. There was similar anguish when he bought the *Boston Herald* in December 1982 for $1 million plus up to $7 million in future profits, and the Chicago *Sun-Times* in November 1983 for $90 million. In Britain he had bought the *Times* and *Sunday Times* in 1981 and now produced 30 percent of the country's national newspapers.

From 1985 the accepted history in half a dozen Murdoch biographies runs like this: Murdoch bought 20th Century–Fox studio in Hollywood, then a chain of television stations called Metromedia, then launched Fox as the first new television network since 1959. He bought *TV Guide* for $3 billion, merged the HarperCollins publishing group, overturned the British trade unions by moving his Fleet Street papers to an industrial site at Wapping, and then almost went broke in December 1990 because a little bank in Pittsburgh refused to roll over a $10 million loan. The Pittsburgh bank incident is the best-known Murdoch story in the world. *Institutional Investor* broke the story. The *Financial Times* added a few more details. Then William Shawcross made the story famous in his biography, *Murdoch*.

But what if it didn't happen like that? What if instead of being a carefully planned grand strategy, Murdoch's great empire building across the globe in the 1980s was just a really bad dream that kept coming back to haunt Murdoch, as he kept making bigger and bigger gambles, scrambling to escape from a calamity created for him by junk bond king Michael Milken? Like a man carrying a flagpole over his shoulder in a glassware shop, every time Murdoch turned to address a new problem, he set off a another wave of chaos somewhere behind him.

The figure of Rupert Murdoch always appears blurred and half-formed until you set him in opposition to something. In the 1980s he is best defined by his rivalry with Ted Turner. The 1980s represented the first wave of the information revolution that would so drastically reorder the U.S. media industry. Turner and Murdoch, perhaps by accident as much as anything else, emerged as the clearest and most farsighted media players in a confusing decade. Their strategies and their timing were strikingly similar. But only one of them emerged from the 1980s with his media empire intact and independent. Pioneers are the first casualties of any revolution. The question has always been how Rupert Murdoch survived.

*   *   *

Robert Edward Turner III was born seven years after Rupert Murdoch. His bipolar disorder makes him closer in personality style to Robin Farquharson than to Murdoch. After inheriting one of America's largest billboard companies, Turner did well building up a couple of television stations. But his real success came thanks to a lawyer named Gerald Levin who headed a tiny pay-television operation called Home Box Office, part of the Time Inc. empire. On September 30, 1975, Levin triggered a huge change in the U.S. television industry by renting satellite time to carry the Muhammad Ali–Joe Frazier fight, the so-called Thrilla in Manila, to cable customers in New York, Mississippi, and Florida. This was a breakthrough, because for the first time a cable program was to be shown simultaneously across the country. Until then the cable operations that had sprung up across America could show only videotapes and programming that cable operators received via expensive microwave links. The cable operators had a lot of channels but nothing to put on them. Levin showed that, if cable companies bought an earth station, they could receive all sorts of programming via satellite to put onto their cable nets. For the first time cable offered not just clearer pictures but a clearly better product than local free-to-air television. The huge growth in cable viewing that this would produce would change the balance of power in the American media. And some of the biggest opportunities lay in providing the new programming.

Within months of Levin's historic broadcast, Turner moved to set up an uplink station that would broadcast his Atlanta television station, WTCG, to an RCA satellite. Any cable operator with an earth station could pull the signal down and rebroadcast Turner's superstation as a cable channel all over America. And they did. That single move would eventually make Turner a multibillionaire. Despite their differences, Murdoch and Turner did have some points in common as two moguls-in-waiting. They both had an intuitive feeling for where media was heading. They were both superb game players. And they both liked sailing and they both liked winning, though not necessarily in that order.

They didn't like each other. For two decades the two men have pursued one of the most high-profile feuds in the business world. The only account of its origin was a curious story that Turner Broadcasting executives gave to a Turner biographer, Bibb Porter, about a drunken speech by Turner after the Sydney-to-Hobart yacht race in 1979, where he humiliated Murdoch, whose boat had gone aground. The story is fine, except that the race was in 1983, Murdoch wasn't in it, and it was Turner's boat that went aground. But there was a speech, and alcohol had been consumed.

The Sydney-to-Hobart is one of the world's top three offshore races. It begins on December 26 each year and offers sailors a 650-mile adrenaline rush, surfing down the east coast of Australia across Bass Strait to Tasmania. In the 1998 race seven sailors drowned in abysmal conditions. Larry Ellison, owner of the software giant Oracle, won that race on his boat *Sayonnara,* with Lachlan Murdoch on board as a crew member. Ellison said that at one point, facing sixty-foot waves and winds touching a hundred miles per hour, he was sure he was going to die.

What is less widely known is the postrace institution known as the Quiet Little Drink, a title that the Cruising Yacht Club spokesman that year called "the greatest misnomer of all times." Indeed, the previous year a local newspaper had run an editorial that began by saying, "Go home, foul-mouthed drunken bum yachties."[4] That was before the editorial writer *really* got snippy. The Quiet Little Drink lasts anywhere from one to four days and includes a competition where crews attempt to beat the standing record for the number of jugs of rum and Coke (a 60/40 mix) that a crew can consume in twelve hours. In 1983 the existing record was 134 jugs, set two years before. The winning crew—which that year was Turner's—traditionally begins proceedings by downing twenty jugs of a cocktail mix made from two liqueurs and milk. While no one has ever accused Turner of having a drinking problem, he has a legendary ability to party. One of the enduring images of the 1977 America's Cup defense was of Turner sitting on the deck of *Courageous* after winning the last race, dripping wet, swigging rum and aquavit. When his mother on the wharf called, "Teddy!" he waved back, "It's okay, Mommy, I'm just sipping." That was before he fell over at the press conference.[5]

Another Sydney-to-Hobart race tradition, one that on occasion blurs the boundaries with the Quiet Little Drink, is a more formal affair, the postrace dinner. A number of speeches are made, including one traditionally made by the skipper of the winning boat. In 1983 that was Turner, who had been called in from sailing retirement to skipper an eighty-foot British boat called *Condor.* Turner won the race on protest after *Nirvana,* an eighty-one-foot yacht owned by New York television executive Marvin Greene of Reeves Communications, forced *Condor* aground in the last minutes of the race. Which was how Ted Turner came to be getting to his feet to deliver a long and rambling speech in which he vented his displeasure not toward Greene or the crew of *Nirvana* but toward the man he believed was a sponsor of *Nirvana,* Rupert Murdoch. Turner went on and on about Murdoch, sitting down only after delivering unpardonable offense—at least in Turner's own eyes.[6]

If only Rupert Murdoch had the faintest clue of what was going on. It had been his habit to spend Christmas at his Cavan cattle property in Australia with the family. He was there this year, but his mind was firmly focused on the other side of the world. That summer Stanley S. Shuman, executive vice president of Allen & Co. and Murdoch's investment banker since 1976, had introduced him to Steve Ross, chairman and chief executive of Warner Communications. On December 1, 1983, News Corporation announced that it had bought 6.7 percent of Warner. Ross told Murdoch to back off. On December 29, several hours after *Condor* ran aground, Steve Ross ambushed Murdoch by pulling off a cute little exchange of stock with his friend Herbert J. Siegel. Siegel's Chris-Craft Industries would pick up a 19 percent stake in Warner Communications, in exchange for

Warner taking a 42.5 percent stake in the Chris-Craft group's string of television stations. Warner now had a major new shareholder to help fend off Murdoch. But more important, it meant that now Warner controlled a small chain of American television stations. As a television investor, Warner had the protection of Section 310 of the Communications Act of 1934, which decreed that alien companies, like the Australian-owned News Corporation, could hold no more than 25 percent of its stock. Warner had been Murdoch-proofed.

Rupert Murdoch's response was rage. The bitterness of his childhood, his political experience at Oxford, and his father's death; his fierce struggles in Adelaide and Sydney against rivals with political muscle and greater resources; his rejection by London society and the torrid newspaper wars in New York—all this had stoked a deep wellspring of anger that he carried within him. It was anger looking for a target. "It's a tone he adopts—he feels the world is out to get him," Clay Felker once said.

Murdoch turned to his New York law firm, Squadron Ellenoff Plesent & Lehrer. The senior partner, Howard M. Squadron, had been a key part of Murdoch's U.S. deals since he'd bought the San Antonio papers in 1983. But recently much of the work had been done by the head of corporate at Squadron Ellenoff, Arthur Siskind. Not for the earnest toilers at Squadron Ellenoff the Socratic maxim that the unexamined life is not worth living. Like most lawyers, they had found that the unexamined life was exactly what their clients were looking for. Squadron Ellenoff was the soul of discretion.

Over the New Year Squadron and Siskind launched a legal blitzkrieg against Warner Communications in state and federal courts challenging the Chris-Craft deal and accusing Ross and the rest of the Warner Communications board of racketeering. The civil cases that followed were remarkable only for the extraordinary legal invective that Murdoch's lawyers spun off—one judge called it a corporate form of feudal warfare.[7] The cases were duly thrown out, but the ferocity of the Squadron Ellenoff legal onslaught eventually induced Steve Ross to buy back Murdoch's Warner stock. Murdoch took a $41.5 million profit, plus $3 million for his interest bill and $5 million to cover Squadron Ellenoff's legal expenses.

The same emotions—and much of the same cast—would resurface thirteen years later in Murdoch's battle with Turner to run Fox News on the Time Warner cable network in New York. In 1983 as in 1996, Turner's diatribes against Murdoch were sparked by a perceived threat to Turner's Cable Network News (CNN). The boat race just gave Turner an opportunity to vent his feelings. "He sat in that very chair a year ago," Turner said in January 1984. "He was talking to me about Cable Network News. He likes it very much."[8] Murdoch liked CNN too much for Turner to be comfortable.

Hollywood, February–May 1985

A year after the boat race Turner and Murdoch had come to remarkably similar conclusions about where the future of media lay. The only changes in the U.S. media industry since the 1940s had been the decline of afternoon newspapers, the reshuffling of media owners, and the minor inroads made by cable companies. The last new television network to be formed had been ABC in 1948. Wholesale changes were about to overtake the industry, initially through the huge advances forged by cable operators. But whatever changes the new world of media would usher in, the ground rules would remain the same. Media is about two things: content and a distribution system to deliver that content to consumers.

The future that both Rupert Murdoch and Ted Turner saw in 1985 lay in the big Hollywood studios and the free-to-air television networks. The studios' film libraries and production facilities offered huge programming content for the media revolution that was unfolding. The television networks provided the biggest distribution platform in the world for new programming. What no one had tried yet was to put these two elements together.

On March 21, 1985, News Corporation announced it was buying half of the 20th Century–Fox movie studio from oilman Marvin Davis for $250 million. Murdoch spent the rest of that week in Los Angeles at Michael Milken's high-yield conference for clients of junk bond issuer Drexel Burnham Lambert, the so-called Predator's Ball. That week at a cocktail party associated with the conference, Murdoch spoke with the head of Fox, Barry Diller, and with John Kluge, an old friend of Murdoch's who had a chain of television stations called Metromedia and a little debt problem. Within days Murdoch had decided he wanted to buy some television stations as well.

On March 13, a week before the Fox deal, Warren Buffett and the Capital Cities group had bid for the ABC network. Ted Turner had been working for months to put together a deal to move on CBS or ABC. He couldn't match the Capital Cities bid for ABC, but on April 18, four weeks after Murdoch had announced his deal to buy half a movie studio, Turner stood on the stage of the grand ballroom of New York's Plaza Hotel to announce that Turner Broadcasting System was bidding for CBS. CBS mounted a long and torrid takeover defense that culminated in a crippling $1 billion stock buyback announced on July 3. Fighting off Turner would leave CBS crippled and vulnerable to another corporate raider, Laurence Tisch. Turner fought on through July with his bid for CBS, but his enthusiasm for the fight was waning.

Murdoch's and Turner's paths continued to cross. On May 2, two weeks after Turner went public with his CBS bid, 20th Century–Fox announced it was buying Metromedia from John Kluge. After an already contracted sale of Kluge's Boston television station went through, Fox would be paying a net $1.55 billion for Metromedia's six remaining stations. The week before Turner learned of the nasty surprise that CBS had planned for him with its stock buyback on July 3, Murdoch received some bad news of his own: He had lost his partner. Marvin Davis was insisting that Murdoch buy him out of both the Metromedia deal and the remaining half of 20th Century–Fox.

In the last week of July News finally announced what had been an open secret for months—that it planned to use the Metromedia television stations to launch a new television network, Fox. The news almost coincided with a CNN report on July 29 that Ted Turner had given up on his CBS aspirations and was meeting with executives at Kirk Kerkorian's MGM/UA studio. On August 7 Turner signed a deal to buy the MGM studio for $1.6 billion.

Both Murdoch and Turner finally had their hands on a movie studio. Murdoch had the basis to launch a new network. Turner had a secure source of films for his existing superstation. And neither man had enough money to hold on to his prize. As a result of what they had already done, both companies were nearly broke.

The only way to get financing for either of these deals was to go to Michael Milken. But Milken would struggle with them. Despite the sophisticated rationale that Milken produced for high-yield debt, at heart his junk bond deals were bridging loans, expensive money for a takeover or a management buyout. Once the deal was done, the borrower needed to replace the junk debt by selling off parts of the business, injecting new capital through a stock offering, or tapping new lines of credit in the target company. It was an effective way to break out the underused wealth hidden away in large companies. Junk bonds weren't effective if, like Murdoch's and Turner's companies in 1985, the companies you were buying didn't have undervalued assets that could be stripped off and you were making a strategic investment that could take five years or more to pay off.

On March 26, 1986, after much arm twisting, Milken financed Turner's MGM deal with $1.2 billion in junk bonds. Kirk Kerkorian, the vendor, had agreed to accept $220 million in preference shares as part of the price. The problem for Turner was that Kerkorian had to be paid dividends on his preference shares in Turner Broadcasting System (TBS) stock rather than in cash. If the TBS stock price fell below $15, Kerkorian would be issued even more TBS stock to compensate. The farther Turner's stock price fell, the more likely it was that Kerkorian would end up controlling Turner's company. By March 1987, with his stock price spiraling down, Turner was desperate to raise money to renegotiate the remaining junk bonds and to pay out Kerkorian. John Malone, now at Tele-Communications Inc., organized a summit of cable company leaders, who agreed to invest $550 million in Turner's company. One reason the cable guys were ready to save Ted Turner was their fear that if they did not, CNN might fall into the hands of Rupert Murdoch.

"I had three choices, oddly enough, for investors," Turner told the National Press Club in 1994. "One was Rupert Murdoch, and I appreciated his offer very much. And the other was General Electric, and the other was from the cable operators. Well, it wasn't hard to decide who I wanted to go with."

The rescue package came at a price. The cable companies, worried by Turner's history of impetuosity, demanded veto power over any decision he made. If he wanted to spend more than $2 million on anything, even on his beloved Atlanta Braves baseball team, he had to get their approval. "Like I wanted to imperil the company," Turner complained later. "Remember, every move I've made, not one of them turned out to be a wrong move. I mean, I'm not talking about how I ran the Braves for ten years. That was a disaster."[9]

For the next decade, besides picking up a couple of independent film studios, Turner continued to hatch new schemes, but none of them came to anything. His cable partners blocked them all, to Turner's chagrin. Turner's role as *enfant terrible* of American media was on ice.

*   *   *

The question is, how did Rupert Murdoch escape falling off the same precipice? A survival story is the inverse of a whodunit. At the top of a deadly thousand-foot drop, the victim is found mysteriously alive and unharmed. The question that the detective has to solve is, did the victim not fall, or wasn't he pushed? Murdoch faced a much more daunting challenge than Turner's. At least Turner had started off with the right nationality. Murdoch was an Australian buying U.S. television stations, raising twice as much debt, and facing huge other problems in his media group.

So Murdoch's great American run began, not in March 1985 when he swooped to buy the first half of 20th Century–Fox in Los Angeles, but six weeks earlier in New York, in his penthouse apartment on Fifth Avenue. On February 10 Murdoch flew his British executives to New York for the weekend for secret talks about moving his British newspapers—the *Sun,* the *News of the World,* the *Times,* and the *Sunday Times*—from his hugely overmanned and highly unionized printing presses on Fleet Street to a new facility he was building at Wapping, in the London Docklands. Instead of printers from the Society of Graphical and Allied Trades, he planned to employ members of the less militant electricians' union. He would need a lot fewer of them. News already ran some of the most profitable newspapers in the world. The wages Murdoch would save at Wapping would be worth another $150 million a year in profits to him—a sum that would pay the interest bill on a huge mountain of new debt.

The downside was that the move would be a blatant challenge to the power of British trade unions. If Murdoch lost this fight, he could wave good-bye to Britain and the profit machine that his British subsidiary, News International, had become. He would be forced out of the U.K., and News Corp would almost certainly go broke. There was no halfway mark here. It would be either a huge success or a momentous failure. Success would depend on the tightest secrecy, and Murdoch and his British execs discussed how to maintain security and create smokescreens to draw attention elsewhere.

By late February Murdoch had signed a contract with Atex, the Boston electronics firm that would supply the Wapping computer terminals for the journalists, and he had met Eric Hammond of the EETPU, to draw up plans to hire staff secretly. From this point Murdoch was committed. So three weeks later, as he turned to launch his assault upon America with 20th Century–Fox in Los Angeles, Murdoch had absolutely nothing to lose. But no one knew about it. Murdoch was like a gambler who keeps buying more chips, while nobody at the casino realizes that he has run out of credit. What does a smart gambler do when he has nothing to lose? He doubles his bets. Wapping and the doomsday deadline were Murdoch's warm little secret as he turned his attention to Hollywood.

Of course, the commitment worked the other way as well. The more Murdoch was forced to pay for 20th Century–Fox and then Metromedia and then to launch the new Fox television network, the more committed he was to making his move to Wapping. Murdoch was prepared—and by now he was required—to push through with a change at Wapping that would overturn the British industrial relations system, simply to finance a new American television network. He was committed to overturning the social system in one country to pay for a commercial venture in another. And it didn't stop there.

The common thread in all of Murdoch's deals in 1985 was that each move he made—buying 20th Century–Fox and Metromedia and building the Wapping plant—had the effect of getting an inordinate number of people all over the world seriously upset with him. The list of the discomfited, beginning in Washington and moving east, ran like this. Murdoch needed to take American citizenship and convince the Reagan administration to give him some slack on foreign ownership laws. Then he had to show the Federal Communications Commission (FCC) that both he and the company that would control the Metromedia stations were American. Unfortunately, while *he* could change nationalities, it was a little harder for News Corp to do the same thing. Murdoch also had to convince the FCC that he should be given a waiver to the U.S. cross-media laws to allow him to continue to own the *New York Post* and the *Boston Herald,* as well as the local television stations he was buying. Then he needed to placate his existing bankers, while at the same time raising the net $2.7 billion he needed for 20th Century, Metromedia, Wapping, and the $350 million deal for Ziff Davis magazines that he had settled in January 1985.

In London Murdoch needed assurance that British prime minister Margaret Thatcher would back him in his battle at Wapping with the immensely powerful printing unions that had dominated the British newspaper industry for so long. By late 1985 Thatcher was already facing challenges to her leadership over her move to sell the Westmoreland helicopter company to an American defense group, of which Murdoch was a director. In the process Thatcher had ditched her own government policy and her defense minister, Michael Heseltine. The question by January 1986 as Wapping opened was not just whether Thatcher owed Murdoch any favors but, because of the Heseltine factor, how long she would be around to give favors.

In Australia, for light relief, Murdoch needed to placate Prime Minister Bob Hawke, whose nose was out of joint because he had given Murdoch privileged status as an Australian in his local media deals. In July 1979 Murdoch had testified before the Australian Broadcasting Tribunal (ABT) that although he held a U.S. green card on the basis that he was a resident alien living in New York, he still qualified as an Australian resident for the purposes of the Australian Broadcasting Act and had obtained absentee ballots by signing declarations that his "real place of living" was his Cavan property in New South Wales. On that basis the ABT had allowed Murdoch to hold two Australian television licenses as an Australian resident. But that decision had opened up a new dispute with the Australian Tax Office over his personal income tax returns from 1975 to 1982, in which he had sought partial relief from Australian tax on the grounds that he lived principally in New York. After his testimony before the ABT, the Australian Tax Office had queried whether Murdoch also fitted the definition of an Australian resident in the Tax Act and whether the source of his income was Australia or elsewhere.[10]

The bottom line: Murdoch had a political problem, a financial problem, and a legal problem. This wasn't a percentage game—he could win most of these battles and still go down. He needed to win virtually all of the battles. The difficulty was that what he was proposing to do was politically impossible and looked like financial suicide. And to boot it was probably illegal.

"I am very proud and grateful to be sworn in as an American citizen," Murdoch said at his swearing-in ceremony on September 3, 1985. His wife Anna and their three children would be naturalized quietly several years later. A decade later the FCC would find that News Corp had probably breached the alien ownership provisions in the way it bought the Metromedia television stations, but no sanctions were imposed.

In 1985 what Murdoch needed was for everyone to get off his back for long enough to let him make these deals work. Like any conjurer, he needed a suspension of disbelief. If, realistically, the deals were not viable, he needed to fashion his own realities. What News Corp was doing, who Rupert Murdoch was, would depend on to whom he was talking. He would practice his own version of virtual politics, convincing Ronald Reagan and Margaret Thatcher of his deeply right-wing affiliations, while assuring the Australian Labour prime minister, Bob Hawke, of his special support. His was virtual nationality—since 1986 he has described himself as an American or as "at heart" an Australian, as the occasion demanded. To help Americanize News Corp in 1985, Murdoch bought more stock to lift his stake in the company to 50.1 percent. Within weeks of receiving FCC approval for the deal, Murdoch sold the extra stock again, so as to be able to tell the Internal Revenue Service that for tax purposes News Corp was Australian-owned.

Murdoch's lawyers would pioneer a form of virtual law that allowed him to assure the FCC in 1985 and every year since then that the Metromedia television stations were American-owned because he and Barry Diller owned 75 percent of the voting stock of 20th Holdings Corporation, the holding company for the stations, and thus he and Diller controlled the stations. At the same time the News lawyers would tell the U.S. Securities and Exchange Commission that News Corp, a foreign company, controlled 20th Holdings. It held 99.9 percent of the company as nonvoting stock and could force Diller and Murdoch to sell the voting stock back to it at any time. Then there were the virtual finances that Murdoch used to convince his bankers that they should keep lending.

The really critical part to working with virtual realities is that the separate

worlds must never collide. While Murdoch's change of nationality, his relationships with politicians, and the battle that saw him finally forced to sell the *New
York Post* to satisfy cross-media laws all provoked storms of media coverage, the
controversy that all these issues stirred up obscured one basic fact. The key element of this deal to purchase 20th Century–Fox and Metromedia was not the
politics, the patriotism, or the legalities—it was financial survival. A decade later
the businesses it would spin off would be worth $40 billion. The issue that would
make or break Murdoch was always going to be finding the money to make the
deal work—and to allow News Corp to stay solvent.

A major money-raising exercise is a little like a carnival shell game. The speed
of the movement and the dazzling sleight-of-hand obscure the pattern of strategic
advances and retreats. In the end all the observer knows is that a large amount of
money seems to be disappearing rapidly down a small hole. What made Murdoch's
1985 shell game particularly engrossing was the way the master players, Michael
Milken and Murdoch, for all their marvelous dexterity, still managed to misplace
$3.6 billion. How could Michael Milken and Rupert Murdoch miscalculate so
badly? The difficulty arose because when Milken came through with the money
for Murdoch's Metromedia deal, as with Turner he linked the repayments to the
stock price.

In 1985 the underlying problem for both Turner and Murdoch was that they
weren't big enough to do these deals. Under U.S. accounting standards News
Corp had net assets of $166 million. Murdoch had told his banks he would not
borrow more than 110 percent of his assets. So in theory he could borrow only
$175 million. He actually needed to borrow $2.7 billion. The only solution was to
raise more capital by issuing stock, as Turner had done with the cable companies.
But that move had cost Turner control of his company. How could Murdoch avoid
the same outcome?

The solution was quite clever. First, between 1984 and 1987 Murdoch's finance
director, Richard Sarazen, used a loophole in Australian accounting standards
to revalue the masthead of News Corp's newspapers by $1.5 billion. This change
produced a jump in the balance sheet that allowed Murdoch to borrow another
$1.6 billion. Arthur Siskind and the legal team at Squadron Ellenoff solved
the other half of the problem. To buy Metromedia, Murdoch needed to raise
$1.15 billion in junk money from Michael Milken. It was, as Siskind later told
American Lawyer, "an extraordinarily complicated and very unusual financing."[11]
Siskind's twist was that instead of treating the loan as junk bonds, News would call
it preferred stock. While in essence it would be a $1.15 billion loan, it would ap-

pear in the News Corp balance sheet as a stock issue—as an asset rather than a liability. "Under Australian [accounting principles], a preferred stock, even though it is designed to have all the attributes of debt, would be treated for accounting purposes as equity," said Siskind. "I always referred to it as a 'junk preferred.'"

This meant not only that News Corp could borrow $1.15 billion through Michael Milken. It also meant that after the increase in assets from this slick piece of bookkeeping, News Corp could go out and raise *another* $1.2 billion in bank debt.

It was really very clever, and the lawyers at Squadron Ellenoff were pretty happy about the whole deal. But the honeymoon was short, because in early 1986 the Milken junk issue turned out to be a complete disaster. It began with an industrial revolution at Wapping that proved a little too successful.

Wapping's Casualties

London, January 1986
In any grand strategy, the difference between success and failure often comes down to who is telling the story. In January 1986 Rupert Murdoch embarked upon an industrial campaign that would transform the finances of his media empire. It revolutionized the newspaper industry in Britain and arguably broke the back of the British trade union movement. Its influence would reverberate in workplace relations across Europe and leave a deep scar on British domestic politics. Yet for Murdoch the results were equivocal. This masterstroke that was his financial salvation also did more than anything else to commit Murdoch to years of financial crisis.

At seven-thirty P.M. on Friday, January 24, 1986, the 5,500 print workers who produced Murdoch's British newspapers—the *Sun, Times, Sunday Times,* and *News of the World*—voted to strike over plans by News International to move its papers to a new plant at Wapping. As they filed out, each printer was handed a notice of dismissal. If News International had decided unilaterally to retrench the printers under British labor laws, it would have had to pay them more than £120 million in retirement and long-service benefits. Dismissing them in a strike meant News could pay them nothing.

The fight over Wapping was an archetypal technology war. Since the early 1970s the newspaper business had been buffeted by technological advances, witnessing the disappearance of the linotype machines that had set each line in hot lead, the rows of page galleys in the compositing room, and the mysterious and terrifyingly noisy vacuum tubes that had sucked containers filled with editorial copy from the newsroom to the printers. Instead, a computer typesetter produced a photographic image of text that was cut up and glued to a page for photographic reproduction. Soon these pages would be replaced by computer pagination, in which a journalist assembled entire pages on a computer screen.

The casualties of this technological change would not just be old equipment and newspaper mystique. The trade of newspaper compositing—one of the oldest in industrial society—would disappear. Several hundred thousand people would discover that their chosen career path had no future. The process was inescapable, inasmuch as no one has ever found a way to resist technological change indefinitely or to remain in business when someone else is doing your job faster, better, and cheaper. All that remained to be decided were the conditions and timing under which the change would be made, how smoothly it would come, and the degree of comfort that employers would offer to a large workforce that would walk away without a livelihood.

The British printers' unions were not an easy group to like. They had used their industrial muscle to ensure that they remained in charge of the entire production process, insisting that any editorial typed in by a journalist must be keyed in again by a printer, negating much of the advantage of a computerized typesetting system. They had also created corrupt workplaces that were overstaffed, sometimes by fictitious employees, where slowdowns, wildcat strikes, and even sabotage had become commonplace. But changing this system presented huge problems.

Rupert Murdoch decided to move his newspapers from their separate locations on Bouvery Street and Grays Inn Road to Wapping, a site that he had bought in 1978 and rebuilt in 1984. News International told the printers' unions that in view of their opposition to Wapping, for the time being it had shelved plans to move its existing newspapers there. Instead it would use the new plant to launch a paper called the *London Post*. In legal actions the following year, lawyers for the printers' unions would argue that the *London Post* was a complete sham, "a smokescreen behind which [News International] carried out a plan, already conceived, to transfer the existing titles to Wapping without the unions and to sack their existing labour force at minimum cost to themselves," as Justice Stuart-Smith put it.[12] After testimony by two News executives, Stuart-Smith found that this serious allegation could not be sustained, and counsel for the printers "very properly withdrew it." This had a somewhat terminal effect on the printers' argument that News had come to the court with "unclean hands."

These were confusing times. Andrew Neil, then the editor of the *Sunday Times,* clearly had the wrong end of the stick when he later wrote that "the *Post* was a ruse: it was never meant to happen," that "the pretence of the *Post* had to be maintained," and that it was "a ruse thought up by Rupert himself."[13] Refreshingly, not everyone needed a cover story. According to Neil, the peculiar view of the world at the *Sunday Times* ensured that when James Adams, one of its senior editorial executives, began disappearing for large periods of time to prepare for the move to Wapping, some journalists assumed he had been doing his bit for flag and country by freelancing for MI5. It was not every newspaper where the security services seemed the obvious alternative vocation.

By September 1985, with presses installed at Wapping and members of the electricians' union ready to run them, Murdoch had hardened his stand, setting a three-month deadline for a new agreement with the printers' unions. The unions wanted an assurance that their members would not be sacked until retirement age, but they later dropped this demand and made other concessions as they sensed the ground was shifting. At the final meeting between Murdoch and the printers' unions on January 23, 1986, the unions appeared to be in a state of panic. While they offered significant concessions for any move from Grays Inn Road to Wapping, Murdoch's view was that it was too little too late. Nothing was printed on the Friday night after the printers walked out, but on Saturday night the *Sunday Times* and the *News of the World* went to press at Wapping and went out on trucks from an Australian-owned transport company, TNT Limited, which was being paid £1 million a week to distribute the papers. Those who were there on the first night at Wapping paint a fearful picture of a raging Murdoch hassling and intimidating subordinates. "You fuckwit! You bastard! Get this fucking newspaper out!" he railed at James Adams.

Events unfolded with all the gritty immediacy of a major industrial confrontation: there was shouting, semi-riots, assaults, death threats, abuse, and harassment, with flares, rocks, and missiles thrown at the buildings. On one night protesters knocked down forty yards of the twelve-foot iron railing fence topped with barbed wire that ringed Wapping, but they didn't breach a second defense line of heavy rolls of razor wire. Each day between 50 and 200 protesters would be outside the Wapping main gate. On Wednesday and Saturday nights the numbers would climb to 700 or more and on occasion to 6,000 or 7,000. The longer the dispute lasted, the larger the crowds grew. On January 24, 1987, the first anniversary of the dispute, more than 10,000 protesters clashed violently with 1,200 police.

The TNT trucks brought in to distribute the newspapers from Wapping were a popular target for protesters. In the first four months protesters broke 92 wind-shields on TNT delivery trucks, rammed another 16, set fire to two, slashed five sets of tires and damaged another 84 trucks. Today the passions and bitterness that drove the Wapping dispute appear remote. The relics are old courtroom transcripts, statistics of violence, and dry arguments about whether words such as "Scab, we will get you" amount to a threat. Geoffrey Richards of Farrer & Co., the News International lawyers, had reminded his client, "Since the very first day I was involved . . . I have advised that, if a moment came when it was necessary to dispense with the workforces [at Fleet Street], the cheapest way of doing so would be to dismiss employees while participating in a strike or industrial action."[14]

Eventually, in an agreement worked out in early 1987. the 5,500 printers who had worked for News for an average of fifteen years were paid about £50 million, or £620 for each year served. Other Fleet Street papers quietly negotiated similar concessions with the printers' unions. The legacy of the fight over Wapping, however, was not so easily settled. Whatever the rights or wrongs of the dispute, its passion left its mark on the national psyche.

Wappping had a lethal effect on Labour Party politics in the U.K. Faced with what was arguably Britain's greatest social convulsion of the decade, Labour politicians found themselves in no man's land, opposed to the confrontational and opportunistic tactics of News International yet unable to defend the working record of the printers or the violence of the protesters. Whichever way Labour politicians leaned, however, their record was marked by the experience. Labour would remain out of power until it appointed a leader who had taken a determined position of noninvolvement with Wapping. Tony Blair would know better than anyone the danger that that conflict carried.

*   *   *

The importance of Wapping to Britain and its contribution to the Labour Party's woes were incidental to Rupert Murdoch. His success there had created a financial problem. Wapping was only a sideshow in Murdoch's attempts to raise the money to buy the Metromedia television stations and launch his Fox network in the United States. Success would really depend upon Michael Milken at Drexel Burnham Lambert finalizing Murdoch's issue of $1.15 billion of junk prefs.

When Milken's debt raising closed on March 6, 1986, after being delayed twice, a little-noticed provision had crept into the News Corp issue. The debt would remain the same for three years. But after that, how much the lenders were paid back would begin to depend on the News Corp share price. If the share price went up 50 percent, the debt owing on the junk preferred stock would go up 50 percent as well. So it was important that the News Corp share price didn't do anything crazy during this time. Murdoch was gambling that his stock price wouldn't go up.

As journalists at Wapping agonized over whether to cross the picket lines, the new presses continued to crank out Murdoch's newspapers. By February 1986 investors had begun to realize just how much money Murdoch was going to make from the move. The outcome from the riots, the nightly confrontations, and the abuse would help propel News International's operating income from £38.4 million in 1985 to £150.2 million in 1987. The News Corp share price drifted up over $6 in January 1986. When Michael Milken's junk preferred issue closed on March 6—the date that fixed the base price for paying back the preferred stock— News Corp's ordinary stock was hovering above $8.50. Two months later News Corp stock hit $16. By March 1987, a year after the Milken junk issue, News Corp stock, after allowing for a share split, had hit $35. In other circumstances this increase would be cause for celebration. But just as the stock price had gone up fourfold, the long-term cost of repaying Milken's junk preferreds had gone up fourfold as well. Unless Murdoch could find a way to refinance, Michael Milken's little poison pill would eventually raise the debt from $1.15 billion to $4.7 billion. It looked like the most expensive company loan in history.

As a desperate alternative, if Murdoch could not find the cash to pay off the junk debt, he could pay off the junk holders with News Corp ordinary shares. But this would dilute his own stockholding down to 9 percent, and he would lose control of his company—as Turner had. Murdoch had left an indelible mark on two countries. In America he had overturned the media business by starting a new network, and in Britain he had revolutionized newspaper manning levels and broken the power of trade unions. The aftereffects of those two changes would reverberate through both countries for years. But the troubling thing was, it still wasn't enough. If by March 1989 he hadn't found some way to refinance the Milken preferreds, then he could forget the stock price and the paper wealth. The game would be over.

This was why, in December 1986, Murdoch found himself in a takeover battle for his father's old newspaper company in Australia, the Herald and Weekly Times (HWT) group. On the surface it looked like Murdoch was finally about to have his revenge on the company that he believed had treated his family so shabbily after his father's death. But while sentiment and revenge were a major part of this deal, the money trail showed a different picture.

Murdoch in this deal was like a master magician working the crowd, ostentatiously handing out shiny coins to members of the audience. When he returns to the stage, he gestures theatrically before opening his cloak to reveal that all of the coins are mysteriously back in his pocket. By sleight of hand he has ended up with all the money. Rather than money, Murdoch was handing out shares that would end up back under his cloak.

In January 1987, Murdoch won a $1.8 billion takeover battle for the Herald and Weekly Times group. About a third of HWT shareholders took cash for their shares. The rest took News Corp shares and convertible notes. Paying them in shares looked like a risky move for Murdoch, because the extra stock would dilute his stake in News, and he would lose control. But the biggest shareholders in HWT were three newspaper groups that HWT itself controlled. More than half of the News Corp stock that Murdoch issued for the takeover ended up in these three companies, which after the takeover Murdoch controlled as well. So rather than diluting his hold on News Corp, Murdoch actually ended up with tighter control on his empire than before.

The big stock issue for the HWT takeover meant that Murdoch no longer needed the Milken junk preferreds. They had been dressed up to look like equity to keep his bankers happy. Now there was real equity in the accounts. News Corp promptly paid Milken off, using a conventional bank loan. Murdoch ended up with 70 percent of Australia's newspapers and revenge on his father's old company, but that was just a side benefit. The financial heart of the deal was a debt-restructuring exercise. Murdoch was taking over a country's media industry to help his balance sheet.

There was one hiccup. The bid for HWT had been bitterly contested by a South African entrepreneur, Robert Holmes á Court. Murdoch had been forced to buy out the biggest shareholder in HWT, which turned out to be the company his father once owned, Queensland Press, which held 24 percent of HWT stock. The announcement that Murdoch's private family company, Cruden Investments, would buy Queensland Press was the move that clinched victory for Murdoch in the HWT battle, which in turn got Michael Milken off his back.

To get some perspective on this: In June 1982 Murdoch's entire stockholding in News Corp was worth $52 million. By March 1985 it had climbed to $300 million. Two and a half years later the Murdoch shares were worth $3 billion. And while that was paper money—the stock market had discovered virtual wealth long before anyone else—the political power that went along with it was quite real. Murdoch had already overturned the American media industry to start up his new

Fox television network. He had needed to move to Wapping and overturn the British newspaper industry to pay for his American adventure. Now, to help Murdoch with the debt blowout produced by Wapping, it was Australia's turn. National boundaries had ceased to matter for him. Murdoch would do a deal wherever in the world it took him, creating social shock waves in as many countries as he needed, in order to survive.

There was only one problem: Despite its paper wealth, Cruden Investments didn't have any money. Its only income was $8 million a year in News Corp dividends. It had raised $400 million debt to acquire 56 percent of Queensland Press (the other 44 percent was now owned by News Corp), but where was Cruden going to find $60 million a year to meet its interest bill? Murdoch had swapped the Milken debt problem in News Corp, the public company, for an even more threatening debt problem in Cruden, his private family company. The Milken debt was a virus that had just switched hosts. Nevertheless it looked as if Murdoch had scraped through. The only way that he could run into problems in late 1987 was if share prices suddenly dived.

5

THE PARTY LINE

Manhattan, October 18–23, 1987

O
N OCTOBER 18, 1987, New York was enjoying the last hours of a lazy Sunday afternoon in late fall. The first snowstorm had hit the Northeast two weeks before, but no trace of it remained. New York was back up to 71 degrees and bathed in sunshine. The leaves were in full color along the Connecticut shore for the benefit of day-trippers. Otherwise October 18 was a slow news day. For the media, Sunday is a nothing day, really.

The lack of excitement in New York was in contrast to—even in spite of—the intense concentration that was being poured on the city from around the globe. On the other side of the world it was already Monday morning. From New Zealand to Australia, to Tokyo, Hong Kong, and Singapore, brokers, portfolio managers, and major investors were hunkered down in briefing sessions before the financial markets opened. On the previous Friday, after the Asian markets closed, Wall Street had suffered the biggest points drop in its history. The Dow Jones industrial average had dropped 108 points, more than half of it in the last hour of trade. That plunge had followed another disastrous day on Wednesday, when the Dow had dropped 95 points. It was down 9.5 percent in three days. So in the early hours of what was for them Monday morning, the best and brightest analysts in Asia and the Pacific were concentrating on just what was going through the minds of New York brokers and funds managers, in their homes in Westchester and western Connecticut, as they enjoyed the last of that warm Sunday. When Wall Street opened fifteen hours later, which way would they jump? Was the correction over? Was anyone feeling lucky? Was it safe? Monday was always going to be a bad day for the Asian markets. The Asian analysts had to intuit whether it was just medium bad or doomsday. They chose poorly.

One of the mysteries on that quiet Sunday afternoon, in the lull before the storm, was what Rupert Murdoch was doing in New York. By rights he should have been in Australia. On the Friday two days before, News Corporation had held its annual meeting in Adelaide. For once, the chief executive was a no-show. Richard Searby, Murdoch's longtime friend and the News Corp chairman, presided over the annual meeting on October 16, but it was a lackluster affair.

In the normal course of events, Murdoch would have ripped through the News Corp meeting—a perfunctory annual ritual that on a slow year stretches as long as fifteen minutes—had a cup of tea with shareholders, and then flown to Sydney for a road show with Australian analysts to boost his stock. Murdoch would then spend the weekend at his Cavan property west of Sydney with Australian execs and family, before heading back to the United States late on the Monday. This was what Murdoch did every year when the News Corp annual meeting came around. He would usually drag some of his senior lieutenants along with him, on the general principle that into every life a little South Australia must fall. So in the normal course of events, on Monday night Murdoch would have been trapped on a plane in the middle of the Pacific, unable to do anything to stave off the initial paralyzing panic that seized his bankers when the world's stock markets went into free fall.

For some reason Murdoch broke with his pattern of thirty-four years. Because he didn't go to Adelaide, he also didn't go to Sydney or to Cavan. Instead he was in New York, with his family in their penthouse on the corner of Fifth Avenue and East Eighty-eighth Street. In the next four days, his decision not to go to Australia that year would save Rupert Murdoch's empire from imploding. It was one of the luckiest decisions he would ever make. It would allow him time to make one of the worst—and best—deals of his career. But what had kept him here?

A range of possible reasons could have kept Murdoch in New York. He might have stayed to meet with Peter Kalikow, the real estate developer who was talking about buying the *New York Post;* or with Pearson executives, who were agitated that he had just snatched 15 percent of the U.K. media group. But it's unlikely. One clue to Murdoch's movements was his position as a rising star on the horizon of the rich and famous. There may have been other secret Murdoch machinations; but whatever else was happening, one piece of business was very clear. Like any good New Yorker, Rupert Murdoch had stayed in town to party.

The press previews for the Forbes 400 list for 1987 hit the newsstands the week of October 12. Each year *Forbes* magazine publishes its list of the four hundred richest people in the world. The list has become one of the major markers of personal and corporate power. At the head of the list, Sam Walton, officially America's richest human that year, with $8.5 billion from his holding in Wal-Mart stores, was not happy. "I could kick your butt for ever running that list," he said to *Forbes* testily.[1] Others in the ranks of the rich and powerful were not so averse to a little public adulation. John Kluge was listed in second place with "at least" $3 billion—in large part due to his fortunate sale of Metromedia to his friend Rupert Murdoch.

Rupert Murdoch had just joined the billionaires' club. *Forbes* valued him at $2.1 billion, the eighth richest person in America. He ranked equally with Warren Buffett. Murdoch was the star performer among the twenty-three new billionaires and a personal favorite of Malcolm Forbes. Allan Sloan, now the Wall Street editor for *Newsweek,* had resigned from *Forbes* after it refused to publish an article in which he argued that Murdoch's empire was built on sleight of hand and Australian accounting practices. The list of newly megarich also included a young software developer and Harvard dropout named Bill Gates, trailing Murdoch at $1.1 billion.

Unhappily, by the time *Forbes* magazine hit the streets later in the week of October 18, Murdoch would no longer be a billionaire. The News Corp stock price that is the basis of his wealth was about to fall into a deep dark hole. He himself would stave off bankruptcy by the barest of margins, hanging on to his worldwide media empire only by his fingernails. But even as misfortune beckoned, he still had this hour in the sun.

New York loves a party the way Hollywood loves a secret. On Tuesday night, October 13, Malcolm Forbes held a cocktail party. Strictly speaking, it was a book launch. Forbes, David Mahoney, and Shirley Lord had joined together in the Forbes building to help their friend David Brown, the film producer and husband of *Cosmopolitan* editor Helen Gurley Brown, to launch his new book, *Brown's Guide to Growing Gray.* They did it out of gratitude for the way Brown had encouraged each of his hosts to write books. When it came to dialing up the corporate A-list to get the party off on the right note, Malcolm Forbes knew exactly who to call. The guest list featured a string of the big hitters who were about to feature in the Forbes 400 list.[2]

John Kluge was there. So were Laurence Tisch, Donald Trump, and Ronald Perelman. And so was Rupert Murdoch. There, in the winners' circle, was the man who hates parties, graciously consenting to make an appearance. The absurd $3 billion that Murdoch would pay for Triangle Publications the following year would show that he was as susceptible as anyone to being included in the inner circles of the American establishment. Forbes's party was Murdoch's triumph.

After all the mud that had been thrown at him over the years, he had finally arrived.

Going to the book launch meant that Murdoch could not fly out of New York for the News Corp annual meeting until Wednesday morning, October 14. Wednesday morning in New York would already be early Thursday in Australia. Murdoch had little more than twenty-four hours to fly halfway around the world to Sydney, change planes, and fly on to Adelaide to make the annual meeting on Friday morning. For a man with a private jet and his own airline, it was probably just possible. But any holdup would leave him hours away in the air as the shareholders got restless. Murdoch didn't take the risk. He stayed in New York after the party.

Tokyo held steadiest on that Monday, down only 2 percent. New Zealand fell 4.2 percent. Hong Kong was off 9.8 percent. The Australian market on the Monday suffered its biggest points fall on record. The All Ordinaries index dropped 80 points, a fall of 3.7 percent, and most brokers went home stunned, but still relieved that the worst of the bad news was behind them. It had been bad, but they had survived. The fall had been contained. Unfortunately on October 19 the action was a long way from being over.

London dropped 10 percent after opening and kept sliding. But it was not until Wall Street opened, just before midnight Australian time, that Australian brokers realized how badly they had got it wrong. Pandemonium reigned. In wild scenes the Dow Jones index dropped 516 points. When the Australian markets opened on the Tuesday morning, the index dropped 500 points—some 22 percent—in minutes. It was a bloodbath that would destroy nearly all of the Australian entrepreneurs of the 1980s.

"I hope someone else is paying—I've just lost a billion dollars," Murdoch quipped at dinner that night in New York. News Corp had been one of the companies worst hit. The share price had touched A$24.50 earlier that month. On Tuesday, March 20, it opened in Australia at A$11. It rallied to close at A$13, but by the following Tuesday panic selling had slammed the price down to A$8.50. And US$1.7 billion of Rupert Murdoch's personal fortune had disappeared. Just like that.

The Week That Never Happened

As far as the popular history of News Corporation and Rupert Murdoch goes, the week of October 19 was a week like any other. News Corp's finances were spread across so many countries that at any time only a handful of people had any real understanding of the group's money trails. The only insights for the outside observer come from timing and the documentary record.

By late September 1987 the correspondence between the Murdoch family company, Cruden Investments, and the Commonwealth Bank of Australia suggests that the bank was getting twitchy about the $400 million Cruden had borrowed nine months before for the Queensland Press takeover.[3] There seemed no major ground for concern. The News Corp stock held in Cruden and in Rupert Murdoch's own private company, Kayarem, was worth $2.1 billion. In addition, Queensland Press held News Corp convertible notes from the Herald and Weekly Times takeover worth another $530 million. The Cruden debt, which with interest payments was now close to $475 million, didn't seem so bad.

That was before October 20. When News Corp shares crashed to A$11 in the first minutes of trading in Australia, Murdoch had dropped $1.2 billion. When the share price hit A$8.50 in the following days, the Murdoch shares in Cruden were worth just $690 million and falling. Queensland Press was down another $320 million on its News Corp notes. The Commonwealth Bank was suddenly stuck with a loan of $470 million with insufficient cashflow to cover the interest bill, secured by shares that kept dropping in value.

The bank had already been twitchy when it had $2.1 billion of security. Watching that margin of safety drop overnight to $220 million is the sort of thing that can put a loan manager into spasm. While the safety margin still seemed large, any forced sale of shares by the Murdoch family to meet the debt would send the News Corp stock price down through the floor, the bank would shoot into losses, and it would be all over for Murdoch.

It was all in the timing. The Australian share market opened at ten A.M. Tuesday morning, and by 10:05 the News Corp share price had self-immolated. Thereafter Rupert Murdoch was toast. But shock waves took time to move out from the market. In New York it was just after six o'clock on Monday evening when the News Corp share price plunged. It is unlikely that alarm bells were ringing for any Australian corporate loan managers until Tuesday. By that time it was after midnight in New York. Red flags would now be attached to Murdoch's personal debt position. But it is unlikely that anyone from the Commonwealth Bank's New York offices in Lexington Avenue would have spoken to Murdoch before Tuesday, October 20 (local time). Probably a meaningful conversation could not have taken place before Tuesday evening in New York time—which was early Wednesday morning at the Commonwealth Bank's head office in Sydney.

Some conversation must have taken place, because just after midday on Wednesday in New York, the Commonwealth Bank took a lien on the Murdochs' penthouse on East Eighty-eighth street. The only official record of this move is a grubby, fading docket in the city register of New York County. The docket is signed by Keith Rupert Murdoch and Anna Maria Murdoch, and it is stamped 12:23 P.M., Wednesday October 21.[4]

Two days after the crash, why was Murdoch's bank taking security over his home? The timing of the New York mortgage suggests the bank was making a margin call on Murdoch, slapping security on any personal assets that were handy. What Murdoch needed—and what, because he was in New York, he was able to provide—was something to stall the bank with. Just over twenty-four hours later, something happened on the other side of the world that solved Cruden's debt problems.

By this time it was Friday morning in eastern Australia. In Brisbane Keith McDonald, the chief executive officer of Queensland Press, was preparing for a board meeting. Since the takeover by Cruden, Queensland Press had run operationally as part of the News group, and its board was dominated by News Corp execs. Early on the morning of Friday, October 23, three days after the crash, a senior News Corp executive called McDonald to suggest that Queensland Press might like to buy 42 million News Corp shares from its parent, Cruden, at A$16 a share.[5]

The deal was way over market price. News shares opened that morning at A$13.80 and closed at A$12.80. By the following Tuesday the price had hit A$8.50. But Queensland made the purchase. Even at its best moments that Friday, it was paying $65 million more than the market price. By Tuesday it was paying a 90 percent premium. That is to say, it was paying $475 million for shares that had a market value of just $252 million. On Tuesday's closing price, Cruden was receiving a $222 million premium. As News owned 44 percent of Queensland Press, the premium given to Cruden was costing News Corp shareholders up to $100 million.

Queensland Press would earn $2 million a year in dividends from this new investment. Its interest bill on the loan would come to more than $75 million a year. The sale price seems all the more remarkable because it looks like Cruden was a forced seller. It had rising debt, no cash flow, and falling security. Selling the shares to any other buyer but Queensland Press would have cost Murdoch control of his empire. But while Murdoch would have known this background, the Queensland Press directors and their advisers didn't. Their point of view was that this was a unique opportunity. If, as the managing director of News Corp, Rupert Murdoch had reason to believe that Queensland Press was buying shares from his family company for more than their current value, or that the deal could have been bettered, it was up to him to say so.

Most of the Queensland Press board heard about the deal for the first time on Friday morning, but they had agreed to it by lunchtime. John D'Arcy, chief executive of the Herald and Weekly Times, who sat on the Queensland Press board, raised concerns about the price. "The deal was basically to benefit Rupert Murdoch," he said later, though he believed the transaction was quite legal. The directors were not aware of Murdoch's dealings with the Commonwealth Bank in New York the previous day.[6]

Later that day in New York, Rupert and Anna Murdoch signed over further personal security to the Commonwealth Bank.[7] Cruden's debt problem had been solved. Black Monday had been a nasty fright for Murdoch, but now it was back to operations as normal. "I dropped two bills—but it's only paper," he told News Corp executives airily several weeks later.[8]

Rupert Murdoch didn't see anything unusual in the deal:

> In late 1987, [Queensland Press] was given the opportunity to acquire approximately 42 million News Corporation shares from Cruden Investments. . . . The board took up the opportunity. . . . No member of the Cruden Investments board or member of the Murdoch family participated in the [Queensland Press] board's decision, or was present when it was made.[9]

News Corp has always been at pains to stress that helping Cruden out was not the major aim that the Queensland Press directors had in mind. While correspondence from the Commonwealth Bank said that it was, that was merely the bank's view. In fact the directors' sole motivation was to make a profitable and strategic investment in "probably the most dynamic media enterprise on planet earth."[10] Earlier that year Queensland Press had acquired News Corp convertible notes at A$18.75 after independent advice. Thus A$16 was a reasonable price to pay for News Corp shares on October 23 because market price was affected by "short-term hysteria."

Unfortunately the short-term hysteria lasted six years, and it took that long for the Queensland Press investment to move out of the red. In tumultuous times Queensland Press directors would have been guided by the views of its two shareholders, both of which were controlled by Rupert Murdoch. And Murdoch wasn't complaining. News Corp continued to prop up Murdoch's control of the empire. In addition to the 21 percent of News Corp stock now held by Queensland Press, Murdoch also shuffled another 4 percent block of stock issued in the Herald and Weekly Times takeover into an off-balance-sheet company called Dexenne. By the middle of 1988 News Corp had $1.2 billion secretly committed to propping up Murdoch's control of the empire.[11]

News Corp raised a new A$1 billion loan with the Commonwealth Bank, of which half went to Queensland Press to cover its deal with Cruden, which settled in Sydney on the night of December 8, 1987.[12] The Commonwealth Bank syndicated parts of the Queensland Press loan among Australian and Japanese banks. A little piece of it even ended up with an American bank that had just opened an office in Brisbane. It was called Pittsburgh National. By 1990 Pittsburgh had had its fill of Australian bad loans and had closed its Australian office.

∗ ∗ ∗

To recap: Murdoch had not been able to afford his great move in 1985–86 to buy 20th Century–Fox and the Metromedia television stations and to launch the Fox network. To pay for it, he moved his British newspapers to Wapping and triggered a year of violent industrial confrontation. The Wapping success produced a new debt problem that he tried to solve by taking over the Australian newspaper industry. When that plan went wrong, he was forced into a deal that left a crippling debt in his family company. Then in the deals after Black Monday 1987, Murdoch flipped the problem back to News Corp. Cruden's loan problem was now once again News Corp's lurking debt crisis. And nobody knew. News Corp shareholders had no idea how closely their company's future was now tied to the problems of Murdoch's private world.

Perhaps the most damaging part of this arrangement was that it all had come so easily. Rupert Murdoch had had the scare of his life, but thereafter he ignored the warning, and in 1988 the Great Acquirer embarked upon his biggest spending spree yet. In June 1988 he announced that he would be setting up a hugely expensive new satellite television service for Britain called Sky Television, challenging the government-approved British Satellite Broadcasting (BSB). On October 31, 1988, News Corp announced that it was buying Triangle Publications from Walter Annenberg for $3 billion. Triangle published *TV Guide* and *Seventeen* magazines. The same month Murdoch ordered 39 giant MAN Roland presses for his newspapers in Britain and Australia for $450 million.[13] A month later he spent another

$350 million mopping up the rest of the publishing company William Collins, which he later folded into the U.S. publisher Harper & Row to form HarperCollins, together with U.S. educational publisher Scott, Foresman, which he bought for $455 million.

Murdoch would spend 1989 and 1990 fending off his looming financial problems, as News Corp spiraled down and his bankers lost patience. Eventually it all caught up with him. At the end of 1990 Murdoch got caught in a worldwide credit squeeze. This time there was no hiding the crisis.

London, December 6–7, 1990
In the last hours of Thursday, December 6, 1990, Rupert Murdoch almost went broke. Such moments are rare in modern finance: Major corporate failures are usually well telegraphed and tend to be prolonged. The warning signs are a lingering decline, a slow downward spiral. Rarely does a determinative moment mark the transition from survival to bankruptcy. In general, huge corporations do not live or die on the outcome of a single telephone call.

But December 6 was Rupert Murdoch's moment, as he sat in the offices of Clifford Chance, the London lawyers for Citibank, preparing to make a phone call. Within hours News Corporation was due to be placed in liquidation. It would be the end of the empire, the end of thirty-seven years of struggle and fighting, of endlessly recreating himself and his company, of juggling realities and possibilities, of forging a media group that reached around the world. And Rupert Murdoch could save it all, it seemed. He could turn the crisis around with just one telephone call to the president of a bank in Pittsburgh. Once the call was placed, everything would depend on Murdoch's powers of persuasion. If he could convince the Pittsburgh banker to hold off, to give him a little time to solve his financial problems, Murdoch and News Corporation would march on. If Murdoch's charm failed, the empire faced fragmentation and dissolution. Those sitting next to him said later that Murdoch's hands were shaking as the connection was made. But the voice on the other end of the line was only a secretary. The banker in Pittsburgh was refusing to take his call.[14]

Murdoch was in London because his media empire had run out of other people's money. That wasn't a huge problem—it had run out of other people's money before. But now News Corp was due to repay a A$1 billion loan that it had taken out three years earlier. It was falling due on the other side of the world from London, on what was already Friday, December 7. News Corp didn't have the money to repay the loan and wanted to roll the debt over. When the Australian loan had been syndicated, by chance a small piece of the loan had ended up across the globe with Pittsburgh National Bank. Pittsburgh National had taken on 1 percent of the debt, a modest A$10 million. A debt rollover normally is a smooth procedure for professional bankers. All concerned charge a hefty fee, and the money goes through without even touching the sides. That is, it does so unless one of the lenders begins to worry about getting their money back. Then the whole rollover process clogs up, and it all starts to stick. Pittsburgh National wanted its A$10 million back. They gave Murdoch a sticky roll.

Murdoch and his key senior legal and financial executives, together with a crisis team from Citibank, had spent the whole day wrestling over the loan with bankers around the world. Murdoch had begun the day in Zurich talking to Credit Suisse, before flying to Heathrow. Australian banks had put up most of the resistance to the rollover that was falling due that day. Then the Japanese banks had dug in their heels and refused to extend the loan. After a titanic struggle Murdoch's advisers at Citibank and at the British merchant bank Samuel Montague had talked the Australian and Japanese hardheads around. They would roll. The battle was won. The fates that guide banking destinies had decreed that today was not the day Murdoch's media empire would crash and burn. That wouldn't happen for at least another week and a half. Today the fight was over. If only Pittsburgh knew that.

David DeVoe, News Corp's new chief financial officer, had called the chief loan officer at Pittsburgh National from Murdoch's London apartment that afternoon, asking him to roll the loan. The request should have been a mere formality, but the Pittsburgh loan officer had refused the request point-blank. He didn't want DeVoe's assurances—he just wanted News to pay him his money. Murdoch later described the moment to his biographer, William Shawcross: "We said, 'We can't [pay off the loan]. You know what that means. We'd go out of business,' " Murdoch said. "The loan officer said, 'That's right.' We said, 'You're telling us to liquidate our company?' And he said, 'Yes.' "

Murdoch's last option that evening was to try an end run around the chief loan officer and call his boss, the president of Pittsburgh National. When he called from the Clifford Chance offices, the bank president's secretary put him back to the chief loan officer.

For nearly three millennia, one of the cornerstones of Western and Greek narrative has been a belief in the day of reckoning. No matter how high Icarus flies, there comes a moment when he falls to earth; when Achilles meets Hector; when Oedipus meets the old man on the road. Macbeth's vaulting ambition o'erleaps itself and falls on the other side. History catches up with us all. Hubris must be called to account—the grand vision inevitably collides with reality. There are no exceptions—our doom is inescapable. It is an entirely postmodern notion that a protagonist may confront his moment with destiny and walk away; that he may endure his worlds colliding, his past rising up to bury him, and yet not perish. So what is one to make of the fact that Rupert Murdoch survived the certain disaster that threatened him on December 6? For the postmodern hero, there is no date with destiny—there is only a weary endurance through the latest in an endless series of crises that stretch out of sight behind and before him.

For News Corp, life had become a mesmerizing sequence of near-death experiences. The group had been in crisis since October 4, the day that David DeVoe sat down nervously with seven of News Corp's chief bankers in the News International boardroom at Wapping in London. DeVoe had been chief financial officer at News for all of one month. News Corp's legendary finance director, Richard Sarazen, had been moved out of the job in early September and given the title of senior executive vice president. He was still a member of the chief executive's office, but he had no more direct input into News Corp finances.

In January 1990 DeVoe had been appointed deputy chief financial officer, just as News Corp's lines of credit were beginning to dry up. A $750 million bridging loan on January 1 was News Corp's last before a global credit squeeze took hold. It fell due for repayment on June 30. News paid back $250 million and received a three-month extension on the balance to September 30. Just before the deadline DeVoe, as newly appointed chief financial officer, had asked for a one-month extension. The meeting at Wapping the following Thursday, October 4, was called by a group of angry senior News Corp bankers who wanted an explanation and some serious reassurances that the sun was still shining in the News Corp universe.

David DeVoe is an unostentatious man. While the typical career history that News Corp published on each of its directors could fill two pages, DeVoe's biography ran to seven lines. As he cleared his throat at the Wapping meeting, the bankers before him knew already that he was not the showman Sarazen had been. But they were not expecting that this quiet unassuming man would diffidently tell them a horror story. DeVoe said that News Corp had a temporary cash problem. It had more than $7 billion in unsecured bank debt. On top of that it had another $3 billion of trade creditors. It was due to repay $2.6 billion by next June—and it wouldn't be able to make that payment. In fact, the mountain of money that News Corp had already borrowed would not even ensure that the group survived the year. News Corp needed another $600 million just to keep going. Would this be a problem? At some point in the mass of figures and schedules that poured forth, it became apparent that News Corp would have a future only if the bankers in that room could organize a rescue party.

By Friday the shouting had dropped a few decibels and the bankers had agreed on a rescue plan, to be coordinated by Citibank and Samuel Montague. News Corp needed to reschedule $7.6 billion of debt held by 146 institutions around the world. The bankers' chief problem was that the group's international structure had been set up specifically to prevent any takeover by the banks. News Corp's debt was unsecured and flowed through a series of offshore companies whose convoluted ownership structure would make bank efforts to secure assets horribly complicated. In a liquidation the banks faced years of expensive court actions in exotic parts of the world to sort out which assets belonged to which banks. The rescue plan that the banks settled on instead was a debt override agreement that gave News Corp the extra $600 million in working capital that it needed and three years to pay back its entire debt. No one bank was to be allowed to withdraw, to get its money back, until they all did.

The important thing to remember in any bank rescue operation is just who is being rescued. In a bank rescue the chief object of compassion and the worthy recipient of succor is not the hapless borrower but the banks; and inasmuch as the rescue is organized by the leading bank, the most worthy recipient of all is the leading bank itself. The rescue operation mounted by *les misérables* in the pinstriped suits would cost News Corp $150 million as a flat fee. The banks would get all of their money back by 1993, and in the intervening three years News Corp would pay them $2.3 billion in interest payments. The chief difficulty was that those banks and institutions that had the least money at risk tended to feel the least urgency for the rescue and to suspect quite correctly that those with the most to gain were the senior banks. They wanted the seniors to pay them out. But the senior banks were playing hardball, insisting that if even one little bank was paid out early, it would trigger a stampede for the exits that would hurt everybody.

In the three months it took for the debt override plan to be adopted, News Corp kept running into repayment deadlines as different sets of loans matured, giving any bank in that loan the capacity to put the entire company into liquidation. Even one tiny default—and some of the banks that held out were owed as little as $2.5 million—would trigger cross-defaults that would overwhelm the company. On October 31, when the original one-month rollover fell due, Murdoch almost went broke. There was a lynching party in Sydney on November 15, when a crew of ornery Australian bankers went into a meeting with Murdoch and other News Corp executives determined to take a serious bite out of Rupert Murdoch. But they turned out to be candy. Once they were in the charm zone, they became as diffident about challenging the Murdoch vision of the future as four decades of bankers before them had been.

On November 30 Murdoch almost went broke again. There was a crisis on December 3, but then it was clear sailing—until December 6 and Pittsburgh. Of course at the end of that terrifying afternoon and evening, Pittsburgh folded. After the loan officer at Pittsburgh National told DeVoe he wanted to put News Corp into liquidation, John Reed, the chairman of Citibank, called the Pittsburgh National chairman to warn him of the dangers to the entire banking system and to Western civilization if News Corp crashed. When Murdoch called Pittsburgh, before he could speak the loan officer was assuring him that he had thought about his conversation with David DeVoe and "we don't want to be difficult." He would roll. End of the Pittsburgh problem.

*   *   *

For Murdoch and News Corp, it was on to other battles, other cities, other bankers to cajole. These scenes would haunt Murdoch for years. During November he called his elder son, Lachlan, and pulled him out of Princeton to be with him in London as he made the endless rounds of bankers. As Lachlan, then nineteen years old, walked home with his father down Fleet Street at one o'clock one night after a long haggling session, he wondered why his father seemed so stressed and dispirited. "I wanted to put my arms around him and hold him up," he told the *New York Times* later.[15]

The crises continued. There was some smart work in New York on December 21, then Murdoch nearly went broke again the night before Christmas. He had another date with near-insolvency on New Year's Eve, paused for a brief respite, then in early January 1991 was back to almost going broke again.

By then he was getting used to it. The entire ordeal lasted 116 days. And then at two-fifteen on the morning of February 1, 1991, it was over. The whole series of rolling crises that had made up Murdoch's great debt crisis was finished. The banks had all signed up on the rescue package, the debt override agreement was secured, News Corp had its three-year breathing space, and Murdoch had survived.

Later, strangely, when News Corp executives and bankers felt free to talk about their four-month ordeal, they talked about Pittsburgh. They told *Institutional*

Investor and then the *Financial Times* in London about the fears of that night. Murdoch told his biographer, William Shawcross, about how the Pittsburgh bank president had refused to take his call and about his need for a stiff drink afterward. It was a classic tale, with a moral that could vary according to whoever was telling the story. The Pittsburgh affair was an example of how a mighty international empire could be brought to its knees by a minor mistake or incident, the One Fatal Flaw. Alternatively it underlined the Frightening, Inescapable Power that even the smallest bank could hold over a huge multinational company. Most of all it was a story that showcased Rupert Murdoch's phenomenal capacity to survive, his ability to face his date with destiny and walk away.

The most remarkable aspect of the Pittsburgh incident was its timeless quality. The story had no past and no future. For all the News Corp executives' willingness to recount the affair as an anecdote, as a colorful *episode* in the rich tapestry of unraveling disaster that was its debt crisis, the same executives proved reticent when it came to giving details about the history of the Pittsburgh loan. How had the money been raised in the first place? What was the original loan used for? For all intents and purposes, the track of the Pittsburgh money was lost in the crisscrossing web of hundreds of intercompany loans that form the way News Corp conducts its business on any day at hundreds of points around the globe. End of story.

At the time the only suggestion that there was more to the Pittsburgh affair came in an odd series of conversations on the other side of the world. The *Sydney Morning Herald*'s banking writer, Karen Maley, had been covering the News Corp debt crisis for two months. Her adroit courting of Australian bankers involved in the debt override operation had given her a steady flow of inside information about how different banks were responding, particularly the unhappy minor banks. On Sunday, December 2, she spoke to several bank executives who for the first time raised their concern that not all of the money covered in the debt override agreement was for News Corp. According to the so-called Dolphin Memorandum, which was the blueprint for the rescue plan, $450 million of private debt owed by the Murdoch family was being mixed in with News Corp's corporate debt in the debt override agreement. The senior lenders were eager to do this, as they previously had loaned money to both News Corp and the Murdochs. The smaller lenders who had had no exposure to the Murdochs didn't see why the two sets of loans should be mixed up. Maley's sources were concerned that money that belonged to News Corp's shareholders (or more to the point, to News Corp's bankers) might be used to pay off Rupert Murdoch's personal debts.

On Thursday afternoon the same bankers alerted Maley to a problem with a large loan that was falling due for repayment the next day; they were particularly reluctant to let that debt be rolled over. The unhappy borrower was Queensland Press. This was an intriguing twist to the debt crisis, but it needed confirmation. Then Maley got lucky. Late on Thursday afternoon she put in a call to Keith McDonald, the chief executive officer of Queensland Press in Brisbane. "I couldn't believe it when he picked up the phone," she said later.[16] McDonald confirmed that Queensland Press had a loan falling due the next day and that there had been discussions about it with the banks, but he dismissed any suggestion of a serious problem.

Allowing for different time zones, it is clear the Pittsburgh crisis on December 6 (London time) and the Queensland Press rollover on December 7 were the same deal—McDonald did not realize how much his future would soon depend upon an unknown bank executive in Pennsylvania.[17] McDonald, who also sat on the main News Corp board, was supremely confident when he spoke to Maley. He gave no indication that he was going to lose any sleep over the loan that night or even that he or anyone else would need a stiff drink afterward.

What made this so unusual was that News Corp owned only 44 percent of Queensland Press. The desperation in London over whether Pittsburgh would put News Corp into liquidation had been triggered by a dispute about debt in the Murdochs' private companies. This was not quite the story that News Corp told *Institutional Investor* and the *Financial Times*.[18] No one was ever told that the Pittsburgh crisis was the result of the murky deal Murdoch had done three days after the 1987 crash.

Then there was Citicorp's insistence that the whole basis of the debt override was that none of Murdoch's banks could be paid off. "We are where we are" and "Nobody gets out" were the two rules that the Citicorp team had hammered down the throats of bankers around the world. But this insistence wasn't strictly accurate. In Australia, according to minor lenders, the Commonwealth Bank had drawn up a list of minor lenders in its syndicates, particularly its Queensland Press syndicate, and quietly taken out any bank that was owed less than A$10 million. An account manager with one of these minor lenders recalls a meeting with a Commonwealth Bank loan manager in which he expected to be told firmly that he wouldn't be seeing any of his money in the Murdoch debt. Instead the Commonwealth Bank man handed him a check to pay off the loan.[19] Pittsburgh National's A$10 million loan was just above the payout point. Not surprisingly, Pittsburgh wasn't happy.

News Corp was just as reticent about what happened next.

In late March 1991 the chief legal officer in Queensland for the Australian Securities Commission, Robin Chapman, walked down the short corridor at the ASC's Brisbane office to see her boss, Queensland commissioner Barrie Adams. The ASC (since renamed the Australian Securities and Investments Commission) had been in existence for just three months as Australia's new corporate watchdog.

Chapman had been looking at a 1987–88 deal in which Queensland Press had bought a parcel of News Corporation shares from the Murdoch family company, Cruden Investments. In 1989 Chapman had helped to rewrite the Australian laws that restrict a company from buying its own stock, or from lending money or giving financial assistance to another party to buy its stock. Based on the scanty details on file, Chapman told Adams she suspected that by doing this deal, Queensland Press had provided money to Cruden that paid for the Queensland Press takeover.

Adams struggled to understand the complex legal issues and corporate structures that Chapman was explaining to him. Eventually he shifted in his seat a little and asked the billion-dollar question: "If we took the view that News Corporation shareholders were disadvantaged by the deal, what would be the effect if we forced them to reverse the transaction?"

The room went silent. This conversation took place just weeks after the debt crisis. Murdoch was still hanging on to his empire by his fingertips. Reversing the deal could trigger a financial crisis for Cruden and put the News Corp debt override agreement into default. To raise money, Murdoch would have little option but to sell most of his News Corp shares. Such a forced sale would depress the News Corp share price even further. The likely result was that Murdoch would not only lose control of News Corp but also go broke. And News Corp itself would hit the wall.

"We can live with that," Adams said easily. "If that is what we find is appropriate, we're comfortable with that."[20]

Of course the issue wasn't that simple. What the ASC would decide to do at the end of its inquiry was one thing. The more immediate problem was what the market would *expect* the ASC to do, if investors knew about the inquiry, while Murdoch struggled to obtain $7 billion in new debt and capital raisings to pay off the debt override agreement in the next two years.

In mid-1991 an ASC investigator described the case as the state's highest priority after the pursuit of fugitive entrepreneur Christopher Skase. It was later downgraded into a documents-only investigation. "It's a routine matter," an ASC spokesperson said in late 1992. "They [the Murdoch companies] got their knickers into a knot."[21] The ASC resolved that no legal action would be taken. Instead, in January 1993 it wrote a draft report that was sharply critical of the Queensland Press deal. It made no comment about the mortgage on Murdoch's penthouse—the ASC had never heard about it. The inquiry also did not look at the price at which the deal was struck. The ASC staff hoped to have the final report tabled in the Australian parliament by June 1993, but the inquiry was overtaken by events. No final report was written, and the matter lapsed. Thus those involved in the Queensland Press deal were exonerated.

The last word went to Murdoch's Australian lawyer, John Atanaskovic, who on March 3, 1993, wrote a scathing response to the ASC's draft report on its investigation. Atanaskovic declared flatly that the ASC was wrong in its interpretation of law and had not shown that the sole or dominating purpose of Queensland Press directors in approving the stock deal in 1987 was improper. Further, he said, by failing to call witnesses, the ASC was depending on a documentary record that was incomplete, when it sought to portray unease among Queensland Press directors about the deal.

"I do not believe that, at the end of its consideration of the matter in 1993, the ASC did in fact consider that Queensland Press might have been providing financial assistance for its own takeover," says Atanaskovic.[22]

It was the runaway News Corp stock price that took the steam out of the ASC inquiry. In late 1993, when the inquiry was finally closed, News Corp stock (allowing for share splits) hit A$48. Queensland Press, which had bought its stock for A$16, was now sitting on a spectacularly successful invesment. As News Corp's stock price continued to rise—the A$16 shares were worth A$160 (adjusting for share splits) in March 2000—Queensland Press became News Corp's private little bank, Murdoch's lender of last resort. It also had become his golden parachute. If Murdoch ever tired of running the empire, selling the News Corp shares held by Queensland Press would offer a spectacular exit.

6

THE FUGITIVE

London/Jerusalem

B Y 1991 NEWS CORPORATION'S AVERSION to paying corporate income taxes had become legendary. Since 1986 its tax bill had averaged less than seven cents on each dollar it reported in earnings. Murdoch's huge U.S. investments to buy Metromedia and 20th Century–Fox and launching the Fox network—with debt that was funded by his operations in Britain and to a lesser extent Australia— had allowed him to structure the News Corp empire around holding companies in the Bahamas, the Cayman Islands, the Channel Islands, and the British Virgin Islands—in short, almost any offshore destination that shared an enlightened view about the need to pay taxes. This archipelago of tax havens allowed Murdoch to channel News Corp's money streams away from high-tax areas like the United States, Australia, and Britain. As the Citibank rescue team had found, it also made News Corp's corporate structure unbelievably complicated. By discouraging Murdoch's bankers from wanting to liquidate assets because the ownership was so hard to unravel, that complexity had helped save the empire.

In the months that followed Murdoch's 1991 debt crisis, his empire continued to battle for survival. In a world full of skeptical bankers, disaffected investors, and incredulous analysts, News Corp kept its own counsel and inched its way back toward solvency. There were dark and far-flung corners in News Corp that did not need to see the light of day, including most of its tax archipelago dealings. While News Corp had always been happy to talk about the low-tax profits it made, it was much more reluctant to talk about how it achieved the tax savings or about the men and women who ran this secret side of News Corp. The subject was clearly marked private and off-limits, a corporate no-go area—as indeed it is for most multinationals that use tax havens. But the downside to a corporate obsession with confidentiality is that sometimes a company can choke on its own secrets.

For all the ingenuity of tax lawyers and accountants in New York and London, multinational corporations depend for their smooth running on a relatively small number of middle-management executives running subsidiary companies around the world, as well as the community of expatriate lawyers and accountants living on the tax haven islands to administer the offshore subsidiaries as directors and company secretaries. The bigger and more far-flung the corporation, the greater trust and responsibility that executives in its outposts carry. People entrusted with the routine tasks of moving money from one offshore account to another have to be up to the task. What is best for the company must be uppermost in their mind. In 1991 Rupert Murdoch's empire was plunged into crisis when it was confronted with the specter of a criminal in its no-go zone. An American-Israeli executive had set out to defraud News Corp, and it was perhaps inevitable that he used the archipelago to hide his tracks.

One of Rupert Murdoch's great strengths is his ability to recognize the merits of a really good idea. This ability is generally marked by the speed with which he tries to hire the person who put the idea to him. The result is that at any time News Corp is surrounded by a cloud of consultants who do not fit into any clear management structure and whose status is judged only by their access to Rupert Murdoch. So it was that on March 22, 1987, Bruce Hundertmark, an Australian entrepreneur, technology consultant, and one-time diplomat and academic who had known Murdoch since 1971, found himself having breakfast in Murdoch's apartment on St. James's Place in London. Discussion was difficult because Murdoch was continually interrupted by a stream of telephone calls from around the world, including one from the Australian prime minister, Bob Hawke, who called to tell Murdoch the secret date for the Australian election. (Hawke, who had just allowed Murdoch to take over the Australian newspaper industry, confidently asked for Murdoch's support. Murdoch replied, "Well, Bob, what's in it for me?")

By the end of this muddled breakfast, Hundertmark had become a consultant for Sky Television, the tiny satellite broadcaster to Europe that Murdoch had been backing since the early 1980s. Sky was going nowhere, so its executives played a fairly minor role in the ranks of Murdoch's advisers. All the same Hundertmark found himself playing dangerous corporate politics. For the next year News Corp's chairman, Richard Searby, refused even to talk to him. "I was offered no line of communication within News Group and no form of supervision except directly from Mr. Murdoch," he said later.[1]

The chief of News International, Bill O'Neill, took Hundertmark aside to explain. "Would you like me to draw for you an organization chart for The News Corporation Limited?" O'Neill asked. He drew on a blank sheet a large circle with a dot at the centre. "This is Rupert," he said, and pointed to the dot.

"Here is the rest of us," he said, and he ran his finger around the circumference of the circle. "Everyone works directly for Rupert."

News International executive John Dux told Hundertmark that the corporate culture was like the court of Louis XIV, the Sun King. Hundertmark had no difficulty identifying himself as the unwelcome new royal favorite. When he began to put investment ideas to Murdoch, the chairman of Sky Television, Sir James Cruthers, who was also a News Corp director, warned him to be careful. "Rupert is the only in-house entrepreneur" allowed at News, Cruthers said.

Hundertmark was interested in high-speed encryption. In 1977 three professors at the Massachusetts Institute of Technology, Ronald Rivest, Adi Shamir, and Leonard Adleman, had come up with a better way of keeping secrets. In many ways the possibility of secrecy—the idea that one can make something appear or disappear, to look other than what it is; that one can hide the real meaning of something to the world at large, while ensuring that under the surface the hidden message is always accessible for the select few—has always been a critical element of social organization. In the modern world the groups who most need to keep secrets, to control flows of information, to make things appear or disappear at will, are media companies. Information and entertainment are commodities, and like all commodities they must be protected from unauthorized use. The encryption system developed by the three MIT professors—now called RSA, after their initials—has two parts or keys. There is a public key that is used to encrypt a message. Anyone can have the public key. But only the person who holds the private key can decrypt the message.

In the early 1980s Adi Shamir moved to Israel. At the Weizmann Institute of Science, Shamir and a Dr. Fiat developed the Fiat/Shamir encryption algorithm. In the mid-1980s the Weizmann Institute and its commercial arm, the Yeda Research and Development Company, were looking at ways to make money from Shamir's algorithms. In 1987, when Hundertmark came looking for ideas, Yeda's commercial push was being handled by an Israeli-American named Michael Clinger, who had a remarkable marketing background in high-tech business.

One feature of almost every relationship that Michael Clinger had ever had was his ability to win the person's confidence. Obviously intelligent, there was something about him that inspired trust. "He was a real charmer, and I genuinely liked him," said Don Osur, an American executive who had another impression when he was left with the task of turning around one of Clinger's failed ventures.[2] Physically Clinger was unimpressive—a stodgy figure with a wide face and large glasses. He looked like a math teacher. But perhaps the geeky appearance was part of his charm—and he was certainly charming. It helped that at thirty-six years old Clinger was already independently wealthy. His social skills were enhanced by his wife, Niva Von Weisl, a former model who became one of the leading lights of Jerusalem society after the couple moved from New York to Israel in 1987.

By February 1988 Hundertmark had convinced Murdoch to invest $3.6 million in developing Shamir's encryption process. Hundertmark and Clinger set up a News Corp venture that traded as News Datacom, in which they held a minority stake. Avoiding taxes was an issue from the start, and the entity they set up existed somewhere in between the legal and tax reaches of Tel Aviv, London, and Hong Kong. The business was based on a research company in Israel called News Datacom Research (NDR), but the holding company, News Data Security Products (NDSP), was based in Hong Kong. A News Corp company in Bermuda, News Publishing, owned 60 percent of NDSP; Adi Shamir owned 10 percent; and the Weizmann Institute's commercial arm, Yeda, owned another 10 percent. The remaining 20 percent was held by International Development Group, a company owned by Clinger and Hundertmark based in the Dutch Antilles.[3] Under the shareholding agreement for News Datacom, each shareholder would have preemptive rights to buy the other shareholders' stock if they wished to sell out. It was a very modest operation, and a great idea looking for an application. That all changed four months later.

In mid-1988 Murdoch's empire was wobbling along in its customary fashion. The Fox television network in the United States was hemorrhaging money, and Richard Sarazen told reporters that if the losses continued, News Corp would have to dump the new network. A day later Sarazen was saying he had been misreported. In February 1989 Fox chief Barry Diller would claim that in the second half of 1988 Fox was actually breaking even. It wasn't the last time Fox finances would vary depending on whom you talked to.

In Britain in June 1988 Murdoch's tabloids were doing themselves proud. The *News of the World,* in between stories about Princess Anne's husband, Captain Mark Phillips, and his candlelit dinners with his Canadian public relations manager, and an orphaned puppy that was being breast-fed by a sturdy British housewife, had covered itself with glory with a story about a tribe of perverted cannibals in Papua New Guinea called the Chimbu. The local arm of the News Corp empire duly reprinted this story in Papua New Guinea's capital, Port Moresby, and forty irate Chimbu tribesmen descended on the British High Commission looking for the name of a good libel lawyer. Contrary to what the *News of the World* had claimed, the tribesmen complained, they were neither perverted nor cannibals. They did not torture their children nor engage in stone-age sex rituals nor practice ritualized homosexuality. They also didn't cut off the heads of rivals and eat their brains after smearing themselves with blood. The *News of the World* must have been confusing them with British headhunters—or perhaps British tabloid journalists—was the general gist of the Chimbu complaint. The *News of the World* was unruffled. The paper had long perfected the defense used by Christine Keeler in the Profumo scandal defense to all such complaints, which in this case was to ogle the indignant noncannibal and sniff magnificently, "Well, they *would* say that, wouldn't they?"

Murdoch was also feeling out of sorts after losing the *New York Post*. As part of the Metromedia deal in 1986, he had picked up Channel Six in New York, which put him in breach of the cross-media laws prohibiting media companies owning a television station and a newspaper in the same city. Murdoch had persuaded the FCC to give him a temporary waiver while he worked out what to do with the *Post*, which was still making losses. He had been confident that the FCC would give him a permanent waiver, on grounds of public interest, until a late-night Senate amendment in December 1987 led by Senators Ernest Hollings and Teddy Kennedy removed the power of the FCC to extend temporary waivers. The amendment was later overturned by the Supreme Court, on the grounds that it was a law which was targeted "with the accuracy of a laser beam" at just one man: Rupert Murdoch. However, the court decision came too late to save the *Post*. Murdoch had been forced to sell, and in mid-1988 he was feeling depressed about it. He did what he always did when facing adversity: When the going gets tough, Rupert Murdoch goes shopping.

He was busy amalgamating Harper & Row with William Collins Plc in Britain to form HarperCollins. He was about to spend $3 billion buying *TV Guide* and Triangle Publications. He was also spending a fortune on new printing presses. And then, on June 8, he stunned a dinner in London sponsored by the British Academy of Film and Television Arts by announcing that he was about to transform his little European satellite operation, Sky. The new Sky would use a medium-power Luxembourg satellite to launch four unauthorized channels to Britain in eight months' time. (Five months later News Corp would still be talking to the

Russian space agency about renting Russian transponders.) Up until this moment the partners in British Satellite Broadcasting (BSB), the consortium that in December 1986 had won an exclusive license from the British government to run a satellite television service, had believed they had the field entirely to themselves. Murdoch's proposed launch date meant that Sky would be operating months before BSB was ready. "We are seeing the dawn of an age of freedom for viewing and freedom for advertising," Murdoch announced. This was "the dawn of television's new age and the most dramatic innovation in broadcasting since the launch of commercial television in Britain more than three decades ago."[4]

It is difficult to appreciate just how knuckleheaded Murdoch's decision was. His broadcasting experience had been limited to owning a few television stations in Australia and launching a new television network in America the year before, a network that continued to bleed his empire. Sky was to be based upon a low-power European satellite operation that Murdoch had owned since 1982, which had virtually no viewers or advertising and in five years had gracefully lost £30 million. Murdoch had absolutely no experience in pay television. So his model for the revamped Sky would continue to be free-to-air television, based on advertising revenues. Murdoch planned to beef up Sky's existing general entertainment channel, buy sports programming from a new channel called Eurosport, have a news channel, and form a joint venture with Michael Eisner at Disney that would include a movie channel.

Murdoch believed that people would be pounding at the doors, wanting to shell out £200 for a satellite dish. His business model, which had *catastrophe* written all over it, would indeed have been a disaster epic—if Hollywood had not rallied to save Murdoch with a solid dose of outraged paranoia. The movie business is built around the issue of copyright, on making sure that the only people who get to see a moving picture are the paying customers. Without such safeguards, copyright pirates, as they have shown, can make three times as much money from a movie as the copyright holder. Studios were willing to show their films on free-to-air television stations—after every other possible market had been tapped, from cinema to video to cable—because TV could be controlled. Beyond a forty-mile radius from the television tower, even *Gone With the Wind* begins to look like the Great Alaskan Snowstorm of 1954. By comparison, a satellite's reach is limited only by the curvature of the earth. The idea of broadcasting movies from a satellite across the major land mass of Europe, where they could be picked up and pirated by *anyone* with a satellite dish; of mixing markets and blurring the distinctions that allowed the studios to extract the maximum dollar of revenue from every territory where their films were shown; all sparked fear and loathing in the sensitive hearts of movie executives. In case the movie houses didn't get it, in November 1988, Sky's British satellite rival, BSB, took out a full-page advertisement in *Variety* with a skull-and-crossbones pirate flag and an open letter underneath: "Dear Hollywood, don't let Rupert feed your product to the pirates. . . ."

Late on November 9 Murdoch called Hundertmark and told him he had to change Sky into a pay-television service. This posed a bit of a problem, because Murdoch had already committed to using the old PAL European television format, but no one had ever encrypted PAL. Murdoch hoped that Paris-based Thomson Consumer Electronics could solve the problem. Hundertmark told him News Datacom could come up with a more flexible and more secure system for controlling access to Sky based on smartcards. VideoCrypt, as it would be called, would be ready for production within six months—a record time for producing high-tech hardware, which relied on some heroic assumptions.

Murdoch wasn't interested. "Don't talk to me about fucking smartcards!" he said. "You are interested in the technology. I am interested only in the result, and there must be satisfactory pay-television systems existing already in the world without you introducing your News Datacom." But in the end Hundertmark persuaded Murdoch to make this huge gamble on his untried technology. In fact he suddenly became Murdoch's most important adviser. After eighteen months of News Datacom being ignored by News Corp management, overnight everything changed. "Everyone wanted to influence and control events that were now of interest to Mr. Murdoch," Hundertmark said later. "There was vigorous competition for my then established position as a confidante to Mr. Murdoch."

Murdoch asked Hundertmark who should run Sky. His adviser suggested Australian television executive Sam Chisholm (the man who would later turn BSkyB around). But in 1989 Murdoch dismissed Chisholm as someone who "had grown old too early." Instead, he said, "I've got it," and picked up the telephone. "Andrew, come over and see me." And so Andrew Neil, the then editor of the *Sunday Times*, became head of Sky.

Neil didn't get along with Hundertmark, who in turn described Neil as "controversial, difficult, technically unaware, and without experience in television." But Neil had a powerful patron in Irwin Stelzer, an American consultant best known as director of regulation at the American Enterprise Institute and adviser to power companies. In 1989, while he was first cultivating a rising British Labour politician named Tony Blair, Stelzer was on what is reported to have been a $1.5 million–a-year contract as a consultant to News Corp. By March 1989 Stelzer had become involved in Sky and had begun a move to push Hundertmark out. Stelzer also wanted to scrap the News Corp/Disney joint venture on Sky. On April 20 he telephoned Hundertmark and told him he had convinced Murdoch that the joint venture should not proceed. He pushed for his own recommendations to run the News Datacom arm, then went to Israel "wooing Professor Adi Shamir," as Clinger put it. The balance of power had changed again.

Sky went to air on time in February 1989. Its rival BSB had to postpone its own launch by six months because of problems with the encryption chip in its set-top box. Sky could fix the holes in VideoCrypt later, not by replacing the whole set-top box but just by issuing a new smartcard. Replacing the cards regularly— every three months was the plan—would also thwart hackers who wanted to pirate the Sky signal. "Without [Hundertmark's] drive, Murdoch could not have put numerous things together in time," one of those involved in the launch later commented.[5] Besides saving Sky, Hundertmark in setting up News Datacom had created what would eventually become a billion-dollar money-spinner. But despite his success, other courtiers now had the king's ear. Stelzer and one of his protégés, Gus Fischer, another consultant to News Corp who had helped resolve a press problem at Wapping, were critical of Hundertmark's strategy, his appointments, and his tendency to make independent decisions without consultation. Hundertmark had collapsed from overwork at Christmas 1989. In April 1990 Murdoch wrote to Hundertmark suggesting he resign. Exhausted and ill, he returned to Australia.

Gus Fischer was now chairman of News Datacom. Hundertmark's replacement, Tom Price, was a friend and former employee of Fischer's without college or technical education, who had sold paint and finishing products around the world for twenty years. Earlier Fischer had pressed Hundertmark to employ Price, whom he described as being "as honest as the day is long." The drawback to this arrangement was that with Hundertmark gone, no one in News Corp's management had any technical knowledge of just what News Datacom did. In effect the operating side of the business was largely under the control of Michael Clinger in Jerusalem. This was unfortunate because in late 1989 Hundertmark had come across an unhappy secret. A former partner of Clinger's had sent Hundertmark a damning set of documents.

*   *   *

Michael Cornelius Clinger, it appeared, had defrauded almost everybody he had ever come in contact with. He was born in England in 1952, but by the 1970s he was living in New York working as a credit analyst with the Chase Manhattan Bank. In 1974 he left Chase Manhattan to work for a Swiss medical supply company. Four years later he agreed to become a business partner of Deborah Rothfield, who wanted to form a company to market surgical lasers called Advanced Surgical Technologies. Clinger took up the idea, but Rothfield claimed he never gave her the half share they agreed upon. When he sold the company three years later, he pocketed the entire $3 million. He then moved on to a new laser-distribution company called Endo-Lase. In January 1984, as chairman and chief executive of Endo-Lase, Clinger floated the company on Wall Street for $3.5 million. The profits he reported to shareholders were fictitious right from the start. After sixteen months the stock had risen from $2 to $18, largely on the back of dodgy profit numbers and creative accounting.

The wheels began to fall off several months later, when the Securities and Exchange Commission (SEC) queried the Endo-Lase accounts. Clinger jumped ship in June 1986 at the insistence of the company's bankers, and two months later Endo-Lase filed for Chapter 11 bankruptcy protection. "Lots of innocent people lost their life savings on the stock," said Don Osur, who built a successful business out of the remains.

In July 1987 the SEC charged Clinger and two other Endo-Lase executives with defrauding investors, falsifying accounts, and insider trading. The three did not admit or deny the charges but settled the case by agreeing to pay back $814,194 in illegal profits, of which $810,600 was to come from Clinger, plus an undisclosed amount raised from the company's stock and bonus money. Facing a barrage of class-action suits from Endo-Lase stockholders who had lost their shirts, Clinger decided not to stay around to face the music. "Mr. Clinger left the country and went to Israel," said the senior counsel of the SEC's Division of Enforcement, James Mann.[6]

Bruce Hundertmark, who at this time was still at Sky, now knew he was in business with a major-league hustler. He told Clinger he had seen the SEC finding. He sent the SEC documents to the News Corp lawyer in London, Geoffrey Richards at Farrer & Co., on November 9, 1988, just hours before Murdoch called Hundertmark for help changing Sky into a pay-television service. Clinger himself says he discussed his legal problems with a senior News Corp executive, who was unconcerned and referred to legal actions taken against Rupert Murdoch in locations around the world. News Corp denies that any such conversation took place. Geoffrey Richards declined to comment.[7]

News Corp had enough crises elsewhere that needed Murdoch's attention. He had planned to run the movie channel as a joint venture with Disney, but just before Sky was launched, Michael Eisner pulled out of the venture on the grounds that Murdoch's *Sun* newspaper was running pictures of topless page-three girls holding satellite dishes with the Sky and Disney logos.[8] Sky said Eisner got cold feet because the bidding between Sky and BSB for movie rights from other studios had grown too rich for his comfort. Murdoch was furious with Eisner and sued Disney for $1.5 billion. Meanwhile many of the Sky set-top boxes had proved faulty, with fuses that needed to be replaced. The smartcards were put together at Sky's Livingstone site in Scotland by News Gem Smartcard International, a joint venture between News Datacom and the French technology group Gem Plus. But many of the cards also had faults. Although Sky was launched in February 1989, the encryption operation was not up and running until twelve months later. Still, Sky solved its problems faster than its rival, BSB, which because of its delays developing its encryption chip did not launch until April 1990.

By June 1990 News Corp had written off £235 million in losses on Sky. In the next four months it lost another £48 million. The huge losses were undermining any hope Murdoch had of convincing his banks to fund him out of the debt crisis that was then developing at News Corp. The total cost of Sky had grown to £550 million. If Sky folded, it would be a total loss. On September 27 Murdoch called Peter Davis at Reed International, one of the shareholders in BSB; they had met at Claridges on July 24, when they'd had an inconclusive discussion about merging Sky with BSB. Now Murdoch told Davis he was ready to talk seriously.[9]

After pumping £850 million into their rival venture, the four major BSB shareholders—Reed, Pearson, Granada, and Chargeurs—were just as eager to stop the bloodletting. The BSB shareholders knew Murdoch was in trouble, but they didn't realize how close to the edge he was. On October 4 David DeVoe had his crisis meeting with News Corp's bankers at Wapping. The BSB shareholders did not know that from that point the fate of Murdoch's empire hung on the Citibank rescue plan. During the week of October 14 Murdoch met privately with Ian Irvine, the deputy chief executive of BSB shareholder Reed International, at Cavan, his country property in Australia, to discuss a merger. On October 21 formal talks began in intense secrecy at Lucknam Park, an obscure Wiltshire hotel near Bath. BSB and News Corp executives booked into the Lucknam Park using false names and said they were executives with a company called Melloward.[10] BSB Holdings needed to keep the talks secret because it had just completed a difficult bank refinancing. If news of the merger talks got out, as Granada legal manager James Tibbitts put it, "BSB would not be dead in the water, it would be dead underwater."[11] News Corp faced a different danger. If the BSB partners learned of the dire debt crisis it was facing, they would offer fewer concessions—or they might not do the deal at all, and wait for News Corp and Sky to fall over.

In five days of tough negotiations, the shape of the merger was thrashed out. It would be a fifty-fifty merger between Sky and BSB, which would be run by News Corp. Despite BSB's reluctance, the new venture, BSkyB, would stick with Sky's ancient PAL technology and dump the high-power DMAC signal used by BSB. The decision would force Britain back to the old PAL television system for a decade. The problem, as the BSB shareholders had discovered, was that a pay-television service lives or dies on its encryption system. BSkyB would not own the VideoCrypt technology that was so important to its future. VideoCrypt was supplied by News Datacom Security Products, which was owned by News Corp and the Israelis. What would happen if News Datacom withdrew the technology? The BSB shareholders had already agreed to take only a half share in BSkyB, though they had invested more than Sky. They had conceded that News Corp would run BSkyB. News Datacom offered News Corp yet another way to squeeze the partnership.

The talks continued through the next week. Unknown to the BSB shareholders, News Corp almost went broke on October 31, when the one-month rollover of a $500 million loan fell due. The BSkyB merger was finalized forty-eight hours later. It was announced at nine P.M.—even before the BSB board approved the deal. Justice Arden would later find that late on Friday afternoon a BSB board meeting had been called for eight P.M., but the meeting to approve the merger was not held until two A.M. on the Saturday morning—and that meeting was later found to be invalid.[12] Both sides immediately began the delicate task of briefing Downing Street, regulators, media analysts, and bankers. The briefings continued through the following week, as the new chief executive of BSkyB, Sam Chisholm, descended like an avenging angel upon the BSB head office.

Chisholm had landed in London to run Sky on September 13. Short and pugnacious, Chisholm stood just five feet three inches tall on his tippy-toes. His style was personal—joking, persuading, shouting, in your face. Despite a serious lung condition he was a heavy smoker. He was alternately described as abrasive

and rude, or as charming and a pushover. A former floor-wax salesman, he had
gone into television and worked his way up to head Australia's National Nine
Network, which was owned by Kerry Packer. Chisholm had transformed Nine
into Australia's leading network with a swaggering management style that mixed
fear, flattery, and a talent for the grand gesture. There was a Good Sam and a Bad
Sam. The Good Sam had an intensely loyal cadre of executives and on-air talent
and was famous at Nine for lavish spending. "Winners have parties, losers have
meetings," he told staff. The Bad Sam had a sign on his desk at Nine that said, "To
err is human, to forgive is not my policy." Some people thought he was kidding.

Within hours of taking over BSkyB Chisholm began sacking staff. In the next
eight months estimates of the indirect casualty toll would go as high as three thousand. Two satellite operations with two sets of head offices, uplink centers, satellite transponders, television studios, and maintenance and administration staff all
had to be slashed. The need for secrecy remained paramount. News Corp, in the
middle of its debt crisis, had decided that it would not be appropriate to tell its investors how much of its investment was being written off as a loss. News accountants took the Sky/BSkyB investment off the group's balance sheet for five months
and treated it as a loan. During that time BSkyB wrote off £750 million in losses,
but News Corp never said a word about this to its shareholders.

*   *   *

Michael Clinger in Jerusalem was still running the most secret part of the
Murdoch empire, News Datacom Research. As head of the encryption operation,
Clinger had become News Corp's official keeper of secrets. Meanwhile in New
York the Securities and Exchange Commission had not forgotten about Clinger,
nor about the $810,600 settlement that he had agreed to pay in July 1987. The
problem, said the SEC's James Mann, was that "Clinger never paid the money."[13]
In November 1990 the SEC ran out of patience. On Thursday, November 8, as
the frenzied lobbying and briefing sessions over the BSkyB merger continued in
London, as Sam Chisholm stepped up his wave of wholesale sackings, and as the
Citibank rescue bid for News Corp stepped up another notch, a New York grand
jury indicted Clinger on fifty-one counts of insider trading, fraudulent accounting,
and obstructing the SEC. A warrant was issued for his arrest. From this point on
one of the most critical arms of News Corp was being run by an international fugitive. Michael Clinger didn't feel abashed by this situation. Nor did he feel any
need to share news of this development with News Corp management, who in any

case were busy with the secret arrangements of the BSkyB takeover and the debt crisis. If anyone could keep a secret, it was Michael Clinger.

In April 1991 Rupert Murdoch made the unpleasant discovery that, after four horrific months of battling with banks to refinance News Corp's debt, he had another banking problem on his hands. After seeing how shaky News Corp's financial position was, BSkyB's bankers were refusing to provide the next round of funding for the struggling business covered by BSB's original loan agreement. The banks wanted the BSkyB shareholders to kick in more money themselves. This was a problem for News Corp because of the tight restraints imposed by the debt override agreement. After another heart-stopping crisis, where liquidation seemed again only days away, the BSkyB shareholders stumped up the cash. To meet News Corp's half share, Murdoch ended up borrowing £22 million through his family holding company, Cruden Investments. Significantly, he raised the money from another Australian bank, Westpac. He had dropped Commonwealth Bank of Australia.

In the course of this restructuring, the BSkyB shareholders hammered out a new shareholders' agreement. One of the biggest issues to resolve was what to do about the ownership of VideoCrypt and the Hong Kong holding company, News Datacom Security Products. The News Corp subsidiary in Bermuda, News Publishing, owned 60 percent of NDSP. How could BSkyB ensure that it would always retain access to the VideoCrypt technology? And given that News Corp had management and board control of BSkyB, how could the other shareholders be sure that News would not demand extortionate prices for the smartcards? The underlying question for the former BSB shareholders was, how much did they trust Rupert Murdoch? Emotions ran high. "It's Rupert's technique to use the power of the management," Frank Barlow of Pearson told Mathew Horsman later. "News wanted to run [BSkyB] as a News subsidiary."

The differences degenerated into shouting matches across the board table between Barlow and Arthur Siskind, the News Corp lawyer and BSkyB board member. "Arthur really couldn't stand Frank—they went at each other all the time," said one director. At one point Barlow shouted at Siskind, "Look, my heart can stand it. Can yours?"[14]

On May 11, 1991, to settle the concerns over VideoCrypt, News Corp agreed to insert the following three clauses in a wider shareholders' agreement. Clause one: Any deals between News Datacom Security Products and BSkyB would be on an arm's-length commercial basis. Clause two: If News Corp's stake in BSkyB ever fell below 33.33 percent, BSkyB could force it to sell its stake in NDSP to BSkyB. Clause three: News International, through News Publishing in Bermuda, would use its "best endeavours" to consult with the Israeli shareholders "as to the possibility" that BSkyB could buy some or all of the News Corp stake in NDSP. In short, BSkyB wanted to buy NDSP, and News Corp would do its best to make it happen.

The problem was, the 1988 NDSP shareholders' agreement meant that any change of ownership required the approval of the other shareholders. So it wasn't clear how News Corp could possibly make the commitment in clause two to sell its stake without the approval of the Israeli shareholders. The Israelis didn't complain because News Corp never told them about clause two. Actually it looks like News Corp never got around to telling the Israelis about clause three either. "I have no evidence of News International having so consulted with the minority shareholders in NDSP," Justice Lindsay found in the Chancery Court in November 1998.[15] This was not a minor omission. Siskind subsequently testified in an affidavit that in late 1991 BSkyB discussed buying News out of NDSP, but "the discussion never became serious." In late 1999 News Corp floated NDS Group, the business into which News Datacom evolved. In March 2000 the market value of NDS hit $5 billion, before it settled around $3 billion. Back in 1991 NDSP was headed for great things, but who would end up with this windfall, BSkyB or News Corp? News Corp's failure to consult with the Israeli shareholders about a share sale to BSkyB meant the big winner would be News Corp. This omission arguably cost BSkyB several billion dollars.

Meanwhile the News Datacom business in Israel was getting out of control. The Israeli staff had a personal loyalty to Michael Clinger and regarded News Corp executives as "merely occasional, uninformed and not always welcome visitors," Justice Lindsay later concluded.[16]

Early on Clinger had hired an accountant friend of his, Leo Krieger, as finance officer both for News Datacom and for the holding company NDSP at $48,000 a year. The two were as thick as thieves. Meir Matatyahu, another young Israeli whom Clinger hired in March 1990, told Clinger in a telephone call:

> You know, it is, how you say . . . shitty company, well, I mean it is not a shitty company but the way that people think, the way that people talk, you can hear it so . . . the standard is so low, it is unbelievable. . . . It's such stupid things . . . but this is it, this is what we have.[17]

Clinger responded:

> Yeah, but you know that is one of the reasons we can manipulate it . . . it
> cuts both ways . . . you know, you have got to keep that in mind . . .
> we would not be doing what we were doing if they were particularly bril-
> liant. . . . It is a headless management with each guy going in his own
> direction and, you know, it has its upside.

Clinger was spending a lot of time in Paris and had become a little hard to contact. He carried a string of passports under different names. He traveled variously
as Michael Clinger, Michael Klinger, Cornelius Clinger, and Cornelius Klinger.
Life on the run had not restricted his lifestyle nor his role as the official face of
News Datacom. In June 1991, for example, he was in Brussels to brief the European Community research commissioner, Filippo Maria Pandolfi, who was trying
to negotiate a new set of broadcasting rules for the European Community market.

   In London Clinger had not hit it off with Sam Chisholm. The Israelis were just
as uneasy about being minority partners with News Corp as the BSB partners
were. Just as the BSB partners feared that News Corp would exploit its control of
BSkyB to its own advantage, the Israeli shareholders feared that News Corp management would channel any profits from the encryption technology toward News
Corp rather than News Datacom. In the eyes of the Weizmann Institute and Adi
Shamir, Clinger was the only defender of their interests. Clinger complained, with
some justification, that BSkyB was buying smartcards at less than cost price
(though this was balanced for the moment because BSkyB's minimum orders
meant it was paying for more cards than it used). The original contract had been
to replace the smartcards every three months, but to cut costs, Sky unilaterally decided to extend the life of the cards—a move that would help Sky but stood to cost
NDSP millions of pounds. Clinger, perhaps rightly, saw it as a breach of contract.
As the quarrel with Chisholm worsened, Clinger threatened to insert a built-in ex-
piration date into the cards, after which they would not function. The two men
had an angry exchange of letters that ended with Chisholm attacking Clinger's
character, refusing to deal with him, and even suggesting he might not be honest.
In those desperate months when BSkyB was fighting for its very existence,
Chisholm had taken the role of the heavy. He was determined to cut costs on all
sides and to chisel price reductions out of all of BSkyB's suppliers—and particularly to renegotiate with Hollywood studios the huge fees for movie rights. In this
bigger picture, Clinger was just a minor irritant.

Chisholm was right, of course. Clinger was robbing News Corp blind. Initially, as we have seen, Sky had manufactured the smartcards at its Livingstone factory in Scotland through News Gem Smartcard International, a company jointly owned with the French group Gem Plus. News Gem had quality problems—up to 12 percent of the cards it supplied to Sky's customers didn't work. Clinger convinced BSkyB to close News Gem and have the cards assembled by a California chip-maker, Bharat Kumar Marya, known as BK. With Clinger's help, BK became the sole supplier of smartcards for BSkyB, through a Jersey company called Phoenix Micro. In return Clinger took half the profits BK made—though the trail of the money was soon lost in the archipelago of tax havens. At BK's request, the pair began using false names in their correspondence; Clinger was Jack Higgins. News Corp remained unaware of Clinger's secret arrangements with BK, but in what followed, it wasn't always clear who was fooling whom.

The larger question is, when did News Corp's senior management realize that one of its most sensitive subsidiaries was being run by a criminal? When asked in June 1996, a senior executive initially said that senior management remained unaware that Clinger was wanted in the United States until mid-1992, after he had cut all links with NDSP. Several months later the same News Corp executive amended the date of the discovery to late 1991.[18] What wasn't clear was *which* News Corp executives knew about Clinger. Given the company's centralized management style, it seems inconceivable that Rupert Murdoch was not told, though when the affair hit the British courts, Murdoch strangely appeared to play no part in the saga. News Corp execs—presumably including Murdoch—claimed they learned of Clinger's arrest warrant around the time they finalized an agreement to buy the Israelis out of NDSP.

By August 1991 Clinger had become too much trouble for News Corp. Peter Stehrenberger, secretary of News International, wrote to the company's chief operating officer, Gus Fischer, about the need to buy out the "nonperforming and disruptive partner" in NDSP. In the end it would be just a question of price. How much would it cost to get this man out of their hair? News Corp wasn't feeling generous. In May the Hong Kong office of accountants Arthur Andersen had valued the company's 60 percent stake in NDSP at between $29 and $33 million. On that basis the combined 40 percent owned by all the Israelis was worth between $19 and $22 million. On September 27 Siskind met Clinger and offered to buy all the Israeli partners out of NDSP for $6 million, plus some further payments out of future earnings. Clinger turned the offer down. Apparently News Corp learned about Clinger's criminal status sometime in the next six weeks, because on

November 6, when the company raised its offer to $12 million in staggered pay-
ments, it came with a demand that Clinger leave the NDSP offices immediately.
Adi Shamir and the Weizmann Institute agreed to the terms. On November 8, exactly twelve months after his grand jury indictment, Clinger cleared out his desk
at the News Datacom offices in Jerusalem and didn't return.

*   *   *

What does a major American broadcasting group do when it discovers it is in a
business deal with a U.S. fugitive? In News Corp's case, the answer was to cut a
better deal. After Clinger left, management set about ratcheting down the sale
price they had just negotiated. Arthur Andersen had another look at the NDSP accounts and decided that, while in May 1991 they had valued 60 percent of NDSP
at between $29 and $33 million, the accounts now showed that NDSP was losing
money on every card it made for BSkyB, its debt was more than its assets, and it
was technically insolvent. It was actually worth nothing. News Corp shared this assessment with the Israeli shareholders and suggested that its previous $12 million
offer was too generous. At a meeting in New York on January 21 (a choice of location that ensured that Clinger did not appear; he was represented by his lawyer)
Fischer told the Israelis that News Corp was cutting the agreed purchase price to
$10 million. Clinger's share, through his IDG holding company, would be $5 million. Clinger hemmed and hawed; then on March 17 he told News Corp that the
whole deal was off.

The News Corp executives were furious. The other shareholders had accepted
the offer, but the whole object of the exercise was to get rid of Michael Clinger.
Now, after months of work, it had all come to nothing. A frenzied series of telephone calls, letters, and face-to-face meetings followed, between Clinger and half
a dozen senior News International executives. News Corp now found itself in a
peculiar situation. It was run and controlled by an American citizen. It regarded
itself as an American-owned company and a good corporate citizen. It had no
power to arrest Clinger; its civic duty lay in alerting U.S. authorities to Clinger's location. But its senior executives and their lawyers were not only meeting with a
fugitive and criminal but proposing to provide him with active support, to the extent of paying him $5 million in cash for his shares in NDSP. Actually their chal-
lenge was to *persuade* him to accept their $5 million.

News Corp executives didn't tell the SEC where Clinger could be arrested,
even when Clinger flew to Britain on April 13. He met Stephen Barraclough,
News International's finance director, and Geoffrey Richards, who had helped set

up NDSP and at various times had acted for News International, for Sky, and as an NDSP director.

No matter how angry the execs were with Clinger, it wasn't in News Corp's interest for Clinger to be arrested. Extradition procedures would drag on while Clinger's assets would be frozen and/or subject to class-action suits, and the NDSP shareholding would become hopelessly complicated. Neither Richards nor Barraclough was an American, and News International is a British company, not subject to U.S. law. So neither man was obliged to assist U.S. authorities. But while News International was not compelled to turn Clinger in, the senior management at News Corp, who in practice had operational control of News International, *were* obliged to assist U.S. authorities, at least by civic duty. If Rupert Murdoch knew that Clinger was a fugitive, as a patriotic American that was where his civic duty lay.

The two sides give different accounts of what was said during the negotiations. Clinger claims that News Corp representatives told him his shares in NDSP were worth very little and that if he didn't sell out, BSkyB would dump the technology; alternatively, News Corp would call in its loans and put NDSP in liquidation. The six News Corp executives and lawyers named by Clinger denied making any such threat. Justice Lindsay found that News Corp had no obligation to inform Clinger that two reports by News International development manager Paul Vatistas had concluded that the £3 that BSkyB was paying for each smartcard was "unrealistically low" because the technology was crucial to BSkyB and the price made no allowance for Israeli research costs. Justice Lindsay accepted the News International view that Vatistas was too young and inexperienced to understand technology.[19]

By May 8 Clinger had agreed to new sale terms. The sale price stayed at £10 million for the 40 percent of NDSP, but News Corp would throw Clinger $560,000 in consultancy fees that Adi Shamir and the Weizmann Institute would not see, as well as further payments based on smartcard sales. Clinger signed a sale contract on May 14, with final settlement due for July 1. The same day NDSP started negotiations with BSkyB about changing the price for smartcards. Two events had changed the outlook for News Datacom's smartcards. On March 9 BSkyB had broken even for the first time and was now making profits, so it could afford to pay more. Second, on May 18 at the Lancaster Hotel in London, BSkyB had won the television rights to the Premier League, a new competition for Britain's top soccer clubs. Within weeks BSkyB had signed up a million people for its Premier League package. They all needed smartcards.

When Clinger, Shamir, and the Weizmann Institute settled the sale of their NDSP shares on July 1, they didn't know that two days before, BSkyB had provisionally approved an increase in the price it paid for smartcards. The per-card price would go from £3 to £4.50 plus a monthly "maintenance" fee of 45 pence. The price had more than tripled: It amounted to £9.90 in just the first year of the card's life. BSkyB would order more than six million cards each year for the next three years and pay more than £180 million. Admittedly BSkyB would no longer make minimum-purchase commitments to take cards it might not use, but even so the former BSB partners now in BSkyB were unhappy when told of the deal in July 1992. Justice Lindsay later noted that Steven Brown, the News International finance controller who had also become finance director of NDSP, "spent some time convincing the BSkyB shareholders who were not in the News group that the price was justifiable."

The buyout of the Israelis' shares had valued the entire NDSP business at $25 million. Seven days later to take advantage of new tax laws, News Corp sold the business into a new offshore British company also called News Datacom for $43.2 million. Given the resale price, the new sale contracts, and the huge price rise for cards, it can be argued that Shamir, the Weizmann Institute, and Clinger received less than their shares were worth. Four years later News Corp would be planning an IPO for News Datacom for $750 million. Four years after that the market value of the company's shares would touch $5 billion. It looks like News Corp fleeced the Israelis—though the British High Court would later dismiss any claim of legal impropriety. But the game wasn't over. The object of the whole exercise had been to get rid of Michael Clinger. As the News Corp lawyers completed the formalities of the sale on July 1, they believed that at last the company was rid of this annoying irritant. But Michael Clinger would prove a lot harder to shake.

THE PRETENDERS

O N A GOLDEN SUMMER afternoon in the Hudson Valley in upstate New York in the late 1970s, Anna Murdoch sat in the garden of the Murdochs' farmhouse in Old Chatham watching the erratic paths of the bees and the yellow jackets and mused on the frustrations of sex and motherhood. They are reading, she wrote, with

> my son sitting snug between my thighs. . . . I hold him at the end of summer . . . now squirming to be off; white soles flashing as he races through the meadow to join the others, crushing wild strawberries and clover with his heels. My own Achilles.[1]

Anna had begun part-time studies at Fordham University and later at New York University, majoring in Greek mythology. Her studies were the basis for the article she wrote late one summer entitled "Motherhood and Mythology: Summer Thoughts on Sex and Creativity," which explored role models for mothers in Greek myths. The outcome of her musings that afternoon would surface, over the following decade, in the three novels she would write. Each of the novels deals with a business dynasty and appears to be shaped by her own experiences and family. But it was in the garden at Old Chatham that she wrote most directly about herself and her children. The most frequently recurring theme in her reverie is that in the midst of plenty she is frustrated and unhappy. At that time she feared that the writing career of which she had once dreamed was over.

By the summer of 1977, when Anna was probably writing, Murdoch had bought the *New York Post* and was filling it with sensational stories of the Son of Sam serial killer, David Berkowitz, of looting and rioting during a power blackout, and of endless politics. At the end of 1976 Murdoch's move to take over *New York* magazine had provoked bitter opposition from *New York*'s founder Clay Felker, who with his wife Gail Sheehy had been among Anna and Rupert's first friends in America.

Murdoch's American biographer Thomas Kiernan, who knew the Murdochs socially, later wrote that their marriage was under pressure at this time. Anna felt frustrated with the end to her literary ambitions that marriage had brought, he said. She was also exasperated by the stories of women who claimed to be on good terms with Rupert. He had become a focus for celebrity groupies. Kiernan says one woman even became a neighbor of the Murdochs at their Old Chatham farm, between the Berkshires and the Catskills, regularly came to visit, and boasted to others of "my importance to Rupert," before Anna angrily banished her. Kiernan claims this period marked a turning point where Anna became far more critical of Rupert, patronizing, and impatient. The tension lasted for several years but later relaxed. "Without saying it in so many words," Kiernan wrote, "Anna Murdoch indicated to me that she and Rupert had reached an accommodation, one of those *ententes cordiales* carved out by sophisticated people who have been married to one another long enough for their familiarity to spill into boredom, if not dislike."[2]

Anna wrote her Old Chatham article in the middle of this period. Elisabeth was ten years old, Lachlan six, James five. Prudence, who loved London, had chosen to finish her education at an English boarding school. Anna and Prudence have always been polite to each other without being intimate. In her article Anna framed her musing around a succession of female figures from Greek myths, whom she posed as role models for motherhood. At one point Anna plays with the argument that the *uterini,* children of the one mother, sharing the same uterus, are closer than those who share the same father.

In Anna's exploration of her relationship to her children, Rupert is ostensibly absent. The only male, the only father figure in Anna's reverie, is the Greek king Agamemnon, who was murdered by his wife, Clytemnestra, because he had sacrificed their daughter to the goddess Artemis. Clytemnestra was later killed by her own son, Orestes. To consider Clytemnestra as a role model for motherhood, as Anna does, is to grapple with the problems of an unhappy marriage—a conflict in which children take sides. Anna notes that Orestes was "a little boy then. Like mine." Clytemnestra's children do not understand why she has become estranged from their father, why she acts to prevent him from harming the children: "Why, then, when [Orestes] grew up did he turn against his mother, the wronged wife, the sorrowing mother?"

It was not the last time Anna would express concern, albeit indirectly, over her husband's influence on the children. Anna emerges as an unhappy and discontented figure. She laments that she has thrown away her productive years for her children and has no time for serious work. She describes the rich scene before her in terms of emptiness. The raspberry canes are dry, stick-looking: "We have eaten all the goodness from them." The leaves are yellow, "the chlorophyll sucked out by the heat of the August days."

Anna's attention turns to the despair she felt about wanting to write. She quotes Tillie Olsen's book *Silences,* which claimed that no mothers—as almost no part-time, part-self persons—had created enduring literature. Anna muses: "Part-person. Parturition. By being whole, have I become less? Has all the creativity I once felt in my pen been confined to that creativity between my legs? A sick joke is woman."[3]

Anna rejects feminism ("I am afraid. I am afraid of modern-day Athenas. They are seducing us with their torches and their songs") and asserts that creativity and motherhood are not exclusive, but her affirmation carries no conviction: "God, I wish I could convince myself, lay waste this cold question which won't leave me alone. Have I given up my best work for them? Is that all there is?"

*   *   *

Philip Townsend, who worked as a butler in the Murdochs' London apartment in the late 1980s, has painted a chaotic picture of the Murdoch household. In an unpublished account of his Murdoch years that he cowrote, he recounts pouring orange juice into guests' coffee, Murdoch apologizing to guests for the menu, and an American chef who was an ex-marine flown to London to cook for an important meal, before flying on to cook on the Murdochs' yacht. The dog that the Townsends secretly kept in the apartment died while the Murdochs were in residence; in order to escape detection, Townsend hid the dog in the large kitchen freezer. Townsend particularly didn't like that Anna Murdoch asked him and his wife to wear uniforms.[4] Townsend's account is all the more colorful for the fact that shortly after *Punch* published extracts of the manuscript, Townsend went to prison for illegal business practices, having started a company selling vegetables.

The Murdochs had a dizzying lifestyle. As a very young child in England, Elisabeth recalled being overjoyed to receive a Shetland pony—only to discover that it was to be the prize for the winning reader in a promotion for the *Sun.* A friend of the children who stayed overnight with the Murdochs recalled that Anna woke them at five A.M. to dress the children to meet their father, who was returning home from a trip. Anna (as she recounted the story to *Time*) often had to reassure the young James that there was nothing wrong with his father's hearing—

he just wasn't listening.[5] James himself (as Anna told *GQ* in 1999) was frustrated that as the youngest he was always served last at the dinner table, and he continually sought to rearrange the table seating to change the serving order. A former executive recalled that James, apparently for similar reasons, hatched complex schemes to persuade his father to let him switch bedrooms. The picture is of a youngest child resentful of his low status.

Amid the peripatetic global lifestyle that Rupert Murdoch pursued for half a century, Anna Murdoch provided the center of gravity for the family. Her upbringing had given her a strong sense of the importance of form. It gave her an impression of aloofness or class consciousness—insisting that she and Rupert be treated with a gravity appropriate to their station. In this respect she was quite different from her husband. But given the degree of uncertainty that attached to much of their lives, an ability to impose structure on domestic life was, for her children, a saving grace.

Although their lives were organized almost entirely around their father's travel schedule and telephone calls, the Murdoch children have always been remarkably close to Rupert. "He is a very good and moral human being, and we are bringing up our children that way," Anna once told the *Washington Post*. "We know what we are about and time is on our side."[6]

In the mid-1980s, however, strains emerged in the Murdoch family. Elisabeth was expelled from her expensive Connecticut boarding school, reportedly for smuggling in a bottle of rum. Lachlan also had a drinking episode. Thomas Kiernan writes that Rupert blamed the children's problems on the intense negative publicity that he had been receiving. Anna, said Rupert, "had buried herself in this novel she's just finished to prove that at least one Murdoch can publish something worthwhile."[7] She pulled her children out of their New York schools and spent a year living in Aspen, where they attended the Aspen Day School.

* * *

Los Angeles, June 1991

In June 1991 the mood among the scores of News Corporation executives flying into Los Angeles for budget talks was one of relief mixed with apprehension. Their relief reflected News Corp's continued existence after the debt crisis. Their apprehension was about the big promises they would have to make as to what they could deliver in the next year.

Among the News Corp crowd was a stocky forty-year-old named Matt Handbury. Handbury had spent a decade in a string of News Corp posts around the world, culminating in his latest position in Sydney running Murdoch Magazines, a small unit that published homemaker and women's magazines. But even after years of hard work he had not been able to shake his nickname as the Man from Uncle. Matt Handbury was Rupert Murdoch's nephew, the son of his older sister, Helen.

"I think he has always been a bit suspicious of family members working in the company," Handbury said later, though over the years Murdoch has had many family members on the payroll.

"I'm a great believer in nepotism," Murdoch told Bruce Hundertmark in the late 1980s.[8]

Handbury was in Los Angeles to tell Murdoch that he wanted out of News Corp. As an exit, he wanted to make a bid for Murdoch Magazines in Australia. When he met his uncle, he said all this. Murdoch was regretful. He took his time. Eventually he said, "Fine." He paused again, and then he said, "You know you could—you could run this. You could head the company up one day if you stuck around."[9]

For a frozen moment the two looked at each other. In the previous four months Murdoch's face had collapsed. Surviving the debt crisis had taken a physical toll on him. Handbury was the eldest child of the eldest child. At that point, of the Murdoch clan he was the only senior News Corp executive, the only family member who could potentially develop a credible business record by the time Murdoch stepped down. Two years later when he described that moment, Handbury still would not be able to keep the regret from his voice. "He did say you could run this," he recalled.

The two men looked at each other, uncle and nephew, and for a moment both knew that this was the truth, that Handbury could indeed one day run the greatest show on earth. He could be the one. He could be king. But they also both knew that Murdoch did not really mean it. Handbury would always hit a family ceiling. The succession issue would be decided by stricter bloodlines. The reins of the fiery chariot would be passed to another pair of hands. Murdoch's successor was still in school.

"But if you want to do your own thing, I respect that," Murdoch continued. The moment passed. Neither ever said it. But the knowledge lay between them.

You owe me.

*   *   *

The issue of the Murdoch succession turns around the moment on January 21, 1948, when Sir Keith Murdoch signed his last will and testament. He was still in the hospital when he dictated the new will, after an operation to remove a secondary cancer in his bowel. As a historical document, the will doesn't shed much light on the family finances, because of the subsequent codicils and settlement agreements Sir Keith added. It is, however, a guide to the shape of the succession that he had in mind. The trustees would be his wife, Dame Elisabeth; Harry Giddy, head of the National Bank, who would succeed Sir Keith as chairman of the Herald and Weekly Times; and his son Rupert.

Under the provisions of the will, the inheritance of his three daughters was to remain locked up in trust into the next generation, providing income for them and for their children. But while that was Sir Keith's broad intention, once a daughter turned twenty-one, the trustees could at any point decide to pay out her share of the estate. The trustees also had a wide brief about where the funds in the estate should go. Sir Keith had already given his eldest daughter Helen £10,000 to buy a house when she married Geoff Handbury. In practice this meant that for many years Helen was the only daughter who ended up with any money from her father. But many years later it would mean that her sisters' final payout was hundreds of millions of dollars higher.

The broad principle was that a major part of the estate's income would go to Dame Elisabeth and the children would receive something like equal shares, but Rupert would have more voting shares to enable him to have "the great opportunity of spending a useful altruistic and full life in broadcasting activities." In the two years that followed, Sir Keith reorganized his corporate holdings around a new family company called Wyamba, which was later renamed Cruden Investments. Cruden's A shares had ten votes each, while its B shares had only one.

In late 1950 the three Murdoch daughters were summoned to Harry Giddy's office at the National Bank. Sir Keith had drawn £50,000 in cash from his account, and in Giddy's office he duly presented gifts of £10,000 each to Helen and Ann, £10,000 for Rupert in Oxford, and £20,000 to Janet. This allocation was to make up for Helen's earlier wedding gift. The children then gravely passed the money back to their father, who issued them shares in Cruden in exchange, and the money went back to the bank to pay down some of Cruden's huge debts. Several settlements like this took place; passing assets over early allowed Sir Keith to reduce some of the death duties his estate would face.

When Sir Keith died in October 1952, his eldest child, Helen, was twenty-three. Rupert was twenty-one; Anne was seventeen and about to take her final school exams; Janet was just thirteen. Cruden Farm went to Dame Elisabeth. The rest of the estate consisted chiefly of the house in Melbourne, the art collection, the two cattle properties, and shares in Cruden Investments; almost everything was sold to repay bank debt and to meet death duties. Rupert was left with 28 percent of Cruden's shares, to be held in a separate trust. They were all A shares, which gave him 36 percent of Cruden's voting rights. Eventually this trust was held in the company named after Rupert's initials, Kayarem. Various settlement trusts that Sir Keith had made before he died accounted for another 35 percent of Cruden's capital and 34 percent of its voting rights; it appears that Dame Elisabeth was entitled to receive the bulk of the income from the settlement trusts. Finally the rest of Sir Keith's estate was held for Helen, Ann, and Janet, who also held a small number of shares in their own right.

Rupert did not initially control the News Limited board; nor did he control the Cruden Investments board, nor the trusts that controlled Cruden. Control lay with his mother. The board of Cruden after Sir Keith's death comprised Rupert, Dame Elisabeth, Harry Giddy, and the general manager, William Jones. With Giddy counseling caution and Rupert ever ready to sound the charge, Dame Elisabeth's vote was decisive. Helen said later, "In those early days after Dad died we would have family conferences around the schoolroom table. There wouldn't be any disagreements with Mum sitting there with her beady eyes. . . . We really were the staunchest of families."[10]

Giddy resigned from Cruden in the late 1950s. To raise capital for News Limited's headlong expansion, Murdoch had a stock issue in 1966, which diluted Cruden's holding. In 1970 Cruden distributed a small portion of its News Limited shares to family members as a dividend. The total inheritance was now worth A$18 million. Eighteen years after Sir Keith's death, this was the first substantial payout that Rupert's sisters had received. It also paved the way for Rupert's first takeover move on Cruden.

In the early 1960s, before Australia switched to a decimal currency, Cruden had borrowed A£1.2 million to buy more News Limited shares, but by the early 1970s its stake in News had fallen to less than 35 percent. To cement their control of News, the Murdochs needed to buy more shares. Rupert was the only family member who could raise the money needed. In the 1988 fiscal year Cruden borrowed A$6 million from Commonwealth Bank and used the money to buy News shares to build its holding up to 43.4 percent. This coincided with an issue of partly paid shares to Rupert's personal company Kayarem, with a total cost of A$5 million. Each year Kayarem would pay off small installments on the shares.[11]

The new shares lifted Murdoch's Cruden stake to 41 percent. This was a pretty good deal for him: for A$5 million he had assured himself of future control of Cruden—and he had the best part of a decade to pay up. He was also entitled to some of the shares held in the settlement trusts that his father had set up. It's not clear whether Rupert had always been entitled to these shares or had bought out some of his sisters' entitlements. But added together with the new partly paid shares that Cruden had just issued, Murdoch now held 54 percent of Cruden's capital and its voting stock. Still, that didn't mean he actually controlled Cruden. In practice that was still his mother's preserve. This was a matter of some importance, because Cruden was about to start earning a lot of money.

Throughout the 1970s the $7 million in dividends that Cruden received was largely swallowed up by the company's financing needs and its share buying. Even after News Limited was reorganized into News Corporation in 1979, the dividend stream continued to be meager. But as Cruden, in line with its shareholding, picked up 44 percent of the total dividends paid, the payout did not have to be high to make a major difference to Cruden. By 1980 Cruden was earning A$3 million a year in News Corp dividends. In 1985 that went up to A$5.2 million, then A$8.1 million in 1987. From 1980 to 1990 the dividend payments to Cruden totaled A$61.5 million. One of the mysteries of the Murdoch dynasty is where that money went.

Most people who come into major money engage accountants, they get a company structure, they start to make investments. They buy new houses or country properties. Murdoch's three sisters showed little sign of this activity. They lived comfortably but not ostentatiously. There was little in their lifestyles to suggest that they owned what amounted to a fifth of one of the world's largest media companies, which had reported profits during the 1980s of more than $3 billion.

Dame Elisabeth has a clear view that wealth does not necessarily make for happier lives. She has always been closely involved with the Royal Children's Hospital in Melbourne, just one of the many causes she supports. "The Murdoch family started by giving us A$5 million to found the institute," said David Denks, who heads the Murdoch Research Institute. "Then the rest of the family joined in a further donation, in which a considerably greater amount was given to the institute." "She has always been a great supporter of charities," one of her nephews said. "That's where the money went." "It drives Rupert crazy," said a friend of the family.

For whatever reason, for much of the 1980s, little money appears to have flowed from Cruden to the sisters. What money there was went to paying taxes, to buying more News Corp shares, to philanthropy, or it remained in Cruden. In January 1987, however, the picture changed. In 1987 Cruden's share capital was just 2.9 million two-dollar shares. As part of the Queensland Press takeover,

Cruden made a bonus issue of 1 billion new two-dollar shares. The shareholdings remained the same, but now the extended family was in no doubt that although they might not be getting any substantial income from it, they were sitting on a A$2 billion fortune. The family had lived with this regime all their lives. But all of Dame Elisabeth's children now had children of their own, many of whom were adults, and they did not always see things in the same happy light. Rupert himself had grown restless with his sisters' shareholdings. "I can't go on making money for all of you forever," he told his mother. "I have to think of my children." The unstable situation that the Cruden share restructure had created would last just three years. While Sir Keith's will had envisaged the family holdings in media being carried into the next generation, it was clear that henceforth the dynasty would continue on more restrictive lines.

*   *   *

In the early 1980s Murdoch gained control of the trusts set up by his father for him in Kayarem. He set up a new structure called the A. E. Harris Trust (a name chosen to be obscure), which would hold almost all of his fortune. The trustees of the A. E. Harris Trust would be accountants and lawyers. Murdoch's control lay in his power to appoint or sack the trustees. This meant that when it suited him, he could say he controlled the trust (as, for example, when he spoke to the FCC in Washington), while at other times he could say he was not the owner of the assets in the trust, as when dealing with government regulators. It was also a structure that would prove rather handy in a divorce.

In the summer of 1990 Murdoch's lawyers came up with a plan to buy his sisters and their children out of Cruden Investments. The price was worked out on the basis that the News Corp stock that Cruden owned was worth A$20 a share, which would value the sisters' holding around A$1 billion. Unfortunately, the buyout plan was overtaken by the debt crisis at the end of the year. The debt crisis was as much a surprise to Murdoch's family as it was to him. After subordinating their interests in News for thirty-eight years, suddenly it seemed as if it could all be taken from them.

On January 15, 1991, the News Corp share price touched A$3.19. At this price, Cruden's subsidiary Queensland Press was barely solvent. It appears that Cruden had guaranteed the bank debt in Queensland Press, which was controlled through another subsidiary, Cruden (ACT). On January 23 Dame Elisabeth and all three of her daughters were appointed directors of Cruden (ACT). It gave them control of the board, as the family became aware of how perilous their situation was. "You'd be wrong to say there was concern about people being left with nothing," said one family member.[12] "There was always absolute confidence in Rupert." The move on to the Cruden (ACT) board was not because the sisters said "we'd better get control of this," the family member said: "It just didn't happen like that."

What was going on? In the middle of these dark days the Murdochs held a family council. It was then that Rupert Murdoch put up a business proposition. Struggling desperately with the biggest crisis of his life, the Great Acquirer still found time to set up another deal. According to sources close to the family, Murdoch proposed buying options on his sisters' shares in Cruden. The sources say that the deal Murdoch proposed valued the News Corp shares between A$7 and A$12, considerably higher than the share price at the time, and it would ensure that the family emerged with something if the company collapsed. But it was far below the family's original expectations.

While News Corp was an empire built entirely on Rupert Murdoch's efforts with no input from his sisters, he has always run it on the basis that the shareholders, the people who own its capital, and not its gifted employees, are entitled to its rewards. In 1992 Barry Diller would leave News Corp for that very reason. Almost half the capital that Rupert Murdoch had used to create the empire was his sisters'. There are several versions of the discussion that followed after Rupert made his buyout offer. Some family friends suggest that parts of the family were unhappy about the price. Others disagree. "No one was banging on the table," asserted one family member soon afterward. "The sisters have always been slavishly supportive of Rupert."[13]

At least some family members accepted the offer. The 1990 Cruden annual report had shown that Helen Handbury's children held a small number of Cruden shares in their own right. By June 30, 1991, they were no longer the beneficial owners of the shares. When Matt Handbury flew to Los Angeles to tell his uncle he wanted to get out of News Corp with Murdoch Magazines, he was really telling him how he wanted to spend the buyout payment. "There's been a bit of money that's going around," Handbury said at the time.[14]

In the summer of 1992 Rupert and Anna and his three sisters and their husbands went on a luxury ocean cruise to Alaska. During the trip the family finally worked out a deal that would leave Rupert's family as the sole owners of Cruden. In addition to the sisters' payouts, Murdochs' nephews and nieces would end up with A$20 million apiece. Murdoch said privately, "Some will piss it against the wall and some will turn it into $200 million."[15] The total buyout price was about A$650 million, but it included an escalation clause linked to the News Corp share price. Finally the empire was all Rupert's—at least in name. Once he had convinced his family to sign on the dotted line, however, he was left with the same problem his father had faced more than forty years before. He had secured his children's inheritance; now how was he going to pay for it?

PART III

AMERICAN JIHAD

8

LOST IN SPACE

Denver, August 10, 1995

IN THE SUMMER OF 1995 Rupert Murdoch flew in to Denver Airport to talk to John Malone. The two men had been having these summits for years. Behind closed doors they would discuss the state of the world, sketch out new alliances, and wheel and deal. Their encounters evoked a heady atmosphere of suspended disbelief, of infinite possibility. Malone and Murdoch facing each other across a table are two of the most powerful reality-shapers alive. "I think he's the most brilliant financial mind I know, as a financial engineer," Murdoch said of Malone in 2001. "I find him a pleasure to deal with. He's a very shrewd investor . . . he's a good individual and a good citizen and a good person to have as a friend."[1]

If there is a single relationship that defines Rupert Murdoch, it is his rivalry and friendship with John Malone. The two men almost like each other. If only they could afford to. Their relationship is based as much on deep distrust as it is on mutual respect. In 1972 Malone and his wife Leslie moved west from Connecticut to Denver to run a fledgling cable network called Tele-Communications Inc. (TCI) for a cable entrepreneur named Bob Magness. TCI had such chronic debt problems that for years Magness and Malone made sure their offices always had a back door, so they could evade overzealous creditors. Leslie Malone, like Anna Murdoch, struggled with the demands created by her husband's heavy workload. Both men remain close to the technical side of their industries, Murdoch with his detailed knowledge of newspaper production, Malone with his degree in engineering and doctorate in operations research from Johns Hopkins. For years Murdoch and Malone have performed a delicate and accelerating dance around each other, composed in equal parts of rivalry and cooperation. Vertical integration was really just "all about trying to catch Rupert," Malone maintained stoutly in 1996. "John's just saying that to take the attention away from himself," Murdoch responded. "I should think we are all responding to John Malone. Dancing to his tunes. I still do sometimes."[2]

Malone, like Murdoch, knows the disappointments in store for anyone who bets his or her future on technology. It was Malone in 1992 who promised that he was on the verge of offering five hundred channels to his cable subscribers. Four years later five hundred channels seemed as far away as ever. Malone's hardware supplier, General Instruments, and its subsidiary Jerrard Electronics were struggling to overcome huge technical hurdles to produce a digital set-top box that could handle the new digital universe. The relationship with Jerrard, where Malone once worked, had grown strained. In late 1997 Malone was filling in a hole in the program at a convention of cable company execs when he gave an impromptu version of the old story about a woman who goes to a psychiatrist to complain that despite surviving three husbands, she had never consummated a marriage. The first husband had been a traveling salesman, Malone said, and he never got home and was killed by a bus. The second was a college professor who used to write about it and talk about it but never got around to it and died of a heart attack. And the third? "That's easy," the woman says, in Malone's telling. "He's a Jerrard salesman—and he keeps telling me how good it's going to be when I get it."

In 1995 Murdoch was once again a shining orb in the firmament of the rich and powerful. In the four years since his debt crisis, he had recreated himself as a corporate entity and an American persona. *Time* magazine now rated him as the fourth most powerful person in the United States, just behind the president, the head of the Federal Reserve Bank, and Bill Gates at Microsoft. *Vanity Fair* had Gates and Murdoch taking turns each year for the top spot in what it called the New Establishment in America, heads of the new power elite and the most powerful private citizens in the world.

Murdoch had taken just twenty-eight months to throw off the spending shackles imposed upon him by the banks in the 1991 debt override agreement. He had paid them out with new long-term debt and a little judicious capital raising. Fox was now established as the fourth U.S. television network, and Murdoch had the *New York Post* back again. In Britain his satellite broadcaster BSkyB was a runaway success, and Murdoch was working on clones of BSkyB around the world. One of them, Star TV in Hong Kong, had a satellite footprint that stretched from the eastern Mediterranean across India and all of Asia. Murdoch ran cable networks in Australia and New Zealand and had satellite plans for Latin America and Japan. Only North America eluded him. Which brought him to his friend in Denver.

For months Murdoch and Malone had been hitting the most expensive piece of God's little heaven back and forth like a tennis ball. Theirs was an exhibition match in space that almost no one else in the media industry even knew was going on. And if they did, who cared? At the close of the twentieth century, space was suffering from a bad press. Blame Hollywood. Filmmakers hate space the same way they love New York. In celluloid realities New York is the place where you must go; space is the place you must leave. Science fiction movies have done to our nursery-rhyme picture of twinkling stars what Steven Spielberg and *Jaws* did in the 1970s to the idea of nipping down to the beach for a moonlight dip and a quick bite. Space is not for the fainthearted. Hollywood has made the image too vivid: astronauts adrift in the cosmos, the ship's sensors gazing blindly, spinning down in a decaying orbit. From the Robinson family's travails to Sigourney Weaver's too-close encounters with aliens, space narratives have always been escape stories. *Apollo 13* presents the prospect most hideously—the spacecraft out of air, oxygen, and power, racing against the clock, making emergency repairs with chewing gum and sticky tape; will Tom Hanks get back in time to watch the kids' school concert? One of the great revelations in *Apollo 13,* at least for bankers and senior media executives, is that the sound of air escaping from a spacecraft has an uncanny similarity to the sound of enormous wads of high-denomination bills spontaneously combusting. You hear that noise in the space business, and you *know* it's going to be expensive.

John Malone had never been much of a space man. He was the guy with his feet on the ground, the big man with the crooked grin who always looked like he was on the verge of doing something downright tricky. Malone was the man who decided what went into the television sets of one in every four U.S. cable households—and what didn't. In three decades he had shown a remarkable ability to stay several steps ahead of everybody else in the media business. His unfailing acumen was one of the certainties of life. In any investment market, from moon dust futures to vacuum-packed coffee beans, you could bet your life that at the end of the day Malone was not the guy who would end up outside the airlock door.

And yet he had this communication problem. The two communication satellites he was worried about were not lost—they were not even in space. They were in a shed, or at least in whatever General Electric uses to store satellites that have no place to go. They were half a billion dollars of hardware resting between engagements, as they say in the entertainment business. The person whom Malone needed to get them out of there was his old sparring partner Rupert Murdoch.

Malone is not big on office furniture. TCI's office decor, at that time, was

Middle American Corporate Spartan. The conference room was glass walled, and the table in the center of the room was black, matching the chairs. In each corner of the room stood a rubber plant. Rubber plants must have been created for media companies. These sturdy little growths flourish no matter how much abuse they receive and even manage to project a little artificial reality of their own. Interior designers love them for their bright, shiny appearance and the positive energy that their leaves give off. That and the fact that office cleaners can apply shiny green polish directly onto the leaves. When the plants have been left unwatered for two weeks with the lights turned off, polish is just the thing to put a little virtual pep back into some wilting positive energy.

It's an enduring image: Murdoch, Malone, and the rubber plants. We know about the foliage because sitting at the end of the table was a journalist, Ken Auletta of *The New Yorker*.[3] Thanks to Auletta, we know who was at the meeting, who did the talking, what they said, how the deals would work, and what the paperwork was about. Auletta's account provides wall-to-wall coverage and sound bites. But it tells you nothing about what really happened. Auletta was there watching it all, and he didn't have a clue what was actually going on—because when the reality wizards are conjuring, things are never quite what they appear. Unseen in that meeting, John Malone performed one of the all-time great escape routines. He was facing a double threat, from Rupert Murdoch on the one side and from Michael Eisner at Disney on the other. He saved himself by setting Murdoch and Eisner at war with each other. To understand what Malone did, you have to know the storylines that led to the meeting.

*   *   *

Earlier in 1995 Rupert Murdoch had had an unpleasant encounter with the Federal Communications Commission. The FCC wanted to know why, in almost a decade, News Corp had never mentioned the fact that its Fox network was owned by a foreign company. A year before, prompted by consistent complaints from the NAACP, the FCC had begun making low-level inquiries into 20th Holdings, the company that held the Fox television licenses and network. After the FCC's third request for information, News Corp produced financial details that showed that, while each year since 1986 it had been assuring the FCC that 20th Holdings was owned and controlled by American interests, this was not strictly accurate. The reality was closer to what News Corp had been telling the SEC regularly over the same period. News Corp, a foreign company in the eyes of U.S. law, owned 99.9 percent of 20th Holdings as nonvoting stock. In 1986 Rupert

Murdoch and Barry Diller had paid just $750,000 to buy 75 percent of the voting stock, so that News Corp could claim that Americans controlled the company. But News Corp could reclaim the voting stock anytime it chose. The Fox accountants told the SEC that News Corp clearly controlled 20th Holdings. But decisions by the U.S. Supreme Court in 1986 and 1987 had indicated that this sort of corporate structure did not meet the foreign ownership test for owning U.S. television licenses.[4]

In early April 1995 Murdoch was facing a major problem. In December 1994 the FCC had launched a full-blown investigation of Fox's ownership. The issue was whether Murdoch and News Corp had shown a lack of candor with the FCC about the foreign ownership level when it bought the Metromedia television stations in 1986. The biggest risk to Murdoch from the inquiry was that the FCC could recommend a formal hearing into whether Fox's licenses should be revoked, a fight that could tie up Murdoch and any U.S. plans in regulatory knots for years. Despite intense lobbying efforts by Murdoch to convince Congress and the FCC to drop the inquiry, the outlook for Fox looked grim. But in late April 1995 Murdoch produced a stunning turnaround.

On April 19, 1995, the FCC's Mass Media Bureau staff reported on the Fox inquiry to the FCC commissioners. FCC leaks revealed that the report found that Murdoch and News Corp were indeed in violation of the foreign ownership laws with Fox but had not deliberately concealed the foreign shareholding from the FCC. Rather, the report concluded obscurely, News Corp had not been as forthcoming as it might have been. News Corp hadn't told, and the FCC hadn't asked. A copy of the FCC staff's confidential memo that was leaked to the *New York Times* included a draft order imposing a $500,000 fine on News Corp and orders to cut its equity in its television stations to 20 percent. The real sting was that such a selloff might force News Corp to pay hundreds of millions of dollars in capital gains taxes. The staff report said of the present Fox holding: "We can think of few circumstances that could be more intuitively contrary to the Congressional interest in safeguarding national security." Making an exception to the foreign ownership rules for Murdoch was "inconsistent with the public interest in this case."[5]

For all that, the FCC's finding was regarded as a coup for Murdoch; the alternative he had been facing was so much worse. "Murdoch has evaded the death penalty—now all he's doing is plea bargaining the size of the fine," said Andrew Schwartzman, head of Media Access Project, a Washington-based public interest law firm.[6]

"This is pure speculation about [an FCC] staff recommendation, but if it were true, it's outrageous," a Fox official responded. "We would be surprised if the commission would follow such a recommendation, but if they did, we would fight it at every level."[7]

The next two weeks were filled with stories (which FCC chairman Reed Hundt denied) of heavy infighting among the FCC commissioners over the final report. Three of the five commissioners—James Quello, who oversaw the original Fox deal, and Republicans Andrew Barrett and Rachelle Chong—opposed any sort of sanctions for Murdoch. Only chairman Hundt and Democrat Susan Ness were holding out for some sort of punitive measure. On Monday, April 24, two key Republicans weighed in. Congressman Mike Oxley (Ohio) described the FCC inquiry as bogus. "I don't know what their beef is, frankly," he said. Jack Fields (chairman of the House Telecommunications Subcommittee) repeated an earlier promise that his staff would review the outcome of the Fox probe and threatened a "top to bottom" review of the FCC.

The FCC commissioners were due to make a finding that week on another Fox deal, to buy a Green Bay television station, WLUK-TV. Fox was again using a foreign funding structure, so the FCC ruling on Green Bay would show which way the FCC would jump on the whole Fox question. April 26 was a wild, confused day at the FCC's Washington offices. Early that afternoon FCC staff told reporters that a decision on Green Bay would be announced later that day. Then they said it was held up. Hundt had agreed to support the majority decision of Quello, Barrett, and Chong supporting Fox, but Ness was holding out. "The situation is very fluid," said one staff member. It was "a give and take decision . . . among various FCC offices to reach a unanimous 5–0 decision" on both Green Bay and Fox.

That was Wednesday. The Green Bay deal was approved Thursday, though Commissioner Ness complained the deal clearly violated the spirit of the ownership restrictions. There was still some groundwork to be done on the larger Fox finding, but a week later the five commissioners had come into line. On Thursday, May 4, Reed Hundt announced a unanimous decision by the commission. Fox was in technical breach of the law but had not misled the FCC. Fox was invited to apply for a public interest waiver on the foreign ownership ceiling. The threat to Fox was all over. News Corp would not even receive a fine. Murdoch had arrived at the hearing room forty minutes early to hear the result, flanked by his wife Anna, his daughter Elisabeth, and Elisabeth's husband, Elkin Pianim. He was tearful afterward as he read a prepared speech. "The bottom line is we're very happy about most of it," he said. "We are gratified by a fair and full review. The merit-less, wild and malicious charges of some of our competitors seem to have been rejected along with their requests for punitive sanctions."[8]

What was Murdoch thinking, in those desperate days in April when it looked as if he could lose his television network? No one knew that, even when things looked blackest, Murdoch had been working on an escape plan. If he had to sell his Fox television network, he was ready to set up a satellite broadcaster. He could transform his empire by pulling a little ruse on his friend John Malone. Murdoch's Plan B went unnoticed because with all the hoopla over the Fox result, little attention was given to the other big FCC decision that week: the sad lament of Daniel H. Garner.

*   *   *

Garner was a radio station operator and former rock concert promoter in White Rock, Arkansas, in 1982 when he heard about a new satellite technology called Direct Broadcast Satellite, or DBS. To be more accurate, what Garner heard was that the FCC was giving away orbital slots in space that could be used to operate high-power DBS satellites. Nature had not given Garner a dashing figure. Reporters called him pudgy. He was a chain smoker. He had no experience in satellite television, and no money worth speaking of that he could use to start a satellite service. But he was incredibly tenacious. With a bit of support from Arkansas governor Bill Clinton, together with Congressman Wilbur Mills, the ex-chairman of the House Ways and Means Committtee, and a former adminstrator with NASA, James M. Beggs, Garner founded a new company called Advanced Communications. In 1984 Advanced Communications emerged from the scrum of applicants at the FCC with a scrap of paper that gave Garner rights over a piece of real estate in space.

If you take a map of North America and draw a line starting a hundred miles east of Phoenix, Arizona, and running north to the eastern edge of Yellowstone National Park and on into Canada, passing east of Medicine Hat, you will have a rough marker for the line that geographers calls 110 degrees west longitude (110WL). For the most part it is rugged country, marked with the tight elevation contour lines that mapmakers use to denote extremely mountainous terrain. There are not a lot of cable customers on 110WL. Rupert Murdoch would later make it one of the most expensive lines in the atlas.

High-power satellites using the so-called Ku-band broadcast frequencies pump out so much power that to prevent interference with one another, international convention requires that they be kept at least nine degrees of longitude apart. At ground level in North America this is about 350 miles. In space it works out to a minimum of two thousand miles of separation. This means that there are a limited number of satellite slots that can cover all of the continental United States, known as CONUS slots. Too far east or west, and the curvature of the Earth blocks off part of the country from the line of sight that the satellite needs for its broadcasts. If you spend half a billion dollars putting up a satellite, it is a bit dismaying to find that half your audience can't receive its transmissions. If you want a chance at getting a return on your investment, you need to reach as many people as you can. After the various orbital slots and frequencies were parceled out with Canada and Mexico in the 1980s, CONUS slots were reduced to just three: 110WL, 101WL (350 miles to the east), and 119WL (350 miles to the west). Each slot carries the right to broadcast more than thirty-two transponder frequencies. So there are ninety-six frequencies in total. If you want to run a big U.S. satellite television operation, these are the slots you have to have.

Daniel Garner picked up the orbital slot at 110WL and all but one of the thirty-two transponder frequencies that went with it. Of the three CONUS slots, Garner's was the plum, because if you pointed your satellite dish at either of the two CONUS slots next to it, you could pick up 110WL as well without having to adjust your dish. This made Garner a natural partner of whoever owned the other two slots. He would be the guy they wanted to buy out when they expanded. Garner didn't have a satellite to put up in his slot—in fact he would never have a satellite. But there is nothing like a free satellite license to give any self-respecting entrepreneur that warm all-over feeling.

Garner spent the next decade trying to interest someone in buying his slot. DBS was still a pipe dream. The *Arkansas Gazette* agonized politely on the etiquette of describing Garner's supporters as "participating dreamers" or just flakes. It was hard to take the venture seriously. Charlie Ergen at EchoStar was interested and in 1992 paid Garner a $1 million deposit to buy the slot, but the two men could never come to terms. Garner offered the slot to Bert Roberts at MCI in December 1993, but Roberts didn't even reply. It was, an MCI executive said later, "one of the most bone-headed decisions we ever made."[9]

Several events changed Garner's prospects. In 1993 antitrust action by the U.S. Justice Department forced cable companies to make their programming available to noncable competitors, including satellite services. The same year Murdoch's BSkyB operation in Britain began to make serious profits. For a time at the end of 1996, BSkyB's stock would be worth more than all of News Corp, its 40 percent shareholder. Meanwhile in 1994 the launch of America's first DBS service,

DirecTV, by General Motors' Hughes Electronics became the most successful electronic sales phenomenon in U.S. history. In the first year alone 1 million subscribers rushed out to buy DirecTV's pizza-sized dishes. Given time, DBS would become the most potent threat that America's cable companies had faced.

These developments had not gone unnoticed by the cable television industry. In 1990 the five biggest U.S. cable companies—TCI, Time Warner, Comcast Corporation, Cox Communications, and US West/MediaOne—launched their own medium-power satellite service as a partnership called Primestar. TCI and Time Warner had the largest stakes, each holding 21 percent of the partnership. The cable companies were acting to counter a satellite venture called Sky Cable that Hughes Electronics was trying to get off the ground in a venture with NBC, Rupert Murdoch, and a cable company, Cablevision. As one cable executive noted at the time, the cable companies "would like DBS never to happen." But if DBS was inevitable, the cable companies wanted a part of the action. Primestar was pushed principally as an alternative for isolated customers beyond the reach of the cable networks and in the first year attracted just twelve thousand subscribers. Another cable employee noted that one of the goals of launching Primestar was to "[d]o our best to keep core services (basic cable programming) off Hughes DBS to minimize long-term competitive bypass threat." The other idea was to keep a short rope on John Malone, to make sure he didn't go anywhere.[10]

Primestar owned eleven of the thirty-two transponder channels on the DBS slot at 119WL. It wasn't enough channels to mount a major satellite service. Then in September 1994 Malone did a deal with Daniel Garner to buy his 110WL slot for $45 million in stock. Malone promptly ordered two high-power satellites for Garner's slot for $600 million (which his partners in Primestar would pay for). Malone now controlled thirty-nine of the ninety-six CONUS transponders. He was poised to become the biggest satellite broadcaster in America—or maybe just to make sure that no one else became the biggest satellite broadcaster in America. And it had hardly cost him a cent. It was all working like a dream—up until the moment when the FCC stepped in.

On April 26, 1995, Scott Blake Harris, the head of the FCC's new International Bureau, broke with previous FCC practice and announced that no extension would be granted for Garner's license. As Garner's company had failed to put a satellite into its slot in the time required, the FCC was reclaiming the 110WL license. Malone's and Garner's satellite slot was gone. Their little piece of space had been lost. And Malone's whole master strategy for meeting the satellite threat to cable was lying in pieces on the ground.

The curious part of Harris's decision was the timing. He announced it just as the FCC debate over Fox and Green Bay reached its climax. It was the day that Harris's boss, Reed Hundt, realized that whichever way he voted, there was at least a 3–2 majority among the FCC commissioners to exonerate Murdoch. That was the "very fluid" afternoon, as FCC staff talked of "give and take" among the various FCC offices, that Hundt switched his vote. The day Hundt gave up the fight on Murdoch, his agency reasserted its authority by giving John Malone a black eye (though Harris said he did not consult Hundt).[11] Markets run on appearances, and to outsiders it looked like the FCC was stiffing Malone because of the concessions it had had to make to Murdoch. But there was another twist to this tale.

Back in 1993, Bert Roberts, the head of long-distance telephone company MCI, had received a call from Michael Milken, the former head of bond trading at Drexel Burnham Lambert. Milken was now out of jail and teaching at UCLA's business school as part of his rehabilitation. Milken asked Roberts to come speak to his class. When Roberts arrived, he found that Milken had invited another speaker as well, Rupert Murdoch.[12] With Milken as matchmaker, the two men formed a friendship, which by early 1995 was ready to turn into something much closer. On May 10, six days after the FCC cleared Fox on the foreign ownership inquiry, Roberts and Murdoch unveiled their new strategic alliance. MCI was to invest $2 billion in News Corp and set up a string of new joint ventures together.

Malone was at a cable convention in Dallas on May 10 when news of Murdoch's MCI alliance was announced, to sudden silence across the convention hall. Cable executives were stunned. The TCI execs pulled into a tight huddle at a table in the middle of the convention room to confer. Initially Malone would not speak with reporters who were present. When he did, he looked visibly shaken.[13] "I'm not worried about Bert Roberts, but Rupert scares the hell out of me," Malone said. "He's my partner, incidentally."

What shook Malone was not just that Rupert Murdoch had found a way to shake down Bert Roberts for a couple of billion dollars. Malone realized immediately that this was an ambush. The MCI deal hadn't just come together in the last week. Murdoch had been planning this all through April. At the very time when the FCC had seemed about to end all of his U.S. ambitions, Murdoch had been working on his next campaign.

Rather, what shook Malone about the Murdoch-Roberts alliance was that it was Roberts who had convinced the FCC days earlier to block Malone's satellite license. MCI had powerful friends in the Clinton administration, and through March and April Roberts tapped them all. MCI argued that the cable companies in Primestar wanted the satellite slot only to prevent it from being used by other DBS operators to mount a threat to cable's monopoly: "The channels at 110WL represent the only remaining block of frequencies that can be used to provide viable DBS service. If the FCC allows these to be transferred to [Primestar], it would be like hiring the wolf to guard the sheep. . . . Cable television will have fought off its latest challenger, and consumers will be forced to pay higher prices with fewer service options." Roberts made it clear that he wanted the 110WL slot for himself, and he was ready to pay for it. But all that time he had been finalizing a linkup with News Corp, the biggest satellite operator in the world. Whatever Roberts said, the satellite slot was always going to end up with Rupert Murdoch.

That day in Dallas when MCI's deal with News Corp was announced, you didn't have to be Oliver Stone to be a conspiracy theorist; to suspect, in the ruins of the cable companies' plans for a satellite license, that there had been a second shooter on the grassy knoll. The way the cable guys read it, while Bert Roberts had been firing the guns against Garner and Primestar, Rupert Murdoch had been the one loading the bullets. It was a stunning reversal. Reed Hundt had been taken in as much as anyone. Murdoch had won every battle with the FCC that month.

And John Malone? He was stuck. He had lost his satellite license. He had $600 million worth of satellites on the way and nowhere to put them. He had to find some way to deflect Murdoch. And now Michael Eisner was going off the reservation.

*   *   *

On July 31, 1995, Disney's CEO announced a $19 billion deal to buy Capital Cities/ABC. Surprisingly, Eisner said that the biggest attraction in the deal was getting hold of ESPN, the world's major pay-television sports channel, valued in the deal at $5 billion. Eisner later told Disney stockholders that ESPN was "practically worth the cost of the acquisition itself. OK, OK, I'm stretching the meaning of the word 'practically.' [But] ESPN . . . is a brand that we can expand and enhance. . . . Indeed, it may turn out that ESPN will be worth the cost of the [Capital Cities/ABC] acquisition itself."[15]

Eisner kept saying ESPN would be worth at least $19 billion, after he launched half a dozen spin-off ESPN cable channels. It did not take cable operators long to figure out that if ESPN ended up worth $19 billion, it would be because of the extra money that Eisner planned to extract from them for carrying the new channels. John Malone was the biggest cable operator, so the biggest chunk of the big new profits that Eisner was forecasting would come from him. That wasn't

Malone's only problem. ESPN was already the national carrier for most of the big U.S. sporting leagues. For its new channels, Disney would need to broadcast more local matches, more college games, more hometown teams. This would mean invading the turf of the regional sports networks that currently covered these games for cable. And the biggest owner of regional sports networks in the United States was John Malone, through his Prime Ticket nets. So Disney's takeover of ESPN was doubly bad news for Malone. Malone needed someone to run defense on Disney, to keep Michael Eisner's ambitions in check. That was where his friend Rupert came in. Ten days after Eisner announced the ABC deal, Malone and Murdoch sat down across a table in Denver. This curious meeting in the middle of the 1990s would prove one of the most significant media encounters of the decade.

*   *   *

Malone and Murdoch's August 10 meeting covered the world, setting the future media agenda for whole continents. It lasted four hours. Ken Auletta sat throughout in growing discomfort, as he later wrote, battling with his desperate need to go to the bathroom. He wouldn't go outside to relieve himself, because he was afraid that if he did he would not be allowed back in the room. It goes without saying that no one else left the room. Bladder control is one of the lesser-known upper-management skills. The common thread that Malone drew, as he and Murdoch carved up the world between themselves among the rubber plants, was the need of each man to reduce the potential for conflict with the other. Malone made the point again and again. Less overtly, in deal after deal Malone was drawing Murdoch closer to himself, aligning News Corp's interests with his own. The closer the two partners were, the more costly it would be for Murdoch to cross Malone. This defensive strategy was driven by the subject that neither man was ready to address directly that afternoon: the vanishing satellite license. The issue hung invisibly in the air between them. Murdoch had pulled the first $1 billion out of Bert Roberts at MCI just eight days before. Malone thought he had just negotiated a deal with the FCC to win the satellite license back for Primestar. How hard was MCI—for which Malone could read Rupert—going to push to derail this new deal?

Murdoch began by asking Malone indirectly if Ted Turner was interested in selling CNN. Malone told Murdoch he had no chance. Malone didn't want to talk about CNN; he was there to nail a deal on sports. He wanted Murdoch to put his f/X cable channel into a joint venture based around Malone's Prime Ticket regional sports networks. It could be promoted to advertisers as a real national cable network, boosted by affiliates around the country to an audience of 35 million cable subscribers. With any luck Charles Dolan at the Cablevision cable group, who owned the other major group of regional sports networks, would join the venture. Putting all the little nets together as a national sports network would provide the first real challenge to ESPN. It could actually make money.

It would also put Murdoch on a collision course with Michael Eisner's growth plans for ESPN. Murdoch and Eisner could fight it out, which for Malone was the object of the exercise—though he wasn't going to spell this out to his partner. It was a typically ingenious defense and containment strategy on Malone's part. Murdoch's comment a year later had a real edge: "I should think we are all responding to John Malone. Dancing to his tunes. I still do sometimes."

In hindsight, Malone might have picked a more manageable partner than Rupert Murdoch. Bringing Murdoch in for cost containment was a little like asking Alaric the Visigoth for advice on urban renewal. The Fox Sports merger was consummated in April 1996, and Murdoch promptly went on a dizzy buying spree for sports programming rights that within a year had proved way too rich for Malone. By 1997 Malone wanted to get out of Fox Sports completely.

Fox Sports was just a part of the August 1995 meeting in Denver. Malone and Murdoch had much wider horizons to peruse. Besides the sports venture there were alliances to make in satellite television in Latin America, with Brazil's largest media group, Globo Organization, and Mexico's biggest broadcaster, Grupo Televisa. Each venture would cost more than a billion dollars. Sky Latin would quickly become the dominant satellite service in the region, leapfrogging its way through South America country by country. In Europe there was some horse-trading over running Malone's programming on BSkyB, and prospects to discuss for satellite services in Asia, particularly Japan. At some point Malone tried to talk Murdoch into buying a 5 percent stake in Time Warner, to put the media company into play. The proposal came to nothing, because even as the two men spoke, Gerry Levin was courting Ted Turner for a merger.

As Murdoch flew out of Denver, it seemed little had changed. But Malone had achieved what he set out to do. Two years later Murdoch and Eisner would collide on schedule with a shower of fireworks. Malone would never get his satellite license back, but with Malone's encouragement Murdoch had become so deeply invested in his new cable channels that when he made his first great satellite play in 1997, he would find that Malone had tied his hands neatly behind his back. After all their history, how could he complain?

HERB ALLEN'S PORCH

Sun Valley, Idaho, July 11, 1996

A MONG THE CROP of wild rumors and far-fetched tales that swirled around Rupert Murdoch in the American summer of 1996, the wildest and most far-fetched was the story that Murdoch did not really exist.[1] He had died years ago, the yarn went, sometime during the 1990 debt crisis. Since then the chief executive's role at News Corporation had been played by half a dozen Murdoch look-alikes. This was the reason for the contradictory strategy moves coming out of News Corp in the last twelve months. Indeed, watching Murdoch during this time was like watching a contortionist under a strobe light. The strobe throws up a series of disconnected and wildly improbable positions: *Flash flash flash.* Which is the real Murdoch?

The answer, on a mild July evening in the mountains of Idaho, was taking the air on the porch, talking quietly, and watching the richest man in New York, Ron Perelman, the fifty-three-year-old proprietor of Marvel Comics, Revlon, and the New World Entertainment television chain, chomp his way through his cigar. Clearly the figure next to Perelman was the real Rupert Murdoch, because he was talking about spending $2.5 billion.

Despite Murdoch's impression of perpetual motion, his American rivals seemed to be passing him by. In the second half of the 1990s the future of mega-media in the United States—and the rest of the world—was being shaped by a series of huge mergers. Recent moves by Walt Disney Company, Time Warner, and Viacom had been worth $44 billion. Among the big four media companies, when it came to pulling out the pocketbook, News Corp had been positively frugal. Murdoch was about to fix that. In the next twelve months he would commit to deals totaling $10 billion, scattered across the American media landscape, as he bet the empire again. In 1997 these deals would spark brutal, wide-ranging media turf wars. It began with this uneasy exchange with Ron Perelman at Herb Allen's annual media and business conference.

Each July Herb Allen summons the cream of America's business and media executives and their families to the ski resort near the tiny town of Ketchum, population twelve hundred, for a five-day mix of business presentations and resort leisure. The fifty-six-year-old head of the investment bank Allen & Co., Allen was America's premier media investment adviser. His family was worth at least a billion dollars, thanks to the smart media deals it did in the 1970s. The annual conference is aimed at mainstream business as well, but after kicking it off in 1983, Allen made it the most significant business ritual for U.S. media in the 1990s. It is a compulsory road station in the titanic struggles shaping the information superhighway. Not that anyone calls it a superhighway. "The country creates a tidal wave, and some people get to ride it," Allen told *Vanity Fair*, with appropriate old-money diffidence and the confidence that comes from making your money a decade before anyone else in the room.[2]

"This is where smart people go to talk to each other, not the rest of the world," said one veteran. Barry Diller, who started up the Fox network for Murdoch and at the 1996 conference was CEO of Silver King Communications and trying to start up another network, called Allen "the gatherer of circus animals."[3] "There are very few places where that many gigantic egos are so fungible," says Diller. (Fungible is originally a legal term; its use in media circles reflects how much time media executives spend talking to lawyers.) "It's a bazaar," Allen said in 1999. "And you can spell that both ways."[4]

The guest list at the conference looked like the score card for the U.S. media industry for the 1990s, a roll call of survivors in the corporate battles to control the country's content and distribution systems. The media business has always been a contact sport, but in the 1990s the underlying fear of the future had given the battles a ferocious edge. So far not many of the megadeals had worked very well. But whatever the result, everyone came to Sun Valley. The winners and losers ended up at Herb Allen's retreat sitting together cheek by jowl.

Bill Gates, the founder of Microsoft, had been coming religiously for years, even in the dim distant past before he became a billionaire. John Malone was always there. Highly influential, Malone had remarkable reach. Through Tele-Communications Inc. he controlled one in every four American cable boxes and through Flextech more than half the cable boxes in Britain, while through Liberty Media he had interests in 23 percent of U.S. cable programming. His cavalier attitude with the nation's elected representatives had made him the cable guy that politicians loved to hate. In the days when they were still speaking, former presidential candidate Al Gore had described Malone as the Darth Vader of the cable industry. At Sun Valley Malone was spruced up to be user-friendly.

Barry Diller was there in 1996, frostily avoiding Sumner Redstone of Viacom. In late 1993 and early 1994 Diller and Redstone had waged a bitter bidding war for Paramount Pictures, a war that Redstone finally won after raising his bid close to $10 billion. In one of the strange outcomes that mark modern debt financing, Redstone raised the money in part by spending another $8.4 billion buying the Blockbuster video store group. Paying for Blockbuster with stock meant that Redstone could borrow more money to buy Paramount. In 1996 two things were apparent: The Paramount-Blockbuster deal hadn't worked for Viacom; and at seventy-three Sumner Redstone was as obsessed as ever with outplaying Rupert Murdoch.

Michael Eisner of Walt Disney Company, still on a roll from the $19 billion deal he had stitched up the year before to buy Capital Cities/ABC, was a surprise absentee. But Time Warner chief exec Gerald Levin was there. Either Levin was days away from losing his job, or he was about to pick up a whole new pack of cards—it depended which way you read it. Levin had taken the helm of Time Warner almost by accident in 1992, after the death of Steve Ross, who was the architect of the 1989 deal to merge Time Inc. and Warner Communications. The most notable move in Levin's career was still his groundbreaking decision back in 1975 as head of Home Box Office to use a satellite link to beam coverage of the Ali-Frazier boxing match in Manila down to cable operators across America. With his quiet East Coast manner, Levin remained a fierce exponent of the future for interactive cable programming. In effect he had bet Time Warner's future on cable. But the trial of Time Warner's interactive technology in Orlando had recently flopped. Six years after the merger that formed it, Time Warner was still struggling under its huge debt, and business reporters were speculating on how long Levin had before he was dumped by his board. The ace that Levin still held was the deal he had worked out with Ted Turner the previous year to merge Turner Broadcasting System into Time Warner. The deal was due to be finalized in September 1996. But then in 1996 who wanted more cable assets?

The four principals in the new DreamWorks SKG studio were at Sun Valley: legendary filmmaker Steven Spielberg; record industry leader David Geffen; Jeffrey Katzenberg, the brilliant head of Disney's core animation business until he fell out with Michael Eisner in September 1994; and Paul Allen, the man who cofounded Microsoft with Gates in 1975. Another familiar face at Sun Valley was Edgar Bronfman Jr., the forty-one-year-old head of Seagram, who a year after buying the MCA studio for $5.7 billion also held nearly 15 percent of Time Warner and the seeming ability to prompt an anxiety attack for Gerry Levin almost at will.

Rupert Murdoch, himself a longtime regular, was back after a break in 1995. He couldn't make it that year because he had been busy holding a News Corp management conference on the other side of the world, at his Hayman Island resort on Australia's Great Barrier Reef. The 1995 clash of timing with Sun Valley was a product of the schedules that dictated when Murdoch's chief guest, British Labour leader Tony Blair, could get there. The superb speech that Blair gave was indicative that he believed that he needed his friend Rupert as much as Rupert needed him. Murdoch's decision to get up close and personal with Blair would not pay off until two years later, when the Labour leader came to power in Britain heading a party that for almost two decades had demonized Murdoch's media grip on the U.K. Blair would be promoted by Murdoch's transatlantic adviser, Irwin Stelzer, as the first Labour leader since the 1970s who could say Murdoch's name without shuddering and making the sign of the cross.

The Sun Valley list went on and on, about 130 executives all up, plus wives and children. Some were there because of the superlative opportunities to network; some for a vacation with the children; some because they were afraid of offending Herb Allen. Everyone was represented: the film studios, the television networks, the cable companies, the software companies, the microchip manufacturers, the new DBS operators, the agents, the content producers, and the investors.

If debt funding had become less fashionable in the 1990s, no one at Sun Valley seemed aware of it. The legacy of the superdeals that had forged Time Warner, Viacom, and the big cable groups had been crippling debt payments. Ironically, among the major players Murdoch was the man with the least debt—and the man bankers still worried most about. So did his peers, for different reasons. As NBC president Bob Wright interjected in 1996 in a Sun Valley debate about the future of communication, "That's not the question! The question is, 'Where's Rupert?' "5

John Malone was the other danger man in this crowd. Together with Bill Gates and Ted Turner, he and Murdoch were the only real builders at the big table. The rest, like Michael Eisner at Disney, Gerry Levin at Time Warner, and Sumner Redstone at Viacom, were basing their strategies for the future largely on fitting existing pieces of media together to form bigger blocks, on the synergies of multibillion-dollar acquisitions. Creating new media assets is a much trickier busi-

ness. The advance of Bill Gates and Microsoft in all directions had a certain inevitable and predictable quality that in the end looked likely to bury all of them.
Ted Turner had the required maverick quality, but his ambitions had been held in
check through the 1990s, first by his cable shareholders and then by his imminent
merger with Time Warner. Only Murdoch and Malone had the capacity and the
resources to think outside the box on a grand scale. Only they had the imagination
and recklessness as well as the authority as principals to take the big gamble that
could turn an industry around. If anyone could meet the challenge that Microsoft
would pose to established media groups in the next decade, it seemed it would be
these two.

Such was the power of the guest list. The 130 executives in attendance were the
major players who were shaping the future of the world's media—at least that was
what the hype around the conference claimed. The prize they were fighting over
was the 200-million-plus consumers which made up the single-language media
market in the United States. The pool they played in was so big that whoever won
the U.S. megamedia wars of the 1990s would create a juggernaut too big for anyone else in the world to handle. The battles were all about form and content,
about distribution and programming, but no one knew just what the successful
mix of these two would be. For Herb Allen, bringing these violent rivals together
for a house party every year requires the skills of an illusionist, enough legerdemain to maintain the illusion that these men are not robber barons squabbling or
mafiosi on a coffee break from the endless turf wars. Rather, this meeting is a fraternity, a gathering of colleagues, an enlightened get-together of the powerful, the
far-sighted, and the worldly wise. Just good ol' boys whoopin' it up.

Herbert Allen doesn't believe any of this himself. While he respects the power
of these individuals, "[i]t's no different from people fighting over railroads," he
concedes engagingly. "People hunting money and power have pretty much the
same style."[6] The remark is an exquisite class marker, the delicate distinction
between the zookeeper and the exhibits. This is not to deny the power of the
Allen & Co. magic. Unlike the in-your-face public style of the 1980s, the under-
score here is mellow: cozy little meetings, good family fun. The entrepreneurial
mood of the 1980s was signaled by Drexel Burnham Lambert's client conferences,
the annual shindig for Michael Milken's junk bond clients that became known
as the Predator's Ball. Much of the original cast is here, but heavy hitters don't
do that stuff anymore. In the 1990s at Sun Valley, it is more like Masters of
the Universe Do Brunch. Media moguls at summer camp. Whatever way, it's
showtime.

* * *

Down at the airstrip, airport manager Rick Baird was on a nice little earner. His backlot was filled with a billion dollars of airplane. Sixty-odd aircraft had flown in for the conference. About half were Gulfstreams, for which he charged $25 a night hangerage. The rest were Learjets, which paid $15. It came to, say, $1,200 a night all together, not to mention the cost of topping up the fuel tanks.[7] Baird was a gatekeeper on the information superhighway. His airport was virtually the only way to enter Sun Valley, outside of a three-hour car drive. Airports are one of the certainties of the information revolution. Shaping the future of world media requires more than just ego, imagination, and dangerously high levels of testosterone. It requires a corporate jet.

It is the minimum requirement. The geography of power has been infinitely dispersed; the superhighway has a thousand different trunk routes. And these players are road warriors. Media brush wars flare at a hundred different spots across the continent, at thousands more sites around the world. The players fly in after the advance party, they do the deal, and they are gone. Thus the choice of location is the first of the many forms in Herb Allen's annual illusion. Allen & Co. will go to enormous lengths to recreate the informalities and the comforts of home. The first requirement is that this is not happening at home or at work but at some in-between space. The events of the next five days must take place in Idaho, not Los Angeles or New York. So the pleasures on the mountain will be underlain with the whiff of aviation fuel. The virtual realities these players will create are, of necessity, high-octane dreams.

Transportation is just one part of the seamless web that Herb Allen spins for his famous week. Hundreds of little details are part of good form, from the bright red fleece-lined Allen & Co. jackets for everybody, to the private security force to ensure privacy. And delicate questions of protocol must be resolved: Who will join the private meals at the Allens' house? Who will sit on the panels for the sessions? Who gets not to sit next to Bill Gates?

The twelve-hundred-odd population of Ketchum alternately ignore or disapprove of "Herbie and the boys." After a decade and a half of rubbing shoulders with billionaires in the street each summer, they remain hugely unimpressed.[8] "They come in all the time, they're just nice folks," Fonda Peters, a clerk at Main Strip T's in Ketchum, told a journalist kindly in 1999. On reflection, she thought there was something that set them apart from her other customers: "They're all short."[9]

This was a low blow. If the media industry agrees on one thing, it is that size does matter. Cutting down short poppies, lopping any upstarts, any threat of competition, is one of the things the American media business has become good at. As Michael Eisner once said of his former lieutenant at Disney, Jeffrey Katzenberg, "I think I hate the little midget."[10] There is the story about Ted Turner (which he denies) that when he was unhappy with one of his employees who was on the short side, he ordered one of his executives to "stand him on the desk, look him in the eye and tell him he's fired."[11]

Annie Liebovitz, the photographer who first shot all the big names at Sun Valley in a thirty-thousand-mile odyssey for *Vanity Fair* in 1994, has a different take on her subjects. She found they were control freaks. They were all *in charge.* "I felt that [the common theme is] the negotiating factor," she said later. "There was a lot of negotiating. And there was also a great sense of control." Her 1994 portrait of Bill Gates she described as "boy with a computer, boy with a machine." Gates had been engrossed in his computer throughout the shoot, up until the moment he turned around and she took the shot. Ted Turner, clearly her favorite subject, agreed to fly up to Montana to his ranch for a shoot. Liebovitz shot cable king John Malone on a dirt road with satellite dishes going up nearby, and Gerry Levin fiddling with a prototype joystick for interactive television. She didn't like Ron Perelman, for reasons she didn't elaborate. Rupert Murdoch agreed to take Liebovitz out with his wife Anna on his 158-foot yacht, the *Morning Glory,* which he sailed himself. "It's funny, he and his wife said that, if they lost everything else, they didn't care, as long as they could just have the boat. The boat was their life."[12] Murdoch married his third wife, Wendi Deng, on board *Morning Glory* in New York harbor in June 1999. He sold the boat several months later.

Herb Allen taps the local population in Ketchum each year to appear as props for the grand performance. Local teenagers are hired to look after the executives' children. (Baby-sitters on the information superhighway earn a thousand dollars for the five days.) Arrangements are made with local stores to provide the country-western gear that guests will need for the wagon ride and western barbecue on Tuesday night.[13]

On Wednesday afternoon families can go whitewater rafting down a six-mile course on the Salmon River. The organized social events are not compulsory. One impromptu side trip back in 1990 began with a little mishap over the basic ground rule of the river, the one about how when whitewater rafting, the important thing is to stay in the raft. Even Rupert Murdoch doesn't walk on water. Flailing wildly, the world's only real global media baron made it back above the surface of the

Salmon River a hundred yards downstream. While slightly bedraggled, Murdoch apparently was none the worse for wear.[14] Elsewhere at Sun Valley there is a golf course and tournament, there is fly fishing, horseback riding, hiking, skeet shooting, and a tennis clinic. Transportation is by chartered buses. Allen & Co.'s bomb squad tries to be unobtrusive as it checks the undersides of the coaches.

Then there's playtime. Friday night is the awards banquet at Herb Allen's big house, with Allen & Co. managing director John Schneider master of ceremonies. The roasting he stages with oversize props is all good clean fun. This year Jeffrey Katzenberg had already set the mood earlier in the day. While speaking as a panelist in a discussion on the state of the entertainment business, he whipped out a Supersoaker water cannon and shot at all and sundry.[15] This would have been a lighthearted, spontaneous gesture, except for the care with which Katzenberg had arranged for his aides to conceal the water cannon in place beforehand. In this league not even humor can be left to chance. Back at the dinner, Schneider traditionally handed out boxing gloves to conference attendees who were at war with each other. This year he used sandwich boards with pointed messages. In 1994 Gerald Levin picked up an inflatable life raft in the shape of a Seagram's bottle, after Bronfman at Seagram built up a threatening 15 percent stake in Time Warner. Bronfman showed what a sport he was by bussing Levin soundly on both cheeks. That was the year superagent-turned-Disney-executive Michael Ovitz, that Hollywood wag, produced an orangutan with a microphone, trained to imitate Schneider as he speaks.[16] In later years Schneider would hand Sumner Redstone from Viacom a "Team Viagra" T-shirt. For David Geffen and Jeffrey Katzenberg, two of the cofounders of the DreamWorks SKG studio, he would have two DreamWorks dolls: "You wind them up and nothing happens!"[17] In 1996, amid the many gags, agent Jeff Berg, head of International Creative Management, was presented with a two-foot vibrator—after Ovitz's move to Disney, Berg was subsequently dubbed "the biggest prick in Hollywood." It was all happening with these wild guys, and *Vanity Fair* was graciously allowed in to take photos and write color on the new masters of the universe.[18]

In this atmosphere of clubby bonhomie it wasn't surprising that in 1993 Jeffrey Katzenberg, then still head of Disney studios, smelled a deal in the air when he spotted Turner Entertainment president Scott Sassa playing tennis with the CEO of Castle Rock Entertainment, Alan Horn. And sure enough Ted Turner later bought Castle Rock (one of the only deals his cable company partners allowed him). And in 1994, while Michael Eisner at Disney was getting his first chest pains, which would require emergency heart surgery days later, Paul Allen, co-founder of Microsoft and a heavy metal fan, got talking to music mogul David Geffen about art. As the friendship prospered, Allen ended up putting $500 million into DreamWorks.[19]

And it was entirely appropriate that at the 1995 conference, while Time Warner's Gerald Levin indicated he was moving more toward becoming a content company (he wrapped up the deal to buy Turner Broadcasting five weeks later), Michael Eisner was walking up Wildflower Lane when he chanced upon investor Warren Buffett coming out of Herb Allen's house. It was one-fifteen P.M. on Friday, July 14. Eisner was still fired up after an impressive presentation on Disney's improving divisions. He had been looking for Tom Murphy, the CEO of Capital Cities/ABC, which he had been trying for years to buy, but was now on the way back to the airstrip to fly home to California ahead of Disneyland's fortieth anniversary celebrations. Buffet, who was the largest shareholder in Capital Cities/ABC, was about to meet Murphy and Bill Gates for a round of golf. Such was the magic of the moment that in a few minutes' conversation it was apparent that finally both Eisner and Murphy were prepared to be flexible over what they wanted. The merger was announced two weeks later on July 31. At $19 billion it was the second-largest merger in U.S. corporate history, making Disney/ABC a $50 billion colossus.[20]

*   *   *

But that was all last year. In 1996 the conference and most of the crowd were flat. The week before, 20th Century–Fox had released *Independence Day* to crowded cinemas across the United States. The sci-fi film, which showed an invasion by alien spacecraft—vast and mysterious shapes heavy with menace overshadowing American cities—would go on to become one of the biggest-grossing films of all time. It would be outshone, however, by a historical drama funded by Fox and Paramount that would begin filming a week after the Sun Valley conference. Its director, James Cameron, had told Fox he was sure he could make *Titanic* for less than $100 million. Filming began badly on the Newfoundland coast when someone slipped angel dust into the crew's clam chowder.

The question at Sun Valley was what to make of this little summer interlude, this engaging piece of virtual reality that Herb Allen had created in this lonely place. Did it mean anything at all? Was its significance merely as a media construct created by Herb Allen and Graydon Carter, the editor in chief of *Vanity Fair*? In 1994 Carter, in his efforts to forge a role for *Vanity Fair* as a "magazine of the world stage," had advanced the line that the leaders of the U.S. media industry were, as he put it, "the pioneers that have made America sort of the first superpower of the Information Age."[21] Their economic and political muscle made this group the country's new power elite, the new establishment. Sun Valley was the fraternity clubhouse for this new order, as Carter portrayed it each year since then. Such was the impact of the *Vanity Fair* coverage that by the end of the 1990s journalists from all over the world were staking out the conference each July, with television anchors making live crosses to Sun Valley several times a day for up-dates on what was happening. By then Sun Valley as a media event had become something quite different, perhaps barely recognizable, from the perceptions and memories of those who actually took part.

The idea that the men and several women at Sun Valley were masters of the in-formation revolution implied that they were also masters of their own destiny—that they actually had some idea of what they were doing, of where they were going. Regrettably, promoting this idea proved impossible, because as time would show, the new establishment at Sun Valley in 1996 had barely a clue about the wave of change that was about to hit them. The bubbling explosion of the dot-com revolution would surprise them more than anyone. They were actually old media. Even Bill Gates got it wrong. In the mid-1990s Gates was still committed to de-veloping the Microsoft Network for online users rather than building a browser for this strange new thing called the Internet.[22] In 1996 Herb Allen, the world's premier media adviser, had not yet touched a computer. In 1999 he confessed, "Andy Grove [the head of Intel] sat me down in front of a computer for the first time two years ago. He showed me how to turn it on, what to do. It was like see-ing electricity for the first time."[23] Allen went on at some length to stress that he immediately saw all the possibilities of computers and was now completely on top of the new media.

While the new establishment at Sun Valley may not have known where they were going, their power was such that it didn't matter. They controlled the biggest media combines in history, and when eventually they realized that they had been left behind by new media, they would play a mean game of catch-up. Bill Gates could get it wrong about the Internet and yet still win the race to produce the world's dominant Internet browser, though not without some cost to Microsoft. Cable operators could misjudge their markets, promise hundreds of channels that never arrived, and squander money on interactive experiments, yet still end the decade with unrivaled reach and power.

The wave of megamedia mergers was unleashing huge new forces on the world's information economy. In films, books, and television, in cable, in sports, in

newspapers, magazines, and radio, the struggle between the media giants was po-
larizing the entire playing field. No area was too small, no undertaking too minor
to escape this competition for influence. There was no single battle for supremacy,
no final resolution; in the postmodern world there were only endless turf wars. All
of these skirmishes had to be fought. But for those left standing earthbound, the
strategic picture was often hard to see. Watching a modern media war can be a
little like living in a small highway town on which two rival gangs of motorcycle
riders descend. After a short, violent confrontation, both groups roar off into
the distance. Rattled townsfolk left behind can only mutter cautious queries like
"What was that?" and "Are you sure they're gone?"

In 1996 the media wars were still to come, and the vision thing was looking
a little dim. Michael Ovitz, the new Disney president under Eisner, came to
Sun Valley in the hope of sitting down with Jeffrey Katzenberg, Disney's former
studio chief.[24] Ovitz wanted to try to work out Katzenberg's differences with
Eisner and his huge lawsuit. But somehow the meeting never happened. Instead,
the action took place on Thursday evening, July 11, on Herb Allen's porch. Barry
Diller later claimed to have brokered the encounter, telling Perelman to button-
hole Murdoch, while advising his former boss on how to handle Perelman.[25]
So after dinner and over cigars Rupert Murdoch and Ron Perelman talked.[26]
Murdoch had known that this moment was coming for more than two years—ever
since May 1994, when he paid $500 million for a 20 percent stake in Perelman's
New World Communications. He had just hoped Perelman would wait a little
longer before cashing out.

Ronald Perelman is not Rupert Murdoch's kind of guy. About the only points
they have in common are large amounts of money and Michael Milken. In the
1980s Perelman was a longtime Milken client who at one point had a Drexel
Burnham Lambert consultant working out of his New York townhouse. Milken's
advice and, more important, his money-raising machine had made Perelman the
richest man in New York—and perhaps in the entire country. Unlike many of the
1980s entrepreneurs, Perelman had proven highly skilled at turning around companies like Revlon and Pantry Pride. In the mid-1990s Perelman's fortune was estimated at $4.2 billion. His corporate style was aggressive. At the personal level a
court-appointed psychiatrist would later note that Perelman had been in therapy
since 1991 to handle anger.[27] His love of the high life, his fondness for actresses,
and the absence, after a decade and a half of journalistic scrutiny, of any evidence
of a sense of humor within the Ronald, as he was called, had made him a gossip
writer's dream. Perelman's spectacularly acrimonious divorce and support battles

from 1996 to 1998 with his third wife, former Democratic fund-raiser Patricia Duff (chronicled gleefully by Murdoch's *New York Post*), and his readiness at one point to hire President Clinton's favorite pizza-delivery girl Monica Lewinsky at Revlon, would add luster to the legend.

In 1996, despite his enormous wealth, life was not going swimmingly for Perelman. In addition to his marital problems, corporate raider Carl Icahn had made a cheeky raid to try to wrest control of Marvel Comics from him. Also, he needed money for casino investments in Las Vegas and Atlantic City. Perelman had known Murdoch only as a fellow rider on the Michael Milken money merry-go-round. In 1984 and 1985 Murdoch had attended the Predator's Ball. It made an unlikely scene, the Australian who hated parties, mingling in the crowd of nouveaux super-riches. In 1994, while still performing forty hours a week of community work as a condition of his parole after a prison sentence for violating U.S. securities laws, Milken had had another big idea for media. Perelman had used the public company he controlled, New World Communications, to buy up a string of television stations. New World had twelve stations, ten of which were CBS affiliates. Milken convinced Perelman he could make a lot of money by flipping his television stations' network affiliations. Then Milken reintroduced Perelman to Murdoch.

At the beginning of 1994 Murdoch's Fox Broadcasting Company (FBC) had broken the CBS stranglehold on Sunday-afternoon football by offering an outrageous sum for the right to broadcast National Football League (NFL) games on eighteen Sundays a year. CBS had balked when Murdoch bid $1.58 billion for the four-year contract—CBS was already losing heavily on the existing contract. Murdoch's deal with Perelman in May 1994 came as a bombshell for the big three networks: News Corp invested $500 million for a 20 percent refundable stake in New World. In return, Perelman flipped his twelve stations to become Fox affiliates. CBS couldn't believe it. When New World Communications CEO Bill Bevins called Tony Malara, the CBS president for affiliate affairs, to tell him New World was switching affiliations to Fox, a scandalized Malara asked, "Which market?" It took a little while to sink in that New World was flipping stations in all of its markets.[28]

The big three networks, faced with a flood of defections to Fox by their affiliates who wanted the Fox NFL games, found only one way to retain their reluctant troops: to throw money at them. "Rupert is driving the other networks crazy," Ted Turner reported later that year. NBC had been cutting down the payments that it made to affiliates from $200 million a year to $100 million in recent years. "Now it's back up to $200 million—and that comes right off the top," said Turner. "And he's done the same thing for CBS and to a lesser extent ABC. And God knows where he will strike next."[29] (Ted Turner might not have known Murdoch's next move, but he had a pretty shrewd idea. If Murdoch was on the prowl with Michael Milken as his adviser, at some point his mind would turn to his old adversary. In mid-1994 Turner quietly put Milken on retainer. If Murdoch was going to make a move on Turner Broadcasting, Turner didn't want Milken loading the bullets.)

"When [the NFL deal] was brought to us, I thought we would get a few affiliates as the years went by," Murdoch told News Corp shareholders a trifle smugly in October 1994. In fact in nine months the Fox network had jumped from 130-odd affiliates to 190. By 1996 it was up to 210 affiliates. "This has caused a tremendous scramble among the other networks," he continued. "We are happy to report that they are spending up to $100 million a year for the next ten years to confirm or to hold on to other stations in their networks to prevent them switching over to [Fox Broadcasting Company]. So, we do have the pleasure not only of having greatly strengthened FBC but [of having] caused some little irritation in other areas."[30] The last line was pure Murdoch. The NFL play had hurt Murdoch's rivals far more than it hurt him. How sweet it was.

The 1994 deal with Perelman was the first, crucial step in Murdoch's campaign to retake American media in the 1990s. It made his NFL play look like a masterstroke, and it transformed Fox into a full-fledged network. And it had worked while New World wasn't earning any money, recording net losses through 1994 and 1995. But in February 1996 Congress had proclaimed the new Telecommunications Act. It lifted the maximum audience reach for a wholly owned network to 35 percent, meaning Murdoch could buy more television stations.

Murdoch was going in the opposite direction from the rest of the industry. The smart money was saying that the way to win the future was to buy into programming. But Murdoch knew that programming wasn't the real key. His whole career in the United States had been like a series of Houdini escape acts. Time and again he had wrestled his way out of the handcuffs, achieved the incredible escape, and taken off the mask—to discover that, at the end of the act, he was once again locked outside the city, hammering to get in. More simply, Murdoch had been blocked by the impossibility of getting the distribution he wanted for his programming. So his strategy was simply an extension of his general corporate philosophy. At the turn of the twenty-first century, appearance dictated substance, form controlled content, and distribution determined programming. So Murdoch was buying television stations before anyone else caught on.

In an ideal world, Murdoch would have liked to keep the New World stake at

20 percent, and buy other stations which could also be flipped to take Fox programming, and in the process overtake CBS as third-largest network. Murdoch knew he would have to buy out the rest of New World sooner or later. If he didn't, Fox would eventually lose the New World stations. Despite the ten-year affiliation agreement, in the end New World would flip them, as sure as God made little channel selectors. This would push the Fox network back into the minor leagues. Yet while New World was definitely a problem for Murdoch, he didn't want to do anything about it too quickly. But Perelman wasn't having any of that. He had been pressuring Murdoch for a buyout of New World since the start of the year. When talks bogged down in April, Perelman took a different tack. Instead of trying to sell New World, word leaked out that he was about to buy more media assets, with a $1.5 billion deal to merge New World with the King World programming and distribution group. New World was about to get much bigger, which meant it would cost a lot more for Murdoch to buy Perelman's company. Whether or not it was Perelman's intention, this news put enormous pressure on Murdoch to act quickly. So this meeting with Perelman at Sun Valley on July 11, 1996, was Murdoch's final chance to snatch the deal back and make it work. It was a purely defensive move for Murdoch. News Corp would not gain a single viewer for Fox from the deal that Murdoch was about the hammer out with Perelman. Murdoch was about to pay $2.5 billion to buy something—access for the Fox network—that he already had. "He had me over a barrel," Murdoch said later.[31] The association had been profitable, but personally Perelman and Murdoch had never been close.

*   *   *

As Perelman sat down to haggle with the Master of Virtual Reality on Herb Allen's porch, he entered the charm zone. Up close and personal, Rupert Murdoch is one of the most persuasive forces on earth. Time and again throughout his career he has wooed and won over the most unlikely foes, convinced the most skeptical and diehard critics to give him their trust, to believe that they are the ones for whom it will be different.

His personal mannerisms help. Murdoch has a way of letting people into his confidence, into the inner circle, as his gravelly, diffident voice casually dissects the world. He puffs out his cheeks as he gathers for a response. The eyebrows peak, he leans forward, and the voice becomes almost a whisper. He lets drop the most devastating information as if it were a casual, bored commonplace. But his mind is always working, shooting out ideas at a hundred miles an hour. And such ideas.

But it is more than just the manner. What Murdoch offers—what Murdoch is offering here to you now—is a piece of the future. The man before you has this uncanny ability to make the future happen, in a way that almost no one else in the world can. The future of ideas and visions he offers makes him almost irresistible to anyone with a spark of imagination. This quality gives him a devastating effect on politicians, particularly on those to the middle and left of center, whose rhetoric depends upon imagination. Murdoch's natural home is deep on the right, and Democratic and Labour politicians understand this in their heads. But often it makes no difference. Murdoch in your face at force ten still takes their breath away with this tantalizing, attainable view of a possible future. This is Murdoch in full seductive mode.

But Perelman wasn't buying. He had taken Murdoch's measure, and for Perelman there was no mystique about the media, there was no magic to the business with which Murdoch could conjure. Perelman rated television stations like property assets. This was all about money, end of story. The first point that Murdoch made was that he was not actually going to pay Perelman any cash. The deal would have to be made in exchange for News Corp's new limited-voting preferred stock. (This was a line of stock Murdoch had issued eighteen months before that essentially had no voting rights. Unlike the Milken junk preferred stock in the 1980s, it was genuine equity.) Perelman would accede to that. But how much would the deal be? Talks between the two had broken down in April over price: Perelman wanted $29 a share for New World, and Murdoch was offering $23 a share. On the porch Perelman came down to $27 a share, take it or leave it. Perelman would walk away with $1.15 billion, a $600 million profit, most of it in the form of News Corp preferreds. In all, Perelman's tough negotiating would gouge another $366 million from Murdoch. Murdoch must have hated that prospect.

The market would certainly hate the deal. It was an outrageous price for a network with a limited upside. If Fox executives could perform miracles at New World, over the subsequent five years the company might become worth almost as much as Murdoch was being asked to pay for it now. But that wasn't the point. Murdoch wasn't paying for product or profits. He was paying $2.5 billion to hold on to an outlet for Fox programming. Behind all the talk of the 1990s about the supremacy of content over form, Murdoch's corporate experience told him exactly the opposite was true. He had content but not enough distribution. After two decades of trying in America, he was still locked out, still clawing for access.

The Sunday night after Herb Allen's conference ended, Murdoch called

Perelman from his ranch in Carmel, California. Against the advice of his own executives, he agreed to Perelman's price. And so the deal was done—just like that. At least that was the public story, graciously eked out to the trade press and later the *New York Times*. That was the big deal, in Sun Valley in 1996. History records it as the last major deal to come out of Sun Valley in the 1990s. Everything that came after that year would just be hype.

But with Rupert Murdoch it's never that simple. There are two rules for negotiating with him. The first is that he is never quite where you think he is. The second is that there is always a deal running underneath the main deal, and another deal running simultaneously underneath that. Ron Perelman would discover the first of these subterranean levels three days later, and it would cost him a lot of money.

Los Angeles, July 14–17, 1996

Hollywood loves a secret. It is *de rigueur,* part of the dress code anywhere north of the Santa Monica Freeway, to be the proud owner of a personal confidence. Or rather, of someone else's personal confidence. There are certain minimum requirements. Like radioactive isotopes, secrets have a high decay rate in northern Los Angeles. Sometimes half-lives are measured in hours. And by definition a Hollywood secret is something that everyone else knows. What other value is there in having a secret?

Rupert Murdoch's particular problem on Sunday evening, July 14, 1996, was that he had a secret that he really couldn't afford to let anyone know about. He had to hold it for only a couple of days—any thought of keeping it under wraps for longer was a hopeless pipe dream. But for those forty-eight hours it had to be that most sentimental of anachronisms, a *secret* secret. One slipup, one indiscretion would cost Murdoch a couple of hundred million dollars.

As Murdoch hung up the phone at his Carmel ranch after sealing the deal with Ron Perelman to buy New World Communications, his poker hand was still only half played. The deal had been stalled since April over the price issue. Murdoch had offered $23 a share, while Perelman hung out for $29, before dropping his demand to $27 a share. All told, News Corp would pay $2.48 billion for New World Communications stock. Perelman's tactics may have increased the price by $366 million and his own personal profit by $155 million, but in the next two days Murdoch would try to get it all back.

Murdoch and Perelman were still stalking each other, still probing for weaknesses, united only by mutual suspicion. It was time to start lawyering up. The legal teams that assembled had forty-eight hours to close a frighteningly big and complex transaction on assets totaling $3.8 billion.

This deal was all about speed. Part of Ron Perelman's squeeze play on Murdoch had been to set up a deal to buy King World Productions, a major television distributor for shows including *The Oprah Winfrey Show* and *Wheel of Fortune*. If Murdoch didn't meet Perelman's price, he would go back to talking to King World. As far as the King World executives knew, their deal was in its final stages, due to be sealed later in the week. Should King World executives catch a whiff of what was happening—that Perelman was planning to jilt them—they would walk. If they walked, so did much of Perelman's negotiating leverage over Murdoch. If the Fox deal fell through, it would cost Perelman more money to placate King World and get the acquisition talks started again. So he had to keep the deal with Murdoch secret.

King World was both a squeeze play and an insurance policy for Perelman in case the deal with Murdoch soured, so Perelman continued the merger talks. The New World board would continue its meetings with the King World directors until late Tuesday to finalize the agreement. But by Wednesday the jig would be up. So Wednesday was Perelman's deadline for the Fox deal—it had to be done by then. In any case, Perelman was too tough a negotiator to give Murdoch any time or room to edge back from this deal. He had a good price, and he needed to keep the pressure on Murdoch to get it all signed up as fast as possible.

But Rupert Murdoch knew something that Ron Perelman didn't: He knew how his own stockholders would react to the deal. Their reaction was important, because this wasn't to be a cash transaction. Murdoch was offering Perelman News Corp stock, a piece of his paper. Stock transactions are a sort of virtual reality. But just how do you value paper?

The key to any stock transaction is timing. Murdoch had agreed to pay Perelman $27 for each New World share, by giving him (and other New World stockholders) that same value in News Corp limited-voting preferred stock. The problem with paying someone in stock is that the price of the stock goes up and down. So in drawing up a stock deal, negotiators have to fix a day on which the stock will be valued. Generally this will be either the day the deal is struck or the day many months later when the deal is settled.

In the United States News Corp stock trades as American depository receipts (ADRs). In the New World deal, the value of the News Corp ADR preferreds was fixed at $18.62, their closing price on Monday, July 15. This price became the benchmark for the entire deal. In the document hammered out by the lawyers, it was agreed that for each New World share, News Corp would issue 1.45 News Corp ADR preferreds (which worked out to $27.01 for each New World share). The ADR preferreds had been trading at $20 just two weeks before (which would value the New World offer at $29 a share), so the price looked good to Perelman.

It looked good to Murdoch too, but for quite different reasons. What had become painfully clear to him in the previous six months was that the Australian institutional funds that still formed the backbone of the News Corp share register didn't like his preferred limited-voting stock. In fact a lot of fund managers hated it. Ever since Murdoch had foisted the preferreds on his shareholders in a bonus issue in 1994, Australian fund managers had treated them like the meningococcal virus. Australian institutions had been bailing out of the preferreds since early 1996, partly out of suspicion over what Murdoch was about to do with them.

The fund managers, Murdoch knew, were going to hate this New World deal. It would confirm all their fears that he would use the preferreds as a form of junk debt, to pay excessive prices for assets. Because of the small size of the Australian market, Australian institutions tend to take larger stakes in public companies than is usual in the United States. This gives them more market clout. So Murdoch knew that after the New World deal he would have some powerfully unhappy shareholders who would punish him by dumping his stock. Once news of the deal broke, the price of the preferreds would drop like a stone. The institutions would be sending Murdoch a signal: Don't mess with us. So Perelman would end up with News Corp stock that was worth a lot less than the $27 that he thought he was getting. Murdoch was planning an ambush—and it would work only if it remained a surprise. If the deal were not finalized by the time the news broke and Murdoch's stock started sliding, Perelman would back out of it, or at least insist that Murdoch gave him more stock to make up the $27 price.

Ron Perelman was in the dark. He might have been expecting a minor price drop in News Corp stock, but not a rout. He did not understand the forms of this virtual transaction. They were the tricky part. If the deal was signed and watertight before any news leaked out, then when the stock plunged, it would be Perelman's loss rather than Murdoch's; Perelman would be locked into a deal to accept the low-price News Corp preferreds. It wouldn't cost Murdoch any less in terms of the number of shares he had to issue, but he would avoid having to issue millions more to honor the price he had negotiated with Perelman, who had to keep thinking he had a good deal until Wednesday morning.

The secret broke with a gasp on Tuesday evening. Joe Flint and Jenny Hontz at

Hollywood's *Daily Variety* heard a garbled version of the deal and began making calls, seeking confirmation. It came as news to the King World board, who were just coming out of late meetings with New World execs.

At that point on Tuesday night, after the news was out, the New World board still had not signed the memorandum of understanding (MOU) that would seal the takeover. The New World executives, if they had been able to give the news their full attention, might have decided not to sign it. But meanwhile, to Murdoch's good fortune, two other megadeals were diverting their attention. On Wednesday the Federal Trade Commission signaled it would approve Time Warner's $7.5 billion purchase of Turner Broadcasting System. And late on Tuesday night, Kirk Kerkorian won the race to snatch the MGM studio, which was being auctioned by French financial group Crédit Lyonnais. Kerkorian had beaten out a range of rival bidders, including Murdoch, for MGM, though Murdoch popped up as a shareholder in Kerkorian's silent partner, Australia's Seven Network. With this much background noise going on, the New World deal slipped through without a problem. The New World board signed the MOU early Wednesday, and the deal was announced with appropriate enthusiasm.

"This acquisition continues the momentum towards our goal to become the leading over-the-air free broadcast television network in the United States, and underscores our commitment to play a major role in this industry for decades to come," Murdoch said in the News Corp press release, in a nicely judged comment that avoided saying anything meaningful.

The line from New World was that the deal had been a negotiating triumph for Perelman over Murdoch. "The bottom line is, they were arguing over price, they had already agreed on strategy," commented one of the New World execs. "For you to come back and get [nearly] the price you were looking for just weeks ago, it's an outstanding chess move."[32]

Perelman's supporter must have been talking early in the day. Over on Wall Street the outstanding chess move was looking more like the expensive end of a three-card monte trick. The News Corp preferreds had begun their predictable descent. The deal had been struck at $18.625 on the Monday close. It eased a little on Tuesday, then dived Wednesday to $16.50. At this level Murdoch's effective price for New World was $23.93 a share. A week later his bid price had dropped even further, down to $22.66. The value for New World shareholders dropped $244 million the day the deal was announced and another $100 million over the following week. Murdoch had won back all of the extra price that Perelman had wrestled out of him. But no one was pointing that out to reporters, who focused instead on the small drop in News Corp's ordinary stock.

It wasn't all loss for Perelman. He had a little insurance that other New World shareholders did not have, because part of his price was paid in cash. That Monday Murdoch had agreed to pay for part of Perelman's shares by taking over existing debt in a holding company. In a series of deals Perelman was to receive $1.15 billion, a profit of about $600 million. About $435 million of that was in debt and cash, which did not go down in value with the News Corp share price. But by Thursday, three days later, the value of Perelman's shares—and his profit—was still down $130 million.

It would have been hard for the senior ranks at News Corp not to have felt some gratification at Perelman's discomfiture. His return was back down around where it would have been if he had taken cash at $23 a share three months earlier. It was all most satisfactory. The warm glow of a happy outcome was cooled by only a slight downside. The Ronald was not happy. Up to now Murdoch's chief share-holders had been a bunch of unhappy fund managers. Now he had a bunch of un-happy fund managers and an eight-hundred-pound gorilla. But that would be next year's problem.

*   *   *

This jousting with Ron Perelman would have been just another piece of corporate chicanery or smart footwork, but Rupert Murdoch is never quite so easy to define. Still another twist lay underneath the New World deal, one that was produced by his complex family relationships. Ron Perelman wasn't the only one who de-pended on the price of the News Corp preferreds: That price had become a criti-cal matter for securing the Murdoch family succession. In July 1996 Murdoch was halfway through the tortuous process of buying the rest of his family out of Cruden Investments. Nor did he really have enough News Corp shares to ensure that his children would control the company. Once he had bought his sisters out, Murdoch would need to husband his pennies to buy more News Corp voting stock. Every dollar would count. In March 1996, to complete the first leg of the family buyout, Murdoch had taken out a A$373 million bank loan through West-pac Bank in Sydney. The only way he could pay off the loan was to sell Cruden's News Corp limited voting preferred stock some years later. Of course, Murdoch could have sold the stock right away, without raising any bank debt. Paying the family with a bank loan like that meant that Murdoch was gambling that the stock price of the preferreds would go up before the repayment fell due—so in the end he would have to sell less of the preferreds, which would leave him with more money to buy News Corp voting stock. He was that confident that the price would go up. In fact, it was imperative that the preferreds' stock price go up. It would certainly be disastrous if it went down—as it had in 1987, the last time Murdoch bet on News Corp stock. A decline in price would have the same result: debt piling up, secured only by a line of stock that was going down.

That was the plan. Then along came Ron Perelman. As Murdoch said, the Ronald had him over a barrel. Murdoch had no choice but to buy New World. There was one small window of opportunity. It was always going to be a tough outcome for Perelman, because he needed to raise money for his casino operations quickly, so he wanted to sell the News Corp preferreds that he picked up in the deal as soon as possible. By contrast, Murdoch's loan repayment and the final installment in the family buyout were two or three years away. Murdoch would have known, that Sunday night at his Carmel Valley ranch when he sealed the deal with Perelman, that this transaction would hit the preferred stock price badly. The public story would be that this deal was a great triumph for Ron Perelman. The in-house story at News would be how the tables had been turned on Perelman. But the personal story underneath everything else was that, as much as Murdoch could enjoy Perelman's discomfiture, the fall in the stock price was hurting Murdoch just as much.

So why did he do it? What is this strange twist beneath the megadeal? The only thing that Murdoch had going for him was a gambler's belief that, even though the preferreds' price would go down, it would recover by the time he needed to pay out his personal bank loan.

"Murdoch's view is that if he is willing to be patient, other shareholders should be patient too," a News adviser told the *New York Times*.[33] Murdoch was fond of describing his business ventures as times when he bet the company on the big venture of the moment—like buying *News of the World* in 1968, or the Metromedia stations and Wapping in 1986, or Sky Television in 1989. But this was not a wager made with Other People's Money. This time, as he had when he bought Queensland Press in 1987, Murdoch had bet the family. It was white-knuckle stuff. But even knowing all of this, that hot night in Carmel Valley, Murdoch took the gamble without a blink.

10

THE APPLE FUMBLE

New York, September 17, 1996

OR MORE THAN A CENTURY Hollywood filmmakers have known that New York is the center of the universe. It is one of the truths that the motion picture industry holds to be self-evident. No one knows quite why this should be so. The best theory is that it is the result of some celluloid wrinkle in space-time. Manhattan Island exercises a profound gravitational attraction that most living entities and large inanimate objects find impossible to resist. Giant gorillas, mutated lizards, alien invasion fleets, romantic insomniacs from Seattle, and huge meteorites all realize instinctively (or at least by the third reel) that if they want to make a splash, New York is the only place to go. Hold New York for ransom, and you'd have the world's attention. Hold Cleveland for ransom, and you'd have, well, half of Cleveland's attention.

The latest round in the eternal quest to storm Manhattan began on September 17, 1996, with a rain front that swept in from Long Island. It had been wet all day, a cold steady rain that turned traffic into a snarling mess. It was still falling as the home team took the field at Yankee Stadium against the Baltimore Orioles. A heavier downpour soon washed the game out, and baseball fans went home aggrieved. In midtown the downpour caught Gerry Levin as he left the Time Warner building to make the short trip up Sixth Avenue for an uncomfortable interview with Rupert Murdoch.

"Good luck," Time Warner president Richard Parsons said to Levin as his boss walked out.

It had already been a long day for Levin. He was twenty-two days away from closing the most important deal of his life. Four years before, after the death of Steve Ross, the legendary head of Warner Communications, Levin had become the head of the world's largest media group. In 1989 Levin had been corporate strategist for Time Inc. in the $14 billion merger that produced Time Warner, but

Ross had been the architect of the deal. By and large the merged entity that Levin inherited from Ross had not worked very well. But in August 1995 Levin had stamped his own mark on the group by persuading Ted Turner to merge his beloved Turner Broadcasting System with Time Warner. It had been a $7.5 billion deal at the time, but the sagging Time Warner stock price meant that by September 1996 the Time Warner stock that Turner and his TBS stockholders would receive was worth $1 billion less.

The merger was due to settle on October 10. While the FCC had approved the deal in July, the FTC had hung tough and insisted on some peculiar conditions, finally giving its approval on September 12. Putting together a big merger is an excruciating juggling act. Not the least problem for Levin to juggle in the last month had been working out what to do with Ted Turner. Turner was about to become Levin's biggest stockholder—he would end up with 10.6 percent of Time Warner. For nearly a year Levin had been working on a management restructuring for the merged group that would leave Turner vice chairman and the most senior figure at Time Warner after Levin himself, without actually having a job.

Turner had been stung by press reports to this effect. Over the Labor Day weekend Levin had flown to Turner's ranch in Montana and discovered an unhappy camper. Turner had a long list of grievances and demands—virtually all of which Levin had been forced to meet. The upshot was that on September 17 Levin threw over his management-restructuring plans and gave Turner a real job, appointing him overseer of all of Time Warner's cable operations in the newly merged group. Turner was now the head of the most important and most profitable division in Time Warner. Like any major announcement in a group the size of Time Warner, Levin's move had sparked a whole new range of forest fires in the management ranks that needed to be put out. So it was late in the day when Levin got to the last item on his agenda, which was to see Rupert Murdoch.

Levin got along well with Murdoch. At least, he didn't get along badly. The two men were polite to each other. Time Warner had cable channels that it wanted to run in Britain on Murdoch's BSkyB satellite service, and Murdoch wanted to run his new Fox News cable channel on Time Warner's cable networks—particularly in New York. At Herb Allen's Sun Valley conference in July, Levin and Murdoch had spoken cordially to each other about their plans and made a handshake deal, as Murdoch put it, to do what they could to provide access for each other's programming in their various ventures around the world.

Murdoch was too ferocious a competitor for Levin to want to cross; his feeling for media was too intuitive to gamble against. Murdoch's abrasive approach to business was almost the complete opposite of Levin's own measured, almost academic responses and buttoned-down style. Murdoch had lusted after Levin's company for more than two decades. When Murdoch first arrived in the United States in 1973, he had briefly contemplated a hostile bid for Time Inc. In 1983 he had made a run for Warner Communications. In 1989 he had seriously considered joining the battle for Time Warner. In mid-1995 John Malone at TCI had tried to talk Murdoch into making a joint bid for Time Warner. But each time the quarry had escaped, and Murdoch had been left scrambling to catch up. Murdoch had no great regard for Time Warner management, which he derided as monolithic and ineffective. But Levin was neither as innocuous nor as flat-footed as he appeared. "He's easily the most underestimated business executive I've ever known," Richard Parsons said in 1997. "He's like a card player who seems like he doesn't know what he's doing, but at the end of the night has all the chips."[1]

Levin, however, suspected that Murdoch still saw him as a lightweight. These and other reasons saw him brave the rain on October 17 to tell Murdoch in person that he didn't have room to run Fox News on Time Warner's cable systems.

Levin returned to Time Warner that Tuesday evening thinking his problems were over. "Actually, Rupert took it very well," he told Parsons.[2] He described the conversation they'd had as brief and polite. Murdoch had even thanked Levin for his consideration in braving the weather. Taken by surprise, Murdoch probably had responded almost by remote control, with the upper-class manners of his upbringing. Certainly there had been nothing on the surface to indicate that hours later News Corporation and Time Warner would be locked in one of the most spectacular turf wars of the 1990s.

But what was Gerry Levin trying to manage here? What was he *thinking*? He had only to look at Rupert Murdoch's history to know that he was walking into trouble. In reality, choosing from among the "what if" alternatives was simple: Whatever Levin did or said that Tuesday evening, the next day he would still have been facing World War III. The only thing he could have done better was to wear a helmet. Of course, that's easy to say in hindsight.

*   *   *

Any Murdoch war is a product of the battles that have led up to it. The cast of characters in the drama that was about to unfold in New York had come together once before, in the last week of 1983. That was the week when Turner's yacht ran aground in the Sydney-to-Hobart race, and Turner launched his great diatribe against Murdoch; when Murdoch was outraged by the deal that Steve Ross at

Warner Bros. had pulled off with Chris-Craft Industries to lock News Corp out of Warner, and had his New York lawyer, Arthur Siskind at Squadron Ellenoff Plesent & Lehrer, accuse the Warner board of racketeering.

New York's mayor, Rudolph Giuliani, was the other character in the drama that gripped New York in October 1996. And he was already familiar with the News Corp lawyers at Squadron Ellenoff because of an event that also took place in the last week of 1983. As chance would have it, during that week, even as Murdoch's lawyers were reaching for the legal hyperbole with which they would attack Warner Bros., Squadron Ellenoff's other major client was taking a more proactive interest in racketeering.

While News Corp had become Squadron Ellenoff's biggest source of fees in the early 1980s, its second-largest client was a rapidly growing defense contractor in the Bronx called Wedtech. Wedtech's corporate strategy essentially was to attempt to bribe every politician, regulator, or government official who came within range of its pocketbook. On its way to becoming one of the major corporate and political scandals of the 1980s, Wedtech gained $500 million of U.S. Defense Department business by claiming that U.S. minorities—in this case, Puerto Ricans—held the majority of the company's stock. At the time of Wedtech's initial public offering in 1983, it became clear that this was not true. Wedtech instructed its new lawyers, Squadron Ellenoff, to find various ways to change the ownership structure "for a limited period of time"[3] that would satisfy the minorities requirement of its defense contracts. The stock would revert to the original owners several years later.

In November 1983 lawyers in Squadron Ellenoff's corporate section, headed by Arthur Siskind, came up with five separate strategies to change Wedtech's ownership structure, but none of them were acceptable to the government. Wedtech management then decided on a simple sale of their stock to the company's Puerto Rican founder, Tony Mariotta. Mariotta would not pay for the stock until two years later, and it would be held in escrow. The escrow agreement was signed on December 27, as Ted Turner tacked down the Australian coast. Siskind was on vacation out of town. What made this sale contract illegal was a side agreement where Mariotta promised he would never complete the deal, and the Wedtech stock would end up back with the original owners. The side agreement made the whole sale document a sham. The Squadron Ellenoff lawyers testified that they knew nothing of the side agreement and would not have worked for Wedtech if they had known. "Mr. Guariglia [the Wedtech president] asked me whether or not he could have a side agreement with Mr. Mariotta where Mr. Mariotta would agree to default," Siskind later testified. "I told him that he absolutely could not, that it was improper, that this was a proposal to be made, this was the proposal everybody had to live up to."[4]

Rudy Giuliani, who was then the U.S. attorney for southern New York, later brought racketeering charges against Wedtech executives, senior government officials, and politicians, based in part on the side agreement. In court proceedings, Giuliani's office would describe Siskind as an "unindicted co-conspirator" in the racketeering case. According to Siskind, this was merely a tactical move that allowed prosecutors to introduce in court a Squadron Ellenoff memo that otherwise would have had legal privilege.[5] But at one point the SEC advised Squadron Ellenoff that there could be a conflict of interest if the firm continued to represent Wedtech. The issue of whether Squadron Ellenoff should be pursued further was reported to be a lively topic in the U.S. attorney's office, where oversight for the case had been assumed by Giuliani's closest friend and aide, Howard Wilson. Giuliani was no doubt relieved that Wilson ultimately decided not to pursue the lawyers for the city's most political organ, the *New York Post,* at a time when Giuliani was contemplating running for the U.S. Senate, though in the end he decided not to.

"At no time did anybody indicate to me that they were considering having me indicted," Siskind testified in 1988. "I never believed I would be indicted in this matter."[6]

Murdoch had had to sell his beloved *New York Post* in 1988, but he and Anna continued to live in their Manhattan penthouse. It took the 1990 debt crisis to make Murdoch leave town. In January 1991, as the battle to save News Corp raged, Murdoch quietly put the Fifth Avenue penthouse on the market, saying he was shifting his home base to Los Angeles, which was now the headquarters of his U.S. operations. Moving to the West Coast helped calm his bankers' nerves, while the money raised from the sale went to fund the first stage of Murdoch's secret family buyout. But while Anna loved Los Angeles, Murdoch felt marooned on the wrong side of the United States and hankered to return east. By 1996 he had fought two battles to do just that. He had won one and lost one. The important one had been the battle to win back the *Post,* a rollicking affair that Murdoch won with the help of Squadron Ellenoff Plesent & Lehrer.

In the years after Murdoch sold it in 1988, the *New York Post* had fallen on hard times. In June 1992 Manhattan district attorney Robert Morgenthau told New York courts that the Mafia had controlled the paper's circulation since 1987.[7] Morgenthau charged thirteen *Post* employees and members of the Bonanno crime family with extortion, coercion, larceny, bribery, and falsifying business records. The ninety-nine-count indictment said the mob had run loan sharking, extorted money from *Post* employees, and sold guns from the loading docks. Some of those charged were alleged to be part of a heroin ring involving the Genovese and Bonanno families. The *Post*'s owner, real estate developer Peter Kalikow, declared bankruptcy in August 1991, but the *Post* limped along until January 1993, when Kalikow's banker, Bankers Trust, pulled the plug.

"If you've ever had the opportunity to have your brains battered in a boxing match, after a while you get kind of numb to it," Governor Mario Cuomo once said of the *Post*'s political coverage.[8] Murdoch had used the *Post* ruthlessly to promote his favored politicians and to savage their opponents. The long list of victims and beneficiaries goes from former New York mayor Ed Koch, whom the *Post* backed; to one-time vice-presidential candidate Geraldine Ferraro, whom the *Post* crucified; to Giuliani, whom the *Post* ferociously supported; to Hillary Rodham Clinton, whom the *Post* described as "a rejected wife," perpetrator of "a veritable crime wave in the White House," who "couldn't find the Bronx unless she had a chauffeur, and couldn't find Yankee Stadium with a seeing-eye dog."

The *Post* was losing $300,000 a week. As the money dried up, its checks for its paper suppliers began bouncing. *Post* reporters were unable to travel—for example, to cover the Oscars ceremony in Hollywood—because its travel agent had stopped giving credit. Photographers bought their own film and paper; reporters paid for their own pens and made notes on the back of press releases because there was no notepaper. In the final indignity, the *Post*'s Washington bureau had its water cooler repossessed. The head of security reported that security guards ostensibly on shift were moonlighting elsewhere and that the building had become the nighttime haunt of drug dealers and prostitutes. This unique New York institution, which *New York Times* editor A. M. Rosenthal had described as "mean, ugly, violent journalism" under Murdoch and which *Columbia Journalism Review* had called "a force for evil," seemed to have reached the end of the line.

Sunday, January 24, 1993, was the day when Peter Kalikow was to announce the paper's final demise. Instead, New York was shocked to learn that in the previous twenty-four hours Kalikow had found someone brave enough, wealthy enough, and foolish enough to take over the *Post* and its problems. This act of civic nobility made the new owner, Steve Hoffenberg, nothing less than a genuine American hero. The man was a monument.

At least that was the prevailing sentiment for the first five minutes after the announcement. Unfortunately it soon became apparent that the only thing monumental about Steve Hoffenberg would be his eventual prison sentence. Hoffenberg was a major-league hustler. Within two weeks, the SEC had launched a civil suit against him for fraud in the biggest Ponzi scheme in U.S. history.

In 1986 Hoffenberg had set up a debt-collection agency that he used as a front to raise money from investors. Investors thought he was paying them handsome returns, but he was merely paying some of their original investment back to them; by calling it profit, he was able to raise even more funds.

By the time Hoffenberg made his January 1993 offer to save the *Post,* he had raised another $400 million from unsuspecting investors. Two weeks later the SEC moved to freeze his assets.

The situation went from bad to worse at the *Post,* because with his funds frozen by the SEC, Hoffenberg brought in a friend as a silent partner. Abe Hirschfeld, an eccentric parking lot developer who liked to call himself Honest Abe, would be convicted of conspiring to murder a business partner in August 2000. "What the hell do I know about publishing? I can't write and I can't type," Hirschfeld said at the time with a shrug.[9] When Hoffenberg's new editor, Pete Hamill, refused to print poetry written by Hirschfeld's wife, Hirschfeld fired Hamill. In scenes that perhaps could take place only in New York, the *Post* staff declared open war. When Hirschfeld held a press conference the *Post* staff interrupted with shouts of "Animal!" and "Liar!" and called him racist and mentally incompetent. Hamill unilaterally rehired himself and published an issue with the banner headline, "Who Is This Nut?" next to a cartoon of the new owner in a straitjacket. It then devoted twenty-four pages to excoriating the character, business history, and curious personal habits of Hirschfeld, beginning with the page-one headline: "*Post* Staff to Abe Hirschfeld—GET LOST."

The *Post* filed for bankruptcy protection on March 15. Hirschfeld now had cold feet over the whole deal. The situation was out of control. No one would seriously consider buying the paper now. Or rather, almost no one. On March 25 Hirschfeld told the *Post's* bankruptcy judge that he would not be putting in any more money to keep the paper running over the weekend. The same day Hoffenberg's lawyers at Squadron Ellenoff put Towers Financial Corporation into chapter 11 bankruptcy—a move that froze the *Post's* accounts receivable, the paper's last hope of raising money. And then—marvelously—a new bidder appeared. He was another Squadron Ellenoff client.

"I am not here as some fairy godmother to pour more money into the paper," Rupert Murdoch assured all and sundry in his downbeat gravelly voice, to universal acclaim. *Post* staff cheered when he visited the newsroom on Monday,

March 29, and appointed Ken Chandler as the new editor (he would later be promoted to publisher). "I am assuming that Mr. Chandler will produce such a brilliant newspaper that the circulation will rise, but I don't expect or hold out any promise of sudden magic," Murdoch said breezily.[10]

New York governor Mario Cuomo and Senator Alfonse D'Amato had been working the phones on both sides of politics to help Murdoch win a permanent waiver from the FCC's cross-media rules to allow him to buy the *Post* and keep WNYW, his New York television station. Cuomo did it with gritted teeth. It took six months of grueling negotiations and brinkmanship. And then it was finished. The *Post* was won. Murdoch was back in the Big Apple. This was his town. Arthur Siskind was "the best lawyer in New York," he declared jubilantly.

That was the battle that Murdoch won. The fight he staged a year later to put a cable channel into New York was the one he lost.

*   *   *

Under the "must carry" provisions of the federal Cable Act, cable television companies are obliged to carry all free-to-air stations on their nets in addition to their own programming. In 1992 the government increased the amount of compensation that the free-to-air stations could charge the cable companies for running their programs. Rather than more money, the big networks instead asked for access for their own cable channels. NBC used this access to launch a low-budget news-oriented channel called America's Talking. In 1994 Fox launched its own light-entertainment cable channel, called f/X. The channel featured a grab bag of shows, from the obligatory breakfast program to a show about pets. "It's the best lineup that $100 million and no brains could buy," scoffed Roger Ailes, the acerbic executive who ran NBC's two cable channels, CNBC, and America's Talking.[11]

Fox launched f/X with 18 million subscribers—more than half of them from John Malone's TCI, who led the way by agreeing to pay an astonishing twenty-five cents a month to f/X for every subscriber. Fox was able to strong-arm other cable companies to take the channel on the same terms, though resentful cablers suspected that it was another one of those special deals that Murdoch and Malone kept hatching and that Malone would be compensated by Murdoch for his trouble with another deal somewhere else in the world.

The major holdout from f/X was the second-largest cable company, Time Warner, which controlled the country's most important cable market, New York. Time Warner's cable execs complained about the quality of the programming and resolutely refused to carry the channel, even when the *New York Post* ran a campaign encouraging its readers to write in to Time Warner to complain. So while f/X was shown around the country, the 1.4 million cable subscribers in New York City never saw it. Of those 1.4 million subscribers, the only really important ones were the advertising executives on Madison Avenue. They were the people who decided whether to put advertising on a cable channel, and it was hard to convince them to put money into something that they had never seen. Round two in the battle for New York had been lost.

*   *   *

In January 1996 Rupert Murdoch announced that in October he would launch Fox News, a twenty-four-hour channel that would stand in opposition to what Murdoch saw as CNN's "left-wing bias." Ted Turner had seen threats to CNN amount to nothing and said, "I'm looking forward to squishing Rupert like a bug."

The old chemistry was still sparking between the two men. "He's ten years older than me, and if the actuarial tables are right, he'll be dead ten years before me, and I'll have ten years of peace and quiet after he's gone," Turner had told the *Financial Times* in 1993.[12] Murdoch replied by sending him a note, "Dear Ted, Let's have lunch before it's too late. Rupert."

"I can't hate him," said Turner when he recounted the story. "I'd like to, but I can't. It's really good to have good, tough competitors. . . . I know he'd like to have CNN, so I have to worry that he'd like to eat me."[13] Relations between the two men had thawed so much that in April 1994 Murdoch gave the keynote speech at a lunch honoring Turner at the Center for Communications in New York Plaza.[14] But the truce didn't last long.

Murdoch told a Washington press conference in February 1996 that Ted Turner had been "particularly energetic" in describing what Murdoch was all about: "I'm reminded of something Disraeli once said to a colleague in Parliament: 'Honorable sir, it's true that I am a low, mean snake. But you, sir, could walk beneath me wearing a top hat.' "[15]

News had become one of the main drivers of television programming, ranking with sports, movies, music, and children's programming as one of the basic building blocks for Disney, Time Warner, Viacom, and News Corp as they worked to turn their program content into worldwide brands. The 1990s had seen a major change in the economics of the media industry. Hollywood now made more than half its movie earnings from international sales. The satellite and cable pay-television platforms that were being set up around the world promised in the same way to offer big earnings for television content producers. It all came down to distribution—to finding a way to make sure the world could watch your pro-grams. News Corp was well on the way to controlling a worldwide distribution sys-tem for its programming, through its satellite and cable operations like BSkyB in Britain, Star TV in Asia, Foxtel in Australia, and Sky Latin in South America. Yet ironically the economics of program production meant that the only way to create a worldwide brand was to succeed first in the huge U.S. market. It was the only way to achieve economies of scale. So the more Murdoch expanded around the world, the more he needed to make it in the United States. And here distribution was much more of a problem.

Time Warner's New York cable system carried seventy-seven channels, of which nine were set aside for the city's use as public, educational, and government channels (known as PEG channels). Another eleven channels were set aside for leased access, and a further fifteen carried the local free-to-air television stations, as required under the "must carry" provisions of the Cable Act. These set-asides left Time Warner with forty-two channels at its discretion. By the time it had allo-cated channels for basic programming, premium packages, and pay-per-view, the network was full. Introducing a new channel, no matter how good, meant bump-ing off an existing channel, a move that would almost certainly annoy a group of its subscribers. This cablers were reluctant to do.

NBC solved the distribution problem by running its own news channel, MSNBC, on its existing America's Talking cable channel. This decision guaran-teed that MSNBC had 21 million subscribers when it launched on July 16, 1996. Roger Ailes, the disgruntled former head of America's Talking and former cam-paign adviser to Ronald Reagan and Rudy Giuliani, quit NBC. Murdoch promptly hired him to run Fox News. Ailes's Republican credentials made him the perfect choice for the conservative political approach that Murdoch favored.

Murdoch could have taken the NBC route. He could simply have converted his f/X channel into Fox News. But unlike America's Talking, f/X didn't run in New York and in any case Murdoch had far more ambitious plans. He had committed f/X to his burgeoning sports alliance with John Malone to run Fox Sports. Instead, for the Fox News launch Murdoch would use one of his most daring stratagems yet. "Money is something you can use to trade to get distribution," said Ailes. "Everybody knows it. Anybody who has the nerve can play that game. This is capi-talism and one of the things that made this country great."[16] To this point the most that any new channel had offered cable companies for carriage was Viacom's offer to pay a $1.20 up-front fee per subscriber to cable companies that carried its reruns channel, TV Land. In April at the National Cable Convention in Los

Angeles, Fox changed the cable television landscape by telling cable executives it was prepared to pay them an incredible $11 per subscriber to run Fox News. To be viable, Murdoch had said that Fox News needed at least 25 million subscribers. At $11 each, that meant he was prepared to fork out $275 million just to get Fox News on the channel selector.

Murdoch's offer shocked the industry and badly rattled his rivals at ABC and NBC. In June he announced a deal with John Malone. At the launch in October, TCI would carry Fox News to 10 million of its 14 million subscribers. According to several reports, Malone had forced Murdoch nearly to double his price. Murdoch would pay Malone $200 million, or $20 a subscriber, and Malone would take 20 percent of Fox News.[17]

This was not quite the act of pure philanthropy on Murdoch's part that it appeared—it was a multiyear contract with sliding charges that eventually would see Fox get its money back. But at the latest level, Murdoch was prepared to shell out half a billion dollars just to buy a news voice. This was quite apart from the costs of setting up a worldwide news operation, with projected operating losses of $366 million before breaking even in the seventh year.

To get to critical mass, though, Murdoch needed Time Warner to carry his signal for its 11 million subscribers. In particular he needed New York. And so in July at Sun Valley he had sat down with Gerry Levin to reach an understanding. Their rapport did not go unnoticed. On Tuesday, July 15, as News Corp lawyers were feverishly putting the New World Communications deal together with Ron Perelman's lawyers in Los Angeles, NBC chief executive Robert Wright oversaw the launch of MSNBC. He told reporters at the press conference that Levin and Murdoch were about to announce a big distribution deal. This was a major problem for MSNBC because while Time Warner had allowed MSNBC to launch on America's Talking, it had warned that it believed the change was a breach of the original programming agreement and that it had the right to pull the channel at any time. If Time Warner did a deal with Fox News, MSNBC would be the easiest channel to dump.

In this already-tangled scene, Time Warner's lobbyists and lawyers negotiated an arrangement with the FTC that was either a masterstroke or another example of a big corporation shooting itself in the foot. The new FTC chairman, Robert Pitofsky, was a Georgetown law school professor with a specialist interest in media concentration. He didn't like the Time Warner-TBS merger, but the politics of the FTC board meant there was not a lot that he could do to stop it. What he settled for was a requirement that Time Warner agree to run another twenty-four-hour news channel to rival CNN, to half of its 11 million subscribers. The requirement was so specific that only Fox News and MSNBC could satisfy this condition. For Time Warner, the appeal of this arrangement was that they were giving Pitofksy something that they were going to do anyway. In fact, Time Warner intended to run both new channels. Joe Collins, the then chairman of Time Warner Cable, wanted the $125 million that Murdoch was prepared to pay for running Fox News, and he also wanted to avoid the huge legal fight that would ensue if he dropped MSNBC.

Levin favored running both news channels in addition to CNN. It was left to Ted Turner, "the madman from Atlanta," to point out just how crazy it was to assist CNN's rivals, when Levin phoned him at the end of August. Because of the FTC's demand, Time Warner was now stuck with taking one of the news channels. But why take two channels? "Ted was railing at him," a Turner executive said later. "He's basically saying, 'It's crazy, you don't want to carry both. You're not taking the long-term view.' He's not swearing, but he can't help himself. 'It's going to hurt the long-term value of CNN.' Plus it would delay the rollout of Turner Classic Movies and delay the Cartoon Network. All while you shoot CNN in the figurative dick. Gerry says, 'Gee, Ted, I don't agree with you.' "[18]

It was part of a much longer litany of complaints that Turner went through with Levin and Richard Parsons at his ranch in Montana over the Labor Day weekend. Levin was caught. When Levin sold the merger to Turner, he had promised him an active role running the group, but in the year since then, he had gradually eased him out of the picture, encouraging him to stay on his ranch in Montana and come in to the office only once or twice a month. Levin already had an unhappy Edgar Bronfman Jr. on his register, controlling 9 percent of Time Warner after the merger. John Malone would hold 10 percent, though for antitrust reasons he was not allowed to vote the stock. Now Ted Turner, who with 11 percent would be the largest stockholder, was steamed at him.

Levin ended up conceding on almost every point Turner raised. CNN would be pulled back from the print news division and run with the cable group. The cable channels would be pulled back from the control of Terry Simel and Robert Daley at Warner Bros. and Turner himself would oversee them. Even the Goodwill Games, Ted Turner's money-losing sporting event, would be given a new lease on life and $25 million promotion. And Fox News? Well, Time Warner has since argued fiercely that the decision to dump Fox News had nothing to do with Turner. In the broader context, this assurance is unconvincing. In any case, on

September 17, after appointing Turner head of cable, Levin went for his little walk in the rain.

*   *   *

Levin's rebuff stunned Murdoch and the News Corp executives. "They were within a half-hour of signing a contract with us, which Mr. Levin assured me was totally on track," said Murdoch. "Then they backed away and said they would rather wait until FTC approval came through."[19]

The realization sank in slowly for Murdoch and the News Corp executives that, despite already spending $300 million and committing to investing several hundred million dollars more, Fox News would launch in twenty days' time with a woeful 11 million subscribers. This was not a viable operation. The Fox News budget projections had predicted the operation would rack up $366 million in losses on top of the start-up costs before breaking even after six years in 2003— but those numbers had assumed Time Warner would be carrying it.[20]

Levin didn't know it, but he had pressed all of Rupert Murdoch's buttons. Murdoch had been outmaneuvered, he had been excluded, and he had been publicly humiliated. He rose up in a cold fury the next day to call Levin back. "What the hell happened?" Levin asked Fred Dressler, head of programming at Time Warner Cable, who had had a similar angry call from News Corp co-chief operating officer Chase Carey. "I came back and everything was fine. Then Rupert called and he went crazy on me."[21] As news of the setback broke, the Fox execs hit the phones to work the press. Time Warner's move was "an enormous breach of faith and a personal affront" for Murdoch, Ailes told journalists.[22] "We were dealt with in a duplicitous manner, and essentially lied to," said Carey. "I don't know how Mr. Levin is going to conduct himself in doing business with people when that is the manner he deals with people."

"We are not going to dignify those vituperative comments with a response," Time Warner spokesman Ed Adler responded.[23]

"We have a contract and we expect them to live up to it," said Murdoch. "If we're not carried by Time Warner here, Time Warner's services will not be welcome on our distribution. We're not signing any contracts to carry them in Britain."[24]

While Murdoch's and his executives' initial response was to attack Gerry Levin, it didn't take long for Murdoch and News Corp executives to detect other fingerprints on the Time Warner knife. It was Ted Turner who had humiliated

Murdoch, they believed, and he had done it in front of an industry audience. Cable executives were on their way to New York for Hell Week, a title that refers more to what cable executives raise than to what they endure. Hell Week was an annual event, a series of industry meetings that would climax in the annual Walter Kaitz dinner on September 25, where Turner's triumphant accession to the head of Time Warner's cable operations and Murdoch's discomfiture over Fox News would be plain in front of nineteen hundred industry figures.

On September 18 Murdoch sat down with Arthur Siskind, Chase Carey, and Roger Ailes to discuss options. The basic question was how wide they were prepared to make this conflict. First, Murdoch could sue Time Warner. But the legal remedies were limited—because despite News Corp's protestations, at the end of the day there had been no contract, only Time Warner's assurance. Judge Jack Weinstein would later conclude in district court, "These were not Adam- and Eve-like innocents slipping naked into the cable television and broadcast jungle to negotiate with each other and the serpent. They were hard-bitten executives steeled in such hagglings. . . . The cajolery, as well as the blandishments, honeyed phrases and assurances that are to be expected in major negotiations of this sort in the media-entertainment field did not constitute fraud."[25]

Siskind ticked off Murdoch's other options for retaliation. News Corp could make trouble for Time Warner at the FTC and challenge the TBS merger on antitrust grounds. "It is quite possible that new evidence could come forward of [Time Warner's] practices and how they have been allocating channels," Murdoch told journalists archly later that week. "There are many people trying to start channels who might have something to say about not being carried by a major cable operator like Time Warner. We are considering our position on that."[26]

Alternatively Murdoch could dump Time Warner's programming in Europe and where possible the United States as well—though the danger was that Time Warner would retaliate and the whole conflict would escalate. "We don't want to burn too many bridges," cautioned Siskind.

In the end News Corp did what superpowers usually do: It decided to fight its battle by proxy. It would call in political favors and twist arms all across town to ensure that local politicians took up arms on its behalf against Time Warner. The first step Ailes proposed was to tap Murdoch's links to the mayor of New York, Rudy Giuliani. In June Giuliani had given News Corp a tax break in return for a commitment to create 1,475 new jobs in New York, 513 of which would come from Fox News. Giuliani would show remarkable tenacity defending those 513 Fox News jobs. The mayor held a very powerful lever. The Time Warner–

TBS merger meant that the city needed to renew Time Warner's cable franchise over Manhattan. This usually straightforward process was due to take place on October 9, after a public hearing on October 7. But the mayor could decide the process was not quite so straightforward. If Time Warner didn't come to Murdoch's party, the city could refuse to renew the franchise.

Ailes put the call in to Giuliani. On Friday, September 20, Giuliani called deputy mayor Fran Reiter to say that Fox had run into a problem with Time Warner that he wanted her to investigate. The situation was "very serious," he said. On Thursday, September 26, as the Fox press war gathered steam, Reiter and the city's counsel, Paul Crotty, met Fox lawyers, who described the problem as an antitrust issue. On Friday, at Crotty's suggestion, Siskind spelled this out in a letter to Reiter, stressing how important the New York market was to Fox News. He urged Reiter to refuse to consent both to the Time Warner–TBS merger and to the renewal of Time Warner's cable franchise agreement in New York.[27]

On Wednesday, September 25, Giuliani and New York governor George Pataki had attended a Time Warner press conference where Levin and Turner announced that the Goodwill Games would be held in New York in July 1998. Time Warner already employed eleven thousand people in New York. The financial fillip the games would give the city should have earned Levin brownie points with Giuliani and Pataki and made him their favorite employer. But Giuliani and Pataki were listening to other voices.

The *New York Post* was its usual strident self in its coverage. Besides running cartoon caricatures of Levin next to scathing articles about the Time Warner decision, it even dropped the CNN program guide briefly—like Time Warner Cable, the *Post* said it was having capacity problems. The personal attacks got to Turner. On September 26, after a lunch with journalists and executives to discuss the Time Warner merger, Turner launched into a virulent attack on Murdoch and his yellow journalism. Time Warner, he said, "doesn't tell its journalists what to write." He went on to compare Murdoch to Adolf Hitler—"Talking to Murdoch is like confronting the late Führer"—and said Murdoch wanted to rule the world. Time Warner, by contrast, just wanted to make money.

"This kind of venal rhetoric has no place in a civilized society," Siskind replied on Friday. "Mr. Turner's statement, which is one more expression of his personal animosity toward Mr. Murdoch, must be viewed as deeply offensive not only to Mr. Murdoch and his associates . . . but to all people of good will."[28]

The Anti-Defamation League of B'nai B'rith complained, and Turner was forced to apologize to victims of Nazism. The *Post*'s response was more robust. It suggested Turner had not been taking his medication and ran a banner headline, "Is Ted Nuts? You Decide." (In late October, when Jane Fonda linked the mayor's support for Fox News to Murdoch's political support for Giuliani and to Donna Hanover Giuliani's on-air job at Murdoch's Channel 5, the *Post* ran a huge picture of Fonda visiting Hanoi in 1972 and dismissed her as "just another scatty-brained Hollywood nude-nik.")

"This is better than the Tyson fight," said John Malone. "This is great comedy to me. Ted Turner hasn't felt so young and energetic in years. He loves a good fight. I would waste no tears on either of these guys."[29]

Believing the whole issue was about Time Warner not having enough room on its channels to run Fox News, Fran Reiter tried to come up with a solution. On Sunday evening she phoned Time Warner's Derek Johnson to say she was "very concerned" about the Fox News situation and that the city might be able to help Time Warner by opening up one of the nine PEG channels set aside for the city's use under the franchise agreement with Time Warner. She asked for a meeting with Gerry Levin or Richard Parsons.

Neither Parsons nor Levin made it to the meeting Reiter organized on Tuesday. Instead they sent Dick Aurelio, the head of Manhattan Cable, to talk to the deputy mayor. The politics of the meeting were going to be a problem. Parsons, besides his history as a Republican aide to Nelson Rockefeller, was a former law partner of Giuliani's and one of the mayor's few high-profile African-American backers. Aurelio, by contrast, was a prominent Democrat. Of the ten people who crowded into Reiter's office, half were lawyers. On Time Warner's side, Aurelio was flanked by Robert Jacobs, general counsel for Time Warner's New York City cable group, and Alan Arffa, Time Warner's outside counsel. On the city's side were: Bruce Regal, assistant corporation counsel; Norman Sinel of Arnold & Porter as outside counsel; and Elaine Reiss, general counsel for the city's Department of Information, Technology, and Communication, which oversaw cable arrangements.

Reiter proposed that Time Warner run Fox News on one of its commercial channels and move one of its "educational" programs onto one of the city's PEG channels. Regal said the parties could "paper over the deal"[30] to make it look like there was no quid pro quo. Time Warner's response was that what the city was proposing was unacceptable and illegal. Its outside counsel, Alan Arffa, began reading provisions of the Cable Act that prohibited the city from dictating the programming that a cable operator should carry. Norman Sinel interrupted him. "You don't have to lecture us on the First Amendment and the law, we know what the law says. The mayor's office is fully aware of the risks involved here. We're willing to take those risks. The question is, is Time Warner willing to take those risks?"[31]

The risk, as Judge Denise Cote would point out a month later, was that the city's proposal might break the Cable Act. The meeting ended quickly, neither side conceding. That night Murdoch hosted a launch party for Fox News in a marquee outside the News Corp offices on Forty-eighth Street that drew an A-list of luminaries including Walter Cronkite, Connie Chung, Barbara Walters, Oscar de la Renta, Governor George Pataki and Senator Al D'Amato. In front of the glittering crowd Giuliani and Pataki officially welcomed Murdoch and Ailes and their new cable operation, which the mayor said was of "incalculable value to the people of the city." (Next morning both Pataki and D'Amato would call Levin to complain about Time Warner's decision to exclude Fox News.) Arthur Siskind made a beeline for Dennis Vacco, the state attorney general, as Murdoch escorted Fran Reiter through the crowd.

Earlier that evening Parsons had called Reiter to say that while he believed the city's actions on behalf of Fox were inappropriate, he hoped Time Warner could avoid a head-on collision with the city. Reiter said the meeting had been "very unpleasant and unnecessary,"[32] because she recognized Time Warner's right not to carry Fox News. But she pushed for Levin to call Murdoch and arrange a meeting. She said she was going to write a letter the next day with a new suggestion, under which the city would seek a waiver from Time Warner to run Fox News directly on one of the City's PEG channels. Parsons said any negotiations would have to wait until after the Time Warner–TBS merger was finalized nine days later, on October 10. Reiter replied that Fox News planned to raise the issue at the public hearing that was to be held the following Monday into whether the city would reaffirm the cable franchise after the merger. She said that "that would be a problem for Time Warner." In addition, the cable franchises were up for their regular renewal in 1998 and Time Warner "would not want the Fox News Channel to cloud the renewal decision."

The pressure on Time Warner was unrelenting, a continuing effort "by fair means or foul," Judge Denise Cote later found, to force Time Warner to carry Fox News. The strategy, it would later be claimed in court, was "to beat Time Warner over the head to force Time Warner to carry Fox News and to retaliate for refusing to do so . . . and to keep beating Time Warner until Time Warner carried Fox News."[33]

On Wednesday Reiter sent Time Warner the letter she had promised. On Thursday Giuliani called a conference with Reiter and the city's lawyers at Gracie

Mansion to review the position. When news of the latest exchange leaked to the press, an angry Gerry Levin ordered his lawyers to send back a terse rejection of Reiter's latest proposal. It was probably on that day, Judge Cote later found, that a decision was made "at the deputy mayor level or higher" that, as Siskind had urged, the city would not re-endorse the Time Warner cable franchise after the merger with TBS unless Time Warner put Fox News on the system.

That night Sinel phoned Arffa and warned that the city might raise antitrust objections to the Time Warner merger. The next day the city wrote again to Parsons urging him to reconsider its position, on the grounds of Time Warner's "good corporate citizenship."

At six A.M. on Monday, October 7, Fox News went on the air with 18 million subscribers, thanks to a string of hastily-cobbled-together distribution agreements with smaller cable companies. That morning, in rowdy scenes, Fox News lawyers launched a broadside against Time Warner at the public hearing over the cable franchise. Two days later the mayor put any decision on the franchise on ice, leaving Time Warner out in the cold. The next day the first subpoenas hit Time Warner. Attorney General Dennis Vacco's office announced an antitrust investigation into Time Warner's cable programming decisions. The same day Fox News sued Time Warner, TBS, and Ted Turner to stop the merger. The suit was "utter foolishness," a Time Warner spokesman said. Ted Turner called the suit "a frivolous piece of junk."[34]

City Hall and Time Warner were now so close to all-out war that there seemed no way to pull back. On Wednesday, October 9, Time Warner received another letter from the city, this one saying that even if Time Warner refused its consent, it planned to run Fox News and the Bloomberg business news channel on its PEG channels anyway. The city included Bloomberg in the scheme to demonstrate that it was not merely favoring Fox News. On October 10 the Time Warner–TBS merger was finally consummated. At 10:48 P.M. that evening, the City began transmitting Bloomberg on one of its PEG channels. It planned to begin running Fox News the next day.

But an hour later, just before midnight, an attorney dropped Time Warner's lawsuit against the city through the mail slot of the federal court in Foley Square. The dispute was about "very fundamental issues regarding freedom of the press and the rights of the people," Richard Parsons said. "The city has basically gone into the news business."[35]

The next morning Judge Cote granted Time Warner a temporary injunction blocking the city from running Fox News or Bloomberg. She ordered both sides to return to court two weeks later. In her subsequent judgment on November 6 she found that there was "compelling evidence" that the city had abused its power and had acted to coerce and to punish Time Warner over its refusal to carry Fox News. "The city's purpose in acting to compel Time Warner to give it one of its commercial stations was to reward a friend and to further a particular viewpoint," she said. Fox News "is not persuasive in its claim that its dealings with the city do not constitute corruption," Judge Jack Weinstein found on April 10, 1997, in the Fox case against Time Warner.

New York was left to wonder at the events that had left Mayor Giuliani, the former mob-busting U.S. attorney, fighting Rupert Murdoch's battle for him with the biggest media group in the world. Why had he been so involved? How was it that so much of the script here seemed to have been written by Arthur Siskind, a man who in the mid-1980s had been under scrutiny by Giuliani's office, as U.S. attorney for New York, in the Wedtech scandal?

"I don't think there was ever any serious consideration given to bringing charges against myself or against Squadron Ellenoff," Siskind said in November 1996. "I spoke to Giuliani at a lunch today and we had a little laugh that anybody could be bringing up that old matter." He was similarly dismissive of any suggestion that Giuliani had favored News Corp in the latest tussle: "Nobody buys Rudy Giuliani."[36]

On Friday, October 18, Ted Turner gave a colorful deposition to the city's lawyers in which he again described Murdoch as Hitler. The legal battle would grind on, but this bout had reached its endgame. Other parts of the News Corp empire required attention. On October 15 Murdoch was in Australia for the News Corp annual meeting, where in the course of an upbeat profit forecast he mentioned that News Corp was a couple of weeks away from floating off part of its Israeli technology and encryption arm. This breezy bit of news generally went down well with the financial press. In fact, the announcement turned out to be a really, really bad idea. It awoke a nightmare from News Corp's past named Michael Clinger.

WIRED

London, March 31, 1995

B Y THE MID-1990s, one of the biggest side effects of the information revolution was that the business of keeping secrets—running a commercial encryption system—was now worth a lot of money. News Datacom and its related
company, News Digital Systems, were valued at close to $1 billion. News Data-
com had become Murdoch's technological edge into the twenty-first century, developing the technology, the set-top boxes to decode his television signals, and the
encryption systems to control the next generation of digital broadcasting. It was
the key to everything Murdoch was planning. With luck it could lock Murdoch
into the new digital environment and lock his rivals out. To safeguard that future,
in 1995 Murdoch launched an extraordinary international manhunt.

The great pursuit began as a result of a meeting in a room at the Four Seasons
Hotel in London. Peter Stehrenberger, the secretary of News International, and
Greg Clark, the president of Murdoch's high-tech arm, News Technology Group,
had shown up for an appointment that even at the time must have seemed peculiar. They were meeting an Israeli lawyer named Abraham Nantel, who had written to Stehrenberger to request the meeting. He wanted to talk about some shady
dealings involving News Datacom. Nantel acted for an Israeli inventor named
Ben Zion Kornizky. Nantel stressed that the decision to approach News Corporation had been his own, not his client's. Nantel, it seemed, had flown from Tel Aviv
to London to see Stehrenberger and Clark on his own initiative. Having come that
far, he had decided that he couldn't make it a bit further to the News International
offices at Wapping. Even at this stage, the affair seems to have been governed by
an obsession with secrecy.[1]

The meeting at the Four Seasons on March 31, 1995, lasted an hour and a
quarter, during which Nantel said that his client, Kornizky, had been "entrapped"

in a business relationship with a ghost from News Corp's past named Michael Clinger, who had taken control of a start-up company that was developing one of Kornizky's inventions. Kornizky was distressed and wanted revenge—which seemed pretty much the reaction of almost anyone who had ever done business with Clinger.

Peter Stehrenberger had been involved with News Datacom from 1989. He was aware of Clinger's wretched history but believed that after the buyout in 1992 Clinger had had no further connection with News Datacom. Nantel told Stehrenberger and Clark that this wasn't true. Through a series of dummy companies in the Channel Islands and other tax havens, Clinger still controlled the assembly of every smartcard that News Datacom produced. He was able to do so because, before News Datacom could program its smartcards for pay-television operators like BSkyB, it paid an outside firm to physically put the smartcards together. News Corp had never realized that Phoenix Micro, the Jersey company that did this work, was controlled by Clinger, who took 60 percent of the profits. News Datacom had tried for years to find another supplier, without success. According to Nantel, Clinger had boasted that, with the help of Israeli accomplices still working for News Datacom, he was inflating the price that News Datacom was paying for the assembled smartcards. In addition, his accomplices were able to ensure that no other manufacturer passed the testing needed to qualify as an alternative source of supply of smartcards for News Datacom. When Tom Price, the London executive whom Gus Fischer had installed because he was "as honest as the day is long," tried a little too hard to find another supplier, Clinger was able to engineer his replacement. The payoff from all this was that, with News Datacom expanding its range of customers beyond BSkyB in Britiain, to DirecTV in the United States, and to other pay-television operators around the world, Clinger could virtually name his own price for supplying the cards. It was a classic scam.[2]

The only evidence that Nantel offered to support these claims was stories that Kornizky had heard and conversations he had had with Clinger. The evidence was circumstantial. But alarm bells were ringing for Stehrenberger and Clark. Greg Clark wrote in his notes on the meeting, "Peter [Stehrenberger] is aware that Gus Fischer recently had a meeting with Leo Krieger [a former News Datacom accountant] when Leo offered information useful to News and damaging to Clinger."[3] The problem was that Fischer, News Corp's former chief operating officer, was no longer on the team. He had resigned two weeks earlier, part of the management exodus that claimed all the News International executive directors except Stehrenberger in an eighteen-month period. Details of Fischer's meeting with Krieger would emerge three years later, when a trainee with one of the legal firms acting for News Corp pressed the wrong button on a fax machine.[4]

Leo Krieger had been Michael Clinger's business partner and closest friend until the two had had a spectacular falling-out over Clinger's wife, Niva Von Weisl. Clinger had walked out on Von Weisl while she was pregnant with their third child and had moved in with a new girlfriend, Daphna Koszniak. Subsequently Krieger developed a relationship with Von Weisl. This enraged Clinger, who began harassing the couple. Clinger fought out a bitter divorce with his wife and married Koszniak. But he continued to harass Krieger and his ex-wife. Krieger responded by blowing the whistle on his former partner. He met with Fischer and told him that Clinger was stealing News Datacom blind, and for $1 million cash he was prepared to supply tapes of bugged telephone conversations to prove it.

Fischer's sudden exit from News put Krieger's claims on hold. It was the Nantel meeting several weeks later that stirred Stehrenberger and Arthur Siskind into action. They renewed contact with Krieger, where their first move was to beat down his price for information. After a little haggling they agreed to pay him $312,500 for his help in the investigation, plus a success fee based on a share of any funds retrieved. An affidavit by Siskind underlined the fevered emotions underlying the case. Siskind told the High Court that part of the reason that News Corp was paying Krieger was "to enable him to take steps to protect himself and Mr. Clinger's former wife, which protection Mr. Krieger believes to be necessary as a result of his co-operation with [News]."[5]

Despite this arrangement with Krieger, Siskind's main hope of proving Clinger's fraudulent behavior lay with Argen Limited, the private investigation firm he had hired to investigate the claims against Clinger. In three decades Argen had carved out a reputation as one of Britain's largest and most discreet private investigation firms, operating in five countries. Financial investigations at Argen were the province of Jonathon Edwards, who had a background as a lawyer, accountant, and merchant banker.

Argen found that Michael Clinger's tracks led deep into the tax haven archipelago. It tracked money flows through the Netherland Antilles, the British Virgin Islands, the Channel Islands, Bermuda, Liberia, and Panama. They obtained confidential bank documents, bank transfer details, telephone records, and restricted court documents, to build up a remarkably detailed picture of where Michael Clinger went, whom he met, and what he said. "We know everything about him," Siskind boasted in 1997. News Corp was able to find out the details of

Clinger's marriage settlement (which was locked in an Israeli court safe) and even the $250,000 Swiss glass staircase he had installed in his $1.5 million home in Jerusalem.[6]

The investigation gave widespread support to Krieger's conspiracy allegations. In February 1996 News Datacom and News International sued Clinger in the High Court in London for £19 million in damages from fraudulent profits. News Corp claimed that Clinger had overcharged News Datacom at least £1 apiece on more than 19 million assembled smartcards. But by 1997 Siskind would be counting the cost of the international manhunt. Legal costs in the eventual trial were estimated at £2 million by a News Corp lawyer, but the real cost of the inquiry was the light that it shone on the secret side of the News Corp empire. For a brief time it put the News Corp archipelago into the spotlight. "There is a message to be sent here," Siskind said when queried about the extent of the investigation. "Despite the economics of the return, we feel very strongly about people who seek to defraud the company. . . . We will not allow ourselves to be extorted by anybody."[7]

In late 1996 journalists were expressing concern about how News Corp had acquired its information on Clinger. Siskind, who oversaw the investigation, had developed a prickly relationship with media covering the case, in particular *Financial Times* journalist William Lewis in London. According to Clay Harris, head of the *Financial Times* investigations unit, one testy exchange between Lewis and Siskind had become very personal. Siskind made a point of showing how much he knew about Lewis's private life. Siskind was convinced he knew the source for a story that Lewis was working on about tax fraud and News Datacom. In conversations with other journalists, Siskind could even quote the dates he said that Lewis had been talking to the man. But Siskind went further with Lewis, to discuss Lewis's recent marriage, where his wife worked, and her job prospects. The inference was: *We know all about you.*[8] Harris's account of that conversation was chilling. Relations between journalists and the people they write about are often heated. But an exchange that extends to family members, made by an executive in one of the world's most powerful media organizations, is something more than sparring. It sounds like a threat.

When questioned in November 1996 about how he had learned details of the personal life of a journalist, and whether News Corp or its agents had had *Financial Times* journalists under surveillance, Siskind and News Corp lawyer Eugenie Gavenchak said that any personal information about Lewis and his family came purely from News Corp's surveillance of Clinger. "We have not engaged in any illegal act. . . . Our instructions [to our agents] are not to engage in any illegal acts," Siskind said.[9]

Clinger suspected he was being bugged. Wiretapping accusations, of course, are notoriously easy to make but difficult to prove, particularly against a media organization whose reporters have routinely assumed false identities and taped private conversations—for example, with Prince Edward's wife, Sophy Rhys-Davies. Clearly the *Financial Times* was not concerned about any suggestion that its journalists had been under surveillance. In late 1996 the *Financial Times* named Rupert Murdoch as Businessman of the Year, with a glowing profile by its media writer, Raymond Snoddy. After Snoddy went to work for Murdoch at the *Times* in London, the *Financial Times* achieved most-favored-nation status with News Corp, with the best access to News Corp's senior executives.

But the emotional temperature in the News Datacom case was running high. In a separate action Bruce Hundertmark had sued Clinger in Israel. He said he was entitled to half of the £5 million Clinger had received from the News Datacom buyout in 1992. A lawyer involved in the case had attempted to commit suicide. Hundertmark was anxious about his personal safety. In late 1995 he had been attacked by two men with knives outside a hotel in Djakarta. Several months later someone had caused $100,000 of damage to his house in Australia. There was nothing to suggest either incident was related to the case, but they had unsettled him.[10]

In mid-1995 the News Datacom case took a curious twist: Clinger developed an acute case of moral sensibility. The Israeli tax authority had been examining his personal tax returns for previous years and suspected him of having underreported his income. The upshot from the conversations that followed was that Clinger, who had already heard whispers of the News Corp investigation, offered to share with the tax man how it was that News Datacom paid so little tax. In 1992 the News Datacom companies had been reorganized as offshore companies that paid for research to be conducted in Israel on a cost-plus basis. Any profits that accrued would be offshore, beyond the reach of the Israeli tax authority. Siskind described this arrangement as standard practice for research companies in Israel, including Intel.[11]

On September 10, 1995, Clinger signed an agreement to assist the Israeli tax authority in its secret investigation of News Datacom. Tax officers and police staged a series of dawn raids on Leo Krieger's home in Jerusalem, as part of twin investigations to determine where the telephone tapes that Krieger had offered to News Corp had come from, and to examine Clinger's allegations that Krieger had evaded personal income tax. In June 1996 Clinger's lawyers disclosed the existence of the agreement in the High Court in London.[12] At the time Siskind said that on several occasions he had asked the Israelis whether they were investigating News Datacom and had been assured they were not. The next thing that happened was that, after a twelve-month investigation, the Israeli tax authority raided the News Datacom offices.

The immediate trigger was Rupert Murdoch's revelation on October 15, 1996, that an IPO for News Datacom was imminent. The new corporate structure would insulate News Datacom's taxable income in a British holding company while realizing more than half a billion dollars in untaxed capital gains. The news galvanized Mas Hachnasa, the Israeli tax authority. By the evening of Thursday, October 17, the Israeli chief of intelligence, Daniel Vash, had signed a warrant to search the News Datacom offices and to hold seven News Corp executives, including Rupert Murdoch, for questioning, on suspicion of tax evasion. The warrant was stamped by the president of the Law Court in Jerusalem. The tax commissioner, Doron Levy, sat on the warrant through Friday as political arguments raged over whether the warrant should be executed. The green light was given by Friday evening, and tax officers were briefed for a mass raid on the News Datacom offices early Sunday morning, immediately after the Israeli sabbath.

The Israelis know how to mount a raid. Early on Sunday morning, October 20, they sealed off the block around the News Datacom office building at Har Hotzvim on the outskirts of Jerusalem. At a time when most taxpayers in the Western world were still tucked in bed in the sure knowledge that the wheels of the tax man, while they grind exceeding small, do not grind on the weekend, seventy-five Israeli tax inspectors thundered through the News Datacom office in Jerusalem. In simultaneous raids they also hit the News Datacom warehouse in Tel Aviv, the offices of three sets of News Datacom lawyers, and the News Datacom accountants.

It was one of the most widely publicized tax raids in history. Radio, television, and print journalists were on hand to record all that happened in loving detail. Newspapers around the world ran pictures of tax officers carrying boxes of documents out of the News Datacom building at Har Hotzvim, on the edge of Jerusalem, with claims that the company had not reported $150 million in earnings. The story was helped by the fact that, ever since the mid-1980s, News Corp accountants, by a number of shrewd but legal financial moves, had made sure that the company never paid more than about ten cents on the dollar in corporate income tax. The accountants had saved News Corp $1 billion in tax payments. Then there was the search warrant itself. Rupert Murdoch's name was on the Israeli document, which meant that he could be held and questioned, but by the time the story was picked up in Britain, the search warrant had somehow (incorrectly) become an *arrest* warrant for the media baron.

Arthur Siskind was called in the early hours of Sunday morning in New York, and Rupert Murdoch in the early afternoon in Sydney, with the news that Israeli tax officers were carting financial records off in trucks. News Corp executives were furious. "Mr. Clinger has the tiger by the tail," Siskind said grittily.[13] News Corp denied all claims, protesting loudly that this was a setup, a piece of mischievous harassment orchestrated by a "former News Datacom executive" who was already on the run from U.S. authorities. Back in 1992 News Corp might have appeared blasé about Clinger's fugitive status, but now its view was much clearer: Clinger had to be put behind bars.

Eventually the frenzied media coverage subsided. No further public statements were made. Several weeks later the Israeli tax officers, wading through the mountain of material taken from News Datacom, made a discovery that while very interesting, had nothing to do with taxes. It would take some weeks more before the Israeli bureaucracy decided what to do with the discovery.

London February 2, 1997

In February 1997 Audley Sheppard had been a London partner at Clifford Chance, one of the largest law firms in the world, for two years. At thirty-six years old, he was a solidly built, reassuring figure for clients, with a faint New Zealand accent that he had retained through a decade of living in Britain. His problem was that, a year into this most bitter of court cases, he still didn't know how much he trusted his client. Trust is not an essential ingredient in the lawyer-client relationship. It becomes an issue only when the lawyer has to go out on a limb for the person he is representing—who in Audley Sheppard's case was Michael Clinger.

In taking on the Clinger case, Sheppard had found himself in a surreal landscape. The court filings on the case in the British High Court read more like a film noir script, at every turn becoming more and more bizarre. They documented a bizarre investigation by News Corp lawyers and private investigators that took them through the tax havens of the world and into the shadowy corners of the global media group itself.[14] Preliminary hearings at London's Old Bailey had raised claims and counterclaims of death threats, violence and intimidation, suicide attempts, blackmail, and doctored evidence. The depth of bad feeling on each side of the case was like nothing Sheppard had ever seen—and the hearing date was still a year away. It wasn't going to get any better. Sheppard had just discovered that someone was tapping his phone. His question on Sunday, February 2, 1997, was what should he do with this information.

Ever since God created trial lawyers (a date that most Hebrew scholars place in the Genesis account somewhere between the parts about lords of the earth and every crawling thing), the British justice system has wrestled with the seminal problem of what to do on Sundays. Starting at nine o'clock on Monday mornings, British courts dispense justice without fear or favor, with a dignity and ritual in keeping with their eight-hundred-year history. They do this right up until Friday afternoon. If the God-fearing architects who designed the system centuries ago had a fault, it is that they took the commandment to rest on the seventh day a trifle broadly. From four o'clock on Friday until nine o'clock Monday morning, the British court system goes into recess. During this time it is difficult to do anything more than secure bail on a drunk and disorderly charge. Officially at least, Britain's judges and their associates, the court system's recorders, its magistrates and administrative staff, its Queen's Counsels, its junior barristers and solicitors, are at rest. And as Isaac Newton long ago observed, objects at rest like to remain at rest.

Nevertheless, if the case is urgent enough and the lawyer is resolute enough, British justice provides a way to obtain an emergency court order. It means approaching the duty judge rostered for that weekend. There are two rules for a young lawyer approaching the High Court duty judge. The first is—don't try it. The second is—if you do, your reasons must be compelling and dire. On Sunday, February 2, 1997, the duty judge for the Chancery Division of the High Court was Justice Evans-Lombe. On Sunday morning Evans-Lombe picked up the phone at his home at Marlingford Hall in Norwich and heard the reference to Rupert Murdoch. From that moment he knew Audley Sheppard had put him in the hot seat. Sheppard told Evans-Lombe that it looked like someone at News Datacom had been running a major bugging and surveillance operation.[15]

Sheppard asked Evans-Lombe for an immediate order restraining News Corp and its lawyers from destroying or disposing of any tape recordings, transcripts, or other records of telephone conversations between Mr. Clinger and his lawyers. Sheppard faxed Evans-Lombe a series of affidavits sworn by Clinger and his Jerusalem lawyer, Michael Kirsch. (Kirsch for most of the previous ten years had been the district attorney of Jerusalem.) According to the affidavits, Clinger had been called to the offices of Israel's National Serious Crime Unit on January 12, 1997. There he had been shown a series of tapes that he was told had been seized by the Israeli tax inspectors when they raided the News Datacom offices three months before. They had been found in the office of News Datacom's managing director, former IBM vice president Abe Peled. According to Israeli newspapers, they were in Peled's office safe.

The tapes found in Peled's office contained recordings of an extensive series of bugged telephone conversations between Clinger and his lawyers and appeared to be the product of a major illegal telephone-tapping operation. Clinger had apparently listened to recordings of fifteen telephone conversations involving himself on a tape marked 23A. Five of these conversations, which had taken place around late September 1996, were with his lawyers at Clifford Chance. Others involved Clinger and his American attorneys. Kirsch later heard the same tapes and verified a rough transcript Clinger had made of his taped conversations. The Jerusalem district attorney confirmed to Sheppard in London that Sheppard's voice was on tapes found in the News Datacom office.

It wasn't just Clinger and his lawyers whose conversations had been recorded. Other tapes, it would emerge, contained conversations among Israeli tax officers talking about their News Corp investigation, and telephone calls from Israeli journalists. Within days the Israeli media would report police raids on several private investigation firms employed by News Corp, including an outfit called Shaffron, run by Reuven Hazak, the former deputy head of Israel's security agency, Shin Bet. Under questioning later by the National Serious Crime Unit, both Peled and Hazak would deny knowledge of any tapes.

Clinger's lawyers were undecided about what to do with this information when they received it in mid-January 1997. But on Thursday, January 30, Clinger had been called back to the offices of the National Serious Crime Unit. While there he said he was shown a fax apparently addressed to a News Corp executive and an adviser, also found in Peled's office in the tax raid. The fax contained a transcript of one of Clinger's conversations with Sheppard.

Clinger's evidence of the fax lifted the matter into a different league. It wasn't the job of the High Court to look at bugging allegations in overseas countries, but a breach of legal privilege—the confidentiality of private communications between Clinger and his British lawyers—was a different matter. Initially it appeared that unnamed private agents employed by News Corp might have gone beyond their brief. But copies of transcripts in the hands of senior News Corp lawyers and executives indicated something more than a rogue operation out of control. It suggested an organized strategy. It also raised the possibility that information that its agents had obtained illegally had reached senior levels at News

Corp, and that News Corp lawyers had not immediately informed the High Court of this unintended breach. At worst, there was a risk that this wiretapping was part of a pattern of illegal activity coordinated at the highest levels of News Corp.

The bugging allegations were dynamite. But were they true? All hell would break loose when the court papers were served on News Corp and Allen & Overy the next day. In angry court scenes the News Corp lawyers would argue flatly that the tapes did not exist and that if they did, then Clinger was the wiretapper. Peled and those allegedly named on Clinger's fax all signed affidavits denying any knowledge of the tapes. In response to a query, Arthur Siskind's assistant, Eugenie Gavenchak, responded:

> If any tape recordings of any conversations do exist, it is clear to us that Mr. Clinger was responsible for making them. If any tapes were indeed found within our company's offices, they were planted there. Mr. Clinger has failed to produce any evidence of this purported fax, other than his own word, the trustworthiness of which needs no comment.[16]

Five years later, Peled gave a completely different version of events to journalist Wendy Goldman Rohm. The way Peled told it, after the tax raid on October 20, 1996, News Corp had convinced the tax officers that Clinger had invented the tax claims against News Datacom. Then Clinger's representatives threatened to fabricate evidence against Peled. "They went to our lawyers and said unless we settled, since I'm so important to Murdoch, they'll cause me major damage and accuse me of wiretapping—a big offense in Israel," Peled told Rohm.[17] The News lawyers had gone to Israeli police with a transcript of the conversation. Two days later the wiretapping tapes were discovered in Peled's offices.

But if this was true, and if News Corp had such an ironclad defense, why didn't they say so at the time? There were certainly fiery exchanges between the two sides' lawyers, as a judgment by Justice Lindsay makes clear. But there was no reference to any threat by Clinger's lawyers, or of going to the police with a transcript. Instead, the News lawyers angrily demanded more details of the wiretapping claims. More remarkably, Peled's account suggests that the tapes were not found in his office during the October 1996 tax raid. As he tells it, the tapes were planted in his office three months later. This means the affidavits by Audley Sheppard of the account given to him by the Jerusalem D.A., and by Clinger's lawyer, Michael Kirsch, when they said police found the tapes in October, cannot be accurate. They must be mistaken or misled. Peled's account requires quite a lot of people not to be telling the truth. In fact, Peled seems to be drawing some sort of giant conspiracy by Israeli officials to fabricate evidence against News Datacom and News Corporation. This is a sensational claim, if it is true. But again, why didn't the News lawyers mention it at the time? Peled is the public face of News Datacom, (or NDS Group, as it was renamed). Why did he wait five years to raise the matter, when the affair had dropped out of the public view, and the only alternative account is an obscure and largely unreported judgment by Justice Lindsay in the British High Court? When asked about this, News Corp, NDS Group and Peled declined to comment.

That Sunday in February 1997 Justice Evans-Lombe was troubled by the scope of the allegations before him. Would senior British and American lawyers really be a party to actions of the sort alleged? It seemed improbable. As a witness, Clinger had little claim to credibility. In relation to other testimony the regular case judge, Justice Lindsay, would later describe Clinger as a skilled liar. But the existence and illegal content of the tapes—found in the chief executive's office in a company whose business is all about secrecy and tight security—had been attested to by Sheppard in London, by the current Jerusalem district attorney, and by Clinger's Israeli lawyer, Michael Kirsch, the former Jerusalem district attorney.[18] What was unsupported was Clinger's claim about seeing the fax, which connected the tapes to the News Corp lawyers. Unless he could produce the fax, this claim would be discounted. At the same time News Corp had its own questions to answer. Clinger was a fraud and a charlatan, but what did that say about News Corp, his former employer, or the way it dealt with its business opponents? From 1990 to the end of 1991, how had Clinger been able to run such an important arm of News Corp's business, representing the company before regulators and senior government officials around the world, *while he was on the run?* Knowingly or not, what part of News Corp's management culture allowed it to employ a fugitive?

The role of the weekend duty judge does not extend to making final judgments. Evans-Lombe signed the interim order Sheppard sought, passing on the job of sorting through the allegations to Justice Lindsay, the judge presiding over the case.[19]

12

THE POKER PLAYER

New York/Denver, February 2–24, 1997

F̲OR A CRISIS JUNKIE like Rupert Murdoch, there is something inspiring about New York, which evokes some of his most brilliant pieces of damage control—intuitive counterpunches that sometimes provide him with a solution before he is even aware he has a problem. In New York Murdoch can be anything and anyone that he wants to be. And on Sunday, February 2, 1997, Rupert Murdoch was a Jewish-American hero.

While Audley Sheppard was planning the application he would make to Justice Evans-Lombe in London, Murdoch had been the guest of honor of the King David Society, the big-money patrons group for the United Jewish Appeal (UJA). Murdoch had been presented with two scrolls of Jewish scripture in recognition of his recent philanthropic efforts. They must have been substantial, as the basic requirement for the lowliest society member is a $25,000 minimum contribution to the UJA each year. The night was just the beginning of the honors for Murdoch the philanthropist. The big news of the evening was that in three months' time the UJA would name Murdoch Humanitarian of the Year. The presentation on May 29 would consist of a gala dinner at the Waldorf-Astoria, where he would again be guest of honor; the night of tributes would climax in a personal tribute from Israeli prime minister Benjamin Netanyahu. The honor was a tribute not just to the lobbying efforts of Murdoch's New York lawyer, Howard Squadron, a former UJA president, and News Corp senior vice president Eric Breindel (a leading figure in the UJA's entertainment and music industries division), after News Corp's Jerusalem tax debacle the previous October; but also to to his own genuine admiration for the Israeli spirit and an untiring campaign by Murdoch since the 1970s to draw close to the Jewish community.

Murdoch himself attributed the bestowing of honors to outrage in the Jewish community over the behavior of Ted Turner in October 1996 toward Fox News, when Turner compared Murdoch to Hitler. He told William Shawcross in 1999, "They were so outraged that they gave me a great dinner, with Henry Kissinger making me Humanitarian of the Year, purely to stick their finger in Ted Turner's eye."[1] What would have been almost as satisfying was that Sumner Redstone, the crusty head of Viacom, who four months before had been planning to sue Murdoch in one of the minor turf wars that the media business throws up, would be UJA chairman for the occasion. The invitations to Murdoch's big night would be sent out under Redstone's name.

Murdoch would not learn of Clinger's allegations, or of the interim orders by Justice Evans-Lombe in London, until Monday, February 3, when Sheppard served the papers on the News Corp lawyers. But it is unlikely that Murdoch would have spent a great deal of Sunday thinking about his Israeli problems even if he had known. Armed with the UJA honor and the personal involvement of the Israeli prime minister, Murdoch had the perfect counter to anything that Michael Clinger could throw at him in Israel.

The problem that Clinger posed was closer to home, in the greater drama that was gripping Murdoch and his media empire in the United States. For no matter how great a media organization's reach or power, no matter how many countries or deals in which it is involved, it remains intensely vulnerable in one area: public confidence. It is not merely a matter of maintaining the confidence of its bankers—though even here News was struggling. It is also a question of probity. Broadcasting licenses around the world are granted on the basis that regulatory authorities believe a media group is fit and proper to be entrusted with such a license. It is a position of public trust. Any accusation that it is involved in illegal activities, such as Michael Clinger had just alleged in the High Court in London, even if baseless, poses a threat to the group's future.

For Murdoch on that first weekend in February, Israel and the UJA and everything else on the empire's agenda was just a sideshow. Because Murdoch was at that moment involved in the ultimate high-altitude property deal, and the issue that had his complete attention was the problem of how to pay for it. Rupert Murdoch had twenty-two days to find $4 billion. Whatever else he did, by February 24 he had to have the money or else have a great story about how he was going to get the money.

*   *   *

The thing about geostationary real estate is that it obeys the rules of property investment everywhere: It begins and ends with position. You pay for the view, and you pay to make sure your view can't be spoiled by developers (or by a high-power satellite parked next door drowning out your signal). And you know that, at the end of the day, the government can make or break your fortune with a rezoning decision. Either way, with terrestrial or satellite real estate, when the government gets involved, you know it is going to cost you money. In September 1995 Reed Hundt used his casting vote at the FCC to cancel the satellite license that Daniel Garner was selling to John Malone. Then in late 1995 the FCC announced that it would auction Garner's license to the highest bidder. The new license carried the right to hang a string of high-power satellites in geostationary orbit 22,300 miles above the line on the map that is 110WL. With digital technology, each transponder could broadcast eight to ten television channels to a pizza-sized satellite dish atop any home in America. Whoever ended up with the twenty-eight transponder frequencies that the FCC was auctioning in the 110WL slot could launch a Direct Broadcast Satellite television service with 280 channels.

The fate of this key piece of America's media future was decided in the drab FCC auction offices on Massachusetts Avenue in Washington on a cold day in January 1996. The two major bidders were John Malone, who through his TCI Technology Ventures was bidding on behalf of Primestar; and Rupert Murdoch. The actual bidder would be MCI, but in the News-MCI relationship, MCI was just the money. The other bidder, Charles W. Ergen, was an unknown.

Back in the 1970s, as the pioneers of cable television were stringing wire along telephone poles, in hock up to their ears so as to connect up another street, another suburb, or another town, another breed of entrepreneur was looking at the sky and dreaming bigger dreams. A cable company could provide subscription television for a town, for a region, or for a state. But if you put a satellite up in the sky, you could broadcast to the entire United States. As a dream, it was all the more appealing because it was hopelessly impractical. The two movements—the cable pioneers and the satellite dreamers—produced two minor but significant waves of migration west.

It had been 1972 when John Malone packed up his family and moved from Connecticut to Denver to run TCI. In 1980 another executive packed up his possessions and headed west. Charlie Ergen was a colorful, knockabout character with an intermittent Tennessee drawl who was once thrown off the Las Vegas strip for card counting. He cultivated the down-home image. A colleague once said of him, "I don't think I've ever seen Charlie with a suit and tie. He wears sweaters and button-down-collar shirts and Nikes. That's Charlie."[2] Stories about Ergen center on his skills at blackjack and poker rather than his Ivy League education or his work in Dallas as a financial analyst for snack-food group Frito-Lay.

The story goes that sometime during a poker game in 1980 Ergen formed the resolve to follow a long-held dream about getting into satellites. His resolve had had its roots (or so he would later tell the story) on the night of October 4, 1957, when as a four-year-old he stood beside his father near their home in Oak Ridge, Tennessee, and watched the world's first satellite, Sputnik 1, streak across the sky, orbiting the earth every ninety-six minutes.

In 1980 he and his wife and business partner, Cantey, packed up and, together with another poker buddy, James DeFranco, headed west to sell satellite dishes. Ergen was twenty-seven. The three partners had $50,000. They went to Denver and opened a shop because they figured, like the cable guys before them, that the mountainous terrain east of the Rockies made television reception difficult. In addition, cable would service only larger communities.

To pick up broadcasts from the low-power satellites in operation in 1980, you needed a satellite dish that cost $30,000 and was ten feet across. If nothing else, it was a conversation starter; after paying a small fortune, your roofline turned into what looked like a deep-space research project. The effect was even more compelling if you lived in an apartment. "We honestly believed people would line up to buy them," Ergen said.[3] Nobody did. Undeterred, Ergen and DeFranco packed a satellite dish on a trailer and headed for Aspen. No one was buying in Aspen either, but two people stopped them on the way to order a dish. Ergen and DeFranco were down to their last $5,000 and were delivering one of the only two satellite dishes they had—when disaster struck. "A gust of wind came along and flipped the dish over," Ergen said later. "It was destroyed."[4] Only the successful sale of the last remaining dish kept the business solvent.

As satellite dishes came down in price and size, Ergen turned to making them himself. By the late 1980s, he had a $200 million international business and had sold almost a third of the million satellite dishes sold in the United States. Originally Ergen's company was called Ecosphere, but he changed it to EchoStar Communications.

In 1983 Ergen heard about a new sort of high-power satellite broadcasting called Ku-band, which could be picked up with a satellite dish only fifteen to eighteen inches across. Ergen believed Direct Broadcast Satellite, as the new system was called, would be a huge money machine. He began acquiring DBS transponder frequencies—even as John Malone was jeering that DBS stood for Don't Be

Stupid. "In Monopoly, the player who usually wins is the person who buys the most deeds," Ergen said. "We have more spectrum than any other DBS provider."

Ergen's spectrum included twenty-one of the thirty-two frequencies at 119WL, and one frequency at 110WL. In December 1995 he put all his hopes on a Lockheed Martin satellite loaded on top of a Chinese Long March 2E rocket—the launch vehicle with the best track record for exploding and killing ground crew. "I was pretty confident but still counting the fingers and toes and breathing a sigh of relief when it went off," he said.

Ergen was set to launch EchoStar's Dish Network with the new satellite on March 3, five weeks after the FCC auction of Garner's old license. He came to Washington for the auction with EchoStar director Jim DeFranco, his old poker buddy. Ergen and DeFranco had no backers and not much money; they were two outsiders who had made it to the big table. "Both of us felt we'd been training our whole lives to be in a big poker game with people like Rupert Murdoch and John Malone," Ergen said later.[5]

MCI lodged its opening bid of $125 million at 9:36 A.M. on Thursday, January 24, 1996.[6] Eleven minutes later TCI topped it with a bid of $201 million. The bidding continued through the morning, a silent affair with bidding teams in separate rooms, lodging bids electronically or using waivers to sit out a half-hour round. Just after lunch TCI made its last bid, at $297.7 million. By three P.M. TCI had run out of waivers and was officially out of the auction. "We weren't going to bid just anything," said TCI senior vice president David Beddow.[7] MCI had the bid at $332 million. Now there was just EchoStar still bidding.

Charlie Ergen was a stayer. Throughout the day he had kept coming back with aggressive calls. At 3:48 P.M. MCI went for the big hit. It lifted the bidding more than $100 million to $450 million. It looked like a killer bid. Ergen exercised a waiver and made no counteroffer in the next round. Such a sum seemed way beyond his financial reach, and the auction looked like it was all over. It was 4:30 P.M. Mercifully, proceedings were adjourned until the next day. Ergen and DeFranco had a night to stew over their next move before they were expected to throw in the towel.

At 9:02 the next morning Ergen came back at MCI with a higher bid. And he kept on bidding. For the executives in the MCI bidding room looking at their electronic screens, working the cell phones for instructions from Bert Roberts and Rupert Murdoch, the auction had become a nightmare. MCI and News Corp desperately wanted to get into the U.S. satellite business, but just how high would the two crazy men in the other bidding room go? Who was really behind them? Or were they just bluffing? "[Ergen] is a smart guy. If he's bidding this high, he has someone else's money behind him. EchoStar just doesn't have the resources," DBS consultant Michael Alpert had said the previous night, before the bidding had reached stratospheric levels.[8]

Was Ergen bluffing? In some ways this question is a little like asking a poker player who has just stared down his opponent what his cards were. Ergen himself denies any suggestion of bluffing. He later said that he had always intended to bid up to $650 million but no further. He didn't have someone behind him, but he figured that he had nothing to lose. If he won the auction, unlike his opponents he would have a satellite ready to launch straight into the slot—though it is hard to see how EchoStar could have paid for the license and not gone broke. If Ergen lost, he would still cost his opposition a bucketload of money. "DeFranco and I, from playing poker, had learned the discipline of not being emotional about what your cards are," he said.[9]

Only when MCI took its bid to $682.5 million just after eleven A.M. did Ergen fold. He had lost the fight. But he had forced MCI and Murdoch to pay an astonishing price for the license.

After lunch Ergen and MCI resumed hostilities over another, less desirable slot, at 148WL. In another day and a half of torrid bidding, MCI forced Ergen from his opening bid of $101,888 all the way up to $52.3 million before MCI folded. Ergen wasn't worried. His stock price jumped 27 percent—unlike MCI stock, which slumped. MCI's winning bid that morning was all the more remarkable because News Corp and MCI would be starting so far behind their competitors. DirecTV, a subsidiary of General Motors, had launched the first DBS service in March 1994 and already had 1.8 million subscribers. Four other DBS services had followed DirecTV—US Satellite Broadcasting, Primestar (which upgraded its existing analogue system to digital), EchoStar's Dish Network, and AlphaStar.

"There is no business model that anyone has seen to spend that much money with three years getting to market and still make a profit," Bob Scherman, publisher of *Satellite Business News*, said on the Thursday night, when MCI's bid was just $450 million.[10] One of the only people who liked the deal was Charlie Ergen. "The price MCI paid was a bargain, it's a very valuable spectrum," he said. This was a message directly to Ergen's bankers. By inducing MCI to pay so much for 110WL, Ergen had triggered a huge revaluation in his own orbital licenses. He had made himself much more bankable.

In starting a new DBS operation, to be called ASkyB, MCI and News Corp would be taking on well-entrenched rivals who had picked up their own FCC licenses for next to nothing. It would be two years and another $600 million before MCI and News could get satellites into orbit and begin their new DBS service, up to four years behind their competitors. MCI had paid a deposit on the license price immediately after the auction. On December 6, 1996, after being held up by various appeals, the FCC announced that the 110WL license was ready to grant. This meant that MCI now had a week to pay up the balance. So it was particularly unfortunate that in November Bert Roberts announced that MCI was pulling out of the partnership and was no longer prepared to provide the $4 billion funding that Murdoch needed.[11]

In hindsight, the breakdown of the relationship between Bert Roberts and Rupert Murdoch looks like pure carelessness. The FCC auction debacle had planted the seeds of disenchantment for Roberts, but it was a series of high-handed moves by Murdoch that had finally soured the alliance.

MCI's withdrawal knocked down the News Corp share price, and the stock continued sliding. The mood among investors was that if God had wanted people to go into space, he would have given them more money. They were worried that ASkyB would become a financial black hole. Its satellites wouldn't be in operation until 1998, and it was unclear how Murdoch was going to pay for it all. Murdoch was already involved in satellite start-ups in Japan, Mexico, and Argentina, and his Star TV satellite operation in Hong Kong was still losing money steadily. He had spent $500 million launching his Fox News cable channel in October. Now there was the ASkyB problem. Financially, Murdoch was more exposed than he had been since his debt crisis six years before. It wasn't life-threatening yet, but negative sentiment for a stock can grow quickly.

Credit agencies were worried as well. The FCC formally granted the 110WL license on December 20, 1996. Three days later, Standard & Poor's announced that it was putting News Corp on negative credit watch. If News Corp lost its BBB credit rating, its debt and stock would no longer be investment grade; they would be junk bonds. News Corp carried $9 billion of investment-grade debt. Keeping that investment status was a condition of the loans. Losing the investment grading would actually put much of the debt into default. It was the nightmare scenario: Murdoch could be facing an instant debt crisis.

Mere mortals and minor media executives flinch at prospects like this. But Murdoch knew all about debt crises. He had been down this road before. So he knew what the solution was. He needed to call a meeting. Two days before the FCC announcement on December 6 that the 110WL license was ready to grant, three hundred fund managers, media analysts and bankers around the world had begun receiving invitations to a special investment conference. Murdoch would host the conference on a soundstage at the 20th Century–Fox studios in Los Angeles on February 24, 1997. News had never before done anything so elaborate. More than twenty News Corp executives would brief analysts and bankers on all aspects of the company and its many ventures and in particular explain the group's U.S. satellite strategy. If analysts would only be patient, all would be revealed. The major effect of announcing the conference was that it bought Murdoch some time. It meant that he had three months to come up with another deep pocket to pay for ASkyB.

Murdoch tried his darnedest to do just that. He approached his satellite rivals, he talked with the telephone companies, he explored an initial public offering to float 30 percent of ASkyB to the American public. Nothing worked. "[Murdoch] extracts so much blood that it's going to be very difficult for anybody to cut a deal with him that makes any sense," one telephone company executive complained.[12]

No one was buying. In the winter of 1996–97 the entire entertainment industry was toast. In the middle of the biggest share boom in history, Wall Street was sick of the entertainment industry's high promises, huge debt levels, and low profits. The growth rate of people subscribing to DBS services was falling, and the cable industry was in retreat. John Malone had frozen TCI's rollout of fiber-optic cable. "Our big capital spending days as a cable company are over," Malone told a Bear, Stearns conference in October, before cutting 2,500 jobs at TCI. Time Warner chairman Gerry Levin had announced that Time Inc. would sell off parts of its cable network because of cable's high capital demands. Time Warner's long-term debt already stood at $17.5 billion. Across the country, after three turbulent years, media mergers were off the agenda. "The fever has broken," one investment banker said.[13]

*   *   *

On February 2, 1997, Murdoch had just twenty-two days to sort out his satellite problems before facing the analysts on February 24. If he didn't have a credible strategy for ASkyB by then, the exodus of investors from his stock would be a stampede, and he would have to write off many of his current ambitious plans. But Murdoch had one last card to play. There was one person in the industry who needed money even more than Murdoch did: his old nemesis, Charlie Ergen, whose Dish Network was now the third-largest DBS operator. Ergen's money problems were growing bigger and bigger with each passing day. Murdoch might finally be able to cut a deal with him. Murdoch's own financial worries were all about confidence. If Murdoch could unveil an alliance with Charlie Ergen, he wouldn't have any more money, but he would have a great story to sell to the analysts.

The timing was tight. So from the moment when Audley Sheppard's High Court injunction landed on Murdoch's London lawyers on Monday, February 3, Murdoch knew he had only days to kick this messy Israeli wiretapping affair out of existence. The scale of what he was about to attempt was too great, and the negotiations he would be undertaking were too sensitive, to be distracted by ugly unproven court allegations that News Corp had been bugging business opponents and foreign governments.

Murdoch already had a containment strategy working in Israel. In mid-January Israeli police had requested an interview with Abe Peled, the head of News Datacom, in whose office the tapes had been found. News Datacom told the Israeli Serious Crime Unit that Peled's duties abroad would keep him from returning to Israel until March. The unavailability of the chief witness would put the Israeli police investigation on hold through February.

Meanwhile in London Murdoch's lawyers launched a ferocious attack on Michael Clinger before Justice Lindsay, the regular High Court judge assigned to the case. They challenged Clinger to produce details to support his phone-taping allegations, including the damning fax he claimed to have seen in the National Serious Crime Unit office. Clinger was not able to do so. He said it was in police hands. On February 10 the High Court suspended any further hearings on the matter until the trial, accepting the News Corp lawyers' assurances that they knew nothing of any bugging.

"It seems to me that the proper approach is to treat the plaintiffs' answer on affidavit that there is no privileged information that has come to or is in their hands as conclusive," Justice Lindsay found. He did extend the injunction on the News Corp companies but reduced this to an undertaking in the case of the News Corp lawyers that any such material, if located, would be presented to the court. The judgment was never reported in Britain. In London bugging was a dead letter.[14]

Within hours of Justice Lindsay's February 10 judgment, Murdoch had telephoned Charlie Ergen at EchoStar's headquarters in Denver to arrange a crash meeting. Three days later Murdoch flew into Denver with a team of News Corp executives to meet Ergen. His great American gamble had begun. He was days away from another one of the worst—and the best—business decisions of his life.

*   *   *

It was an interesting pairing in the EchoStar offices. On one side of the table was Charlie Ergen, forty-four years old, determinedly casual. Opposite him was Rupert Murdoch, the man never seen in public without a white shirt and tie. For all of his career, Charlie Ergen had done things his way. Like Murdoch he was a gambler, he challenged conventional wisdom, he had regularly put the future of his company on the line, and he ran his company like a personal fief. He ran to win. In another lifetime Ergen and Murdoch could even have been friends. But in decades of wheeling and dealing, Rupert Murdoch had never been known to forget a wrong. He took losing money very, very personally. The thing that would always niggle below the surface of any relationship between the pair was that at the auction for the 110WL spectrum twelve months before, Ergen's poker skills had cost Murdoch $350 million—the difference between TCI's last bid and what Ergen had pushed MCI up to. Ergen's bidding had crippled the MCI–News Corp partnership. Murdoch would remember that for a long time.

So it was a measure of the gravity of Murdoch's situation, and his supreme ability to do whatever he needed to do to survive, that this meeting in Denver a year later was even taking place, that he was sitting down with this man who had been the cause of so many of his problems. With him was Chase Carey, who had recently been named co-chief operating officer of News Corp, who still ran the Fox television network; Preston Padden, a former Washington lobbyist who was head of ASkyB, whose work corralling the Fox television affiliates had won him a tough reputation; and Arthur Siskind.

On the other side of the table were Ergen, EchoStar's legal counsel David Moskowitz, and EchoStar executive vice president Carl Vogel. Vogel was given much of the credit by analysts for turning EchoStar into a bankable proposition. Vogel had taken a big risk three years before to leave his position as president of programming at Jones Intercable in Denver to join a shaky satellite start-up. "Some people thought I had taken leave of my senses," Vogel said later.

Each side needed to calculate how desperate the people on the other side of the table were. The EchoStar team knew Murdoch had a problem with ASkyB but didn't realize how poisonous the relationship between Murdoch and his partner, MCI, had become. On the financial side, News Corp's accounting disguised the size of Murdoch's gambles. A week before News Corp had reported a $350 million net profit for the last six months, under Australian accounting, on the way to a healthy 1997 profit. Under U.S. accounting, however, the return for the full year was three-quarters of a billion dollars less than Murdoch had reported, and News was losing money.[15]

EchoStar's situation was even more precarious. The Dish Network had 430,000 subscribers, but it was burning up $5 million a week. Its liabilities were already $70 million more than its assets, and Ergen needed to find another $200 million quickly to pay for his next two satellites. If Ergen didn't find more money by June, EchoStar would hit the wall.

EchoStar needed Murdoch. But corporate deal-making is never just about deals. Something much more personal was at stake here. For Murdoch, winning EchoStar was about winning over Charlie Ergen. Murdoch told Ergen that he shared his vision and wanted to join him. Previously, talks with Murdoch had been about buying Ergen out. Now Murdoch was talking partnership, a meeting of equals, and he was bringing his legendary powers of persuasion to bear. "Charlie, you remind me of myself when I was younger," Murdoch told Ergen over dinner.[16]

"The personal chemistry with Rupert is very positive," Ergen would say days later. "We've known each other for quite a while now, and I have followed Sky's progress in Britain very closely. . . .We matched up personally, we are both individuals who have attacked monopolies and oligopolies."[17]

In formal meetings, over the telephone, and at Ergen's home, the two principals talked about their shared frustrations with the cable industry, their career experiences, Ergen's precarious early days, and Murdoch's own close encounters with penury, including his debt crisis at the end of 1990. Like everyone else in the world, Ergen had heard the story of how a bank in Pittsburgh had almost sent Murdoch to the wall over a $10 million loan. "[He was] one little bank away, and we watched it all, and one of the conversations that Rupert and I had was that it makes more sense to do something today when we are both financially sound than when we are laying on the ground bleeding," Ergen said.

Beyond the pleasantries there was the sales pitch. This meeting was about a merger. Preston Padden had a little survey of twelve hundred cable customers that he would present eleven days later at the News Corp analysts' conference. The survey showed that 52 percent of cable customers, offered the service that EchoStar and ASkyB together would be able to provide, said they would immediately cancel cable and switch to Sky, as the new service would be called. Sky would own seven satellites and 49 of the 96 CONUS transponder frequencies. EchoStar already offered its customers 120 channels. Sky would offer America five hundred DBS television channels of crystal clarity, including for the first time local channels and video on demand.

Ergen would say later, "Our competition isn't so much the other guys in this industry—it's the cable guys who have 65 million people paying for TV today with old analog cable, monopolistic, high-priced, archaic systems. . . . It costs me $5 per person to send signals to everyone in the whole United States. The cost for cable companies to rewire digitally is $600 per home, and they must pass every house in a neighborhood even if the residents aren't customers."[18]

Sky's edge was that, with so many satellites and television channels, it could give customers most of their local free-to-air television stations in the same package. DBS customers would not have to have one system for satellite and another antenna linked up for local stations. At long last DBS, like cable, would be able to offer it all in one system.

Before Sky could do so, however, the U.S. Congress would have to change the law to enable satellites to retransmit local broadcasts—and that would be the tricky part. But Murdoch and Ergen both believed that Congress could be persuaded. The market penetration would be huge. Under the News Corp business plan, Sky would lose $500 million in its first year but would break even in 1999 with 3 million subscribers. By 2002 Sky would be generating $1.2 billion in operating profits. By 2005, subscriber numbers were expected to pass 15 million.

At some point during his series of talks with Murdoch, Charlie Ergen became a true believer. Truth to tell, he always had been, ever since the night he watched Sputnik 1 wobble across the sky. He said later,

> News Corp made sense as a strategic partner because they brought things other people couldn't—satellite capacity, programming content, worldwide expertise. They know more about DBS than anybody, and they brought capital. We made sense because we got them in the marketplace today, as opposed to a year from now. It's certainly an equal partnership, and it's certainly complementary.[19]

There was a little friction on technology. Murdoch wanted the merged venture to use the smartcard encryption developed by News Datacom and News Digital Systems (which had been renamed NDS after the unpleasant publicity of the Israeli tax raid in October). Ergen had made his fortune making satellite equipment and used Swiss encryption technology, which he believed was better and which he wanted to keep. No mention was made of the bugging allegations in the British High Court or the investigation by the Israeli Serious Crime Unit.

There are usually two danger points in any merger negotiation. The first is agreeing on the money. With Sky the money was fixed up. EchoStar stock was at $15, and News and MCI would buy half the company for $1.2 billion at $25 per share and pump in $200 million cash by May. But a real deal-breaker can be the floor plan. No matter how exciting the concept or how appealing the deal, there comes a moment when each member of any negotiating team sits back and begins to wonder what their role will be in the bigger, better enterprise. After the merger happens, where are they going to *sit*? In the new head office, who is going to end up without a chair?

Ergen insisted that he retain control of the new entity. He wanted to run Sky and retain EchoStar management or the deal was off. Murdoch didn't like it and said he would think about it. He flew back to Los Angeles but called Ergen back a couple of days later. They agreed that Murdoch would be chairman, and Ergen would be president and chief executive officer. News Corp would appoint Sky's chief financial officer. David Moskowitz would learn later that his opposite number, Arthur Siskind, planned to have him sacked as soon as the merger was complete.

Murdoch then added a condition of his own. This thing had to be a done deal by Monday, February 24, in time to present it to the analysts and fund managers at the News Corp conference at 20th Century–Fox. Ergen's merchant bankers told him this was madness—there would be no time for a full-scale contract, and announcing a deal with News Corp would cut off any other possible funding life-line for EchoStar. Committing to Sky without a full contract would leave Ergen out of money and completely in Murdoch's power if Ergen's fellow visionary decided to renegotiate the deal. Ergen overruled his advisers and put all his chips on Murdoch.[20]

A binding letter agreement was drawn up and signed on Thursday, February 20. Ergen agreed to use the NDS encryption technology under strict conditions. Under the letter agreement, News Corp and EchoStar executives were to complete their due diligence checks on each other by March 7. Despite the critical importance that News Corp attached to the News Datacom technology in this deal, EchoStar and its due-diligence committee were not told of the Israeli inquiry into News Datacom nor of the police interest in its chief executive. During the due diligence period News Datacom chief Abe Peled would be interviewed by Israeli police on March 2 after a formal caution that he was suspected of wiretapping, but EchoStar was not informed.[21]

February 24, 1997, Showtime

Late on the afternoon of Monday, February 24, four days after the letter agreement between EchoStar and the ASkyB partners had been signed, analysts in the final session of the News Corp conference in Los Angeles were already thinking about catching return flights. It was then that Murdoch and Ergen stood up and shocked their audience of three hundred with news of their Sky deal.

"Our goal is not to be complementary to cable," said Charlie Ergen at the press conference afterward. "We want to *eliminate* cable."[22] "Four years ago the cable industry promised 500 channels, and it's Sky that will deliver on the promise," EchoStar's Carl Vogel said as he stood beside Ergen.[23]

"At that point, the cable guys will be calling for Dr. Kevorkian," said Preston Padden, renamed head of global satellite operations for News Corp. The cable operators immediately rechristened the Sky venture "Deathstar" but would not share Padden's enthusiasm for euthanasia.

Murdoch raised a laugh with a not very cryptic reference to his fight with Ted Turner to get Time Warner to carry Fox News in New York. Sky was all about "access to, not control of, distribution outlets—we never want to be beholden to greedy gatekeepers," he said.[24] Ergen fended off questions about how the deal had been put together. "Rupert may have known about the deal two weeks ago, but I only found out about it a day or so ago," he told News Corp journalists, a little disingenuously.[25]

The most aggressive comments came from Preston Padden. In the past critics who disliked his abrasive style had described him as Rupert Murdoch's attack dog. "Our goal is to come to market with a television product so superior, and a consumer proposition so compelling, that a substantial number of 70 million households stop writing their checks to their current service—usually cable—and start writing them to Sky," Padden told the audience. Afterward it was Padden's speech that those in the audience remembered best and that the cable industry hated most. "The presentation of the deal [by Padden] was the most egregiously stupid presentation by a corporate executive that I've ever seen," said Gordon Crawford, senior vice president of Capital Research and Management Company. "I went up to Rupert afterward and told him that talk was going to cost him a lot. I don't think he realized that the cable industry is this small club of individuals whose net worth is tied up in their companies, and how pissed they would be."[26]

Murdoch laughed and conceded Padden had gone too far, though he himself had been beating the same drum. "We're aiming for the big cable market, 65 million homes," Murdoch told journalists. "We expect to have a good 50 percent of all new satellite customers from here on."[27]

Once again the cable industry was stunned. The prices of cable stocks dived. An industry trade weekly, *Multichannel News*, ran a cartoon of a small cable operator considering two options on a blackboard: "Plan A: Hope Murdoch's plans to air local broadcast signals on Sky aren't realized. Plan B: Build altar; say prayers."[28] Here was the man who had miraculously smuggled Daniel Garner's satellite slot away from the cable operators, who had gouged them on fees to run his f/X channel, who had started a fourth television network from scratch when no one had believed it was possible, who had built the biggest satellite operation in the world, now openly promising to drive them out of business.

John Malone was one of the first to tell Murdoch just how foolish he had been. Malone had known about the Sky merger before it was announced, because he and Murdoch had held another of their regular minisummits in mid-February. As always, their discussions had covered the world. They'd talked about Fox News, Murdoch's interest in buying Pat Robertson's Family Channel, and their satellite joint ventures in Latin America. In particular, they talked about Murdoch buying Malone out of the Fox Sports joint venture. It was a deal that would put a billion dollars into Liberty Media and get Malone out of a hole. His long-time mentor and partner, Bob Magness, had died in December 1996, and Malone was worried about where the controlling bloc of TCI stock that Magness had controlled would end up. With the money Murdoch was offering to buy him out of Fox Sports, Malone would be able to buy out the TCI stock held by the Magness estate—which otherwise would be sold on the market to pay inheritance taxes. Murdoch would have been aware of the huge favor he was doing Malone with the Fox Sports deal. It was during these talks that Murdoch broke the bad news that went with it: He casually told Malone that he was about to announce a satellite partnership with Charlie Ergen.

Malone's lieutenant Peter Barton told *Denver Post* journalist Stephen Keating, "Rupert told us he was doing the deal with Charlie. I remember looking at him and telling him he was nuts. John said, 'Let's move on.' But John was quite pissed about this. It colored the meeting." Malone was less stoic after the theatrical announcement of the merger on February 24. He swore at Murdoch in a meeting several days later. "Rupert," Malone said, "we're trying to sell affiliation on f/X and Fox News and Fox Sports and having you as a partner under these conditions is not an asset."[29]

The question was, did Murdoch and his executives really believe the claims that they were making? "Rupert Murdoch is an old friend," said TCI's new president, Leo Hindery. "I applaud his strategic initiative. I am more than a little annoyed by the anti-cable rhetoric."[30] Hindery had gone to the meeting with Malone determined to clarify if News Corp's "public rhetoric" was the same as its "internal rhetoric."[31] That is, did they mean what they were saying? Hindery went away relieved that they didn't.

Behind all the drama on the Fox soundstage that day, the new partners' real views of the future were more modest than they were letting on. In a year, EchoStar had clawed its way to a subscriber base of 400,000. This was still far behind its major competitor, Hughes Electronics' DirecTV, which had 3 million subscribers. No matter what Sky did with new technology, local programming, and five hundred channels, its internal forecasts suggested that DirecTV would stay ahead of them. The Sky business plan that Murdoch and Ergen announced with such gusto to the world on February 24 was for Sky to have 8 million customers within five years. But this represented only 38 percent of the market.[32] Its DBS rivals—chiefly DirecTV—would have 13 million subscribers. This would be devastating for cable operators, who faced losing a third of their customers. But they would not be losing most of them to Sky. When Murdoch said, "We expect to have a good 50 percent of all new satellite customers from here on," he meant that the aim was merely to keep up with DirecTV. The big threat to cable would come not from Murdoch but from General Motors, DirecTV's ultimate parent. But on February 24 Murdoch convinced the world of exactly the opposite.

A headline in an industry magazine, *Cablevision,* summarized the rising tide of indignation and outrage among cable operators: "Cable to Murdoch: Drop Dead." For the moment the threat of Murdoch had put the operators on the defensive. But it was only a question of time before they rallied, then brought their wagons out of the circle, and mounted a counterattack. In the narrow window of opportunity that this gave him, Murdoch had to find some powerful allies. He needed a political fix; and no matter how daunting the task, he needed it quickly. Success or failure in the battle to make the Sky merger work lay in how Murdoch fared in Washington.

13

DIVIDED ROYALTIES

Washington, March–April 1997

WHEN RUPERT MURDOCH went to Washington in March 1997, he faced one of the most delicate tasks in modern politics. He needed a change in the copyright laws that would allow his Sky satellite operation to beam local television programming down to its customers across the United States—and he needed it in a hurry. He hoped to have the new laws in place by April, tacked on to the end of a $4 billion appropriations bill to fund U.S. troops in Bosnia and disaster relief in the American Midwest.

As one lobbyist put it at the time, "Historically, copyright legislation is the most difficult legislation to get through Congress . . . it will take some pretty creative strategizing for them to get their proposal through."[1] The difficulty is that copyright holders range from local television stations to networks to movie producers to sports leagues. The information economy is based first of all upon an economy of information—of regulating the commercial returns from media. The entertainment industry is based upon tightly defined market territories. If the boundaries are rewritten—and with satellite television boundaries may cease to exist—the immediate questions are: Who pays the royalties, who gets paid and how much do they get paid? Rewriting the copyright laws is like rearranging the deck chairs for everyone in the entertainment industry. Nobody wants to move.

And it was a bad time for Murdoch to be asking for a political favor. In the early months of 1997 a sea change was buffeting conservative politics. The current malaise could be seen most clearly in the woes that had overtaken House Speaker Newt Gingrich. Back when the Republicans had swept to power in September 1994 to win both Houses of Congress, Gingrich had been the man of the hour, the architect of a historic victory. His Contract with America manifesto had been the platform for the Republican revolution, and Gingrich had seemed an unstoppable colossus, a man poised to succeed Bill Clinton as president.

That was 1994. When Murdoch came to Washington in 1997, the picture was not so happy. King Newt was being blamed for a string of Republican disasters. There had been the failed standoff with Clinton that Gingrich masterminded in late 1995, when Congress refused to pass the federal budget until Clinton cut spending. And holdups with Republican legislation; filibustering in the Senate; party losses in the 1996 elections; Clinton's landslide victory to win a second term—all had stirred discontent with the speaker's leadership. In January 1997 the House Ethics Committee fined Gingrich $300,000 for misleading information he supplied during an investigation of his finances. Some Republican kingmakers had begun an internal debate about the virtues of regicide.

One of Gingrich's most vehement critics was William Kristol, a leading light among the new conservatives, the so-called neocons. By March 1997 Kristol was calling openly for Gingrich to resign in the right-wing magazine written for Washington insiders called *The Weekly Standard.* The cover line on the March 20 issue was "Newt Melts," and the issue featured an opinion piece by New York Republican congressman Peter King, who described Gingrich as "roadkill on the highway of American politics." Gingrich was on a trip to China at the time, but he was so incensed at the King article that at Elmendorf Air Force Base on his way home he called Rush Limbaugh's radio program to attack Kristol. "I don't know of any conservative person who is a serious person who isn't, frankly, worried about what's happening at *The Weekly Standard,* and Kristol's passion for destroying Republicans," Gingrich thundered.[2]

The spat degenerated. At a Washington dinner for his political action committee, GOPAC, at the Ritz-Carlton Hotel on April 3, Gingrich defended his record and tried to show that he had regained his old fire and reforming zeal. In passing, he cited the high sales in Mongolia of the book *Contract with America,* which he said had even been distributed by camels and horses. "Isn't it exciting to know that not only in America but in Mongolia, ideas are working," Gingrich said. It was perhaps a mistake that Gingrich brought along a ceremonial Mongolian hat to the conference, a triumph of burgundy velvet and gold shaped like a crown, as the press gleefully reported. "In two years we've come from Contract with America to Contract with Mongolia," Kristol sniffed disdainfully.[3]

The difficulty for Rupert Murdoch in this little spat was that while he needed Gingrich's cooperation to achieve his goal, Bill Kristol worked for him. Murdoch had given Kristol a budget of $3 million to launch *The Weekly Standard* eighteen months before, to give Murdoch an authoritative voice in Washington among the neocons. Murdoch said at the time that he didn't expect to make money from the

Standard; it was "a bit of a hobby." He said he thought it would be fun.[4] There was no indication that Murdoch was telling Kristol what to write, but given News Corp's track record, one could never be sure. At the very least, the question for Gingrich would be why Murdoch didn't rein Kristol in, once the attacks on him started.

* * *

Gingrich's position vis-a-vis Rupert Murdoch had become very peculiar, and it went to the heart of the pressures gripping Republican politicians in Washington. If there was anyone in America whom Gingrich could blame, other than himself, for starting him on the slippery slope that led to his predicament, it was arguably his erstwhile admirer and new friend, Rupert Murdoch. The key to understanding Murdoch's political problems in March 1997 lies in the history of America's conservative politics.

Murdoch has always had a remarkable effect on politicians. Unlike many chief executives, he has made a habit of descending regularly upon Washington to argue his concern of the moment in person. In some conservative circles he has superstar status. One lobbyist told of a legislator who virtually went into shock after running into Murdoch walking through Congress one day. "It was like he'd seen the Second Coming," the lobbyist told reporters.[5] There was a flip side to Murdoch's notoriety. Over the years he had made so many cozy deals with political leaders of all ideological persuasions, and his reputation had so far preceded him, that for his Democratic critics, merely seeing him speak with a politician could raise grave suspicions: Somehow Murdoch must be pulling another fast one.

The American electorate's swing to the right in November 1994 was not simply a matter of choosing different politicians. It was a quest for new ideas. Newt Gingrich came to office on a wave of public hostility toward self-serving incumbents and party machines. Main Street America wanted to see power taken away from the traditional power brokers, including lobbyists, committee chairmen, and committee staff. A major part of the power taken from House and Senate committees was absorbed by Newt Gingrich himself.

The 1994 Republican victory came at a critical moment. The new crop of legislators faced the task of coming to terms with the broader issues facing American society and its economy. Their lofty concern was shaping (or reshaping) America's future. A major part of that future would be determined by the technologies emerging out of Silicon Valley and communications labs around the country. What would be the role of government in the uncharted new world that information technology promised? Did Congress know any more about where technology was going than did the media industry leaders who met at Herb Allen's conference at Sun Valley each July? How did one make sense of the changes that technology were bringing to society? Where did the future lie? These were questions of some immediacy, because Congress was about to embark on the first major overhaul in decades of telecommunications law. Matters of ideology here would translate into market movements worth billions of dollars. The Republican view of technology would be shaped by the conservative policy institutes.

At the end of the twentieth century most visions of the future lay somewhere between two extremes. On the one hand was the dark European pessimism formulated by writers like George Orwell, whose book *1984* painted a future where technology is used to control the populace and Britain is reduced to an outpost named Runway One. The book deals with the nature of power and the way it has come to pervade our intimate spaces; but it is the vision of Big Brother as the hand behind technology, using telescreens in each home to spy upon and brainwash the population, that has become the book's most memorable image. Opposed to that view, at the other end of the soothsaying spectrum, was the long tradition of American optimism, which suggested that with technology the only thing that Americans had to fear was fear itself. It was this latter view that was propagated by the right-wing think-tanks and policy institutes that had driven the Gingrich revolution. Their initial goal was to discredit the pervasive skepticism about technology as Big Brother that Orwell's work had produced.

It was a battle of ideas and worldviews where no quarter would be offered, and there were no noncombatants. When Charles William Maynes retired in 1997 after seventeen years as editor of *Foreign Policy,* he complained that the "nonpartisan specialists" who had traditionally advised policymakers in all camps had been replaced by a new breed of "combat intellectuals": "In today's Washington ideas are no longer tools made available to everybody. Rather, they are weapons crafted for one's political allies."[6]

The conservative policy institutes' views on technology and their pervasive influence, which tended to correspond happily with the views of the technology companies that supported them so generously, can be best appreciated through the words of their most high-profile advocate.

Rupert Murdoch made the best-known political speech of his life in London's Banqueting Hall on September 2, 1993. Ostensibly he was there to unveil a new package of pay-television channels for BSkyB. His address, which would set out his vision for the future of world media, was being broadcast by satellite to little groups of investors and media analysts at sites around the world.

Murdoch told his worldwide audience that they were on the edge of a technological revolution: "For years man has been both beguiled and frightened by new technologies, and with reason." Television was a new medium that could entertain and inform, but it also opened the potential for totalitarian control by Big Brother, as laid out by George Orwell. But a decade after Orwell's famous date, he had been proved wrong. Advances in telecommunications technology had "proved an unambiguous threat to totalitarian regimes everywhere." Telecommunications technology had been critical to the enormous spread of political freedom in recent years:

> I must add (with maybe a tiny touch of regret) that this technology has also liberated people from the once-powerful media barons. . . . The media mogul has been replaced by a bevy of harassed and sometimes confused media executives, trying to guess what the public wants.[7]

Consumers were in control, Murdoch said, and technology was "galloping over the old regulatory machinery, in many countries rendering it almost obsolete."

At least, that is the way the speech appeared in the next day's edition of the *Times*. But Murdoch hadn't quite said it like that. Before launching into the speech, Murdoch had paused to look around at the Rubens paintings that decorate the Banqueting Hall, savoring the moment. "I am particularly fond of *Hercules Crushing Envy,* from which we have suffered much," he began reflectively. "And *Minerva Crushing Ignorance,* from which we have suffered even more." The speech went down well with the satellite audience, particularly the cut-away shots of BSkyB chief Sam Chisholm looking most unamused when Murdoch referred to "harassed and sometimes confused media executives."[8]

The speech was a disaster for Murdoch. A month later the Chinese government, alerted by Murdoch's widely reported comments, dealt with the unambiguous threat to totalitarian regimes everywhere by banning all satellite dishes in China. Murdoch had paid $825 million to buy Star TV in Hong Kong, principally so that he could broadcast to the mainland. The Chinese ban threatened to turn this whole investment into a complete loss. In a bid to assuage Chinese concerns, Murdoch dropped the BBC World Service from the Star platform, but Beijing was unmoved. He spent the rest of the decade attempting to reestablish links with

Chinese leaders, as Star notched up $100 million in operating losses year after year. And Murdoch stopped mixing business with foreign politics. Advocating political change through technology was just too volatile a subject to bring up. When it came to learning painful lessons, Rupert Murdoch never needed to be told twice. Why then, a year after the Banqueting Hall fiasco, had Murdoch returned to the same dangerous ideological ground?

Murdoch was in Melbourne on October 20, 1994 to give the John Bonython lecture at the Centre for Independent Studies, a policy institute modeled on the Institute for Economic Affairs in London. His theme was the arrival of the "century of networking." "Those of us who make our living by putting news and ideas and their audiences together face changes, triggered by science, that are no longer differences in degree: they amount to differences in kind," he said. George Orwell misunderstood the future, Murdoch argued, because he got it all wrong about technology. Ignorance was not strength, as Orwell asserted; freedom was not slavery. Rather than becoming Big Brother, technology was liberating people, producing an anarchistic media environment with no barriers to entry. [9]

This was an area with red flags all over it for Murdoch. Essentially it was the same argument he had made the year before at the Banqueting Hall. He was careful to avoid politics, but if you gave the underlying theme the smallest nudge, you would be back with technology as the great threat to totalitarian regimes. Asian governments could read the subtext of a speech. Murdoch's actions over Star TV and the BBC had shown he was too pragmatic to walk into danger needlessly, and this speech was clearly dangerous. Why then was he playing with fire like this, two weeks before the U.S. congressional elections?

Murdoch drew his argument from the early galley proofs of a book published that month by Peter Huber, a lawyer with a U.S. think tank, the Manhattan Institute for Policy Research. (Huber's thesis had been kicking around in various forums for more than a year and appears to have been the major source for Murdoch's 1993 London speech). Huber had written his book, *Orwell's Revenge: The 1984 Palimpsest,* by using a computer to recombine a wide range of Orwell's works to produce a happier version of *1984,* interspersed with chapters of his own analysis of where the technological revolution was going. In fact Huber had drawn so heavily from Orwell that he ended up paying a quarter of his royalties on the book to Orwell's estate.

Huber argued that *1984* was still the most important book published since World War II: "Orwell's technotic vision still casts a dark shadow over every advance in telegraphy, telemetry, telephony, and television—which is to say, every

facet of teletechnology, every yard of the information superhighway, that is transforming our lives today."[10]

One of the themes in *1984* is the way that those in power in a society can
rewrite history to suit their own ends. Winston Smith, the book's hero, spends his
days at the office rewriting old newspaper clips. That way every Party prophecy is
always vindicated: "Who controls the past controls the future; who controls the
present controls the past." Huber's novel approach was to rewrite the history of
1984 itself, to give the book a feel-good Hollywood ending. Huber's argument was
that technology is essentially anarchistic—and that that proves to be society's salvation. Orwell's unhappy citizens discover that the telescreens that Big Brother
uses to control them are actually interactive. They use them to communicate with
each other. The network becomes in effect the World Wide Web. They develop
street markets, entrepreneurial spirit and free enterprise become rampant, and
authoritarianism curls up its toes and calls it a day.

Huber's focus was on the way technology empowers private citizens. "We are
all becoming broadcasters in our own rights, with our PCs and broadband connections between them," Huber said in an interview in early 1995 on *The Progress
Report with Newt Gingrich,* a U.S. cable television show sponsored by Gingrich's
Progress and Freedom Foundation. "We are all gaining inch by inch the power of
a Dan Rather or a Peter Jennings."[11]

Huber was less clear about the position of chief programmer in this brave new
network. Michael Vlahos, the show's host, asked him, "It seems as though there is
an opportunity for a kind of re-creation of the kind of gatekeeper system, for example, that you have in Hollywood." This question was a gift to Huber, ready for
him to wave away with a stock answer. Instead Huber fudged. The question was
about access to networks, and he ended up talking about good and evil. Technology always amplified both "the power to do it well and honestly" and "the
power to do it badly," he said:

> But there—what it does seem clear to me is that it amplifies the good
> overall. The good and the honest and the productive people get more out
> of it than the cheaters and the malefactors because—I mean, that's just
> the way.

Huber's description of the moral dimensions of the information revolution
must have seemed awkward even at the time. Today it sounds uncomfortably like
a religious position, a statement of faith. One of the pillars of America's freedom

of speech laws is the belief by U.S. courts that good ideas push out bad ideas. It is a given. This belief is what makes freedom of speech possible, and it is why censorship is unnecessary. The paradigm has proved a little less robust when libertarians go on to apply the same concept to commerce and argue that good business practices drive out bad ones—and therefore there is no need for government to regulate business in any way. This is not a given. So are the new media a form of expression or a business enterprise? For Huber, the information revolution was all about communication—so governments should stay out of it. Wall Street, on the other hand, was about to discover that the revolution was really all about business. Technology was the road to commercial El Dorado.

Huber was speaking on the brink of the greatest wealth transfer in human history, the Internet stock bubble that would trigger the giddiest pursuit of money seen in modern times. Probably 1995 was the latest that anyone could still describe the Internet in the disinterested, altruistic terms of its government and academic origins. Indeed, in September 1995 at a Progress and Freedom Foundation conference in Aspen, Huber was described as lamenting that "the current view of the World-Wide Web as a marketplace was that it was full of deceit; a global bazaar full of mistrust." It would not be long, however, he assured his audience, before the transparent nature of the Web transformed into a place for "higher levels of integrity and loyalty."[12]

Rupert Murdoch has been accused of many things in his life but never of being a wild-eyed optimist. His life story has been a struggle against being locked out by media gatekeepers. "I have fought against them all my life," he said of his first monolithic business rivals in Australia in the 1970s. He has described his life as a series of interlocking wars; he likes to refer to his use of sports as a "battering ram" to break into markets. In the mid-1990s he and his rivals were spending billions of dollars to ensure that whatever twist or turn the information revolution took going into the next century, they would hold the keys to the kingdom. It was the reverse of what Peter Huber was arguing. Why then was Murdoch going out of his way in October 1994, at some risk to himself, to publicize and endorse a libertarian philosophy to which in practice he was so fundamentally opposed?

Besides his policy work, Huber was a partner at Washington law firm Kellogg Huber Hansen & Evans, which represented the regional Baby Bell telephone companies in their efforts to roll back some of the restrictions of the consent decrees that broke up AT&T. Huber's high media profile underlined how influential he had become in Gingrich's circle of advisers and as one of the architects of Republican strategy on telecommunications reform. The real attraction of

Huber's thesis was the political agenda it carried. If technology is anarchistic, then any attempt at government regulation is at best futile. At worst it might be detrimental for society as a whole. Huber coauthored an influential study for the Progress and Freedom Foundation released in February 1995 that argued that Congress should allow the Baby Bells to enter the lucrative long-distance market and also to compete with cable companies. "We should do everything possible to unleash cable companies to attack phone companies and unleash phone companies to attack cable companies," Huber said.[13] Most important of all, Congress should abolish the FCC entirely, a cause that Huber championed at every opportunity and eventually turned into a 1997 book.[14] So in terms of realpolitik, Huber's attack on Orwell was really an assault on the FCC.

Rupert Murdoch had never been on the best of terms with the FCC. Each year since 1986, the commission would later conclude, his media empire had misreported the level of foreign ownership and control of the Fox television stations. In 1993, when he spoke at the Banqueting Hall, Murdoch was opposed to the FCC in principle. But Huber's anti-Orwell rhetoric applied nicely to any government involvement in the media. And while Murdoch might be opposed to the FCC only in principle, he had far stronger feelings about the government-owned BBC. His newspapers had been running virulent anti-BBC editorials for a quarter of a century.

Thirteen months later in October 1994, when Murdoch spoke in Melbourne, the FCC problem had grown far more specific. After prodding by the NAACP, the FCC had forced News Corp to disclose for the first time the foreign ownership of the Fox stations. The FCC was mulling over whether to launch an inquiry. For Murdoch, taking up Huber's thesis about technology not only brought him into the policy network around Newt Gingrich; it also provided an oblique way to undermine the federal agency that was investigating him. For libertarians like Huber, it was a natural consequence: If George Orwell was wrong about technology, then a government regulator like the FCC was unnecessary and should be killed off immediately. In Murdoch's view that could not be soon enough. Murdoch pressed the attack on Orwell perhaps out of conviction, but certainly out of self-interest.

In mid-November 1994 the FCC problem grew even more threatening for Murdoch, after NBC launched a strident complaint against the Fox stations. Relations between NBC and Fox executives had become poisonous, with reports of heated telephone calls and an alleged confrontation (later denied) where NBC president Robert C. Wright "jabbed his finger at Mr. Murdoch's chest,"[15] complaining that he had been forced to spend hundreds of millions of dollars to keep NBC's affiliates from defecting to Fox. NBC was pressing the FCC to open a full inquiry into Fox's foreign ownership.

Murdoch was already heading for Washington. Preston Padden had scheduled a whistle-stop tour of the Capitol for late November 1994, three weeks after the Republican landslide win. Padden set up eighteen meetings over three days for Murdoch with Republican and Democratic leaders. While these meetings were purely courtesy calls, it was only natural that the conversations would turn to the FCC inquiry, at least in passing. The key players to see would be Bob Dole, the Senate majority leader; Jack Fields (R-Tex.), the chairman of the House Telecommunications Subcommittee; Thomas Bliley, a Republican from Virginia handpicked by Gingrich to chair the House Commerce Committee; Senator Larry Pressler, the amiable chairman of the Senate Commerce Committee; and the face of resurgent Republicanism himself, Newt Gingrich.

On the hectic Monday afternoon of November 28, 1994, Speaker-elect Gingrich was still operating out of his cramped Capitol office. His new staff would have no offices until he was formally elected speaker two months later. In the meantime his one-room office was awash with papers. New telephone lines were being installed, and some of his aides were operating without desks, off the floor. That afternoon Gingrich arrived late. He took a look at the wild scene in his office and waved his next appointment down the hall to a reception room, which was being set up for a Democratic dinner function.[16] As he walked down the corridor with Rupert Murdoch, Gingrich had no idea how much this new relationship was going to cost him.

In November 1994 the goal for which Gingrich had been striving for two decades was finally within his reach. Ever since the former Georgia college professor had won a seat in Congress in 1978, he had worked tirelessly to discredit the ruling Democrats, attacking their ethics and values. The high point was in 1988, when he had filed a complaint against Speaker Jim Wright. Wright later resigned over a string of ethics charges, including improper benefits from book royalties. In the early 1990s Gingrich's political action committee, GOPAC, had sent monthly audiotapes on tactics and vision to 28,000 supporters. Gingrich's recurring theme was the corruption of the incumbent Democrats and the welfare state. He advised aspiring Republican candidates to use words such as *bizarre, sick, self-serving* and *cheat* to describe liberals and Democrats.[17]

Gingrich was a man of immense energy. In 1994, besides leading his party as minority whip, teaching a college course, and mixing regular television appearances with political speeches and masterminding a sweeping political change throughout America, Gingrich had not neglected his hobbies. He liked to write books. His publisher, Jim Baen of Baen Publications, was finalizing his latest effort, a steamy historical novel called *1945*. Early reports described the book as a bodice ripper, and Gingrich and Baen were toning down some of the bedroom scenes. The following year the book would earn Gingrich a princely $8,000 in royalties. But in June 1994 one of Gingrich's aides, Jeff Eisenach (who had founded the Progress and Freedom Foundation the year before), had set up a meeting between Gingrich and a New York literary agent, Lynn Chu, to discuss a more lucrative writing opportunity. Chu and her husband Glen Hartley represented a high-profile stable of writers including literary critic Harold Bloom and conservatives David Brock, Thomas Sowell, and Irving Kristol. In June 1994 Chu told Gingrich that he could expect to earn up to $2 million from a book that, as he later put it, "described what we need to do to renew American civilization."[18] Gingrich said, in effect, "Get serious."

The book floated as an idea through the summer until August, when Chu had lunch with Adrian Zackheim, executive editor at HarperCollins US, who expressed interest. HarperCollins had a fascination with books by powerful politicians. Previously it had published memoirs by British prime minister Margaret Thatcher, Soviet president Mikhail Gorbachev, and a biography of Chinese leader Deng Xiaoping written by his daughter. "They were very excited, and we were happy to pursue it with them," Chu said later. "We knew they were a good house, they responded to the numbers we were pitching out. . . . Sometimes it all happens one-on-one like that."

By late November Chu and Eisenach had turned the idea into a seventeen-page proposal, *To Renew America*, for Zackheim. The situation was not yet resolved, but Gingrich was facing the pleasant prospect that HarperCollins was about to make him richer than he had ever been. As both sides tell it, the meeting that followed between Gingrich and Murdoch was one of the most confused exchanges in modern politics. It was a seven-figure misunderstanding. Gingrich did not know that Murdoch owned HarperCollins, so he could not know that the man he was accompanying down the corridor was about to pay him $2 million; and Murdoch for his part didn't know that HarperCollins was talking to Chu, so he could hardly be asking for any special political favors.

It was, as Padden described it later, "the most insignificant meeting in the history of the world."[19] Murdoch and Gingrich spoke for about a quarter of an hour. Padden and News lobbyist Peggy Binzell were also present, as was Gingrich's aide

Greg Wright. "It was a ten minute meeting—maximum," Murdoch told Ken Auletta at *The New Yorker.* "We met in the hall, because there were too many people in his office. It was just chitchat. We talked about the chances of his getting his Contract with America passed."[20]

Initially, spokesmen for both men denied that Fox's FCC problems were raised at the meeting. But six weeks later Padden conceded, "Right at the end I interjected that NBC was trashing us all over Capitol Hill, and it was just sour grapes because we were hurting them in the marketplace."[21] As Gingrich recounted the exchange: "They said something about, 'We're in this big fight with NBC,' and I said, 'Fine, I don't care.' I never got involved in individual cases like that. . . . The truth is, I don't remember anything about his problems with the FCC."[22]

Chu told the *New York Times* that she was not formally appointed Gingrich's agent until three days later, Thursday, December 1, "and that's when I immediately began talking money."[23] On December 9, HarperCollins's senior vice president Jack McKeown told dozens of the company's employees at their winter sales conference that HarperCollins had won the Gingrich book with a $2 million advance.

On December 7 the FCC announced that it was holding a formal inquiry into Fox, and Republicans began coming out in support of Murdoch. The next day Mike Riley, a Republican congressman from Texas and a senior member of the House Telecommunications Subcommittee, announced he would be introducing legislation to overturn the foreign ownership laws on television stations. *Daily Variety* reported that Republicans were prepared to rally around the Fox cause, and in the weeks that followed Larry Pressler, Thomas Bliley, and Jack Fields all came out in support of Fox.

Gingrich meanwhile had had second thoughts about the $2 million advance. He had spoken to his friends Alvin and Heidi Toffler and to former secretary of education Bill Bennett, who told him there was more money out there. Only Gingrich's fiction publisher, Jim Baen, told him to take the money and run. On the afternoon of December 20, Chu held a telephone auction with publishing houses including Doubleday, Simon & Schuster, Putnam, and Little, Brown. Such was HarperCollins's enthusiasm for the book that the bid price escalated sharply—so sharply that only one other publisher, Penguin USA chief Peter Mayer, managed to lodge a bid, believed to be about $4 million for one book. HarperCollins won with a deal for $4.5 million for two books, including a Gingrich reader. Again, Murdoch said he knew nothing about the negotiations. "I was telephoned in Beijing on Christmas Eve and told that it had happened," Murdoch told Ken

Auletta in mid-1995. "Howard Rubenstein called me. I went crazy. I knew critics would explode."[24]

This is a curious account. The call on December 24 by Rubenstein, New York's master spin doctor, would not have been to tell Murdoch that HarperCollins had made a rather large publication advance. The call could only have been about damage control, because in the intervening four days the critics had already exploded. On 22 December, Democrat Minority Whip David Bonior had launched a devastating attack on Gingrich with a press conference script that read straight out of pantomime. He began:

> I'm so sorry that I'm late. I know I've kept you waiting, but I just received this gift from Santa before we went away for the Christmas holidays, and I'd like to open it up and share it with you. Oops, it's for the other minority whip, Mr. Gingrich, who will be the next Speaker. It's a check for $4 million from Rupert Murdoch. Would you like to see it?[25]

Bonior suggested a link between the book contract and Republican support for Murdoch and Fox. But was this really the sort of improper payment or bribe that Bonior was suggesting? Gingrich gave every impression that he believed that $4.5 million was the fair market price for his writing, and thus Murdoch was entitled to no special favors. Murdoch says he knew nothing about the deal. Having said that, Gingrich had a history of difficulty in distinguishing between his personal ambitions and his public duties—particularly in using tax-free donations to fund political activities. He had also been criticized for the favourable mentions he regularly gave in his college course to companies that sponsored him.

*   *   *

Murdoch, for his part, had a history of publishing books by political leaders while they were still in power. In February 1995, Murdoch would host a New York launch for a book by Deng Xiaoping's daughter, as well as a thirty-member Chinese delegation to Sydney. After HarperCollins published Gorbachev's biography in 1987, Murdoch had not hesitated to use the leverage this gave him. News International director Bruce Hundertmark remembers meeting a team from the Russian Space Agency at Wapping in November 1988 headed by Eugene Luppov, when Murdoch was considering broadcasting Sky from a Russian satellite: "The Soviets were very impressed at the opportunity to meet *the* Mr. Murdoch, as they put it, and straightened their neckties and jackets before the presentation."

Murdoch told the Russians he wanted a meeting with Gorbachev to discuss a News Corp pay-television service to the Soviet Union.

An improper payment exists in the eye of the beholder. It is a state of mind. It takes only one person in such a deal to feel that it is an improper transaction for it to be an improper transaction for both parties. There is no evidence here that either Murdoch or HarperCollins executives or Gingrich viewed this transaction as being in any way improper. But committing to a book deal of this magnitude proved extremely costly.

In the furor that followed, Gingrich found himself under fire even from Republican ranks for the sheer size of the advance. Eight days later he announced that he would forgo the $4.5 million and settle for $1 up front, with royalties based on book sales. That comedown was not enough to stop a House Ethics Committee investigation into the original book deal. *To Renew America* went on sale the following August, just as Gingrich was testifying about the deal before the ethics inquiry. The book proved to be a best seller, but not enough of a best seller to recoup what Gingrich had given up. Gingrich grossed $1.47 million in royalties for *To Renew America* and another $163,500 on the second book, *Lessons Learned the Hard Way*, for a total of $1.64 million.[26]

Gingrich had always been strapped for money. Now the Murdoch factor had cost him a fortune. If Gingrich had accepted the Penguin bid for $4 million, the deal would not have been such a cause célèbre and may well have survived. But the advance wasn't the only loss. Gingrich's agent Lynn Chu operated on a 15 percent commission. On the royalties Gingrich actually received, that would have come to $245,000. The difficulty here was that Chu had acted in good faith and produced a $4.5 million advance that Gingrich had then declined. She was still entitled to her 15 percent fee of the original deal. That came to $675,000. Gingrich had to pay Chu an extra $430,000.

The repercussions continued. Gingrich was cleared by the Ethics Committee over the book deal, but ethics inquiries are hard to stop. The sheer momentum that the Murdoch controversy had produced meant that the committee kept looking at other complaints that the Democrats had tacked on to the investigation. Without the Murdoch book deal, it is doubtful there would have been inquiries into the secondary complaints, which related to Gingrich's fund-raising practices. This long-simmering inquiry finally resulted in a $300,000 fine imposed on Gingrich in January 1997. At this point, after paying Chu and his cowriter, Newt had netted just $656,000 from *To Renew America*. It was a long way short of his original fond hopes in 1994. And in early 1997, as Gingrich explored avenues to raise the $300,000 he needed to pay his Ethics Committee fine, he realized that his only major prospect for producing big money was from more book royalties. To pay his ethics fine, he needed to write the second book for HarperCollins. (*Lessons Learned the Hard Way* was published in 1998 and earned $163,500 in royalties. Gingrich's career prospects were not helped by his decision to dedicate the book in loving terms to his wife Marianne, when he had been having an affair with an Agriculture Committee clerk and former intern, Callista Bisek, since 1993.) Thus in 1997 Gingrich's financial future once again lay with Rupert Murdoch, the man whose maneuverings had brought Gingrich to this pass in the first place. And now Murdoch's editor at *The Weekly Standard* was making fun of his Mongolian hat.

*   *   *

Gingrich was hardly in a position to criticize Murdoch, whom he had hit up six months before for a $1 million donation to the Republican Party in California. Instead, Gingrich raged against Kristol and his "ABC bosses," a reference to Kristol's regular television spot. So if Murdoch was looking for a political miracle in 1997 to save his satellite hopes, it would not be coming from Gingrich. It was a question not just of whether Gingrich would be inclined to give Murdoch a miracle but of whether he still had the power to pull one off. It wasn't the only setback.

Besides his small team of inhouse lobbyists, Murdoch's biggest ally in Washington was the tobacco industry. He had been on the board of Philip Morris since 1989, while Philip Morris chairman H.W.H. Maxwell had sat on the News Corp board since 1992. The relationship was more than just the natural attraction between a media group and a major advertiser with an image problem. The tobacco industry hired the best lobbyists and spin doctors in Washington, and they had close links with southern politicians. Murdoch's pro-tobacco stance made him a natural fit for the Cato Institute, a high-profile conservative think tank whose major contributors included R. J. Reynolds and Philip Morris. Murdoch joined John Malone on the Cato board in September 1997.

Unfortunately for Murdoch, the malleable Larry Pressler, chairman of the Senate Commerce Committee, lost his seat in the November 1996 elections. The new head of the Commerce Committee was John McCain. While Thomas Bliley, the head of the House Commerce Committee, liked to describe himself as "one of the tobacco industry's best friends," McCain would show himself to be one of the tobacco lobby's worst nightmares: He introduced a 1998 bill that, if passed, would have cost tobacco companies $518 billion. So the tobacco lobbyists were not the ideal advocates for Murdoch's present dilemma.

Murdoch had bolstered his lobbying arm by engaging Parry & Romani Associates. Its star recruit was Dennis DeConcini, former Democratic chairman of the Senate Judiciary Subcommittee on Patents, Copyrights, and Trademarks. DeConcini, like McCain, was one of the Keating Five, a group of politicians who had received donations from Charles H. Keating, who was later convicted of fraud after his Lincoln Savings & Loan lost $2.5 billion. While DeConcini resigned after he was criticized by the ethics committee, McCain escaped largely unscathed. It was still, however, a sensitive subject for McCain. The situation made DeConcini as awkward an advocate for Murdoch as the tobacco lobbyists.

The biggest thing that Murdoch had going for him was the fact that Congress hated cable companies. After all the deliberations that had gone into the 1996 Telecommunications Act, the legislation had turned out to be a disappointment. The Progress and Freedom Foundation and the various right-wing think tanks had assured Republicans that lifting price restrictions would trigger cutthroat competition between cable guys and telephone companies and would lead to slashes in telephone and cable prices. Nothing like that had happened. Moreover no credible rival to cable had emerged, and cable operators had celebrated by raising cable fees by an average of 10 percent in 1996. Many Republicans felt that they had been sold a bill of goods. "If anyone ever says they really believed real [telecommunications] competition was going to come from cable, they are either stupid or disingenuous," said one government insider.[27] One of those most upset was John McCain. On March 6 Murdoch went to Washington to brief him on the Sky merger and the competition it would pose to cable operators. The Baby Bells had done nothing more than make promises about providing competition; Murdoch was about to really do it. McCain was sympathetic but noncommittal.

Murdoch had decided on a crash-through strategy. A conventional change in the copyright law could get bogged down in Orrin Hatch's Judicial Subcommittee on Patents, Copyrights, and Patents and be bounced around other committees for years. Rather than allow that, Murdoch would use his friends in Congress to press the measure as a matter of urgency, tacking it onto an appropriations bill. The downside was that if this strategy failed, the issue would end up back with the disgruntled committee chairman whose power he had tried to subvert.

At McCain's invitation, Murdoch returned to Washington on April 10 to appear before a Commerce Committee hearing into the rise in cable rates. "Congress must clarify that satellite competitors like Sky are legally entitled to carry local broadcast stations the same way that cable and wireless cable systems can do today," he said. He went on to portray himself as the persistent underdog. When Fox TV was launched, he said, "The critics laughed so loudly I still have a slight ringing in my ear." He had launched Fox News six months before, "despite a firmly entrenched competitor in CNN and in another younger but widely hyped competitor, MSNBC." Even if it succeeded, he said, with 8 million customers Sky would hardly put cable out of business: "Sky is willing to risk a $3 billion capital investment to bring consumers a better choice now. If you give us the legal authority, the rest is up to us."

Murdoch is a persuasive advocate. "There is this premise that Rupert Murdoch is the white knight, and that he's the only one who knows how to provide competition," complained Stephen Effros, president of the Cable Telecommunications Association. "It's a silly premise."[28] Meanwhile National Cable Television Association president Decker Anstrom was insisting that Sky had to provide "more specific information about its business plan, about its technology and about the specific legislation it's looking for. Otherwise [Murdoch is] making nothing more than some vague assurances."[29]

Murdoch was touching a chord, but it had become clear by April 10 that he was unlikely to win the fast-track legislation he was seeking. "It's too much, too soon for one person to pull off, even for Murdoch," Lehman Brothers analyst Kim Wallace told reporters. "He'll have to kiss the rings of twenty or thirty people but he will prevail [by the end of the year]."[30]

That same day Orrin Hatch wrote to Senate Appropriations Committee chairman Ted Stevens objecting to tacking copyright amendments onto an appropriations bill, as "copyright issues are complex and deserve a full airing." Murdoch said he welcomed "all the hearings in the world," although "what a delay does is let our competitors catch up with us."[31]

In reality the game was already over. The window of opportunity that Murdoch had been looking for was closed. Typically, the first person to realize this was Murdoch himself. Within a day of his April 10 appearance before McCain's committee, reports circulated that Murdoch had been talking to his cable rivals about cutting a new satellite deal since before he even came to Washington. Murdoch had already conceded that he was facing a humiliating defeat.

*   *   *

For a minor media mogul, this setback might have been debilitating. But running a worldwide empire like News Corp had shown Murdoch that the game always goes on, somewhere else in the world. At the same time that he was wooing Republicans, he was helping to engineer a different political revolution in Britain. In London on March 17, 1997, British prime minister John Major called a general election for May 1. Murdoch's *Sun* newspaper had supported the Conservative Party since the 1970s. On the British election day in 1992, the *Sun* had run a page-one picture of Labour leader Neil Kinnock's head squeezed into a lightbulb. The headline read, "If Kinnock wins today, will the last person to leave Britain please turn out the lights." When Major won a surprise victory for the Conservatives that year, the *Sun* crowed, "It was the *Sun* wot won it." On March 18, six days before *The Weekly Standard* in Washington ran the "Newt Melts" cover accusing Gingrich of not being right-wing enough, the *Sun* began day one of the British general election between Major and Labour's Tony Blair by dumping the Conservatives: "The Sun Backs Blair." Days later in Sydney, News Corp attacked another conservative leader, Australian prime minister John Howard. In the courtly conversational style of local News chief Ken Cowley, it hardly ranked as a threat; more like a promise to be brutal with a fluffy pillow.

*   *   *

By the middle of March the dismayed American cable industry had regrouped. On March 17 it roared into New Orleans, twenty thousand strong, for the three-day annual conference of the National Cable Television Association (NCTA). On the final day Ted Turner took the stage for an interview with Larry King, under stern orders from NCTA chief Decker Anstrom not to trash Murdoch. Nevertheless Turner could not resist a jibe, saying nothing that Murdoch did surprised him, because he had just turned sixty-six and he was running out of time:

> He's got to do it quickly before he passes on. As hard as he works, you know, he could have a stroke or a heart attack at any time. That's OK, isn't it, Decker? This nice man could trip and fall . . . a hundred stories.[32]

Turner should have quit while he was ahead. Instead he went on to defend Time Warner's broken promise to run Fox News on its New York cable net: "You don't have a deal in this country until you have a signed contract. A promise doesn't mean diddly poo. I never sued anybody over a promise. I promised to be faithful to my *wife.*" A little pause followed, as Turner remembered that Jane Fonda was in the audience. "Uh, not this wife. But everybody makes promises they haven't kept."

Turner resolved the minor hiatus that this gaffe produced by returning to his favorite theme: "We're going to make it as tough as we possibly can [for Murdoch], kind of like the Russian army did to the German army. . . . Either he's going to go hungry or we are. He's the one that cast down the gauntlet." Gerry Levin was more prosaic about Sky: "It's never going to get off the ground. It's over-hyped. They have too many problems to overcome."[33] But behind the bravado, the industry was in deep turmoil. "Every meeting we've had, Murdoch is the topic of discussion," one industry official said.[34] What would trigger a rebound in cable stocks? "If Rupert Murdoch gets malaria," said cable industry guru Paul Kagan.[35]

News Corp had $2.5 billion tied up in Fox News, Fox Sport, and f/X in partnership with John Malone. But Malone's warning that cable operators would drop Murdoch's cable programming was being realized. A week after the announcement of the EchoStar merger, Jeff Marcus, the head of the country's ninth largest cable group, Marcus Cable, canceled appointments with News Corp executives to carry f/X on more of his systems. Marcus flatly refused to see Murdoch's people. [36] Malone later testified, "Most of the large cable operators were giving [Murdoch] a slow no on carrying his channels."[37] Like Marcus, they would not even discuss carrying Murdoch's programming. "I don't think, generally, people want to buy bullets for the gun that's going to shoot them," said Glenn Jones, head of Jones Intercable, when asked about carrying Fox News for his 1.5 million subscribers.[38]

The five cable partners in Primestar had met before Turner's speech on March 19. "Time to market is critical to gain market share, blunt ASkyB entry," Malone noted tersely in a memo the next day. Malone's memo suggests that the cable operators would try to minimize ASkyB's impact by delaying the launch as long as possible. Dan O'Brien, the Time Warner representative on the Primestar committee, noted at a partners' meeting a week later, "[ASkyB] will be a formidable competitor." He expected News Corp to have prices lower than everyone else's.[39]

Murdoch was beginning to realize the full cost of what he was doing: The bottom line was that his $2.5 billion stake in cable channel programming was being threatened by his $1 billion investment in satellite television. The programming problems had grown so serious that in late March he went to Malone for advice. Leo Hindery, TCI's determinedly amiable president, described the outcome of the meeting as "both organizations saying, 'Let's talk. Let's not whale on each other.' " Malone was actually a little more blunt than that. He told Murdoch flatly that the whole EchoStar merger proposal was "lunacy."

Murdoch's response, even in the deadening tones of a Justice Department legal document filed fourteen months later, still carries the desperate flavor of that moment. "Well then, help me get out of it; help me find something else to do," Murdoch told Malone. "What is Plan B?"[40]

Malone has never said quite what Plan B was. But on March 26 he discussed Murdoch's options with Bob Scherman's Washington trade publication, *Satellite Business News*. "Rupert is so aggressive that he doesn't really make a good partner," said Malone. He thought the ASkyB strategy would probably work for some markets, saying, "I wouldn't be surprised to see them target a few markets, really drive hard in those markets, and Rupert try to make a deal for distribution." Malone apparently saw Murdoch's strategy as a squeeze play, where the quid pro quo Murdoch was offering was to go easy on pushing his satellite service. "There's some kind of peace in which Rupert gets what he wants, which is broader distribution of his programming networks in exchange for which he's not quite as aggressive [in DBS]."[41]

Malone had outlined the basic ingredients for an armed truce. Murdoch would ease up on the cable industry, and in return the cable guys would run his channels. But a player as sophisticated as Malone could extract more out of this than just the pleasure of seeing his friend Rupert eat a little humble pie. Malone could also use the situation to change the balance of power in Primestar, where TCI and Time Warner each held a 21 percent stake. It was a lever to make Gerry Levin at Time Warner more amenable.

Malone continued:

> You don't take Rupert lightly. It may actually be the kind of rallying cry
> Primestar and the cable operators need in order to really see the threat
> that is there. So Rupert may be doing us a huge favor by pointing out to
> us our vulnerabilities and rallying us . . . I suspect that the external threat
> of Rupert Murdoch to CNN may be about to cause them [Time Warner]
> to be a little more willing to reach the combinations with TCI and the
> rest of the industry and maybe have a united front in Primestar.

For whatever reason, a week and a half after the NCTA conference, Murdoch appears to have concluded that the conflict required a more drastic resolution. It is hard not to feel some sympathy for Charlie Ergen, Murdoch's erstwhile partner at EchoStar, as events unfolded in April. Murdoch's presentation to the Commerce Committee on April 10 was supposed to be the linchpin of his campaign to win Capitol Hill over to the anticable cause. But the following day David Lieberman reported in *USA Today* that Murdoch had had another meeting earlier that week with Malone, where Murdoch had proposed quite a different agenda. He had discussed dumping EchoStar and instead folding ASkyB into Primestar with the cable operators. Bob Scherman at *Satellite Business News* ran the same story. He said Murdoch met with Malone and Hindery in New York on Tuesday, April 8.[42]

What was Charlie Ergen to think? When Murdoch read the *USA Today* story, he left a message on Ergen's answering machine saying that he had not had discussions with the Primestar partners in more than a year. Preston Padden also denied any meeting: "This is someone's fantasy." Then Ted Turner called Ergen to tell him that News Corp officials had approached Time Warner. "He called to say that News Corp was throwing us overboard and that they were meeting with Levin to talk about a Primestar–News Corp deal," Ergen later told *Denver Post* journalist Stephen Keating.[43] Clearly Turner wanted to scuttle any Primestar deal.

In Washington Murdoch's lobbying campaign was dead in the water. The stories that the cable companies had circulated about Murdoch's secret New York meeting with them, whether true or not, had killed any hope of tacking a quick political fix onto the appropriations bill. The stories kept coming. *Multichannel News* also reported Murdoch's offer to fold ASkyB into Primestar. "Rupert's desperate," a senior cable executive said. Primestar chairman Jim Gray, a former Time Warner executive, was dismissive. He said he wasn't in the room when the Murdoch pitch was made. "I haven't heard anything serious like that coming from the partners, and my own view is that there's a low probability that anything will happen in that area," he said.[44]

The question was, if the cable operators had stalled Murdoch in Washington, did they still need to negotiate with him? Having beaten Murdoch, they wanted to roast him, to leave him swinging with a satellite license and satellites that he couldn't afford and no one wanted. Discussions between News Corp and Primestar that spring were handled mainly by Leo Hindery and Chase Carey. Hindery was "a peacemaker. . . . He kept trying to convince everybody that there was more profit in peace than war," Malone said later. Malone was hauled out for the heavy meetings with Time Warner and several other Primestar partners, where he was "a proponent of, at least, exploring whether or not we could make peace [with Murdoch]."[45]

For Charlie Ergen, April brought the slow and bitter realization that his satellite dream team was not going to reach orbit. Murdoch would cast him adrift, into desperate financial straits. The only thing that Ergen had going for him was his sheer cussedness and ornery determination. Back on March 7, EchoStar and News Corp, after taking advice from tax lawyers and the FCC, had agreed to re-structure the deal and draw up a new terms sheet. But lawyers on the two sides could not agree, and draft versions kept bouncing back and forth between them. The worrying thing was that if News Corp took the view that the original letter agreement had been abandoned—as it would—and no subsequent agreement had been finalized, where would that leave Charlie Ergen? What would stop Murdoch from walking away from the table?

Ergen and Padden, who headed News Corp's satellite operations, fought over everything. Padden had planned the Phoenix uplink facility as a landmark. His plans called for the glass-lit lobby to be backed by "a 150-foot-long granite wall of water . . . with finishes of cherrywood, marble, stainless steel, and terrazzo." But Ergen didn't want to pay for granite; he wanted to use linoleum.[46] Since April 7, the day before Murdoch's reported meeting with Malone in New York, News Corp had been insisting that the new Sky operation use News Datacom's encryp-tion and conditional access system. Ergen wanted to continue with the Swiss Nagra SA system that EchoStar used. He argued that hackers had broken the News Datacom encryption. "Charlie said, 'I'm not going to risk my business on this thing,'" EchoStar spokeswoman Judianne Atencio said later. Padden re-sponded that EchoStar was Nagra's only customer, with only 400,000 subscribers. On April 17, in a torrid meeting at EchoStar's headquarters between Ergen and Murdoch and their executives, Padden stormed out. He didn't return.

On April 25 Murdoch wrote to Ergen highlighting the News Datacom issue among a range of issues needed to be resolved: "[News Corp] cannot agree to making a vast investment in EchoStar on the basis of [the Nagra] technology. . . . We cannot go forward in our partnership using this technology."[47]

Meanwhile, EchoStar's stock price had dropped from $27 to $14. The critical date would be May 1, when News Corp was due, under the original letter agree-ment, to make a $200 million loan to EchoStar to keep it going, and file for federal approval for the deal. May 1 was the event horizon, the point of no return for the entire deal. Once Murdoch had put down some hard money, he would be com-mitted. As it turned out, no money was forthcoming for Ergen that day. The rumor mill ratcheted up a cog.

On the evening of May 1, when asked about the Sky deal, Malone responded,

"It's dead."[48] Padden appears to have come to the same conclusion. He resigned from News Corp, telling reporters, "The reality that I did not have a job was apparent nearly to everybody else in the world before I figured it out."[49] It was not an easy parting for the man who a year before had said he was with News Corp "for life," who had regularly had his boss as a houseguest when Murdoch went to Washington.

"From what I understand, Murdoch placed a call to Ted Turner on Tuesday of this week [April 29] suggesting that they make peace," UBS Securities analyst Rick Westerman told CNN. "I understand that Murdoch met with Gerry Levin, the CEO of Time Warner, on Wednesday and there were discussions with respect to the potential satellite relationship going forward."[50]

Ergen was still alive and kicking, nonetheless, trying to revive the deal. The following Monday, May 5, EchoStar demanded that News Corp make good on its commitment to loan the $200 million, to prevent EchoStar from going broke. Though Ergen didn't know it, on Tuesday News Corp sealed a deal with MCI for News Corp to take 90 percent of ASkyB. On Tuesday afternoon, after further exchanges, Chase Carey flew into Denver International Airport, where he met Ergen and told him bluntly that if he wanted the merger to go ahead, he would have to resign. The new venture had to be headed by a News Corp executive, or News would go its own way. Ergen said he still wanted to go ahead but wanted time to consider. Carey said he would call him the next day. But he never made the call. The momentum toward the courtroom had become unstoppable.[51]

On Wednesday, May 7, the first legal skirmishes began. On Friday morning News Corp finally signaled that the alliance was over when six of its employees left the EchoStar offices. That night EchoStar staff drove to the home of the chief deputy clerk for the U.S. District Court of Colorado and filed the paperwork for a writ at his kitchen table. Charlie Ergen was suing News Corp and Rupert Murdoch for $5 billion.[52] The first question was whether EchoStar would stay solvent long enough to get the case to court. The second was serving the writ on News Corp. When process servers could not gain admission to the News Corp offices in New York, David Moskowitz drove out to Arthur Siskind's house in Larchmont to serve it personally. The exchange went badly. News Corp and EchoStar lawyers would spend much of the next eighteen months deposing each other and everyone else connected with the deal. The onerous terms exacted by Ergen when the suit was settled in late 1998 would cost News Corp and MCI $3.5 billion.[53]

And Charlie Ergen? He still thought he knew Rupert Murdoch. For months after the deal came apart, as EchoStar struggled for survival, Ergen would keep that signed agreement with Murdoch on his desk. He would look at it every day and wonder, What could have been? Where did it go wrong? In his darker moments he would wonder whether Murdoch had ever intended to go through with Sky, or whether he had been used as a pawn in a wider game. He would even wonder whether it had all been some sort of hideous revenge for the 110WL auction.

14

THE TESTING OF PAT

Virginia Beach, Virginia, February–June 1997

SOME TELEPHONE CALLS should never be taken. One day in the depths of the North American winter of 1997, Murdoch picked up the telephone and said, "Hello, Pat," though he should have known better.

America's most influential religious figure was on the other end of the line. Murdoch had never made a secret of his admiration for Pat Robertson, the one-time Baptist minister who became a television evangelist, then a politician, while remaining always a businessman. Murdoch had known Robertson since 1986, when Robertson sold his Boston television station, Channel 25, to Fox. "You can say what you like, he's right on all the issues," Murdoch said of him during Robertson's unsuccessful presidential campaign in 1988.[1] Now Robertson was calling Murdoch about another business opportunity.

What was Rupert Murdoch doing? His family background should have warned him of the danger he was facing. Murdoch had had enough Low Churchmen among his ancestors to know the folly of this course. His roots would have told him that it is a basic premise of Protestant free enterprise that you never, ever do business with the preacher. Because when you do, and the preacher gets a fatal attack of scruples, it will cost you a lot of money. In the next four months Pat Robertson's inner struggle to do the right thing would cost Rupert Murdoch $1 billion. It would also play a critical role in resolving the battle for cable networks, the future of satellite television, and the economics of sports. The outcome would be determined by a bizarre string of events that reached as far as a hotel room in Zaire. Even in the topsy-turvy worlds of the Murdoch empire, this outcome would be remarkable. The conflict was a subtle one and must be examined one strand at a time. It begins with the peculiar character of Marion Gordon Robertson, the tall silver-haired figure who has always been known as Pat.

Pat Robertson in his own way is as much a pioneer of the cable industry as Ted

Turner or Gerry Levin or John Malone. Robertson was fresh out of seminary in 1959 when he came to believe that God was telling him to buy a defunct UHF television station in Plymouth, Virginia, for $37,000. Soon after the station went to air in 1961, Robertson hired Jim and Tammy Bakker, a husband and wife team on the revival preaching circuit, to do a puppet show. With the station's finances in disrepair, Jim Bakker launched a tearful appeal that drew in a surge of donations. Subsequently Bakker and Robertson launched a show called *The 700 Club,* which aimed at raising seven hundred supporters willing to pledge ten dollars a month. Robertson never looked back. In 1977 he launched America's first general-entertainment cable channel with a risible sixteen thousand subscribers. Five years later his audience had grown to 15 million, and no one was laughing.

Robertson was part of a wave of televangelists who took America's airwaves by storm in the 1970s and early 1980s. Jimmy Swaggart, Robert Schuller, Jim Bakker, Oral Roberts, and Jerry Falwell became household names. By the mid-1980s Christian preachers had sixty-two national syndicated shows. The virtual realities of modern media held no fears for the televangelists as they contemplated the television programs forged by faith, the cable networks not made with hands. In 1985 a Nielsen survey of the top-ten religious shows reported that 21 percent of America's television households were tuning in to Christian TV for at least six minutes a week, and 40 percent of households watched at least six minutes a month. These huge numbers marked a major social phenomenon. The televangelists "have greater unrestricted access to media than any other interest group in America," sociologist Jeffrey Hadden of the University of Virginia told *Time.* The head of National Religious Broadcasters, Reverend Ben Armstrong, claimed the televangelists had "done what Ted Turner tried to do and Rupert Murdoch wants to do—create an alternative fourth network."[2]

Armstrong's claim was not without substance. Whether you loved or hated television preachers (and most people settled for one or the other), they had become arguably the only noncommercial group to make serious inroads into the American television industry. But already in the mid-1980s waves of change were beginning to buffet them as the information revolution gathered speed. How the virtual cathedral weathered this sea change would say much for the future of independent voices in traditional media. And how the televangelists survived would turn largely on the flamboyant, passionate figure who towered above them all, Pat Robertson, whose audience was almost double that of his closest rival.

The most distinctive feature of Pat Robertson has always been his mouth.

When the Bank of Scotland pulled out of an online banking alliance with him in June 1999 over his outspoken comments, Robertson said, "You can't believe how strong the homosexuals are" in "that dark land" of Scotland. His 1991 book, *New World Order,* described world finances as being controlled by a Jewish-led conspiracy. He advocates using political assassination against foreign heads of state. He sees feminism as a "socialist anti-family political movement that encourages women to leave their husbands, kill their children, practice witchcraft, destroy capitalism and become lesbians."[3] It isn't just gays, feminists, child molesters, and Democrats who arouse his ire (not necessarily in that order). "You're supposed to be nice to Episcopalians, Presbyterians and Methodists," he told the London *Observer.* "Nonsense. I don't have to be nice to the spirit of the Antichrist."[4] Around that time he was quietly shuffled off the Laura Ashley board.

Not that Robertson always means quite what he says. "I have been on TV now for almost forty years, I do a one-hour show every day, and it is easy to make what I believe are malapropisms," he said in 1999, by way of explanation. "I speak from the heart often, and many times these statements needs clarification and if brought out of context can easily be misunderstood."[5]

Robertson's point about context is significant, because if there is one person whose rambling, stream-of-consciousness diatribes bear comparison with Robertson's, it is that other fine southern gentleman, Ted Turner. The similarities between the two men go deeper than sharing a flair for overdramatic language and the outrageous phrase. Each used a public appeal for money to keep his first television station afloat, and each went on to found a cable network. Both men are plugged into a tradition of southern rhetoric that is easy for outsiders to dismiss and underestimate.

Robertson was on the brink of entering politics when Murdoch bought his Boston television station in 1986. Robertson's 1988 bid for the Republican presidential nomination proved one of the pivotal experiences of his career. In nine of the first ten primaries in the South, Robertson beat front-runner George Bush, whereupon Super Tuesday blew away his hopes. Robertson was in Washington for the Bush inauguration in January 1989. He was mulling over his political prospects and his mailing list of 3 million conservative Christian voters when a young conservative activist, Ralph E. Reed Jr., convinced him to found a new religious political group, the Christian Coalition. It would become one of the most powerful supporters for America's move to the right in the 1990s.

Of more immediate importance, problems had developed at the Christian

Broadcasting Network (CBN). In 1988, with Robertson away campaigning, dona-tions raised by *The 700 Club* dropped 36 percent. Who was responsible? The revivalist tradition from which Robertson springs has always struggled with the tension between the natural and the supernatural, between belief in God's power and in personal agency. A popular expression in fundamentalist circles sums up this tension: "You must pray as if it all depends upon God. Then you must go out and work as if it all depends upon you." The big drop in donations to *The 700 Club* made it appear that, at least at CBN, it all depended upon Pat.

"What are we going to do when Pat Robertson is gone?" CBN's chief financial officer, Robert M. Prigmore, said in 1994. "Pat's not going to live forever." "It was an eye-opener of how dependent we are on Pat and the money he raises for the ongoing ministry," CBN director Harold Bredesen said in 1994. "We realized our need for alternate funding."[6]

CBN needed to become more commercial. At the same time the profits that its Family Channel were raking in were beginning to threaten CBN's tax-free status as a charity. The solution to all this was for CBN to sell the Family Channel; the most suitable buyer would be itself. In early 1990 CBN sold the Family Channel to a new company called International Family Entertainment (IFE) in return for $250 million of convertible debt. All of the initial stock in IFE was held by Pat Robertson, who invested $100,000, and his son Tim, who kicked in $50,000. Robertson Sr.'s stock was held by a trust he controlled that would revert to CBN when he turned eighty, twenty years later. One aspect of this arrangement was that, while Robertson would have complete control over the investments held by the trust, he could always say that no matter what he did privately, the money would always end up with CBN.

At this point the Robertson family's returns were minimal. Two years later when IFE and CBN raised $187.5 million in an initial public offering, Pat and Tim Robertson ended up with supervoting stock in IFE worth $62.5 million. CBN and Regent University (the college Robertson had founded) kept on selling down their IFE stock on the stock market. By 1996 the CBN and Regent stock sales had raised $285 million.

Tim Robertson continued to craft the Family Channel into a general-entertainment network that ran old family fare like *Bonanza, The Waltons, The Three Stooges*, and *The Mary Tyler Moore Show*. "I make no bones about it, I am a person of faith, and I have very deeply held religious beliefs, but I don't use the channel as my pulpit," Tim Robertson told the *Boston Herald*.[7] Robertson de-scribed his ideal viewer as a mother, aged twenty-five to fifty-four, who was seeking entertainment suitable for young children but was leery of the content of most TV shows.

The Family Channel went on to cable in Britain in 1993 and to satellite in Latin America in 1995. By then the Robertsons had made the Family Channel one of the top-ten television brands in the world—a fact that advertisers conceded sometimes with gritted teeth. "We buy it [Family]," Grey Advertising senior vice president Jon Mandel told *Multichannel News,* "even though the worst piece of garbage ever run on TV is *The 700 Club.* It doesn't carry commercials, anyway."[8]

By 1996 Pat Robertson had become a man of many parts. From his base in Virginia Beach, besides IFE he also presided over Christian Broadcasting Network, which produced *The 700 Club,* and he also owned a string of commercial ventures that included a hotel, a theme park, an unsuccessful vitamin and cosmetics business, and a retirement village. Nearby was Regent University, and just down the road was the headquarters of Robertson's relief agency, Operation Blessing International.

But in late 1996 press attention was focusing on Pat Robertson's private business interests—in particular his diamond mining operation in Zaire. "I personally funded huge shipments of medical supplies to the refugees from Rwanda as well as the victims of the Ebola outbreak in Kikwit," Robertson said later. "It was obvious that private charity could not sustain the enormous need that existed in the country, and I was attempting to make investments in timber, mining and agriculture which would be self-sustaining. Regrettably, the chaotic political situation in that nation made such ventures impossible."[9]

In the early 1990s Robertson had established a cordial relationship with the brutal dictator of Zaire, President Mobutu Sese Seko, who granted a diamond mining concession on a river in southeastern Zaire to a corporation that Robertson owned called African Development Company. The concession turned out to be something of a dud. Robertson flew in dredges that didn't work, diamond grades were poor, and eventually, after writing off losses that some estimates put as high as $7 million, he pulled out. But the link raised questions about what Robertson was doing in business deals with Mobutu in the first place. Some curious incidents came to light.

Kinshasa, Zaire, March 23, 1993
The door to Leslie Naghiu's hotel room was unlocked, but this didn't trouble him. Even the most dependable of hotel maids can forget to lock a room after she comes in to turn down the sheets, and he was glad to be back in familiar sur-

roundings. He had just completed a trip to the back blocks outside of Kinshasa, through military checkpoints where soldiers had been known to beat up and rob foreigners. That was why he had left his attaché case behind in his room on the nineteenth floor.

Naghiu shuffled into the dark room and felt for the light switch. It wasn't working. He fumbled around and finally located a floor lamp. It was then that he saw the clothing strewn about the room, his large suitcase open, and a man crouched beside it—a man who, even as Naghiu saw him, rose and lunged at him with a knife. In the fierce struggle that followed, the knife caught Naghiu above the ear on the left side of his head, then again on the right forearm. And then Naghiu realized that a second man was coming toward him out of the bathroom. Amid a flurry of blows a wider darkness engulfed him, and Naghiu slumped to the floor unconscious, where his companions later found him.[10]

The incident was revisited in Delaware District Court in February 1996 when Naghiu, who worked for Pat Robertson's Christian Broadcasting Network as "director of executive protection," sued the Intercontinental Hotels group for personal injuries and the loss of $146,000. The money had been in the briefcase stolen from him during the attack in his hotel room in March 1993. According to Judge Murray M. Schwartz, who described the events in the case as "rich with intrigue," Naghiu had flown to Zaire with other CBN staff that month "to purchase diamonds and render humanitarian aid."

Naghiu brought $100,000 in his attaché case. While in Zaire he had received another $46,000 "as proceeds of a diamond transaction," Judge Schwartz found. Robertson said later:

> To the best of my knowledge, [Naghiu's] medical expenses were paid by insurance which we had provided for him, and he was given retirement settlement from our organization to compensate for his severe injury in excess of $500,000. Today I am still at a loss to understand why he did not prevail in the case against the Intercontinental Hotel Company, which, in my opinion, was clearly negligent in permitting one of its guests to be attacked, brutally beaten, and robbed in his room in their hotel.[11]

But Judge Schwartz dismissed Naghiu's claim for compensation against the hotel on the grounds that he had not owned the money that was stolen. He also found it "noteworthy" that the hotel group had twice requested, without success, paper records to show where the money had come from and who owned it, and to prove that it even existed. Further, despite repeated requests, Naghiu had not been able to produce evidence that he or CBN had declared the money when he left the United States, as required by U.S. law and the Customs Service.

It really was most peculiar. Did the money in the suitcase belong to Pat Robertson's private companies, or to the tax-exempt CBN organization, or to Operation Blessing? Why didn't the owner of the money, rather than the man carrying it, bring the lawsuit? If the money was connected with Robertson's private businesses, as seemed likely, what were CBN staff or relief workers doing handling it—and being knocked unconscious for it?

In 1996 these questions seemed to have little significance. There was nothing illegal or improper about carrying a suitcase of money, or trading diamonds. But the virtual cathedral of the televangelists ran on appearances—or at least its leaders seemed to believe it did. When asked about his mining interests in 1999, Robertson explained, "You can look at it one way and say this is a wonderful thing you're doing, taking your money to try and make some profit in order to help people who are desperately poor. The other side is that it is not right. But if I please the Lord and I do what he says then he will take care of me."[12]

But the sort of questions that were being raised about Robertson's diamond operations had the potential to damage the relationship of trust that Robertson, *The 700 Club*, CBN, and Operation Blessing enjoyed with their donors. And donations were the lifeblood of the Robertson group. Robertson was already struggling with bad press because of an ongoing tax audit by the IRS over several million dollars of CBN funds that had been channeled into his presidential campaign in 1988, and the Christian Coalition's ties with the Republican Party. Then there was the lawsuit brought by three members of the Regent University law school, after Robertson wrote an open letter that suggested they were the worst law professors in the history of Western jurisprudence. There had been a messy scene in a Virginia courtroom when a process server had tried to serve a court order to Robertson, chasing him around a table in a conference room, papers and coffee cups spilling over, and some spirited pushing and shoving, while Robertson's bodyguard threatened to beat the process server up. All in all, by early 1997 a little more bad press was the last thing that Pat Robertson needed. This provides one possible explanation for the remarkable turn that events would later take. In the meantime Pat Robertson had had a close encounter of an entirely different kind. In early January 1996 his old friend Rupert Murdoch had telephoned him with an idea. It was a world away from the comfortable values of the Family Channel.

*   *   *

If anyone knew the frustrations of seeking media access in the 1990s, it was Murdoch. He had had to scrap and scrape to win affiliates for the Fox network. He had just committed to launch Fox News, an outlay that would grow to more than $500 million. And at the same time he had decided to launch a cable channel with children's programming called Fox Kids. It was the brainchild of an aggressive Egyptian-born Israeli American named Haim Saban.

Saban, like Robertson, had carved a business empire out of a niche in the media industry, but he had taken a very different route. The international growth of the U.S. entertainment industry has produced opportunities for entrepreneurs at every frontier. The dubbing down of America is very big business. Every time a book or film or television program or song crosses a national or language frontier, it provides work for the little community of specialists who can translate or dub the work, to make it acceptable and saleable in another culture. Saban was a linguistic arbitrageur. He was born in Alexandria in 1944, and his family moved to Israel in the 1950s, where he grew up in modest circumstances. Like many people from Alexandria, he was a polyglot, able to switch at will among English, French, Hebrew, Arabic, Spanish, and Italian.

In the 1970s Saban built one of the largest music businesses in France, then in 1980 moved to Los Angeles. He said later he had had barely enough money to buy a hilltop house in Hollywood and a Rolls-Royce. He scrounged and pushed his way into music work in Hollywood, then into producing a children's show for NBC called *Captain Kidd.* U.S. domestic sales covered the $200,000 cost of producing each episode and gave Saban a $50,000 profit. It was the overseas sales, where he could earn another $70,000, that became the major profit driver of such productions. In 1986 he secured the rights to a Japanese children's action show called *Macron 1,* to be dubbed into English. On the same trip to Japan he came across episodes of Japanese fantasy shows from the 1960s and 1970s, on which he quietly took an option for distribution rights outside Japan. They were pretty horrible to Western eyes, but they had some expensive special-effects fight scenes between giant dinosaurs and huge robots intercut with human figures. The thought stayed with Saban that the figures wore helmets. Once you put a helmet on a figure, it could be anyone underneath.

For the next six years he played around with the idea of producing a cheap-as-dirt children's program by shooting a few scenes of American teenagers changing into bright costumes, then intercutting the special-effects shots from the old Japanese shows of the 1970s. He pitched the idea to a succession of network programmers over the years, all of whom found the idea too awful to contemplate, until in 1992 he found someone desperate to try something loopy and unusual in children's programming. Margaret Loesch, programmer for Fox Children's Network (FCN), loved the idea. In 1985 when she was president of Marvel Comics' television production company, Loesch had actually spotted the same Japanese program—a year before Saban—and had paid $25,000 to have a pilot dubbed into English. U.S. network executives had hated it. "One network executive asked, 'How could you bring us this piece of garbage?' " Loesch said later. So when she signed up Saban to produce another U.S. version of the same show, her colleagues, her staff, and her boss thought she was out of her mind. "They basically thought I had finally lost it," she said.[13] A week before the pilot was aired in September 1993, the new head of Fox programming, Lucy Salhany, watched the video and faxed Loesch to tell her to dump the show. "Maybe I'm too old, but this will be a disaster," Salhany wrote. "You're right—you're too old," Loesch faxed back. "Kids will like it, and I've got a back-up if they don't. Please let me go ahead." Salhany relented.[14]

Over the years Saban had worked through a series of names for the show. The original Japanese name, *Che Je Yu Rangers*, didn't really have the southern California feel he was looking for. *Galaxy Rangers* was an early attempt at a name, but this was also discarded. To beef up the action sequences Saban had contracted to buy footage from other Japanese programs including *Kaku Rangers, Dai Rangers, Spielvan,* and *Metalder* or *Megaman.* Saban included a campy script to pull this hodgepodge of material together and for a name eventually settled on *The Mighty Morphin' Power Rangers.* In September 1993, even as Fox worked on contingency plans for what to do when the show bombed, *The Mighty Morphin' Power Rangers* took America by storm. They became the most popular children's programming in forty countries, on the way to pulling $5 billion in merchandising sales. Power Rangers became the most popular action figures of the decade, beating Batman, Star Wars, and World Wrestling Federation figures out of the park. In 1995 alone U.S. merchandising sales topped $1 billion. World sales were probably double that. *Power Rangers* made FCN the highest-rated children's programming on broadcast television. Only Nickelodeon on cable had higher ratings for children aged two to eleven. The Rangers also made Haim Saban a major Hollywood player.

In 1992 Saban's company, Saban Entertainment, had been a solid little production house. It notched up $48 million in U.S. and foreign sales that year from its stable of children's television programs ranging from Marvel Comics' *X Men,* and *The Tick* ("a garden variety giant 400-pound crime fighter") to *Goosebumps.* The company's net profit was a modest $4 million. In the two-and-a-half-year period ending in October 1995, Saban's operating profits totaled $224 million, driven by the $290 million that the company earned from the Power Rangers. It wasn't the television shows that made the money—it was the royalties from Bandai America, which made the Power Rangers action figures. In 1995 only a quarter of Saban Entertainment's sales came from television deals. Two-thirds of the company's income—or $164 million—came from merchandising and licensing.

Haim Saban had developed a distribution system that could take programming unique to one country and extract profits from it in dozens of countries around the world. He had become an expert at "freshening" old programs with new scripts, voices, and music. He knew that all popular fads have a use-by date, even the Power Rangers, so his stated policy was to refresh the Power Ranger characters by "changing their costumes and ethnicity." Even so, by late 1995 the Rangers had peaked. That was when Saban put the squeeze on Rupert Murdoch.

It wasn't just Haim Saban who had been making money out of the Power Rangers. FCN had earned $85 million from them in the same two-and-a-half-year period. Murdoch wanted to replicate the runaway ratings success of FCN on cable. At the same time that he was planning his Fox News cable channel in late 1995 and 1996, he had a covert operation going to set up a cable channel called Fox Kids. In hindsight, what Murdoch should have done was hang on to Margaret Loesch, who had made FCN such a success, and dump Saban, whose one big hit, the *Power Rangers,* had already peaked. But life never works like that. Murdoch believed Saban's involvement would be critical to the success of the venture. Saban was interested, but he wanted to be an equal partner in Fox Kids. So in mid-1995 Saban and Murdoch agreed to merge Saban Entertainment with FCN. Saban and Fox would each hold just under 50 percent of the new company, Fox Kids Worldwide. Murdoch's merchant bankers, Allen & Co., would hold the rest of the shares, which would keep the deal off the News Corp balance sheet. The deal valued Saban Entertainment at close to $1 billion.[15]

The plan was to float Fox Kids Worldwide within a year, which would give Saban the big cash payout he was looking for. In the meantime Murdoch paid $80 million cash to Saban and the minority shareholders in Saban Entertainment

as "walking-around money." Stan Shuman at Allen & Co. didn't just help to organize the deal. Wearing his other hat as a Democratic Party fund-raiser, he helped
Saban use the payout to become one of Clinton's major fund-raisers in Hollywood,[16]
an outcome that must have been as gratifying to Shuman as it was annoying to
Murdoch.

By the end of 1995 the Fox Kids deal had been hammered out. The only prob-
lem was how the new children's cable channel would be distributed. So in January
1996 Murdoch quietly called his old friend Pat Robertson to put an idea to him.
Robertson's company, IFE, needed cash to upgrade its programming. Regent
University and Christian Broadcasting Network were also strapped for cash.
Murdoch was prepared to pay cable operators to carry Fox News. In a variation on
the same theme, he suggested to Robertson that he would pay IFE to run Fox
Kids on the Family Channel during the day up to six P.M., in a twelve-hour block
of programs. Overnight Fox Kids would have 59 million subscribers, putting it
well ahead of the Disney Channel (with 28 million subscribers) and in striking distance of Nickelodeon with (72 million subscribers).

Robertson liked the idea but didn't commit himself. Instead the IFE board appointed Goldman Sachs to find someone prepared to pump $350 million into the
company. It was an almost impossible task, because on the one hand Robertson
insisted that at the end of the day he had to retain control of the company; that
way, he could ensure that the new management would not drop *The 700 Club*. On
the other hand, John Malone at TCI reminded IFE that he had preemptive rights
over any stock to be sold. He would block any new investor holding a larger stake
than TCI.

Whatever financial structure emerged, Pat Robertson and John Malone both
had to be happy at the end of the day. The struggle to achieve it would throw off
a bewildering series of failed deals—and drive off almost all of IFE's suitors. The
key to following the saga that unfolded is to see in each deal how much money
ended up on Pat Robertson's side of the table—and how much it was going to cost
Rupert Murdoch.

Goldman Sachs talked to NBC, to CBS, and to Universal Studios, but in the
end they all wanted to take control of IFE. Only Murdoch was prepared to leave
Robertson in charge. Goldman Sachs proposed a $643 million takeover scheme.
IFE stockholders would be offered between $20 and $21 a share. Regent Univer-
sity and CBN would walk away with $166 million between them. Pat and Tim
Robertson would not receive any money. They would hold on to their supervoting

shares and 20 percent of the company. The money to fund the takeover would come from bank borrowings, a $110 million cash contribution from TCI, and $350 million from the new investor, News Corp. By August 1996 Murdoch was chafing at the delays and offered to sweeten the deal by pumping another $150 million of subordinated debt into IFE. This brought the total cost to Murdoch of carrying Fox Kids to the Family Channel's 59 million subscribers to $500 million. This was still a much faster and more effective way of getting on to cable than the ten-dollar-a-head inducement Murdoch was offering cable operators to run Fox News.[17]

By December 20, 1996, all parties were ready to draw up a formal proposal. The final meeting was set for Los Angeles during the week of February 3, 1997. But in the interim Pat Robertson got cold feet. Caught between two powerful figures like Murdoch and Malone, Robertson feared that he would lose control of the Family Channel, and if *The 700 Club* survived at all, it would end up rescheduled into the two A.M. slot. At the last minute Robertson refused to sign the papers and called off the deal.[18]

Malone had had enough. He told Robertson he was prepared to step away from the deal if someone made him an offer. At this point the deal was dead. "I think it's firmly on the rocks," a source told *The Hollywood Reporter.*[19] Over more than a year Robertson had proved a demanding, frustrating negotiator. He had picked and fiddled with the details of the deal, trying to pry out more money and greater control. He was just too much trouble. This was the point where Rupert Murdoch should have cut his losses and run. Instead, when Robertson phoned Murdoch in mid-February to talk him into reviving the deal and buying out Malone, Regent University and CBN, Murdoch said he would see what he could do. As he discussed it with Malone, Murdoch decided he could break the deadlock by throwing some money into the pot for Robertson himself. Mistakes like this one are what come from answering telephones.

*   *   *

Rupert Murdoch maintains the frenetic sort of schedule that would put most people on Prozac. But Murdoch's maneuvers in February 1997 were bewildering even by his own standards. In Israel his group had been accused of bugging business opponents and government officials. In Denver Charlie Ergen believed Murdoch was offering him the deal of his life with the Sky merger. Meanwhile Pat Robertson was on the phone demanding a new deal. So was Peter O'Malley, the owner of America's best-known baseball team, the Dodgers, which Murdoch had decided he wanted to buy. In the back of his mind was a coupon-and-inserts business called Heritage Media that he would buy for $1.4 billion on March 17. And then there was the little problem with John Malone.

Malone was angry. The EchoStar merger announcement had come halfway through the convoluted negotiations over IFE and Fox Sports. In trumpeting the power of the new Sky alliance, Murdoch's executives had gone out of their way to describe how they were going to destroy the cable industry—and that would include the largest cable company, John Malone's TCI. The first consequence was that Murdoch could kiss good-bye to any plans he had for buying Pat Robertson's Family Channel. "We were really neutral in it," Malone said much later, of the IFE negotiations. "The only thing we said is that while Rupert was working out his difference with the cable industry, on the satellite side, we wouldn't let any deal happen. Once the satellite deal got worked out, we simply took our foot off it and said, 'It's open to the highest bidder, but it's Pat's call.' "[20]

This is the sort of magnanimous understatement that is made only in retrospect after a peace settlement. At the time the emotional temperature was much higher, the antagonism much stronger. The bottom line was: Nothing was going to happen with the Family Channel as long as cable operators like Malone were facing the Sky merger. Murdoch wasn't taking the pressure lying down. If the IFE deal was off, and cable operators were threatening not to run his programming, then Murdoch wasn't going to buy Liberty Media's half share in Fox Sports that Malone wanted to sell. "We want to remain partners with them," Murdoch told journalists rather archly. "We don't want to lose their carriage."[21]

The script was playing out like one of the remakes of the Hollywood classic where two people who dislike each other are handcuffed together and forced to cooperate. No matter how irritated Murdoch and Malone were with each other, the reality was that they were irretrievably bound together. And both men were too smart not to realize this after the first annoyance had worn off. It was this wider confluence of interests that brought them together again in late March to say, as Leo Hindery later put it, "Let's talk. Let's not whale on each other." It was at this meeting that Murdoch made his plaintive appeal to Malone over the EchoStar deal, "Well then, help me get out of it; help me find something else to do. What is Plan B?"[22]

By that stage, finding a way out of the mess was as important to John Malone as it was to Rupert Murdoch. The satellite and cable industries were looking down the barrel of a crippling price war that could have a devastating impact on the whole communications revolution. More to the point, it would have a devastating impact on Murdoch's and Malone's businesses. So the two men kept talking.

And Murdoch kept talking to Pat Robertson. Under the new deal for IFE that Murdoch put to Robertson, Fox Kids would not be putting any more money on the table than last time; the difference was where the money would go. There would be no general takeover bid; instead all the cash went to Pat Robertson and his assorted interests. No one else would get a red cent. The payout went like this: Fox Kids would buy CBN's stock at $26 a share and Regent University's stock at $24 a share. Malone's TCI would be paid out at $26 a share in convertible notes in Fox Kids. Then Pat and Tim Robertson would sell their supervoting stock for $70 a share. So Regent and CBN would end up with $203 million, and the Robertsons would end up with $350 million, paid out three years later. They would have certain governance rights over the Family Channel. And *The 700 Club* would stay at ten P.M. each night. For decades Murdoch had based his business strategy on the belief that every man or woman has a price. Rupert thought he had his friend Pat pegged. For $350 million, the least Pat Robertson could do was to come quietly.

On April 8 Murdoch joined Fox executives to make a presentation to the IFE board in New York. As Malone would be taking convertible notes, Murdoch would be paying out only $550 million in cash, which was little more than he had been planning to pay previously. The independent directors pointed out that most of the money now went to the Robertsons personally. The board didn't like it, but since the deal was a private one between shareholders, it didn't require board approval.[23]

Malone was also in New York for the IFE board meeting. That was how the two men came to have their famous April 8 encounter that proved so fatal to Murdoch's Washington campaign, where Murdoch reportedly offered to dump the EchoStar merger while offering his ASkyB satellite slot to the cable operators' Primestar instead. Meanwhile negotiations with Pat Robertson had turned a little sticky.

Through April Robertson continued to bicker over the terms of the buyout that Murdoch was offering. Various combinations were floated for the Robertsons' $350 million payout. The Robertsons were conscious that this deal might not be looked upon quite so warmly by the rest of the IFE stockholders, who would receive nothing. In late April Pat Robertson leveled a new demand at Murdoch. Any deal would also have to have something for the rest of the stockholders. They would have to be offered at least $24 a share for their B class stock. This hadn't been part of Rupert Murdoch's plan. The whole idea of buying out the Robertsons was to avoid paying anything to anyone else and getting involved in a full-scale takeover bid. Extending a general offer like that would cost News Corp another $630 million. As the Robertsons also held a swag of B shares and options, it would also put another $60 million in their pockets. If IFE were in play, who knows what other bidders might emerge?

At the start of May, just as Murdoch was grappling with the implications of Pat Robertson's latest demand and killing off his alliance with Charlie Ergen, something remarkable happened. Murdoch and Haim Saban went to meet with Robertson and CBN management on May 2 to work out a final form for the deal, when Robertson made an extraordinary offer. Robertson said he believed it was important to be fair to all the IFE stockholders. That was why he was insisting that Fox Kids should make an offer for all the IFE stock. Even so, it just didn't seem right to Robertson that he should receive $70 a share for his supervoting A stock, when all the B stockholders received only $24 for their B stock. In fact, it was forbidden by IFE's certificate of incorporation, which stated: "In the event of a merger or consolidation [all classes of shareholders] shall be entitled to receive the same per share consideration."

Any decent corporate lawyer could have found a loophole to get around this restriction, but it was a matter of principle. Pat Robertson felt so strongly about the need to be fair to everybody that he was willing to accept less money for himself, so that Murdoch could offer more to the other shareholders. It would not cost Murdoch anything extra; it was merely a redistribution of the payout.

Robertson said later:

> I was offered a substantial premium for the controlling shares of IFE that would have amounted to a huge windfall for my son and me. Instead of taking that personal financial windfall, it seemed only proper that all the shareholders should benefit from the sale on an equal basis with the controlling A shares, and that there would be no control premium offered.[24]

This was a remarkable gesture. Robertson was offering to accept only $40 for his supervoting stock, which would cut his payout by $150 million. Sharing that extra cash with the other stockholders would lift the price they received to $28 a share. While this would increase the payout for Regent University and CBN and the Robertsons' own B stock, Pat and Tim would still end up a long way out of pocket. As a piece of corporate philanthropy, giving away $150 million for the sake of a principle is hard to beat. It is the sort of thing that restores one's faith in tele-vangelism and virtual charity.

But why had Pat Robertson done it? Robertson is a complicated character, whose history shows both shrewdness and sincerity. Which side was at work here? It would be a brave reader who tried to second-guess Robertson's motives in doing anything. But in the critical days at the end of April, when Robertson experienced his change of heart, the Zaire connection had raised its head again. On Sunday, April 27, Robertson's local paper, the *Virginian-Pilot*, ran a major story about three Caribou aircraft that Robertson's Operation Blessing aid agency had bought in 1994 for $1 million. The Caribou were old Vietnam War–era cargo planes to be used for relief work in Zaire. Robertson announced on *The 700 Club* that Opera-tion Blessing was "bringing in a couple of short-range STOL [short take-off and landing] aircraft that can get directly into those camps." He then asked viewers to call a number that appeared on the screen. On another program Robertson said, "There's the medical strike force in Goma with those people and now we've got a little small plane. We're doing a shuttle down to Bukavu so that we can take doc-tors and medicine back and forth from Goma to Bukavu. . . . So please go to your phones. You can participate in Operation Blessing."[25]

The April 27 story in the *Virginian-Pilot* quoted two of the pilots of the three planes saying they remembered one or two humanitarian flights but otherwise the planes had been used exclusively to haul equipment for Pat Robertson's private diamond mining operation. One pilot's flight logs referred to Robertson himself flying on one of the planes where the log entry read, "Prayed for diamonds." Chief pilot Robert Hinkle told Bill Sizemore at the *Virginian-Pilot*:

> We got over there and we had Operation Blessing painted on the tails of the airplanes, but we were doing no humanitarian work at all. We were just supplying the miners and flying the dredges from Kinshasa out to Tshikapa. . . . After three months I had the workers in the hangar take the Operation Blessing off our tails, because I was embarrassed.

A CBN spokesman said that the planes had proven unsuitable for relief work and that Robertson's mining company had reimbursed Operation Blessing for their use. Sizemore's story sparked a two-year government inquiry into whether Robertson or CBN had raised donations under false pretenses. The Virginia at-torney general's office eventually cleared Robertson, who it said did not know that the statements he had made on *The 700 Club* were wrong. Robertson had paid

$572,597 to Operation Blessing to reimburse it for the use of the planes. Some $400,000 of this amount was paid in August 1997, two months after the inquiry began.[26] "I've turned my other cheek so many times, my head is dizzy," Robertson said in 1999 of the *Virginian-Pilot*'s continued coverage of the affair. "This is beyond the pale . . . they've tried to destroy a charity."[27]

No substantive adverse findings were ever made against Robertson, CBN, or Operation Blessing. But the Zaire story had awakened the old concerns about Robertson mixing his personal interests with those of his ministry. It suggested that Robertson had a knack for coming out ahead in any deal. The issue here was not whether using the planes to haul diamond dredges was in any way improper. Rather, since the virtual cathedral depended on public opinion, perceptions were the issue. And Pat Robertson was about to announce a deal where he and his son received $70 for each of their A class shares and walked away with $409 million in total, and everyone else was offered just $24 a share. The *Virginian-Pilot* story touched off a storm of controversy about Robertson's business links.

Six days later Robertson met with Murdoch and made his remarkable offer to share $150 million of his payout with the other stockholders. On one thing Robertson was perfectly clear: His offer to Murdoch was not triggered by the adverse publicity. "My relief efforts in Zaire had absolutely nothing to do with the IFE transaction," he said. "My motive in doing business in Zaire was to help people."[28]

Robertson like Murdoch is a complex character. Even if Robertson was influenced by the Zaire story, it still takes considerable character to walk away from such wealth. "We gave up about $150 million in control premium, but after all, your reputation should be considered more important than money," Robertson said.

Murdoch was in a difficult position. He was depending upon Robertson to provide a home for his Fox Kids cable channel. He wasn't really happy about making a full-pitched bid for all IFE stock. It would cost a lot of money and open the door for other bidders to jump him. But faced with a preacher so obviously struggling to do the right thing by his stockholders, reducing his own payout to increase the price offered to everybody else, it was a little difficult to withdraw.

It got worse. By the week of May 12, stories about the deal were in the press. On Wednesday, May 14, the *Wall Street Journal* reported that a deal was imminent. No mention was made of the original $70-a-share deal that Robertson had knocked back. The *Journal* only noted, with some asperity, that the Robertsons would receive $40 a share while all other stockholders would receive only $26 to

$28 a share. This touched off a new storm of controversy. It wasn't just Robertson's preferential pricing that raised eyebrows. There was a more basic incongruity in this union between the violence underlying Fox Kids' *Power Rangers, X-Men,* and *Goosebumps* and the family values espoused in *The 700 Club, Touched by an Angel,* and reruns of *The Mary Tyler Moore Show.* It was a fairy-tale story line as old as the world: Heidi meets Godzilla, Beauty sells out to the Beast, King Kong runs away with Jessica Lange.

IFE's institutional shareholders were angry at the different prices. Mario Gabelli of Gabelli Funds waxed a little biblical himself. He would vote for the deal "when hell freezes over," he said. IFE's annual meeting was scheduled for the following Monday. On Friday, May 16, two days after the *Wall Street Journal* report, IFE announced that it was in talks with a potential bidder, but that any bid that eventuated would offer all stockholders the same price. Rather than $70 a share, Robertson would now receive only $28.50. The Robertsons would walk away with only $213 million, though the return for Regent University and CBN was up slightly, to $231 million.

For Murdoch, the downside to this new arrangement was that Robertson now had a powerful incentive to extract the best possible price he could for IFE stock. Two weeks before, Robertson had quietly agreed to move *The 700 Club* out of its spot in prime time at ten P.M. each night, back to eleven P.M. This was the stumbling block that had driven off other suitors in the past. With that concession made, NBC, Sony, CBS, and Universal Studios once again began circling IFE— and Fox Kids was now just one of the would-be bidders. But it was Michael Eisner at Disney who became the greatest threat to Fox.

The IFE board played hardball. The Fox Kids bid stood at $28.50 a share. IFE told the suitors the company would open exclusive negotiations with the first bidder to offer $35 a share. The Fox Kids execs swallowed hard and said they would consider it. Murdoch had started this whole ball rolling with an offer to kick in $350 million to get Fox Kids programming onto cable. Even back in February, when the deal had looked dead, Murdoch had been contemplating paying out only $500 million. Now the total payout for IFE had risen to $1.7 billion. Counting in IFE's bank debt, the deal valued the company at an incredible $1.9 billion. Going back to do business with the preacher had cost Murdoch and Fox Kids $1.4 billion. Pat Robertson had suffered probably the most expensive attack of conscience in corporate history.

In the process Robertson had increased the payout for CBN and Regent University from $165 million back in February, to $284 million. Pat and Tim

Robertson's payout for their A and B stock and options totaled $262 million. While Pat's stock was held by a trust that would go back to CBN in the year 2010, Tim would retain $113 million from his original $50,000 investment in IFE seven years before. To his stockholders, Robertson was a hero.

At the end of May it looked like this fabulous bonanza would get even better. Michael Eisner flew secretly to meet Pat Robertson at Virginia Beach, where he offered to top Murdoch's price and bid $37 a share for IFE. It wasn't just that Eisner wanted a cable channel. By this time, frustrating Rupert Murdoch had become a passion with the head of Disney. The Eisner factor meant that the titanic struggles in the spring of 1997 to determine the future of the world's media giants had become a whole new ball game.

15

MAN FOR ALL SEASONS

Los Angeles, January 1997

EVEN LEGENDS MAY COME to grief. For even the greatest baseball players, there is a last season. On a wintry day in January 1997, when the baseball diamond at Dodger Stadium was as cold and hard as the ground gets in southern California (which is not very cold and hard at all) Peter O'Malley announced he was calling it a day: He was selling the Dodgers at the end of the season. The baseball world went into shock. The Los Angeles Dodgers were the best-known and best-run baseball team in the world. In the way that a sporting team can come to symbolize the aspirations and identity of its hometown, the Dodgers were the face and pride of L.A. With marvelous dexterity they also managed to remain the face and pride of New York twenty-three years after Peter O'Malley's father Walter swung a deal with Los Angeles to move the Brooklyn Dodgers three thousand miles away to the West Coast.

For days after Peter O'Malley's announcement on January 7 the press was filled with stories of unimaginable anguish. It was more than just sentiment over a lost ball park and ball team. The Dodgers had become a community undertaking. Sport is a passionate business. Its competitions share some of the characteristics of religious wars in that they are essentially tribal in nature. No slight, no betrayal, no injustice on the part of an opposing team is ever forgotten. And that is true when one is merely discussing sports in general: Baseball is a far more serious matter. It is the heart of the American sporting ethos. Oliver Wendell Holmes Jr., the Supreme Court justice who reshaped the liberal tradition of law in American society, knew this. "We are not mere grubbers in the muckheaps of the world," he admonished his profession, with his eyes firmly set on an enlightened judiciary and the higher good of society. The higher good clearly involved "exhibitions of baseball," which he decreed at the turn of the century were "purely state affairs" and as such were exempt from state and federal antitrust laws. One may conclude either that this was an inspired piece of jurisprudence or that Holmes really liked his baseball.

Baseball heroes like Babe Ruth and managers like the Dodgers' Tommy Lasorda have a quality of Everyman, transformed by a wonderful talent into towering figures. In the first half of the century the laws of symmetry required that to match their larger-than-life players, the owners of baseball teams must be of corresponding size. Walter O'Malley was such a figure, possessing the charm and aggression of the black Irish. In 1958 O'Malley, who left Brooklyn because his plans for a new stadium were turned down, finagled his way into a land swap that left him with three hundred acres of land that had been set aside for cheap urban housing at Chavez Ravine in Los Angeles. The Hispanic Americans living on the land, in a barrio called Palo Verde, were duly evicted, and O'Malley proceeded to build a model baseball stadium there. Its lack of water fountains was an oversight over which he expressed surprise, but it meant that thirsty fans could only buy Coca-Cola or beer from his stalls. It was a maneuver known to movie theater managers as "Coca-Cola plumbing" and won him the nickname H2 O'Malley.[1]

His son Peter was a different animal: unfailingly polite, reserved, precise, and always formally dressed, with a manner kindly but patrician. Peter O'Malley grew up in baseball's First Family and found it hard to emerge from his father's long shadow. But he ran a good ball team. Dodger Stadium kept the price of its tickets low, and it didn't festoon the grounds with advertising or cannibalize the public stands to build lucrative corporate boxes.

In many ways, though, by 1997 Peter O'Malley seemed to have lost his nerve. "I think family ownership of sports today is probably a dying breed," he said on January 7, as he announced his decision to sell. "You need a broader base than an individual family to carry you through the storms. Groups or corporations are probably the way of the future."[2]

The furor over the sale eventually subsided. New York politicians talked about making a bid to win back their Dodgers but never did. Angelenos got used to the idea that a big corporation was probably going to end up with the ball team. But the real consequences were much broader. Unknown to most, the geopolitics of sport in southern California—and in all of North America—had become dangerously unstable. The various emerging alliances that sought to control the sports-entertainment-media business in the United States were on a collision course. They were one small step away from direct conflict. The significance of Peter

O'Malley's announcement on January 7 was that his pending departure would force the business to take that final step on the road to war.

*   *   *

Rupert Murdoch was appropriately diffident about his interest in the Dodgers. At a panel discussion at the International Radio and Television Society in mid-January, he downplayed any interest in bidding for the team, "[b]ut I'm not saying that absolutely."[3] The first call to Peter O'Malley's office came some weeks later: Murdoch would like to have dinner with O'Malley. This was the logical way to start things off, because the biggest hurdle facing anyone who wanted to buy the Dodgers was that they first had to sell themselves to Peter O'Malley. He was selling the family heirloom. This was not a conversation over a business lunch. A potential buyer would require exquisite negotiating skills and would have to use any prop or advantage that would give him the slightest edge. Murdoch's edge was a house.

Barry Diller signed the papers to buy Jules Stein's mansion, Misty Mountain on Angelo Drive, for the Murdochs in September 1986. It is one of the great houses of Hollywood, filled with star-studded history. Celebrity architect Wallace Neff built it in 1926 for Fred Niblo, director of silent films like *The Mask of Zorro* and *The Three Musketeers*. In the 1930s Niblo fell on harder times with the rise of talkies and rented the house out to Nelson Eddy and later to Katharine Hepburn. There, on the splendid lawn, Hepburn played croquet with Spencer Tracy. In 1940 Jules Stein, the founder of MCA (now Paramount Studios) bought it and lived there until he died in 1980. His wife Doris died four years later, and the house went on the market.

The house stands on six acres on a hilltop off Benedict Canyon, overlooking Rudolph Valentino's house, Falcon's Lair. It offers probably the best views in Los Angeles, with a panoramic sweep across the city and beyond to the Pacific Ocean. "It was beautiful, you really had a sense of privacy, of being alone," the Steins' daughter, Jean, said of growing up there. Beyond the high walls, gates, and security cameras a six-hundred-foot driveway leads up to a two-story Spanish-style mansion with a red roof and stone facade. The fourteen rooms are arranged around a circular courtyard with a wishing well and a Chinese elm at its center. Murdoch paid $5.8 million for the house in 1986 and another $2 million for the antiques and artwork that Stein had collected for it. "My wife and I are extremely excited about it," Murdoch said when he wrote to Neff's son about renovating the house after moving in. The house has four family bedrooms, three staff bedrooms, nine bathrooms, a pool, a screening room, two greenhouses, and a formal English garden that Anna Murdoch managed.

It takes more than a bunch of bedrooms and a view to make an impression in Los Angeles, but even by Hollywood standards Misty Mountain was a magnificent setting. It served as a springboard for Anna's charity work that put her on hostesses' A-lists. It dazzled Murdoch's executives when they trooped to L.A. each year for the budget meetings. It was the perfect backdrop for relaxed business dinners, where Rupert and Anna and their guests could stroll around the gardens past the Italian pines or look out over the city from the terrace sipping California Chardonnay. It was a high, airy space where one could talk easily about the big picture. It was a place where a patrician like Peter O'Malley could feel at home around the smell of almost-old money.

Dodgers president Bob Graziano came with O'Malley for dinner at the Murdochs'. The entire evening was a triumph of composure for Murdoch. At the time he was deeply involved in the Sky merger deal with Charlie Ergen. He was still looking to stare down the cable operators who were after his hide, and he was desperate to square off his exasperated partner John Malone, to win over Congress, and to tempt Pat Robertson. And he was doing his best to micromanage the British general election. Somewhere along the line he found time to buy a coupon-insert business called Heritage Media for $1.4 billion on March 18. To have all this in the air, and to put it all aside long enough to be the perfect host and tell Peter O'Malley exactly what he wanted to hear, required extraordinary self-control.

News Corp executive Peter Chernin was there that night, along with Murdoch's elder son, Lachlan. At twenty-five years Lachlan was no stranger to the drama of haggling over sports. Two years earlier he had been part of a small News Corp team that had secretly signed up players in hotel rooms across Australia, as the company mounted a takeover bid on rugby league football. Tonight Murdoch Sr. kept the conversation brisk with a string of questions. "He wanted to know about my family and me and why I was selling the ball club," O'Malley later told the *Los Angeles Times*. "I told him I thought it was too high-risk a business for one family because there was no reason to believe player salaries would level off. . . . I also told him about the tragic relation the owners have with the players. The lack of trust, and the animosity. I told him the truth."[4]

Though Murdoch had hated sports as a boy, as an adult he had quickly realized that sports stories sold newspapers. Reportedly he had never been to a baseball game in his life. Yet on that night he spoke intelligently about the Dodgers' lineup—about Vin Scully; about catcher Mike Piazza, whose contract was coming up for renegotiation; about the Japanese pitcher Hideo Nomo; and about the international prospects for baseball. "I was astonished at his depth of knowledge—with all he's got going on—about the Dodgers," O'Malley told Connie Bruck of *The New Yorker.*[5]

In much the same way that he had with Charlie Ergen at EchoStar, Murdoch managed to tap into O'Malley's dream for the future. O'Malley didn't want a personality to buy the Dodgers. He didn't want to sell the Dodgers as an adornment to the buyer's ego. "He's not dancing on the roof of the dugout, or in the clubhouse filling out the line-up card," he said of Murdoch.[6] His host was able to share O'Malley's enthusiasm for promoting baseball internationally, because with his satellite and cable interests around the world, Murdoch had a unique capacity to take the Dodgers around the world and back. Like many before him, O'Malley described his business relationship with Murdoch as a romance. "The first time we met we had a common interest, a common focus," he told Bruck. The night at Angelo Drive was a "first date."[7]

For Rupert Murdoch, buying the Dodgers was not such a sentimental affair. It was merely an episode in his five-year odyssey to become the uncrowned sports czar of the world. Since 1992 Murdoch had spent $5 billion buying up sports programming rights. He had written off at least one-fifth of it as losses even before the ink dried on some of the contracts. In 1997 his empire was paying more than $1 billion a year for sports rights, yet Murdoch's appetite for sports programming was more voracious than ever.

*   *   *

It had begun at the Lancaster Hotel in London, just before noon on May 18, 1992. In a tense meeting, the chairmen of twenty-one first-division soccer clubs voted by the narrowest of margins to give Murdoch's BSkyB and the BBC exclusive broadcast rights for the new Premier League soccer competition. It was the climax of a furious months-long battle for the rights between Sam Chisholm at BSkyB and Independent Television (ITV). Two hours before the final vote Chisholm had telephoned Murdoch in New York, waking him in the middle of the night. Chisholm wanted to lift BSkyB's bid by £30 million to trump a revised offer that ITV had made an hour earlier. Murdoch gave his groggy approval. Chisholm's late counterbid won the day, so that BSkyB and the BBC won the Premier League broadcast rights for four seasons, for what then seemed the astronomical sum of £304 million.

Looking back, this move seems to have been the sort of corporate masterstroke that is generally stumbled upon only by luck and only by the very bold. Chisholm had been plagued by doubts about whether BSkyB could afford the Premier League rights. The bid would cost BSkyB £76 million a year, less the BBC's payment to run game highlights for its *Match of the Day* program. Chisholm's doubts were soothed within weeks as BSkyB signed up one million subscribers ready to pay £5.99 a month for the sports channel. That came to almost £54 million a year of new income for BSkyB, almost overnight repaying most of the cost of winning the rights. Sports became a huge driver for raising BSkyB's subscriber numbers. As Murdoch said later, "The Premier League was the really big move, it gave us a huge boost. That was a big deal, and it took off straight away."[8]

A year later Murdoch turned his eyes toward America's National Football League (NFL). The Murdoch assault on sports—the transformation of the man who had always hated sports of any kind into arguably the most influential person in sports in the world—came at an awkward time for the North American media industry. The big networks—NBC, ABC, and CBS—were hurting from the inroads that cable television had been making on their audience for two decades. In the early 1990s the big three were scaling down their costs by cutting back on payments to their affiliates, and working to slow down the big growth in sports costs. While network executives were always "slaveringly eager to . . . cut into each other's market share," as Murdoch put it, anyone could see the overall trend here. This was the sort of tacit consensus that game theory predicted, where it was in everyone's interest not to outbid one another. Everyone stood to lose from another cost blowout.

When Murdoch set out to win the free-to-air rights for the National Football Conference, one of the two divisions in the NFL, his first task was to convince Laurence Tisch at CBS, who had held these rights forever, not to bid against him. According to George Vradenburg, a former CBS executive now at Fox, Tisch had to be convinced that "Rupert was a crazy man."[9] In the previous term CBS had paid just over $1 billion for its four-year package of games and had lost $150 million on the deal. That meant that for CBS the rights had been worth only $850 million, or $212.5 million a season. Murdoch blew CBS away by bidding $395 million a season, for a total over four years of $1.58 billion. After that CBS was never in the race. Once Murdoch had won, his first step was to write off $590 million as an up-front loss on the contract. This meant he was actually valuing it at less than the previous CBS deal. (He later reduced the write-off to $350 million, under pressure from investors.) But regardless of how he did the accounting, suddenly Rupert Murdoch was Mr. Football.

The effect of the NFL contract in 1994 was as great for Fox as the Premier League had been for BSkyB. But the ripples spread wider, because by making this outrageous deal work for him, Murdoch forced his rivals to follow him up the cost scale. He had changed the economics of sport. He had shown that the up-front losses in a rights deal weren't important. The critical thing was the ability to leverage off other gains from the rights—in this case, attracting new affiliates to Fox. In 1995 Murdoch stepped up into an even higher gear. In February he won a five-year deal for Fox with the National Hockey League for $155 million. In the next three months he committed more than $700 million to rugby league and rugby union. In November he bid $575 million to share major league baseball rights with NBC for five years. At the same time the regional sports nets that were about to become Fox Sports bid $129 million for cable rights to baseball. Murdoch immediately wrote off $80 million on the Fox Sports deal and another $29 million on college football.

Then there were the deals that got away. In July 1995 the International Tennis Federation backed out of a plan to set up a new tour backed by Murdoch's money. In golf there was also a failed attempt backed by Greg Norman to finance a rival to the PGA tour. Then there were the Olympics. NBC paid $475 million for the broadcast rights for the 1996 Atlanta Olympics. In mid-1996 Murdoch bid $705 million for the 2000 Sydney Olympics, and NBC knew it had a fight on its hands. Eventually it won Sydney with a bid of $715 million. But in the process NBC tied itself into a massive $3.57 billion deal to take broadcasting rights for the five summer and winter games from 2000 to 2008. Thwarted, Murdoch moved his sights across the Atlantic, where the European Broadcasting Union (EBU), on behalf of state broadcasters throughout Europe including the BBC, had bid £961 million for a similar package to NBC's, running to 2008. Murdoch bid £1.3 billion for the package, but the anti-Murdoch factor defeated him. The International Olympic Committee stayed with the European Broadcasting Union. "We sidestepped $400 million to have the assurances of maximum ratings," said Jacques Rogge, head of the European National Olympic Committee. Even in defeat, however, Murdoch had forced the EBU to pay more than it ever had before for sports rights.[10]

The net effect of all this bidding was that around the world the price of programming rights for sports events went through the roof. It constituted a redistribution of wealth from media groups to professional sports associations, clubs, and sport stars. By the end of the decade, the flows of money that this process spun off to sporting groups were so great as to represent a form of social engineering. The catalyst for it all had been the Murdoch effect—his demonstration that these rights were worth far more strategically than previously acknowledged. Whenever media groups bid against Murdoch, they were conscious that they were up against a rival who was prepared to offer what seemed crazy prices. The bidding strategy that this realization produced for media groups in sports rights auctions around the world was simple and brutal: Media groups would bid whatever it took to win the rights. If the cost of the rights proved beyond their reach, they would bid it up to ensure that the eventual winner was saddled with a crippling obligation.

The difficulty in treating sports in this way is that it reduces any sporting code to a financial strategy. The world's love affair with sport, and the qualities that sporting contests can represent, are never quite as simple as they seem. Why does sport arouse such emotion? Four decades after the Dodgers moved to Los Angeles, why do Dodgers fans in Brooklyn still grieve the loss? Why do British soccer fans still feel so incensed about the 1998 battle to buy Manchester United? Murdoch's 1995 foray into Australian rugby would show the danger of forgetting that, at its best, sport is still a matter of the heart.

The Pedant, the Pariah, and the Polo Player

Midway through 1995 Sydney legal circles were enjoying a delicious prospect. After three decades of armed truce, Rupert Murdoch and Kerry Packer were back at each other's throats. A lengthy court battle was shaping up between Australia's two richest sons before a deeply appreciative legal audience.

Kerry Packer is a very large man. He has never actually thrown anyone through the window, but former executives say that on occasion it has been a near thing. One failed business deal in 1988 reportedly ended in Packer wrestling with his former partner on the floor of his office in Sydney. Packer in a rage is a terrifying experience that leaves powerful executives white-faced and shaking.

Packer is entirely without pretension. After his near-fatal heart attack at a polo match in 1990, when his heart stopped for several minutes, he remarked, "I've been to the other side, and let me tell you, son, there's fucking nothing there." Since the late 1980s he has spent much of his time pursuing his passions for polo and gambling, a lifestyle that chews through more than A\$100 million a year. He is alternately the savior and the scourge of casinos around the world, where he has regularly won or lost \$20 million in a single night. Packer is not a gentle man. On one occasion in the high-rollers room in a Las Vegas casino, he turned on another gambler, who was making much of his own importance and his $100 million fortune. Clearly annoyed, Packer passed him a coin and growled, "I'll toss you for it."

Back in 1960 Rupert Murdoch's bouncers had beat the stuffing out of Packer and his brother Clyde, after they and four other worthies had forcibly occupied a printing press owned by the Anglican Church, to prevent Murdoch from buying it. The confused, torrid affair had sins on both sides and left the Packers limping off. In the 1970s, when Kerry took the helm of the Consolidated Press media group after his father's death, he and Rupert had concluded that media moguls didn't do stuff like that anymore. Ever since, they had maintained a wary peace, meeting regularly to hatch elaborate schemes to take over Australia's media, most of which came to nothing. Murdoch was pre-eminent in print, owning more than 70 percent of Australian newspapers. Packer owned the country's leading television company, National Nine Network, which had been built up in the 1980s by Sam Chisholm, before he left to take over at BSkyB.

In 1994, however, powerful forces were testing this relationship. The crisis came to a head over rugby. The game known as rugby is actually two separate games, called rugby league and rugby union. Rugby league is the major football game played in New South Wales and Queensland. While rugby union, the older game, was an amateur game associated in Australia with private schools, rugby league's heartland was the working-class suburbs of inner-city Sydney. In the 1980s and 1990s the game had emerged as a major business linked to clubs funded by slot gaming machines, though its critics claimed the Australian Rugby League (ARL) was hidebound and Sydney-centric. The ARL's slick promotional campaigns featured Tina Turner singing "Simply the Best" from the top of the Sydney harbour bridge or held aloft in the arms of brawny rugby players. For all that, it was still the people's game, and anyone who threatened it risked becoming a social pariah.

In 1995 Murdoch and Packer were locked in a ferocious battle over who would control the game. A case in the federal court would determine not merely who won the dispute but the future of rugby league itself. And the thing that amused Sydney lawyers so mightily was that the case would be heard by Justice James Burchett. Those lawyers who liked to gossip gleefully reported that Justice Burchett had never dreamed of going to a football game in his life. He was bookish. A clever, conscientious judge, his critics said he had a reputation as a pedant, for being supercilious and even a trifle conceited.

The saga had begun on the night of Thursday, March 30, 1995, when the players of the Sydney Bulldogs rugby league team finished a training session under lights at their Canterbury-Bankstown home ground. Their coach, Chris Anderson, told five of them that he had something planned after their showers, that there were some people in the city he wanted them to meet. Late that night he took his leading players to a high-rise office in Sydney's central business district. One of the two men waiting for them in a conference room there was familiar to the players: John Ribot, the outspoken chief executive of the Brisbane club, who was the Australian Rugby League's chief critic. The man beside Ribot was less familiar: the twenty-three-year-old figure of Lachlan Murdoch.

This move had been coming for more than a year. News Corporation had launched a cable television operation called Foxtel with the government-owned telephone giant Telstra, which needed a lever like rugby programming to boost subscriber numbers. Unfortunately, Kerry Packer had locked up all the television rights to the Australian Rugby League until the year 2000. Packer had resold the pay-television rights to Telstra's cable competitor, Optus Vision, in which he had a 5 percent stake. In a meeting with ARL directors on February 6, 1995, Ken Cowley, the managing director of News Limited (News Corp's Australian operating arm), proposed a new league with fewer teams, run in conjunction with News Limited. The ARL refused. While Cowley promised not to pursue a rival competition by stealth, a flurry of secret meetings with clubs followed.

In a meeting on March 23, Cowley, Ribot, and David Smith (the News Limited executive heading the rugby league planning) presented a plan to Rupert Murdoch to commit A$60 million over four years to set up a rebel league competition. Smith's office was subsequently set up as a "war room," lined with schedules of the plan to target the ARL's "core playing strength." Some two hundred players would be offered two or three times their existing salaries to join the breakaway league. Travel documents were drawn up in false names for News Corp executives involved in the swoop, in an operation that was characterized at every turn, Justice Burchett later said, by "secrecy, deceit and suddenness." There was a certain indelicate timing in that this was taking place just as, in Washington, FCC staff were finalizing their report on Murdoch's 1986 Metromedia deal and on whether News Corp's actions were characterized by a lack of candor. At the same time Murdoch was secretly negotiating his alliance with MCI, while in London Peter Stehrenberger was arranging his meeting with Abraham Nantel to talk about Michael Clinger.

On Tuesday, March 28, 1995, News Limited signed up five of the ARL's top coaches on three-year contracts, including Chris Anderson at Canterbury-

Bankstown. Two days later Ribot and Lachlan Murdoch secretly flew to Sydney to target Anderson's team, the Bulldogs, who had won the ARL premiership the year before. Ribot met with Anderson at midday to discuss the plan to bring his players in late that night to sign them up for a new league, eventually called Super League, when Anderson himself would receive two checks for A$50,000 apiece.

The details of what took place that night in the Atanaskovic Hartnell offices are not entirely clear. Justice Burchett did not regard Ribot as a reliable witness. In the state industrial court Justice Brian Hill said that parts of the evidence given by Ribot and Anderson were unconvincing. Lachlan Murdoch was never called to give his account. "I had nothing to do with that," Lachlan said in 1999, when asked a general question about his role in Super League.[11]

What is generally agreed is that Ribot and Murdoch explained News Limited's plan to set up Super League and asked each player individually to sign a playing contract. Players were offered salaries between A$150,000 and A$350,000, plus an immediate sign-on fee of between A$50,000 and A$100,000. "This is Santa Claus in April," Ribot repeatedly told the players. But it had to be signed that night, he said, or they would "miss the boat." Signing was a formality, Ribot assured them, because their club could force them to play for Super League anyway, which was to be an elite competition—"the best of the best." Neither of these statements proved to be true, Justice Hill later found in the state industrial court.[12]

The players had had no idea of what they were walking into. Confronted late at night with complex legal documents that their coach was urging them to sign, they were not able to make outside calls for legal or accounting advice. Ribot later testified that he had expressly offered any player who raised the matter the opportunity to have his manager present but the offer was declined, but Justice Hill later found that these requests "were, in truth and substance, refused by Mr Ribot."

By the time the players went home in the small hours of Friday morning, seven of them had signed up with Super League. The problem for Ribot was that several of them had signed the wrong piece of paper. Two of the players had signed the schedule to the contract but not the contract itself—one of them said later that the only documents he saw that night were a letter from News Limited dated the next day, and the contract schedule. At least four of the international players who signed had omitted to sign the standard terms page. The four subsequently had their contracts overturned by the state industrial court, which found that News Limited had obtained their signatures by "unconscionable dealing" and misrepresentations. "None of [the four] read anything that night," Justice Hill concluded.

The players went home with their sign-on checks but had to wait another three weeks to get a copy of the contract they had just supposedly signed. They were told to deny that they had any connection with Super League and were given a briefing packet that explained how to do it. If a journalist asked them if they were in negotiations with News Limited, the suggested "player response to media questioning" was "There is no point in that, when I have a current contract which I am obliged to honour."[13]

That night was the beginning of a beautiful relationship between rugby players and the legal profession. In the next two years Sydney's senior silks and solicitors would get to know more about the personal idiosyncrasies and behavior of the country's top rugby stars than they could ever have wished. The lawyers took some time to get used to living cheek by jowl, day after day, with large young men with a robust sense of humor who would take to throwing around anything remotely ball-shaped during breaks in court proceedings. The ARL's lawyer, Mark O'Brien, said of the players he represented, "Some of them can't even pack their bags without help."[14]

In the next twenty-four hours News Corp signed up another twenty-six players in raids in Brisbane, Townsville, and Perth for contracts as high as A$600,000 plus signing-on fees of A$100,000—huge sums in the previous rugby league economy. By that stage it had become clear that not all of Super League's new recruits were sticking to the suggested "player response to media questioning." They had been blurting out details, and the story was splashed across the front pages of newspapers across the country.

It is difficult not to feel some sympathy for Geoff Cousins, the former advertising executive who started work for Foxtel's rival, Optus Vision, on March 31. His first morning was a nightmare. He arrived at the office ready to take up a marvelous job as chief executive of a billion-dollar start-up for a new cable service, only to find that his rival, Foxtel, was in the process of pinching all his rugby programming. The new job had become a billion-dollar crisis. Who was he going to call? A dumb question—the phone was already ringing. It was Kerry Packer on the line, and he was furious. It got worse when Packer arrived at Cousins's office in person: He was seven feet tall, and he was waving a checkbook. It soon became apparent that it was Cousins's own checkbook.

The News Limited operation depended upon a quick victory. The A$60 million

budget was not likely to go far if the ARL remained obdurate. What changed the
picture was that by midday on March 31, Cousins's first day on the job, Optus
Vision and Packer's National Nine Network had committed between A$10 million
and A$13 million to support the ARL. Within days this figure grew to A$40 million. Most of that money would come not from Packer but from Cousins. Cousins
had persuaded the Optus Vision shareholders—Cable & Wireless, BellSouth, and
Continental Cablevision—that rugby league programming was more important
for Optus Vision than it was for the Channel Nine Network.

The next day ARL officials, together with Packer's son James, launched a
counteroffensive, pressing large cash payments on rugby players who signed loyalty agreements to the ARL. The battle was joined in hotel rooms and clubhouses
across the country, and it split the league in two, both physically and emotionally.
"This battle split the entire country, fathers against sons, neighbors against neighbors, footballers against footballers," ARL president Ken Arthurson told *The New
Yorker.* "It ruined a lot of lives, mine included. And all because Rupert Murdoch
wanted to control a sport that belonged to the people and was selfish enough to
think he could own it for pay television."[15]

Eventually Super League and the ARL signed up three hundred players
apiece. In an effort to outflank the ARL, News Corp had put rugby league associations around the world on its payroll, beginning with an £87 million deal for the
English Rugby Football League to join a European Super League that transformed rugby league into a summer sport to coincide with the southern hemi-
sphere winter.

The cost of the Super League exercise had soared above A$500 million, and
the affair was headed to the federal court for resolution by Justice Burchett.
Burchett may not have started out knowing much about rugby, but five months of
hearings cured this ailment. What became apparent when he handed down his
judgment on February 23, 1996, was that he didn't like secret meetings or News
Limited's plan to take over the ARL by "infiltration by the back door." He did not
accept the evidence given by several News Limited and Super League witnesses,
and he drew adverse inferences from the failure of Cowley and Smith to appear in
the witness box. He gave the worst serving to Peter Moore, the chief executive of
Canterbury-Bankstown, who was also an ARL director, over his efforts to recruit
Chris Anderson for Super League:

> Mr. Moore had not less than an ordinary appreciation of right and wrong.
> He knew his duty. But, stripped of pretence in cross-examination, he was

revealed as a man who had been overwhelmed by the magnitude of his temptation. He was completely corrupted, and shut his eyes to his obligations to the club and to the [ARL]. But those who suborned the coach, and at least indirectly Mr. Moore, were acting with their eyes open. They knew they were asking officials of clubs to break their contracts . . . and their duty of fidelity. They were using the financial power of News Limited to corrupt targeted individuals.[16]

Justice Burchett froze all further actions by the Super League companies that News Limited had set up until the year 2000, and he left open a claim by the ARL for huge damages. It was a stunning win for the ARL. Arthur Siskind flew to Australia to supervise an appeal process and to see what could be retrieved from the legal debacle. News Limited was still in there punching, with talk of moves to circumvent Burchett's ruling with a new players' league.

The ARL's lawyer, Mark O'Brien, warned of dire consequences if Super League players even held a training session: "The present directing minds of News Limited will be [held] in contempt if this occurs. And that, of course, is Lachlan Murdoch, the man very much at the front of this fight, and Ken Cowley."

When the case moved to the appeals court, the exchanges were just as bitter, as the News Limited lawyers argued that Burchett had been swayed by the "emotive" language used by the ARL's lead counsel, Bob Ellicott Q.C., which had appealed to the judge's heart rather than his head. Ellicott, a former federal attorney general, had argued that there was an "ethical void" in News Corp's corporate culture, together with a belief in "the divine right of supernationals." News Corp seemed to believe "that Rupert can do no wrong, Ken [Cowley] can do no wrong, and Lachlan can do no wrong."[17]

*   *   *

The issue at the heart of the Super League dispute was something that was causing heartache all over the world. What Justice Burchett had to resolve was the complex question of who owns a sport: Is it a commercial venture or a community enterprise? Is it an undertaking based on mutual trust and confidence, or does the competitive arena extend to the way the sport is organized and run? At a more esoteric level, is it important for a sportsperson to be honorable? Ultimately Burchett's judgment seemed to hark back to Oliver Wendell Holmes's turn-of-the-century judgment that baseball was an "affair of state." It was something beyond the common run of human experience; it was an exalted endeavor to which different rules must be applied. Burchett's judgment ran into problems on appeal, in part because of the way he defined the size of a market in applying trade-practice laws; but the heart of his judgment was that the way rugby league was played in Australia by clubs together with the ARL was characterized by "mutual trust that each is pursuing a common purpose." One could call it the love of the sport. It made the ARL the basis of a joint venture that placed fiduciary obligations upon ARL and club executives and employees. The secret meetings and plotting and late-night signings by coaches, players, and club officials breached these fiduciary obligations. In hindsight one might consider that Burchett had constructed an elaborate legal edifice that allowed him to protect an Australian social institution.

Perhaps it is significant that this lofty view was taken by a judge who himself had limited contact with the modern sporting world. On October 4, 1996, the court of appeal transformed the ARL's victory into a crushing defeat. Notwithstanding Ellicott's indignant arguments, the court upheld News Limited on sixty out of sixty-one points of appeal against Justice Burchett's ruling. One of its critical findings was that the contractual uncertainty and internal squabbling of the ARL before the appearance of Super League did not constitute a joint venture based on mutual trust and confidence. Consequently there were no fiduciary obligations of the sort described by Burchett. It followed that the directors of rebel clubs were not necessarily in breach of their duty to the ARL, and the actions of the Super League coaches whom Burchett had criticized so sharply could be seen in a more acceptable light, as looking after the interests of their players. "Perhaps the criticism was too harsh," the appellate judges concluded.[18]

In another of life's little ironies, the appeal judgment was released four days before Fox News sued Time Warner over Gerry Levin's broken promise to run Murdoch's news channel in New York. The appeals court decision in Sydney in effect acknowledged that at the end of the twentieth century sports clubs were a business. Broken promises were regrettable but not illegal. One could as well quote Judge Jack Weinstein's district court judgment in the Fox News case: "They were hard-bitten executives steeled in such hagglings. . . . The cajolery, as well as the blandishments, honeyed phrases and assurances that are to be expected in major negotiations of this sort in the media-entertainment field did not constitute fraud."[19]

The turf war between Packer and Murdoch smoldered for two years. Various peace agreements were brokered during this time with the help of the two heirs apparent, Lachlan Murdoch and James Packer. These agreements foundered amid accusations on both sides of bad faith and broken promises, but there was too much at stake for the conflict to go on indefinitely. The two billionaires had had a marriage of convenience that lasted for three decades. Now both of them were facing difficult succession issues. Their sons' futures could be threatened by a long bruising war. Like two old sweethearts, Murdoch and Packer decided to patch things up, to stay together for the sake of the kids. On January 16, 1997, Murdoch and Packer signed an agreement that gave the National Nine Network the free-to-air broadcast rights to Super League and the right to buy half of the News Limited stake in Foxtel at cost price. "I would be telling a lie if I said I didn't feel deeply wounded and bitterly disappointed," said Arthurson, who retired as ARL president two months later. "It's not really a great way to start the year, is it? Sometimes you really wonder what it's all about." He continued: "It's a pity they couldn't have made the bloody deal in the first place. Then none of this would have happened."[20]

The ARL soldiered on for another season, as game attendance figures plummeted, before bowing to the inevitable and merging with Super League in 1998. In 2000, after News Limited dropped one of the oldest Sydney clubs from the competition, eighty thousand people took to the streets, the biggest protest since the Vietnam War. News Limited had lost an estimated A$300 million on Super League.

*   *   *

The downside to spending $5 billion on sporting rights around the world is that broadcasting contracts expire. The BSkyB contract had given the British soccer clubs more money than they had ever seen. But by the time the rights came up for renegotiation in June 1996, the clubs were convinced that they had sold themselves short in 1992. BSkyB's rivals believed the same thing and they were prepared to offer enormous prices to oust BSkyB. To retain the rights, BSkyB had to pay more than double the previous price, for a total of £674 million. And this was nothing compared with the huge battle looming in the United States when the National Football League (NFL) rights came up for renegotiation.

In the last half of 1997 a strange corporate madness seized the American broadcasting industry. Speculation about the next round of NFL contracts had been bubbling ever since Murdoch stole the broadcast rights to one of the two NFL divisions, the National Football Conference, from CBS in 1993. By 1997 the NFL contract negotiations—the broadcast rights for cable, for television networks on Sunday and Monday nights, and for the different NFL conferences—

had become a blood sport. Michael Eisner at Disney and Rupert Murdoch started meeting with NFL officials in March 1997. Murdoch's success with Fox had convinced the NFL, like the British soccer clubs, that it had undersold itself in its 1993 contracts, which had raised a total $4.4 billion for the four seasons. This time the NFL was looking for real money. "Out of the last negotiations three years ago, there was a feeling in the NFL front office that they undervalued the AFC rights in selling out to NBC (for an estimated $217 million per season)," an advertising executive told *Media Week*.[21]

The existing four-year contract—thanks to the huge price increase that Murdoch had offered for Fox's share of NFL games—had paid $1.1 billion a season for football. The 1997 negotiations doubled that payment to $2.2 billion each season over eight years. Total payments came to $17.6 billion. The rights themselves hadn't changed; it was just that now the broadcasters would pay a staggering $8 billion more for them. It was a straight wealth transfer, from the broadcasters to professional football players, who picked up 62 percent of the NFL's gross revenues. The Murdoch effect—the compulsion for media moguls to keep up with Rupert, or merely the realization that Murdoch had changed the economics of sport—had transferred $8 billion out of the media industry. The stock market values a company as a multiple of what it earns each year. Thus the full effect of the 1997 NFL renegotiation was to reduce the market value of the NFL broadcasters by up to $30 billion. The only people who were not complaining were the players, who would pocket an extra $5 billion.

The biggest loser was Michael Eisner at Disney. In 1993 ABC's *Monday Night Football* and the cable rights shared between ESPN and Ted Turner's TNT had cost a total of $1.97 billion, or $492 million per season. In January 1998 Eisner's ABC and ESPN retained Monday football and pushed out TNT to take all of the cable rights for eight years for $9.2 billion. It came to $1.15 billion per year. The increase in the price of the rights over what ABC, ESPN, and TNT had paid previously came to an extra $658 million per season. That is, each year for the next eight years an extra $658 million would be taken out of Disney's cash flow. In return for that extra payout Disney merely held on to its former position and gained half a season of cable rights. Eisner committed to this monster payment while he was looking over his shoulder, feeling the breath of his rivals hot on his heels. Disney stock peaked in May 1998. While other media stocks continued to soar thereafter, Disney dropped 40 percent in the next year. There was plenty of bad news elsewhere at Disney to explain it, but the NFL rights were a quiet body blow from which Eisner would not recover.

16

THE MOUSE WARS

Los Angeles, January–June 1997

IN JANUARY 1997 Michael Eisner was feeling the first twinges of concern that all was not well within the Magic Kingdom. The warning signs were as yet faint. Earnings at the Walt Disney Company were still chugging along; the stock price would not peak for another year. There had been some little irritation over the departure of Eisner's second-in-command, Mike Ovitz. Eisner had hired Ovitz—his longtime friend, the head of Creative Artists Agency, and the super-agent known as the king of Hollywood—in September 1995. Unfortunately for Eisner, Ovitz's employment contract had an extraordinarily generous payout clause.

In December 1996 Ovitz was fired. Two days after Christmas that year Disney lawyers wrote to Ovitz to confirm a payout of cash and Disney stock options valued at $140 million. It worked out at a little under $10 million a month for Ovitz's fourteen-and-a-half-month tenure at Disney. The termination payment was "larger than even the expert hired by the Disney Board to explain the contract imagined it to be, larger than almost anyone anywhere will receive in the lifetime of any of the parties, and perhaps larger than any ever paid," Delaware Chancery judge William B. Chandler III later concluded.[1] For a group that minds its pennies the way Disney does, it was very disconcerting. It was, as Eisner freely admitted to shareholders at the Disney annual meeting in February, "[n]ot good. A mistake. Won't happen again. . . . Be angry. Be annoyed. God knows I am."[2]

Peter O'Malley's announcement on January 7 that he intended to sell the Dodgers was the next bit of bad news for Eisner. Only months before, Disney had bought a controlling stake in the Anaheim Angels baseball team, unaware that a much more attractive prize would soon be coming onto the market. Now Eisner realized he had bought the wrong ball team.

Eisner's only consolation was to finalize a new stock option scheme for himself on January 11, two weeks after Ovitz's payout, worth $198 million. Not that anyone grudged it to him. In twelve years Eisner had come to personify the transformation of Disney into one of the largest and most profitable media companies in the world. Eisner had started out in the 1960s as a television executive at ABC. In the early 1980s he had gone on to be Barry Diller's second-in-command at Paramount Pictures, until both men had jumped ship—Diller to 20th Century–Fox and Eisner to head the demoralized Disney studios. Eisner made the better landing.

At the time of Eisner's arrival, the glory days of Disney's early years were long over. The company was even considering closing down its animation studio. Instead Eisner and the diminutive Jeff Katzenberg, whom Eisner had brought with him from Paramount, went back to Disney's core business. Eisner (an elaborately casual figure who touched six foot three and on occasion wore socks that were too short) and Katzenberg (a serious figure in black-framed glasses and suits) succeeded in turning Disney's animation business once again into the cornerstone of the entire company, a triumph of Mouse-to-Mouse resuscitation. Besides producing a string of animation hits including *The Lion King, Pocahontas,* and *The Hunchback of Notre Dame,* Katzenberg rereleased a series of Disney animated classics. Eisner extended that increased revenue into overseas distribution and video sales, which in turn drew people to Disney's new theme parks. Then there were the Disney cruise ships. And the Mouse shops. By 1996 Eisner had opened 636 Disney stores around the world to sell the Disney merchandise that was spun off from the Disney films and programming. The company functioned as an integrated whole that had made Disney one of the best-known brand names in the world and incidentally generated enormous amounts of money.

Disney's corporate structure worked like a vine or climbing plant. Eisner kept finding new ways to leverage off the company's brand name, which was based upon its library of animated films. The heart of the Disney empire was thirty-five animated feature films, made at enormous expense over six decades, that could be recycled forever for each new generation of children between the ages of two and eleven. The enormous power that this library gave Disney also made the company extremely vulnerable. Any threat to Disney's animated film business also threatened the taproot of the entire enterprise. If anything supplanted Disney films, the many branches of the empire could wither. The Mouse would fight ferociously to defend its franchise.

The strategy was so stunningly successful that by the mid-1990s the question for Michael Eisner was, what next? As he opined in his 1998 memoir *Work in*

Progress, written with Tony Schwartz, "Success invariably prompts restlessness. Absolute success often corrupts absolutely." Eisner's emergency heart surgery in July 1994 had contributed to his unease. After experiencing chest pain on July 15 at Herb Allen's annual media conference, Eisner had been flown home for a quadruple coronary bypass. He wrote to author Larry McMurtry, "Something has happened to me that is a big deal. My life has a finite sense to it, and there is certainly a hollowness that comes with such realizations. I try not to think about it, but I think about it all the time."[3]

Eisner was still recuperating in early August when a simmering feud came to a head over Katzenberg's determination to succeed Disney's president and chief operating officer, Frank Wells, who had died in a helicopter skiing accident in April. Perhaps the last straw for Katzenberg had been a *Newsweek* article on August 1, based on an interview Eisner had given a month before. Eisner had suggested to *Newsweek* that Disney should be modeled more along the lines of Rupert Murdoch's News Corporation, controlled by a strong leader without a second-in-command. Katzenberg's subsequent departure, which ended Hollywood's most successful working relationship, turned extraordinarily bitter and would consume both men for years. In notes that Tony Schwartz made for Eisner's memoir, Eisner returned again and again to muse over the Katzenberg problem, as it had become. Besides his comment about "the little midget," Eisner went on to claim that "Jeffrey was my retriever." And again: "He was my pompom—I'm the cheerleader."

In the giddy kaleidoscope of deal-making and -breaking, alliance and misalliance that the media industry had become, Eisner stood out as an old-fashioned kind of guy. He was a good hater. Katzenberg had gone on to join David Geffen and Steven Spielberg in launching DreamWorks SKG. The new film studio became the epicenter of the anti-Eisner faction in Hollywood. "He hates us and we hate him," Spielberg was reported as saying. "But he's a businessman. He'll buy our shows."[4]

"The more we go it alone, the better I feel," Eisner told *Fortune* in 1998. "Fighting and suing each other and making love—to me that's too schizophrenic. Either you love somebody or you hate somebody. I can't quite deal with this idea that you love them on Monday and hate them on Tuesday. But that is the business."[5]

The legal battles with Katzenberg over his termination payout would run until August 1997, when Disney settled with an estimated payout of $100 million. Further disagreements over the share of profits to which Katzenberg was entitled from films such as *The Lion King* saw him back in court against Disney. Eisner finally settled in July 1999, paying Katzenberg a further $200 million. Team Disney had spent too much executive time on a fruitless quarrel. But in 1997 Eisner had bigger problems looming.

In the mid-1990s Eisner had pushed the Disney brand about as far as it could go. There was only a finite number of Disney stores and Disney theme parks and Disney cruise ships that the world could handle. The question was, where did Eisner go from there? His view, as he put it to stockholders in the company's annual report in late 1996, was that Disney's history could be divided into three phases. There was the period Before Michael Eisner, which was the dismal history of Disney as a stagnant backwater up until 1983; then there was Early Michael Eisner, which was the twelve-year period of spectacular turnaround; and then there was Resurgent Michael Eisner. That was the new era he had ushered in with his deal with Warren Buffett at Sun Valley in 1995, for Disney to buy Capital Cities/ABC. The deal, which was finalized in early 1996, allied Hollywood's top film studio with America's top television network. Eisner had done it, he said, "to protect the Mouse," to ensure that Disney television programming could be distributed over the ABC network. But the real attraction of the deal, he always emphasized, was in acquiring ESPN, the world's premier cable sports network. ESPN already earned $600 million a year in cash flow. Eisner believed that that figure could grow and that the future for Disney lay largely with the opportunities to expand ESPN, to launch ESPN Zone stores, and to spin off new cable channels like ESPN 2 and ESPN News. So for Eisner sports programming was critical.

By the start of 1997, however, Eisner was beginning to realize the real cost of the company's executive squabbles and management instability in the mid-1990s: They had made him take his eye off the ball. Disney was still churning out strong earnings, but in business after business the growth areas were already staked out. In his own way Eisner was facing a crisis of confidence, a test of nerve every bit as threatening as Peter O'Malley's at the Dodgers. Almost everywhere Eisner looked for new opportunities in 1997, someone else had got there first. What was frustrating was that it was always the same someone. The end result was that, two and a half years later, Michael Eisner would no longer be the blue-eyed boy of Hollywood and Wall Street. The Disney stock price would be in full retreat, and the business press would be openly debating whether Eisner should step down. The natural rise and fall of business cycles and the woes that Eisner brought on himself when he was out of form contributed to his decline, but if there was one person who could be said to have brought Eisner down, it was Rupert Murdoch.

The question is, back in early 1997 what started Eisner's slide? What should Eisner have done to beat off Murdoch's relentless war on the Mouse? The point where Eisner's slide became irreversible is easier to locate: It was that moment in January 1998 when he committed a $9.2 billion blunder and bought NFL rights. Why did Eisner do it? What made him so desperate? What was it that left Eisner with nowhere to go except to pull out the checkbook, swallow hard, and sign off on a deal that he knew would cripple Disney's earnings?

*   *   *

Eisner's prospects in January 1997 didn't look too bad. In films Disney, under Joe Roth, who had left Murdoch's 20th Century–Fox to replace Katzenberg as Disney's studio head, remained the most profitable studio. Fox in turn had hired Bill Mechanic from Disney to work under Peter Chernin, chiefly for his overseas marketing savvy. After the success of *Independence Day,* Mechanic and Chernin appeared to have stumbled badly with a lavish film directed by James Cameron. Production of *Titanic* was running late, and Hollywood gossip had costs blowing out from $100 million to beyond $250 million.

Meanwhile Jeffrey Katzenberg at DreamWorks had been hiring animators from the Disney studios for million-dollar salaries. In the process he had doubled the cost to Disney of making animated feature films. Such films were the company's lifeblood: *The Lion King* had grossed $761 million at the box office for Disney, another $500 million in video sales, and $225 million from consumer products.[6] Eisner could blame Murdoch for this new threat. In March 1994 Bill Mechanic at 20th Century–Fox had hired two former Disney animators, Don Bluth and Gary Goldman, to build a $100 million animation studio in Phoenix, Arizona. Fox's move had sparked a new interest in animated films by the major studios. By the end of the decade animated films would account for a quarter of Hollywood film production. Warner Bros. built a new studio and beefed up its animation staff from 140 to 400. DreamWorks built a $150 million studio with 400 employees. Fox's first film, *Anastasia,* was due out in September 1997. Eisner planned to bury *Anastasia* in a Disney sandwich, releasing Disney's latest children's film, *Flubber,* and re-releasing *The Little Mermaid* back to back to coincide with the *Anastasia* launch, to lock up the children's audience. *Anastasia* had cost $50 million to make. Disney's strategy ensured that the Fox film grossed only $63 million at the U.S. box office. Three years later Fox would close its animation studio in Phoenix. In Hollywood, you don't mess with the Mouse.

In television, the ABC network's ratings were slumping. Eisner was depending in part on a couple of new Fox-produced hits, *The Practice* and *Dharma and Greg,* to put the network back on track. Here again it looked like Eisner was a couple of steps behind the pace. Peter Chernin had convinced Murdoch to go after the top-ten television comedy writers. Chernin offered these writers two or three times their existing salaries, with contracts worth between $10 and $15 million, to come up with new ideas for shows. Fox ended up with half a dozen of the people it was targeting. In 1995 Fox had spent $17 million on writers, but in 1997 it ballooned to $60 million—probably more than News Corp's total payroll for journalists.[7] In the process Fox also blew away the production budgets of its rivals, who had to match the offers to hold on to their writers. "We knew we were going to screw up the business a little," Chernin conceded to *Fortune.*[8]

Chernin's strategy had paid off with shows like *Ally McBeal* and *The Practice* by Michelle Pfeiffer's husband David E. Kelley, and writer Chuck Lorre's *Dharma and Greg.* With other hits like *Buffy the Vampire Slayer* and *King of the Hill,* by 1999 Fox had twenty-nine prime-time television series in production. Like filmmaking, producing television series is a huge gamble. Most series bomb and are not renewed the next year. For the first three years the shows that survive are produced at a loss. But once a show reaches that magic three-year point, it can be syndicated—and then the show can be very profitable indeed. *King of the Hill,* for example, sold for $4 million an episode. That translates into $104 million for a season of twenty-six programs, almost all of it profit. Murdoch had gambled hundreds of millions of dollars making television programs. With any luck, in five years time he stood to make billions.

Logically television series production was an area where Disney and ABC should have been expected to excel, especially now that Congress had lifted the decades-long ban on Hollywood studios producing television programs. But Murdoch already had the ground staked out. "This has nothing to do with attacking Disney," a News Corp spokesperson said when asked about the growing rivalry. "We are entering businesses we find attractive."[9]

The real clash was over sports.

*   *   *

In late September 1996 David Hill, the garrulous head of Fox Sports, pulled off a minor coup. Even before the L.A. Dodgers came onto the market, he bought the Dodgers' local pay-television rights. Hill was an Australian who had been called in to run Murdoch's new American sports division in 1994 after his success as sports chief at BSkyB. For $6 million Hill picked up broadcast rights for forty-five Dodgers games per season from a failing wireless pay-television service in California called Tele-TV. The Dodgers rights gave Fox Sports West (FSW) cable in southern California an embarrassment of riches. The network already broadcast the L.A. Lakers, the L.A. Clippers in basketball, the Anaheim Mighty Ducks in hockey, and the Anaheim Angels in baseball. In order to fit the Dodgers into the crowded lineup, Fox Sports West announced that it was launching a second cable sports channel.

Fox Sports West 2 (FSW2) launched on January 27, 1997. Besides the Dodgers, it carried the Clippers, the Mighty Ducks, USC and UCLA basketball and football, horse racing, and high school sports. Apart from the Dodgers, these were games for which Fox Sports already held the rights. The economics were simple: Fox West Sports had 4.2 million subscribers paying a dollar a month for the channel, for a total of $50 million a year. The only extra programming cost to run FSW2 would be the $6 million a season for the Dodgers. Against that, FSW2 would charge seventy cents per subscriber per month—that is, extra annual revenue of up to $35 million. This looked like a windfall.

It was unfortunate that the Dodgers' season didn't start until April. FSW2 launched in January, in the middle of the hockey season. The timing meant that in the early weeks the channel's major draw was the Mighty Ducks, which were owned by Disney. The Ducks were indignant that to watch them you had to buy FSW2. For Disney, the Ducks were no ordinary team to be messed with. They had gone way beyond sport—they were a branding exercise. Fox Sports was messing with Disney's sporting mascot. Disney was counting on the Ducks and the Anaheim Angels as the cornerstone for the regional sports channel it was planning, ESPN West. So FSW2 was bad news for Disney. Again Rupert Murdoch had got there ahead of Michael Eisner, to launch his own California sports channel. Just to rub salt in the wound, he was launching the channel with Disney's pride and joy, the Mighty Ducks. Disney executives began calling their lawyers.

In February 1997, with Pat Robertson blowing hot and cold on the Fox Kids deal, tempers rising in the London High Court over Michael Clinger's wiretapping allegations, and Rupert Murdoch lining up to meet with Charlie Ergen, the Mighty Ducks sued FSW2 to force them to put the team back on FSW. Three weeks later, on February 24, as Murdoch and Ergen were announcing their Sky merger on the Fox studio soundstage, Fox Sports returned fire with an antitrust suit against Disney for inciting cable companies not to carry FSW2.

The affair played out with all the moral outrage that typifies a media turf war. In the Orange County Superior Court the Mighty Ducks claimed they had contracted for games to be shown on FSW with 4.2 million subscribers, and that moving them to FSW2, which had less than 300,000 subscribers, voided the contract. The Ducks' greatest concern was for the fans. In the U.S. District Court nearby, the Fox federal antitrust suit claimed a conspiracy by Disney and ESPN, who wanted to use the Ducks and the Angels to start their own new network.

Disney had made false and disparaging comments about Fox Sports' rights to telecast the Angels and Mighty Ducks, Fox Sports claimed, and had deceived cable operators into believing that FSW2 would not be able to deliver its scheduled programming. "Disney has enormous leverage over cable operators," the writ said. Because of its extensive programming interests, "Disney is in a position to pressure, punish and reward cable operators."

Behind the colorful claims, the problem for FSW was that the cable companies were refusing to pay for another sports channel that they didn't want, even when FSW offered the first year for free. This opposition intensified after the threat of Murdoch and Ergen's Sky rose above the horizon on February 24. Disney and Fox continued maneuvering for position through the spring. Disney was reported to be bidding to buy the Los Angeles Clippers, to have three California sports teams on which to base its planned sports channel, while Murdoch was in talks with the Lakers and the Kings, but nothing eventuated. Fox Sports offered $100 million for rights to Angels and Ducks games for the next ten years, but Disney wasn't interested.[10] "It's not a personality war per se, not like Ted and Rupert," a media chief executive said. "It's that every ball field they show up in, the other guy's there. Inevitably a rivalry builds up."[11]

Everyone agreed that this was so very not-personal. It was not conflict so much as healthy competition. With the judges still out on FSW2, attention switched to the next stage of the competition: the pursuit. It involved a race to find a man in New York named Charles Dolan, wrestle him to the ground, then offer him $850 million. The winning side—and this was the tricky part—had to convince Dolan to take its money.

*   *   *

Dolan ran America's sixth-largest cable company, Cablevision. John Malone had been feuding with him forever. Malone and Dolan had both built up remarkably similar regional sports networks. While Malone's Prime Ticket networks, which became the heart of Fox Sports, were based in California and the American South, Dolan's Rainbow Media sports networks were based in New York, Chicago, and Boston. In 1994 Dolan beat Malone in a furious bidding war to buy Madison Square Garden from Sumner Redstone at Viacom for $1.075 billion. The Garden, its sports teams, and its sport networks gave Dolan an unassailable position in New York, with broadcast rights locked up for all the city's major teams. Dolan's partner, the ITT hotel group, had funded most of the Garden deal. When ITT put its half share in the Garden up for sale in February 1997, Dolan insisted he had preemptive rights to buy ITT out for $765 million. Dolan was to settle the deal on June 19, when he needed a bank credit line of $850 million.[12] Cablevision was already hopelessly overleveraged, with $3.9 billion of debt, so Dolan needed to find someone else to come up with the money.

The Fox Sports and Rainbow Media networks were "two halves of a $100 bill" that Malone and Dolan couldn't put together, according to Cablevision executive Marc Lustgarden. Malone's hope in 1995, when he proposed the Fox Sports merger, had been that Rupert Murdoch would be the "rubber joint" between himself and Dolan, but so far it had not worked. If a deal could be done, though, the result would be a merged network of regional sports channels that had national coverage. It would be, finally, a solid threat to Disney's ESPN.

Not that Disney was worried. In 1998 ABC/ESPN president Steve Bornstein told HBO, "I kind of look at Fox as a big mosquito."[13] Beneath the disdain, however, winning Rainbow Media had become as important to Michael Eisner as it was to Rupert Murdoch. In one stroke a Rainbow deal with Eisner would stop Fox Sports' expansion plans in its tracks and give ESPN a solid platform of regional sports networks. Chuck Dolan, however, would prove an elusive quarry.

Back in Los Angeles Murdoch's concern to secure the future of Fox Sports West 2 had prompted his dinner invitation to Peter O'Malley. O'Malley in turn invited Murdoch to watch a game at Dodger Stadium and eat a Dodger Dog when the season kicked off on April 1. The sale of the Dodgers was finally hammered out over three hectic days of negotiations, from May 8 to May 10, for $311 million. Life had become impossibly complicated for Murdoch. In the first days of May he had wrestled with the death-throes of his merger with EchoStar—and also with Pat Robertson's extraordinary call on May 2 asking Murdoch to give him less money in the bid for IFE and the Family Channel. On May 6 Charlie Ergen had been left on the tarmac at Denver International Airport, waiting in vain for Chase Carey to call. On May 7 the legal battles with EchoStar had begun. News Corp execs were deeply enmeshed in the Dodgers negotiations on the evening of Friday, May 9, when Ergen was lodging his $5 billion lawsuit. As if all of this were not enough, April 28 had been Rupert and Anna's thirtieth wedding anniversary. "We had five days in Bermuda," Anna said unhappily several weeks later. "It rained."[14]

Peter O'Malley's announcement on Monday, May 12, that he was seeking permission from major league baseball to begin sale procedures with Murdoch triggered fresh outpourings of public grief. L.A.'s ball team was to be run by a multinational company. Would the Dodger ethos be forever lost? Was Rupert Murdoch colorful enough? columnists pondered. Was he enough of a character for this sacred trust? The wilder reports suggested he didn't even like baseball. The general consensus was that Murdoch was too much a faceless businessman to run the city's pride and joy. The ball team needed someone who was more of a pirate.

Throughout May Rupert Murdoch kept moving the troops forward, making the deals, but he was desperately vulnerable. He had lost MCI's financial support. He had blown away the EchoStar merger with Charlie Ergen. This left Murdoch with a satellite license and operation and no partner to pay for it. And his programming was blocked on all sides. The media was full of stories of Murdoch's humiliation. The only people who could save him were the cable operators who owned the Primestar satellite operation—and they hated him. They weren't buying Fox News, they weren't buying Fox Sports, and unless he could resolve his problems with Pat Robertson, they wouldn't be buying Fox Kids. By April Murdoch had realized that he was in trouble with his EchoStar plan and had made the leap to join his enemies. But no one at Primestar seemed ready to catch him.

Primestar's medium-power DBS operation was the second-largest satellite service in the United States, with 1.8 million subscribers. It was a partnership owned by the country's five largest cable companies: John Malone's TCI, Gerry Levin's Time Warner, Comcast Corporation, Cox Communications, and the MediaOne group. In seven years of squabbling, the Primestar partners had almost never been able to agree on anything—not even the simple process of turning the partnership into a company. Their distrust of Murdoch was matched only by their distrust of one another. The basic problem they faced, however, was that no matter how much they disliked Murdoch, they needed the satellite slot at 110WL that he had wrestled off them two years before. To get it back, they would have to agree to merge Sky into Primestar.

Leo Hindery at TCI lobbied the Primestar partners to drop their resentments and do a deal with Murdoch for his satellite license, which would solve all the problems. Hindery was "a peacemaker. . . . He kept trying to convince everybody that there was more profit in peace than war," Malone testified later. Most of the resistance came from Time Warner. Malone himself was wheeled in for the tougher meetings, where he said he was "a proponent of, at least, exploring whether or not we could make peace [with Murdoch]."

Murdoch was insisting that before he did a deal with Primestar, the cable partners would have to contract to run his cable channels. The cable operators wouldn't do this, but by mid-May there was talk of an informal agreement about the channels. Murdoch wasn't going to get any money for the license either; instead he would have to take a complicated package of quasi-equity that would leave him with a 33 percent share of Primestar but no voting rights. It was almost ludicrous, the terms the cable partners were insisting upon, to ensure that some way, somehow, Murdoch did not pull another Houdini act on them, whip off the handcuffs, and waltz off with control of their company. What was definitely ludicrous was that, despite all these precautions, within a year it looked like Murdoch and Malone had set up a structure that, if not for the intervention of the Justice Department, could have allowed them to do precisely that.[15]

Malone argued Murdoch's position to his partners: "It just really says, 'Hey guys, I'm not Darth Vader anymore. If you carry my programming, you won't be subsidizing the enemy and, therefore, feel free to treat me as a friend, not as an enemy.' "[16]

By Monday, May 19, Hindery was so hopeful that a deal could be reached that he told Goldman Sachs analysts that "he expected news soon that would calm competitive concerns about satellite versus cable." At the Time Warner annual meeting the same day, Gerry Levin was saying the reverse: "Time Warner is not standing in the way of any agreement [over Murdoch and Primestar]," he said. "There is no agreement. There's nothing to be stood in the way of."[17] It didn't help that the previous Friday Judge Weinstein in New York District Court had thrown out most of the Fox News case against Time Warner, dating back to the previous October.

Murdoch's future now hung on a knife's edge. For months he had kept any number of balls up in the air. There was ASkyB and the satellite license, there was Fox News, there was the Family Channel, there was Haim Saban at Fox Kids, and Fox Sports, the fracas over Fox Sports West 2, the pursuit of Chuck Dolan, and the Dodgers. It had been a great show, but the curtain was going down. Murdoch had about two weeks to finish the juggling act, to bring all of these balls safely to earth. And now Michael Eisner was on his case.

The Dodgers had been the big wake-up call for Eisner. Now that Murdoch had the Dodgers, no matter which way the Mighty Duck court cases went, the future of Fox Sports West 2 was assured. Would Eisner and Murdoch face off directly, now that each owned a baseball team? "Well, he and I won't unless he improves his batting average," Eisner told the *New York Times*. "But I hope the Angels end up in the National League—then we'll kick Rupert's butt, right here in Chavez Ravine."

"We generally can't compete with Rupert on costs," Eisner told *Fortune*. "He's a much bigger gambler than we are—and by the way, it's paid off for him. I'm more a sleep-at-night kind of executive."[18]

Eisner was never going to be as acquiescent as he sounded. At Team Disney the corporate culture was that Disney executives didn't talk about their competitors; they talked about their "enemies." In New York Fox Sports was offering Chuck Dolan an $850 million investment in Rainbow Media. Eisner put another $100 million on the table to trump Murdoch's bid. During the week of May 19 Eisner also contacted Pat Robertson to do due diligence on IFE's accounts. The IFE board had said it would enter into exclusive negotiations with the first bidder to offer $35 a share—which happened to be Fox Kids. Eisner threw another $100 million into the pot and said he was ready to offer $37 a share. It was never quite clear why Eisner suddenly wanted the Family Channel. The major reason seemed to be that Rupert Murdoch wanted it.

Is a media battle personal? It's "completely personal," Eisner now told *Fortune*. "I mean, it's not really personal, but—I always felt from the time I was trying to fix Tuesday nights at ABC in the 1970s that it was personal. I gotta win. I gotta get the best programs on the air. My problem is, I like [rival media executives] and I've known them forever . . . Rupert is totally charming."[19]

"More intelligently, it's about business," one cable executive said as the Disney-Fox competition intensified. "But it's looking like a fight."[20]

It was unfortunate timing for Eisner to be making overtures to Pat Robertson just then. On May 1 ABC had screened the controversial episode of the *Ellen* sitcom in which Ellen DeGeneres's lead character comes out as a lesbian. Robertson was supporting a campaign by Christian fundamentalists to punish Disney's moral laxity by boycotting its products. "God has little obligation at the present time to spare America, because we are polluting the world with our television programs, our movies and so forth, our books," Robertson had said on *The 700 Club* eighteen months before. "We are polluting the whole world. We've made the world drunk, if you will, with the wine of our fornication."

Admittedly, Robertson had also had harsh things to say in the past about Fox shows and had called for an advertisers' boycott on *Married . . . with Children.* Gary David Goldberg, the producer-writer of *Family Ties,* once put the cynical industry view: "Left to their own devices, the three networks would televise live executions. Except Fox—they'd televise live naked executions." Thankfully this view had never seemed to affect Robertson's relationship with Murdoch.

While Eisner was making forays against News Corp, Rupert Murdoch was away on *Morning Glory.* To make amends for their rained-out anniversary in Bermuda, the Murdochs had flown to board the yacht at Hamilton Island on Australia's Great Barrier Reef and spent the week of May 20 cruising the Whitsunday Passage, the idyllic spot that was used for the movie *Dead Calm.* Running a media war from a boat moored somewhere off the coast of paradise can be hell. But that was why Murdoch had put so much communications gear into the yacht.

Murdoch's telephone negotiations inched forward. By May 23 Chase Carey and Hindery were reported to have hammered out a rough agreement to sell ASkyB to the Primestar partners. The following Monday UBS Securities analyst Rick Westerman was calling it "a done deal." The next day Primestar itself confirmed that merger talks were under way. The most promising sign was that one of the Primestar partners, Cox Communications, agreed on May 27 to carry Fox Sports West 2. Days later another Primestar partner, MediaOne, also signed a ten-year deal to carry the channel.

If Murdoch was facing his Waterloo, it still wasn't clear whether he had been cast as Wellington or Napoleon. So it was that Thursday evening, May 29, found him back in New York, putting on his best togs before heading for the Waldorf-Astoria. With all of Murdoch's grand plans still up in the air, the great night had finally arrived when the United Jewish Appeal was to induct him as Humanitarian of the Year. More than a thousand people had braved the crowd of protesters outside—five separate groups were waving placards—to gather in the Waldorf-Astoria's grand ballroom for a dinner dance. There to greet them was the master of ceremonies, the duchess of Richmond herself, Liz Smith, gossip writer extraordinaire for the *New York Post.*

"I like Rupert Murdoch," Smith told the assembled dignitaries. "He's not just the best game, he's the only game in town. Hell, he is the game." "I will undoubtedly be described as kissing Mr. Murdoch's ring," she conceded, but continued undaunted. "The future will lead us to the continued rise of the Murdoch news empire, where creativity will reign, energy and enterprise will dominate, and loyalty will bear its ancient Old Testament meaning."

There was "not a single person in the world who is more deserving of this honour [than] . . . my friend, Rupert Murdoch," the evening's chairman, Viacom chief Sumner Redstone, assured the $1,000-a-plate crowd. "If you don't know Rupert as well as I do, believe me, it's better to have him as a friend than as an enemy. Ask Gerry or Ted. They're not here tonight."

Privately Redstone was less averse to a little rivalry: "I do share [a similar] sort of background with Rupert," he said at the time. "But people say I want to emulate him. I don't want to emulate him. I'd like to beat him!" Redstone was actually still vying against Murdoch as a late bidder for IFE. Whatever was said over dinner, by the next day Viacom had pulled out of the race. Pat Robertson himself had shown up at the UJA dinner. With a neat display of ideological suppleness, he had managed to put aside for the night his views on worldwide Jewish conspiracies.

Israeli prime minister Benjamin Netanyahu in a videotape segment saluted Murdoch's newspapers and television interests for their "commitment to the battle for truth" and their support for Israel. The crowd ended the night on the ballroom floor, while Natalie Cole sang "Midnight Sun." The UJA raised $2.3 million.

For Murdoch the next morning it was back to the war zone.

Murdoch had until Monday evening to commit to an unconditional bid for IFE. But over the weekend a new snag emerged. The IFE board met at six-thirty on Monday evening to be told that Fox Kids had not met the deadline. Talks would continue, but Murdoch's exclusive rights to negotiate with IFE were over. The board was now free to accept a higher bid from Disney. Michael Eisner wanted his own exclusive negotiating period, starting with a bid of $37 a share. To help clarify their thoughts, the IFE board approved a special $100,000 payment for each of the directors—themselves.

Relations between News Corp and Disney worsened. "It got pretty ugly," said one executive involved in the negotiations.[21] All that stood between Michael Eisner and victory here were Pat Robertson and John Malone, who still had veto rights over any stock sale by the Robertsons. The sticking point was again *The 700 Club*. Robertson had agreed to move the program out of prime time, to eleven P.M. For $37 a share and $1.9 billion, Eisner felt entitled to dump *The 700 Club* altogether. Robertson refused. On Disney's side, the sleep-at-night kind of executive wavered. With no concession from Robertson, the price was too high.

Eisner's fight to do a deal with Cablevision was going no better. Chase Carey had put together a complex deal where Fox Sports paid $850 million for a 40 percent stake in Dolan's Rainbow Media and Madison Square Garden. Chuck Dolan was ready to take it, despite a higher bid from Disney that reportedly went as high as $1 billion. "Eisner is pulling his hair out," an ESPN executive told the *Los*

Angeles Times. "A network of regional channels would have been the perfect complement to ESPN. It would have given us local footage and saved enormously on production costs."[22]

Why would Dolan turn down Eisner's higher bid and go with Murdoch and Malone at Fox Sports? Various reasons were advanced, but the most convincing was that Chuck Dolan had discovered that he had a new best friend. It all came together for Murdoch in a remarkable forty-eight-hour period. On Monday, June 9, Malone sold Dolan some of TCI's best cable systems, in the New York metropolitan area. It was a cash and stock deal worth $1.1 billion that left Malone holding a third of the shares in Dolan's Cablevision Corporation. It was the beginning of a beautiful relationship. Cablevision stock doubled overnight. It would take another two weeks to finalize the Fox Sports deal with Rainbow Media, but there was no more talk of doing a deal with Disney. "At this point, the regional war is lost," a Disney executive conceded."[23]

On June 11, two days after Malone's deal with Dolan, Primestar finalized the $1.1 billion deal to buy Sky from Murdoch. At noon that day the IFE board was told there was now no further holdup for Fox Kids to buy IFE, and the takeover agreement was announced forthwith. Cox Communications signed up a long-term deal to take Murdoch's FSW2 sports channel in California. A string of other cable deals to carry Fox News followed.

Suddenly Rupert Murdoch was in the clear. He had done it. Through his daring alliance with Charlie Ergen, he had taken on not just the cable operators but most of the American media industry as well. And he had been beaten. Yet he had forced the cable guys to swallow their resentment and take him back. He had recovered more than he had lost. He had no voting rights in Primestar, but he still owned a one-third stake in the second-largest satellite DBS operation in North America. He had finally achieved financial viability for Fox News. He had ensured that Fox Kids would roll out on the Family Channel as "a great international children's network," on one of the widest distribution channels in the world. And with Fox Sports he had broken through to build a national network out of a bunch of regional nets, based on loyalties for local teams, that could eventually threaten ESPN. "We are extremely confident it will be very profitable," he said.[24]

After Shocks: The Winners and Losers

With the end of the 1997 Murdoch Wars, the American media industry had remade itself—out of its own fears. On the whole the outcome was positive, which just goes to show the widespread social benefits that can flow from a media-business culture that runs on angst, corporate anguish, and high levels of personal animosity. No one really understood the consequences of that culture's obsession with defeating one man. Even after Rupert Murdoch and the cable industry had signed their corporate peace agreement in June, none of the participants had any idea of the chain reactions they would trigger or of the flood of capital they would release on Wall Street. For many media investors in the second half of 1997, the first warning that the earth had moved was when they looked up and saw an advancing wall of money.

In July at the Sun Valley conference Murdoch sat down with Gerry Levin and Richard Parsons and worked out a deal under which Time Warner would run Fox News in New York. The agreement was announced on July 23. Ted Turner hadn't liked the Primestar deal with Murdoch. Keeping the Hitler comparison alive, he said the deal was "just like Munich." Now Turner decided he could live with Fox News: "What Martin Luther King is to brotherhood, I am to the cable business." Turner's commitment to brotherhood and universal suffrage was given a little assistance when Fox lifted its objections to Turner's TBS, which had just changed from a superstation into a paying cable channel, continuing to carry games of Turner's Atlanta Braves baseball team.

Wider moves were afoot in the media world. On June 9, the same day John Malone unveiled his new alliance with Charles Dolan at Cablevision, Bill Gates at Microsoft pulled off another surprise. He announced a deal to invest $1 billion into the Roberts family's Comcast Corporation. Malone later came to believe that it was part of a wider strategy by Gates to covertly bid for the TCI stock owned by the heirs of Malone's late partner, Bob Magness, to snatch control of Malone's company. It didn't really matter if this was true; for Wall Street the critical thing was that Sky, the Murdoch-Ergen threat, was no longer hanging over cable companies. Also, Bill Gates was now so confident that the future of the information revolution lay in cable networks that he was putting out serious money to get involved.

Sky proved to be the unmaking and remaking of Rupert Murdoch. That spring there was more at stake in the titanic struggle than just another corporate deal. This would be one of the turning points for communications at the turn of the century. Sky was the nightmare that cable operators had been dreading for a decade. Whether it worked or not, Sky offered a very different future for America and for the information revolution. If it had succeeded, Sky would have decimated the cable industry and turned cable executives into dinosaurs. If Murdoch had won the legislative changes he was seeking from Congress, he could have spread the cable industry on toast. While Sky would cost $3 billion in start-up funds to cover all of North America, cable companies would spend $3 billion to put fiber-optic cable into just 3 million homes. The *Economist* magazine likened the cable networks to the canal systems of the nineteenth century—expensive constructions that were out of date as soon as they had been constructed.

Even if Sky failed, it would still have pulled enough revenue from the cable operators to force radical cutbacks in their grand plans to roll out fiber-optic networks. Fiber-optic cable had been one of the two constants of the information revolution, along with faster microchips. It was an industry law: While the processing speed of computer chips doubled every eighteen months, the amount of data that fiber-optic cable could carry doubled every twelve months. But cable was expensive. With Sky creaming off the cable companies' profit margin, they would not have been able to afford a wide rollout of upgraded cable. There would be no rewiring of America.

This fact carried profound consequences, because the future that Murdoch was offering America was not fully interactive. Geostationary satellites could not carry full two-way Internet broadband access, telephony, and eventually video telephones. In 1997 it seemed that all of these things would require either fiber-optic cable or wireless telephone technology, which was still years away, or the high-speed DSL telephone connections that the Baby Bell telephone companies seemed to be backing away from. With his EchoStar deal in February 1997, Rupert Murdoch was offering America a very different future, an immediate alternative that would push the future of communications in a new direction. The information highway had come to a fork.

The thing to note here is that satellite services were always going to be a threat to the cable industry, with or without Murdoch's Sky. The critical thing that Murdoch did was to trigger a knee-jerk response in the cable industry that overwhelmed the DBS threat and locked up the key DBS satellite slots for the next two years. What changed the future of media was not what Murdoch attempted but the response he provoked. Murdoch's contribution to history was to be defeated.

Eleven months later the Justice Department would step in to try to reverse the tide, with an antitrust suit to undo the deal that Murdoch and Malone had so painfully negotiated. The suit claimed, quite understandably, that the only reason the cable operators who owned Primestar wanted to buy Murdoch's satellite slot was to prevent anyone else from using it. But the government intervention would be too late. The changes brought in by this summer of 1997, by the American media industry's overwhelming obsession with beating Rupert Murdoch, would be irreversible. The earth had moved.

The ripples spread wider. In the cable companies and the telephone industry, two huge blocks of capital had been rushing at each other for more than a decade. Inevitably they would become competitors. If the threat of satellite scared the cable guys, this was nothing to the anxiety that a cashed-up cable industry could inspire among the Baby Bell telephone companies. What would the telephone companies do when cable customers started to use their cable connection to make telephone calls? The future that this conflict promised was alive with possibilities.

Once Sky was history, what followed was like watching a landslide in slow motion. With satellite no longer a threat, Bill Gates's investment in cable signaled that he believed this was where the future of communication lay. In effect, Murdoch had closed the back door for cable, while Gates had opened the front door. It forced Wall Street to reappraise the way it understood media. The result was huge rises in stock prices for cable companies. It was a win for everyone involved in the Sky fight—even for News Corp. In April 1997, with hostilities at their peak, the seven biggest cable investors—TCI, Time Warner, Comcast, U.S. West, Cox, Cablevision, and MediaOne—together with News Corp had a total market value of $74 billion. A year later their stock prices had more than doubled, and the group was valued at $159 billion.

That was just for openers. In June 1998 the biggest telephone company in the United States, AT&T, saw the growth in the cable companies and began a new wave of telephone-cable mergers by bidding for TCI. That set off another round of rises for cable company stock prices. By July 1999 stock in the original group of seven cable companies (including those now merged into AT&T) together with News Corp was worth $338 billion. In two years stockholders had grown $265 billion richer. Microsoft's market valuation meanwhile jumped from $117 billion in April 1997 to touch $514 billion in July 1999.

This all happened as Internet revenues were taking off, and as the huge growth in Internet business captured Wall Street's imagination. It was no coincidence that the AT&T merger with TCI coincided with the start of the Internet stock craze. AT&T was going to use the cable networks for local telephony—and to give its customers broadband access to the Internet. The merger convinced Wall Street that America would have the new fiber-optic networks that it needed to under-write the e-commerce of the next decade—and even if the new cable guys didn't do this, it was now clear that someone else would. America would be rewired, the future dominance of the Internet seemed assured, and Internet stocks jumped $570 billion in the six months from October 1998 to April 1999.

Investors call this phenomenon a virtuous circle. The more that the various arms of the communications revolution converged—the television, the telephone, and the computer—the higher the prospective profits were for everyone concerned, as one sector fed off the other. The tidal wave of money swept along computer and chip makers, software groups and telephone companies. It even made Charlie Ergen at EchoStar richer than his wildest dreams. By April 1999 the indirect effects from this chain of events had topped $2 trillion—a sum equal to 25 percent of America's gross domestic product and arguably the largest transfer of private wealth in history.[25]

The wealth came in the form of higher stock prices rather than cash payments. It seemed particularly apposite that the technological revolution that began by promising the paperless office ended by delivering paper profits. But they weren't all paper. About $10 billion in new cash was pumped into Internet companies for working capital in the first half of 1999 alone. Arguably just as significant, this new wealth triggered a change in thinking, a radical shift in the way the corporate world viewed its future. For most executives in 1997, online commerce was an exotic option with no great relevance beyond e-mail. The six-month Internet boom that began in October 1998 changed that assessment, buried it under a mountain of new money. By mid-1999 the online future had become a dominant obsession for business. The world would never be the same.

Neither Murdoch nor his defeat was the direct cause of this remarkable confluence of events. At the end of the twentieth century huge new forces were coming together in the American economy. Yet in a strange way the Murdoch Wars became a catalyst for the process. Beating Murdoch broke the technological and financial logjam in multimedia. It changed financial perceptions. Did Rupert Murdoch intend any of the consequences? He wasn't looking to change the world when he flew in to Denver to meet Charlie Ergen. He was just angry at Ted Turner for shutting him out of New York, and he needed a trophy deal to show the analysts. Murdoch's guiding light is not Machiavelli—he leaves that to John Malone. Murdoch is much more attracted to Faust. He does what he has to do.

In any case, the game in 1997 had moved on. Wherever Murdoch moved that year—in baseball, football, or basketball, in film, in children's programming, in books, even in the coupon inserts you get at the supermarket—he triggered a landslide. If Murdoch's satellite gamble determined where the information super-highway would go, his content deals would determine what ran on it.

Michael Eisner was the major loser in these wars. Skirmishes between Disney and News Corp continued through the year until January 1998, when Eisner, the sleep-at-night kind of executive, committed his company to the biggest sports deal in history: a $9.2 billion rights contract with the National Football League. Eisner had beaten off Murdoch's ambitions to extend his grasp on the NFL, but the huge price made the victory pyrrhic. When Murdoch first snatched the NFL rights from CBS in 1993, Larry Tisch had learned how painful it was to emerge from a battle with Murdoch as the loser. As the Disney stock price began its downward spiral in 1998, Eisner would learn how much more painful it could be to come out of the battle as the winner.

PART IV

MURDOCH'S
ARCHIPELAGO

17

THE TROUBLE WITH TONY

London, 1998

ALMOST A YEAR after he became prime minister of the United Kingdom, Tony Blair learned, as Rupert Murdoch had before him, the perils of accepting long-distance telephone calls. The Italian prime minister, Romano Prodi, had called to clarify some details about schedules for European Union meetings that Blair would chair. The date was Wednesday, March 18, 1998, a detail that gave a curious historical twist to their conversation. The two men never revealed exactly what was said, and nothing more would have come of the call. But five days later, on March 23, a Turin newspaper, *La Stampa,* reported the conversation and claimed that in the middle of an otherwise mundane discussion of European Union business, Blair had raised the subject of Rupert Murdoch. Murdoch had just offered Silvio Berlusconi, the Italian opposition leader, £4 billion to take over Berlusconi's Italian television network, Mediaset. *La Stampa* claimed that Blair had asked Prodi if the Italian government would block the deal.

The next day, Tuesday, the *Financial Times* also reported that Blair had intervened on Murdoch's behalf when speaking with Prodi. Blair was in Paris when the story broke. Murdoch was in Los Angeles, where he and Anna had attended the Academy Awards that Monday night. It was one of the last public appearances of the Murdochs' marriage. *Titanic,* despite early pessimism, had become a huge box-office success on the way to grossing more than $2 billion. It also won nine Oscars, including three for director James Cameron.

It took some time to get a coherent account of the telephone conversation with Prodi from Blair's office. Blair's press secretary, Alastair Campbell, briefed British journalists that the story that Blair had intervened on Murdoch's behalf was "a complete joke" and "C-R-A-P, balls." He later said that he had been misreported, and he denied reports in the *Financial Times* that he had said Murdoch had not been mentioned. He declined to say what had been discussed by Blair but said,

"This was not a conversation about Rupert Murdoch." When Campbell was questioned later about his comments by a parliamentary subcommittee, he said, "I described [the *FT*] story as a joke and I happen to think it was a joke. I think it is the oddest form of intervention to sit in your office waiting for a phone call from the Italian Prime Minister."[1]

The private secretary who sat in on the phone call was unavailable in Paris early in the week the story broke and later was said to be in the Middle East. Blair's office backtracked steadily as further details of the call came to light. His cause was not helped when the British embassy in Rome confirmed the conversation. Blair told reporters he had certainly not been doing Murdoch any favors: "There is no question of offering assistance to anybody. I treat Mr. Murdoch no differently from anybody else in respect of any business with British interests."[2]

On Friday, March 27, the *Times* confirmed that Blair had intervened on Murdoch's behalf. The *Guardian* reported that Murdoch had been boasting "to his peers" about the incredible level of access he had with Blair. When Murdoch asked Blair for his help, even the pressures of Blair's government presenting its first budget on March 17 had not distracted the British prime minister. Blair had called Murdoch back two days later with news that the Italian government would not view the deal favorably.

The *Financial Times* quoted a News International executive who had been suitably impressed: "Rupert's access to the Prime Minister is pretty amazing. We were all a bit bowled over."[3] News Corp issued a huffy disclaimer from New York: "It is perfectly common for major businesses to enlist the heads of government and heads of state on issues of this sort." Blair's position was to stress that as British prime minister he was prepared to go in to bat for the interests of *any* British concern. "I have made it clear that BSkyB will be treated no differently from any other company," he added.

The incident gave Tony Blair's government its worst week in the House of Commons since it had come to office eleven months before. The criticism came from all sides. The Labour chair of the Public Administration Committee referred to "the rather unedifying spectacle of half truths and non-denial denials" in the government's handling of the issue. Backbenchers like Norman Baker, the member for Lewes, ventured a little heavy humor: "It seems that the Prime Minister is very much in bed with Mr. Murdoch, and I do not envy the Prime Minister in that respect."[4]

Blair wasn't the only one feeling the heat. The Prodi affair came just as a month of torrid press coverage of Murdoch's empire had been about to subside. While Murdoch had always shown himself to be impervious to whatever was thrown at him in the press, this time he had been forced to go on the defensive, to make more public statements than he had in a decade. The raw emotion in some of his outbursts that month indicated something of the personal stress he was under and what a year of constant crisis had cost him.

Three separate disasters had come together to produce this horror month for Murdoch. The common feature in each of them was the strength of the link that Murdoch had forged with Blair. It was a complex relationship that had been evolving for three years. The key to understanding it is the more complicated set of relationships between Blair, Murdoch, and the American who had become so influential on both of them, Irwin Stelzer.

Stelzer, who grew up in a poor Jewish neighborhood in New York, founded a highly successful international consulting firm, National Economic Research Associates (NERA), in 1961. NERA specialized in antitrust, electricity, and telecommunications issues. In 1983 he sold the firm to Marsh & McLennan and took a sabbatical in Aspen, the Colorado ski resort.[5] Stelzer found himself living in the exclusive Starwod Community next door to one of his best friends, Rupert Murdoch. Stelzer was also one of Murdoch's most trusted advisers, not merely on economic matters but in Murdoch's broader view of the world. Stelzer's views on society reflected and shaped Murdoch's own. He had arguably done more to color Rupert Murdoch's internal landscape than anyone else. It was said the two men got along so well together that they once talked about building a tunnel to join their two houses, though their wives were not as enthusiastic.

In the late 1980s Stelzer's consultancy arrangement with Murdoch and News Corporation was reported to be worth more than £1 million a year.[6] Bruce Hundertmark, the man who set up News Datacom, recalled meeting Stelzer at lunch with Andrew Neil at Murdoch's London apartment in March 1989. Stelzer, Hundertmark said, "assumed an air of superiority and great authority in all matters although as far as I ever knew he was never appointed to any position in News."[7]

In addition, Stelzer wrote columns for the *Sunday Times* in London, the *Post* in New York, *The Weekly Standard* in Washington, and even a column in Australia for the Queensland Press flagship, the *Courier Mail*, which gave him a voice and public profile that any economist would die for. Writing for such different audiences required a degree of rhetorical flexibility. In Britain, Stelzer argued unceasingly that embracing the European Monetary Union (EMU) and adopting the euro as currency would take away British jobs and be bad news for Britain. On the other side of the Atlantic he took the view that the EMU could threaten New York's position as the world's financial capital and would be bad news for the United States.[8] After his Aspen sabbatical Stelzer went on to lecture at Oxford and run an energy program at Harvard University. At some point he was also a managing director at the Rothschilds' investment bank. After Harvard he joined the world of right-wing think tanks with a stint as director of regulation at the American Enterprise Institute. In 1998 he moved to the Hudson Institute in Indianapolis.

Friends describe Stelzer as highly likable with a formidable intelligence. He is a phenomenal networker. He has a gift for spotting bright young (or not so young) men and becoming their patron. One effective way he furthered their careers was to introduce them to his friend Rupert Murdoch. Stelzer became close to Andrew Neil of *The Economist* in the 1970s; in 1983 he arranged for Neil to meet Murdoch and recommended Murdoch make him editor of the *Sunday Times*.[9] Stelzer, who often wrote or cowrote Murdoch's speeches, was also an admirer of Peter Huber of the Manhattan Institute, whose views on the need to deregulate the telecommunications industry (and the shortcomings of George Orwell) meshed neatly with Stelzer's own. It is likely that Stelzer wrote both Murdoch's speech at the Banqueting Hall in London in September 1993 and the speech on Orwell in Melbourne the following year.

Stelzer was also a strong supporter of Charles Murray, whose book attacking the American welfare system, *Losing Ground*, triggered a decade and a half of legislation to reduce welfare payments. Stelzer, who had introduced Murray's ideas to Murdoch, arranged for the *Sunday Times* to pay for Murray and his family to spend a month in Britain to write a series of articles about a crime-ridden British underclass that he called the "New Rabble" and the need to cut welfare support for unmarried mothers. Stelzer also arranged, after Murray had been paid for this work, for the *Sunday Times* to slip Murray another $10,000 check on top. An appreciative Murray described Stelzer as "the godfather."[10] Murray addressed News Corp executives at a management conference in Aspen. On one occasion when Murray visited Stelzer in Aspen, Murdoch sent his Gulfstream to pick Murray up. In 1993 Murray's warnings of a developing white underclass led to a flurry of political moves to deny welfare to unwed mothers.

In 1994 Murray was stirring up controversy again with *The Bell Curve: Intelli-*

gence and Class Structure in American Life, a new book he cowrote with the late Richard Herrnstein of Harvard. It tackled the ticklish topic of connections between race, class, genes, and intelligence. Its central thesis was that the technology-fueled economic boom of the late twentieth century had created a meritocracy, a new upper middle class whose members' advancement was due entirely to their own skills and abilities. In the technological society the stairway upward was open to anyone with intelligence. Some people were smarter than others, and they became rich because of it. Others stayed poor because they were less intelligent—a cognitive underclass. It followed, Murray said, that the reason the majority of blacks in America were poor was that they were less intelligent. This discrepancy reflected differences in intelligence between different races. *The Bell Curve* suggested that some people would always be at the top. Murray believed that affirmative-action programs penalized smart white people and produced a distorted and unfair society. Attempts to redress the genetic balance, such as education programs in the ghettos, in Murray's view, were a waste of money.

Murray was resurrecting in modern form a bleak social outlook that has surfaced whenever wide economic moves trigger social changes. It is the rhetoric of the new winners. History suggests that when a new group climbs the class staircase, their first move is to lock the stairwell door behind them. The Murdochs have always believed in the superiority of their own genes. In December 1999 Rupert Murdoch made a speech in Oxford where he emphasized the importance of IQ and genetic inheritance. The *New York Post* has a history of receiving criticism for inflammatory coverage of blacks. But by late 1994, when *The Bell Curve* appeared, Murdoch had a black son-in-law. In September 1993 Elisabeth Murdoch had married Elkin Pianim, whose father was a prominent Ghanaian dissident.

Of all Irwin Stelzer's bright middle-aged men, his greatest discovery was Tony Blair. When Stelzer reviewed John Kenneth Galbraith's *The Good Society* for the *Times* in 1996, he argued that while the book had "a few kernels of wisdom," it had not shown "so much as a nod in the direction of studies by social scientist Charles Murray. . . . In this area of public policy the good professor appears less well read than Tony Blair."[11]

As a young backbencher in the British Labour Party, Blair had stayed aloof from his party's fervent anti-Murdoch rhetoric during the Wapping dispute in 1986. He told Andrew Neil at the *Sunday Times,* "I hate the print unions even more than you."[12] In the late 1980s he caught Stelzer's attention because of his opposition to the Conservative government's moves toward nuclear energy, away from the country's traditional reliance on coal. Blair saw the issue in terms of employment, while Stelzer by conviction and from his long-term association as a consultant with U.S. energy companies acquiring Britain's coal power stations, saw coal as more efficient. Stelzer wrote several columns praising Blair as an up-and-coming star of the future. The casual links deepened after Blair became Labour leader in 1994. Eventually the two began having regular meetings to discuss Labour policy. They became so close that the *Guardian* speculated that Stelzer had become a paid consultant to the Labour Party. Stelzer did not comment.[13]

According to Andrew Neil, Murdoch met Blair for the first time on September 15, 1994, in dinner in a private room at Mosimann's restaurant in Belgravia. The dinner was arranged by Gus Fischer, but it is difficult to believe that Stelzer did not play a part. Stelzer also reportedly arranged for Blair to address the American Enterprise Institute in Washington. In July1995 Blair flew to Australia to address a News Corp management conference at Hayman Island on the Great Barrier Reef. There he made it clear that he had dumped Labour's longstanding policy to force News International to reduce its media holdings. Murdoch observed in his opening remarks before Blair spoke, "If the British press is to be believed, today is all part of a Blair/Murdoch flirtation. If that flirtation is ever consummated, Tony, I suspect we will end up making love like two porcupines. Very carefully."[14]

Through 1995 and into 1996 Stelzer produced a series of columns written in the tone of a disinterested spectator that grew ever warmer toward Blair. Stelzer considered gravely the charge that Blair was another Clinton clone or even Clinton Lite. He then went on to argue the contrary, that Blair should be seen as Margaret Thatcher's natural heir: "I know Tony Blair . . . Blair is one of Thatcher's children. And I think he knows it."[15]

In the summer of 1996 Stelzer wrote a remarkable tribute to Blair for *Public Interest*, a conservative journal edited by Irving Kristol. The article was based on an interview that Blair had given at Easter, in which he said he was an ecumenical Christian. Stelzer went on to argue that Blair had led a revolution in the British left: "Christ in, Marx out." Stelzer took Blair's somewhat diffident comments and his decision to send his children to a Catholic school and discovered Blair as a man who "has room for Christ in his Christianity." Blair was a modern reformer, Stelzer proclaimed, who had put the Methodist chapel back at the center stage of the Labour Party. He had put "sin"—a concept that Stelzer linked with "the undeserving poor"—back into political discourse. He would "leave it to the theologians and philosophers" to debate what Blair actually believed:

One thing is clear, however: the leader of Britain's left-wing party finds it acceptable, politically, to profess his Christianity and to look to the New and Old Testaments for a central core around which to develop his political program. Of necessity, that requires a cultural stance not very different from that of America's Christian Coalition.[16]

Stelzer had already concluded that Blair was Margaret Thatcher's ideological heir. Now in this highly crafted essay he set up a parallel between the ecumenical faith propounded by the leader of the British Labour Party and the fundamentalism of America's religious Right. It was a juxtaposition that less agile minds than Stelzer's might have missed. Stelzer had produced a dazzling piece of rhetoric with the apparent aim of convincing the American right wing that Blair was almost one of them. The question is why the ideological gymnastics were necessary. What made the American view of Blair so important? As the article kept returning to the Christian Coalition, the most obvious answer was that Stelzer's real target was the Christian Coalition founder, Pat Robertson. At that period there was a suggestion Stelzer was anxious to obtain Robertson's good opinion of Blair, which could in turn influence Murdoch's support for the Labour leader. This may be so. Then again, in many ways the juxtaposition that Stelzer proposed was eerily similar to Rupert Murdoch's own description of himself as a product of Methodist roots and Catholic leanings.

By early 1997 Blair had convinced Murdoch that he would not move against News Corp's interest once he was in power and that he would hold off from joining the European Monetary Union. On March 18, 1997, the first day of the election campaign, Blair and Major woke up to the realization that the earth had moved. Murdoch's *Sun* newspaper, after nearly two decades of backing the Conservative Party, had changed horses.

On April 14 Labour's media spokesman, Lewis Moonie, announced that a Labour government would relax rules on cross-media ownership, allowing large newspaper groups like News International more opportunities to own broadcasting groups. Labour also would not support widening the tax net for commercial television to include BSkyB. Blair probably would have won the election with or without the backing of Murdoch's papers, but their support arguably turned a probable victory into the largest majority in history for the Labour Party in the House of Commons. Murdoch's support continued after the May 1 election. Blair reportedly dined privately with Rupert and Anna Murdoch twice before the election and hosted them at the prime minister's residence at Chequers on several occasions in the following year. But in early 1998 the price for this special relationship was beginning to become apparent.

* * *

Three separate strands came together in February and March 1998. The first was Murdoch's ongoing quest to swing a deal with Silvio Berlusconi. Italian politicians had been agitating to pass a law to ban politicians from owning television stations. It would either force Berlusconi to retire from politics or would turn him into a forced seller of his half share in Mediaset. Murdoch had already tried and failed to extend his empire into France; he was still battling and getting nowhere in Germany. Italy would prove no easier. In December 1999 Murdoch would sell his yacht, *Morning Glory*, to Berlusconi for £4.5 million, apparently in a bid to cement a friendship. Whatever his sentimental attachment to the boat may have been, business was business.

The second strand was the price war that Murdoch's News International newspapers had been waging in Britain since 1993. In stage one of the price war, Murdoch had slashed the cover price of the *Sun*, in a successful bid to restore its flagging circulation to 4 million. But the move turned into a disaster when the price of newsprint doubled. Just when News International was poised to capitalize on its higher sales, it found its newsprint supplies were restricted. It was losing money from the price discounts and the higher paper price; without extra supplies of newsprint the *Sun* could not print enough copies to capitalize on its gains. Murdoch's strategies generally have two parts. First there is the great gamble, the big outlay that risks the empire or the division, like the decisions to launch Sky Television and Fox News or to buy the NFL rights. The second part—the critical part—is the payback, the period when the huge returns that justify the gamble are secured. The newsprint crisis meant the *Sun*'s price war had no payback.

Murdoch's British executives protested to him that the newsprint problem was not their fault—newsprint for the group was ordered from New York. But for whatever reason, Murdoch proceeded to stage one of his periodic management culls in Britain. News Corp's chief executive officer, Gus Fischer, went in early 1995, and News International managing director John Dux went in March. At the end of 1995 only two of the thirteen executive directors of News International remained: Murdoch himself and company secretary Peter Stehrenberger.

Stage two of the price war involved cutting the cover price of the *Times* to ten pence on Mondays, and forty pence on Saturdays. It was an aggressive move to steal market share from the Tony O'Reilly's *Independent* and Conrad Black's *Daily*

Telegraph. According to Dan Colson, deputy chairman and chief executive of Telegraph Group, in 1993 Murdoch had told Sir David English of Associated Newspapers, "Don't worry about the *Telegraph.* Leave them to me. I'll put them out of business for you."[17] Colson estimated that the *Times* price-cutting alone cost News International £30 million a year, for a total £150 million over five years to 1998. Hit by the newsprint price rise and the discounting it had taken to counter the *Times* price cuts, the Telegraph Group's earnings dropped from £60 million in 1993 to £1 million in 1996.

In late 1997 backbenchers in the new Labour government were concerned enough about the threat that Murdoch's price policy posed to the future of newspapers like the *Independent* to agitate for legal bans on anticompetitive pricing. Against them, Murdoch's supporters argued that he was merely doing what any good businessman would do. On November 12, with talk in the air of Parliament passing an amendment to trade practices legislation to outlaw predatory pricing in the newspaper industry, Murdoch was unrepentant. He told reporters at the BSkyB annual meeting, "No way will I call a truce. No one else wants to call a truce. They insult me every day, so they can go to hell. People do not much seem to like competition in this country." But just to be sure, Murdoch made an appointment to see Tony Blair at Downing Street the next day.

In February 1998 Blair drew criticism from Labour ranks by opposing the amendment on predatory pricing, which was passed in the House of Lords. On February 9 rebel Labour members of the House of Lords combined with other parties to amend the government's new competition bill, bringing it into line with legislation in the United States and Australia. The amendment banned any "abuse of dominant position . . . if it may reduce the diversity of the national newspaper press in the United Kingdom by reducing, retarding, injuring or eliminating competition."

The *Times,* in an editorial headlined "The Enemies of Success," complained: "We have initiated a pricing policy that has increased the market for broadsheet newspapers by 14 percent, brings more buyers and readers to ourselves and many of our competitors, countering an international trend of decline." The *Times* did not wish to destroy the *Independent,* as had been claimed, the paper argued. "We would only say that those who wish to keep this title alive have chosen a market-distorting route that will guarantee the continuation of its current state of death-in-life. If that is press freedom, it is the freedom of the specimen jar for the insect."[18]

Tony Blair then announced that his government would not support the amendment, and it was not passed in the House of Commons. But the debate had rekindled many of the old passions about Rupert Murdoch that the Labour Party had held for two decades.

The third strand in the controversy that engulfed Murdoch in Britain in the spring of 1998 began with a secret meeting on July 3 the year before. A week after stitching up Fox Sports' $850 million deal over Madison Square Garden in New York, Murdoch headed for Hong Kong for the handover ceremonies of the former British colony on June 30. After the formalities he had been granted a meeting in Beijing with Zhu Rongji, one of the Chinese vice premiers and the man tipped as the next prime minister. It was a moment that Murdoch had been working toward for nearly four years, ever since the Chinese government abruptly banned his Star TV satellite broadcasts in China, in the wake of Murdoch's indiscreet comments in London that technology was "an unambiguous threat to authoritarian regimes everywhere." Westerners had found two approaches possible in dealings with China. When Disney released Martin Scorsese's film *Kundun* about Tibet, Beijing had publicly chastised Disney and threatened to pull Disney's plan for a theme park in China. In response, a group of Hollywood's creative elite held a widely covered press conference at which they released a public letter of protest to Chinese ambassador Li Daoyu. The Chinese backed down.

The alternative strategy was appeasement. In April 1994 Murdoch had dropped the BBC World Service in the face of Chinese criticism of its coverage. "The BBC was driving them nuts," Murdoch said later. "We're not proud of that decision. It was the only way. . . . The truth is—and we Americans don't like to admit it—that authoritarian countries can work. . . . The best thing you can do in China is engage the Chinese and wait."[19] This remark was a long way from his position in the 1980s, when he had told *Sunday Times* editor Andrew Neil that he believed Britain should lob a "warning nuke" into a Chinese desert as a wake-up call over Hong Kong.[20]

In 1995 HarperCollins published the biography of Deng Xiaoping by his daughter, Deng Rong, and Murdoch personally escorted her to the promotional press conferences in the United States. The difficulty with appeasement was that in Chinese eyes it created a loss of face. When Murdoch was shown in to see Zhu Rongji on July 3, 1998, it appeared to have been a second-best option. Initially the editor of the *Times,* Peter Stothard, had been promised an interview with President Jiang Zemin, in return for hosting the board of the *People's Daily* on a tour of Britain, providing first-class air travel, and arranging interviews with senior British politicians. This promise was downgraded into an interview with Vice Premier Zhu, which had not gone happily. Stothard never filed a story about it.

Murdoch's interview with Zhu appears to have been tied into this process. When Zhu saw the head of News Corp, he felt sure enough of himself to pull Murdoch's chain a little. Zhu broke though the usual exchange of pleasantries via an interpreter to address Murdoch in English. He had heard, Zhu said, that Murdoch had taken out U.S. citizenship when he wanted to operate a television network in America. Would he consider taking out Chinese citizenship to further his interests in China?

Murdoch was clearly taken aback. Zhu watched his reaction for a moment, then turned to his entourage behind him and repeated the question in Chinese—to general mirth.[21] Murdoch hung in there slugging. He told Zhu that broadcasting via digital satellite "would be a powerful means to provide information, education and medical services to the population, which is scattered across this vast country."[22] The year before, Murdoch had launched the Phoenix Channel, a Mandarin-language channel beamed from Star TV's satellite owned 55 percent by Singapore Chinese and business interests in China close to the Red Army. While it was ostensibly still illegal to receive satellite broadcasts, Star was claiming to have 36.5 million viewers. Murdoch wanted to turn that claim into officially approved distribution across China's cable systems. Zhu gave Murdoch an attentive audience, but six days later, as Murdoch headed back to the United States for the Sun Valley conference, nothing was immediately forthcoming. In August the Chinese government released fifty-five new regulations banning foreigners from holding television interests.

The breakthrough came in September. Phoenix was granted formal sanction to be carried on two cable channels in Guandong and Guangzhou provinces, reaching 2.5 million people. It was still only the tiniest of toeholds, but it was the first official approval for Murdoch. "I don't think the Chinese in any way will expect us to be agents of propaganda," Murdoch said that summer. "They certainly don't want us to be agents of subversion, and we have no intention of being that."[23]

"There is a great deal of change happening in China, and on present indications we are getting a much warmer welcome," Murdoch told shareholders at the News Corp annual meeting in Adelaide on October 7. A week later the *People's Daily* reported that the Chinese Ministry of Foreign Affairs had granted approval for Sky News to open a Beijing office. When Chinese president Jiang Zemin made a brief visit to the United States at the end of the month, Murdoch was reported to be one of the business leaders who would fete him. Murdoch was in the audience at the Waldorf-Astoria in New York on October 31 to hear Jiang speak. Two days later he bobbed up at another Jiang address at the Beverly Hilton in Los Angeles.

Murdoch's growing interests included an information technology joint venture with the *People's Daily*, with an Internet homepage called ChinaByte. When Jiang visited Australia in 1999, Murdoch's *Australian* newspaper published an entire section of the paper in Chinese for a week. In 1998 there was even talk of Murdoch buying a soccer team, Dalian Wanda, the top team in the Chinese National Football League. Back in December 1997 the Hong Kong papers were full of Murdoch's most daring gambit yet. He had been speaking to executives from China Central Television (CCTV) and Communist Party officials about broadcasting CCTV's Channel Four via satellite to Europe and North America. Murdoch had offered nine of News Corp's satellite transponders to broadcast the propaganda channel for three years, free of charge. The strength of the gesture was that it was a straight gift, with nothing requested in return. CCTV officials did not answer press queries on the deal. In January 1998, at this critical moment when events in China finally appeared to be turning his way, Murdoch focused on a new problem.

In the early hours of July 1, as Hong Kong was still celebrating the handover ceremony the previous night, and the last governor of Hong Kong, Chris Patten, was relaxing on the royal yacht *Britannia* in Kowloon Harbor, HarperCollins secured a deal with agent Michael Sissons to publish a forthcoming book by Patten, *East and West,* for a £125,000 advance. Eddie Bell, the portly, cigar-smoking executive chairman of HarperCollins UK; the head of trade publications, Adrian Bourne; and the trade publisher, Stuart Profitt, had won the book with a bid that fell just under the level that required approval from HarperCollins in New York.

Even at the time it was a brave decision. A chill wind was blowing through the publishing house. Earlier that month, Anthea Disney, the chief executive of HarperCollins' parent, News America Publishing in New York, had dumped 106 book contracts. Seventy of the authors involved had not made their completion deadline, while another thirty-six were deemed noncommercial. "Let's clean house," Disney said, on the way to writing off $270 million from the HarperCollins balance sheet. While the contracts were paid out, authors and agents saw the move as a breach of trust.

It was a mark of the internal power balance at HarperCollins that when Disney ruthlessly pruned the publishing lists in the United States, Eddie Bell showed no sign of following suit in London. Bell was forty-eight years old, a gruff Glaswegian who had survived for eight years as head of HarperCollins.

Whatever befell the Patten book later, Bell exhibited no shortage of courage at the outset. He committed to the book, although it was common knowledge that

Murdoch detested Patten. Later that month, after returning from his meeting with Zhu Rongji, Murdoch took Bell to task over the Patten deal, expressing "extreme displeasure," as Profitt later described it. Patten was badly out of favor in China. The government-controlled press referred to him variously as a "criminal of a thousand antiquities," a "serpent," a "drooling idiot," and a "perfidious whore." When the editorial writers were really cross, they called him a "tango dancer."

Bell risked his boss's ire and remained committed to the book. Later that year Murdoch again complained to Bell, but Bell remained resolute. In January, however, Bell's position became untenable. According to Andrew Neil, Murdoch was furious that despite raising the matter with Bell twice already, the book contract had not been canceled. "Kill the book!" he ordered Anthea Disney in New York. "Kill the fucking book!"[23] Murdoch denied this version of events.

Bell continued his rearguard action, resisting a move that he saw as folly. He wrote to Disney on January 20, "Following your instructions to relinquish rights, I have given considerable thought to the potential ramifications of such action. The more I have thought about this, the more concerned I have become. I felt therefore that I must write to ensure that you are fully aware of the ramifications of not publishing which are potentially serious for News Corp and HarperCollins. KRM [Keith Rupert Murdoch] has outlined to me the negative aspects of publication."[25]

Bell had included a report by Stuart Profitt, the publisher of the trade division who would be editing the Patten book, that described the first six chapters that he had just received as "probably the best written and most compelling book I have read by a politician since I came into publishing." Bell quoted advice from HarperCollins's public relations agency that dropping the book would be a disaster, then went on to discuss PR strategies to contain the damage. He concluded by asking Disney to confirm that she had passed the memo to Murdoch.

Anthea Disney flew to London to discuss the matter on Monday, January 26. Profitt, who was aware of the ax hanging over the book, heard nothing further that week. On Thursday he proceeded as planned with a dinner for fifty-five booksellers and HarperCollins staff at the Savoy Hotel to introduce them to Chris Patten, who had flown across from France. Profitt introduced Patten and described *East and West* as "the most intelligently written book I've read by a politician in 15 years of publishing."[26]

On the following Tuesday Profitt had still heard nothing of the Disney meeting of the week before and went to his immediate superior, Adrian Bourne, to ask about it. Bourne said he also had heard nothing. But on Wednesday, Bourne asked Profitt to come see him the following day. At that Thursday meeting Bourne said he and Bell had decided to drop the Patten book, not because of the meeting with Anthea Disney but because they both judged that the book did not conform to the outline "or indeed inspire us from a commercial standpoint." He said that "the text was disappointing and that it was not worth what we had paid for it." Bourne then asked Profitt if he had his support in the decision. When Profitt said he would have to think about it, Bourne handed him a gagging letter drawn up by Harper-Collins's lawyers. "It is imperative that you make no communication with any individual employed by HarperCollins about this decision, and of equal importance is that you make no approach to any outside body or individual . . . that this decision has been made."

On the Friday Profitt asked for written reasons for the decision to cancel the book contract. The following Monday he asked again in writing and was promptly suspended from his position. A week later HarperCollins leaked a story to the *Mail on Sunday* that the Patten book had been "dumped for being too boring." At this point the story was playing out as planned. HarperCollins's public relations advice in New York had been that the whole affair would blow over, in the same way the Disney decision to ax 106 book contracts the previous June had. It would be a tempest in a teapot. What the New York spin doctors had overlooked, however, was that the decision to suspend Profitt over the problems he was making about the Patten book was made on the day that the House of Lords was passing its amendment aimed at reining in predatory commercial practices in the News Corp empire.

On Friday, February 27, the *Daily Telegraph* ran details of the saga and the writ that Patten had lodged against HarperCollins for breach of contract, as well as a writ that Profitt had just lodged for constructive dismissal. It even reproduced Eddie Bell's letter to Anthea Disney of January 20. In a statutory declaration prepared for the legal action, Profitt said that the reason given for dumping the Patten book was "clearly not a true or sustainable position and it is not one which I can support, as I have been asked to. . . . To do so would have meant . . . both lying and doing enormous damage to my own reputation. Though I have some sympathy for Eddie Bell, he has tried to make me the scapegoat. He has chosen the wrong man."

The furor that followed awakened all of the anti-Murdoch phobias of the past. One of the world's largest publishing houses had decided to impose draconian censorship in order to pursue Murdoch's commercial interests elsewhere in the world. It came just as the House of Lords was debating a predatory pricing policy that was pursued by News International and that sought to make the *Times*

Britain's best-selling quality newspaper. And at this critical time the *Times* declined to run the Patten book story. On the Saturday it carried a small story giving News Corp's response to the claims, denying any attempt to make changes in the book. "As is well known, the editors of News Corporation publications are free to express their opinions and often have been critical of the Chinese, as well as other governments," News Corporation said.

The *Times* media editor, Raymond Snoddy, said later that the lack of coverage was an "unacceptable error," but his attempts to interview Patten, Bell, and Murdoch had failed. By Tuesday, March 3, the paper's editor, Peter Stothard, was saying that he had thought the Patten book was "a pretty minor story" but he might have "underplayed it." The hapless Stothard was then hit by reports in the *Daily Telegraph* of claims made two months before by the *Times*'s former East Asia editor, Jonathan Mirsky, that the *Times* had gone soft in its reporting on China. "From four days after the handover [in June] until the end of September, the readers of *The Times* would have thought that Hong Kong had been lifted up to Pluto. . . . *The Times* has simply decided, because of Murdoch's interests, not to cover China in a serious way."[27] "Contrary to [Mirsky's] statement the China coverage of *The Times* is wholly and solely in the hands of the Editor," Stothard responded, "I have never taken an editorial decision to suit Mr. Murdoch's interests, nor have I ever been asked to."

Labour backbenchers were muttering about referring the original *Times* takeover in 1981 to the Mergers and Monopolies Commission, on the grounds that Murdoch had not honored the pledge of independence for the paper that he had given when he bought it. "It's worrying this man has such immense power," Thurrock MP Andrew Mackinley said. "There's an overwhelming case for his U.K. media empire to be broken up by legislation." "I'm concerned about the concentration of media ownership and the way owners interfered in editorial policy," the chairman of the Parliamentary Labour Party, Clive Soley, said.[28]

To some extent this reaction was just the usual list of suspects sounding off about their favorite demon. A more pragmatic response came from Gerald Kaufman, the man who led the investigation into Murdoch for voting irregularities at Oxford in 1952. Kaufman, now chairman of the Culture Select Committee, dismissed any talk of an inquiry: "This does not seem to be an issue about public policy. It is an issue of public controversy."[29]

On March 3, Rupert Murdoch responded to the barrage of criticism. After a brief stopover in London, he gave an interview to Snoddy in a car on his way to Luton airport. Murdoch described the Patten book deal as a "cock-up," a mess, and put the blame on the senior executives at HarperCollins for not being more forthright in handling the issue. Murdoch told Snoddy:

> I did not tell people to try and censor the book or invent excuses not to do it. I said, "Why don't you go and say we would rather have someone else publish this and if there is any chance of losing money we will make it good?" They chickened out and got themselves into the position where they were inventing reasons why they just didn't want to publish it which were nonsense, leaving me in a completely inexcusable position.[30]

Murdoch said the HarperCollins executives had "screwed it up." As a result Stuart Profitt, who was a very good editor, was able to take up the "position of a martyr" and Patten's agent, Michael Sissons, was able to "work it for a lot of publicity to sell a lot more books." Murdoch believed that no one had been hurt by the furor "except us in a PR sense because our people cocked it up at the end. I just regret that our people weren't more forthright about it at the very beginning when I was with them."

This response appeared inadequate in the face of the moral outrage that was being hurled at Murdoch. As reports came in of other books on China that HarperCollins had put on hold, some of the publishing house's leading authors began talking about jumping ship. Three days later, on March 6, HarperCollins settled its lawsuit with Patten and expressed groveling contrition. In an agreed statement, HarperCollins "unreservedly apologized" for any suggestion that *East and West* was rejected for not being up to proper professional standards or for being too "boring." HarperCollins said it accepted "that these allegations are untrue and ought never to have been made."[31]

Rupert Murdoch weighed in to say that there had been no winners or losers in the controversy. "Mistakes have been made and we all share responsibility," he said. "I have total confidence in the proven talents and abilities of Eddie Bell and the entire publishing team. . . . Eddie, Adrian Bourne (managing director) and Adrian Laing (general counsel) have had a difficult few days but I know that their professionalism, experience and above all their determination will take the company successfully forward."

Patten's agent, Michael Sissons, remained unimpressed. "Mr. Murdoch's comments of Tuesday and yesterday offer an insight into his mind," Sissons responded. "Clearly the notion of a graceful apology does not come easy to him. He acknowl-

edges a 'cock-up' and adds that 'mistakes have been made and we all share the responsibility.' That, I suppose, is one way to describe a malicious falsehood con-
cocted with the sole purpose of protecting, mistakenly as it turned out, the wider
interests of the empire. Moreover he cannot resist a sneer at all of us who have
raised the matter."[32]

By and large the HarperCollins admission took the sting out of the debate. But
Murdoch was concerned enough about the collateral damage to his interests to
meet with Tony Blair. According to a News International executive, the meeting
took place at the end of February. Quentin Davies, the Conservative member for
Grantham and Stamford, later told the House of Commons that Blair hosted
Murdoch at the prime minister's country house, Chequers, in the first week of
March. Other reports identify the date as Sunday, March 8. Whatever was said
during that visit, clearly the personal chemistry between the two men was still
strong. Murdoch was reassured about his high standing with the prime minister.

*   *   *

On Monday, March 16, Murdoch met with Silvio Berlusconi, the Italian opposition leader, and offered him £4 billion for Mediaset. Murdoch gave Berlusconi
seventy-two hours to think it over, then retired to a villa in Milan to wait for the response. Murdoch is not a man who takes forced delays well. He fidgets. As he
waited, his concern grew that even if Berlusconi agreed to the deal, the Italian
government might intervene to stop its leading television network from falling
into foreign hands. Murdoch badly needed to know if it was worth proceeding
with this bid. But who was he going to call? By Tuesday, March 17, his thoughts
had turned to Tony Blair. It was exactly a year since John Major had called the
British election, and Murdoch had made the groundbreaking decision to back
Blair. On the anniversary of this decision, Murdoch decided to call in a marker.

Two weeks later, as criticism of the Prodi incident burned hot, Blair told the
House of Commons, "As for newspaper proprietors, I meet all of them regularly,
I know all of them. I regard that as a sensible part of being the leader of a major
political party. As a matter of fact, I have no illusions about any of them. They are
all highly able, highly ruthless and dedicated to the success of their businesses, as
I am dedicated to the success of mine."[33]

It was a statement that seemed to be as much about describing Blair's view of
himself as of any newspaper proprietor. Learning to live with Murdoch was a
piece of realpolitik to which the architects of New Labour had committed at least

three years before. On May 12, when the amended competition bill went back to Commons for the second reading, the government announced that it would vote down the amendment on predatory pricing.

The most damaging issue to arise from the weeks of controversy was not that Murdoch, like many newspaper proprietors before him, dictated the editorial policy and news coverage of the publications that he owned, nor that he was prepared to intervene to ensure that his publishing house did not print books on certain subjects. The underlying conflict was rather that Murdoch's media empire, News Corporation, was a multinational conglomerate whose corporate objectives did not necessarily correspond with Britain's national interests. Murdoch's concern about the threat that price wars posed to Britain's quality newspapers was in part directed at undermining Conrad Black and winning control of an Australian newspaper chain. And Murdoch's international media operations had an agenda to present to the world the Chinese government's view of itself.

In 1999, when NATO aircraft mistakenly bombed the Chinese embassy in Belgrade, the coverage on Murdoch's Phoenix Channel was so stridently anti-British that the British embassy in Beijing lodged a complaint. In the United States News Corp was still struggling against its larger rivals. In the rest of the world, the picture was quite different: The issue was whether multinational media groups like News Corp were now too big and powerful for politicians in medium-sized economies like Britain's to control. This concern was not to impute particular malice or ill intent to Rupert Murdoch or his companies. It was rather to acknowledge that at the turn of the century, large multinational corporations had come to pose a rising threat to national sovereignty and that Murdoch was on the very edge of that wave. Just how little control national governments had over Murdoch was shown most markedly in News Corp's money trail. It was concern over this money trail that had triggered a secret meeting in Sydney three months before.

*   *   *

Just before Christmas 1997 a secret task force of tax officers met in Sydney to devise a strategy to monitor News Corp's international money movements. As well as Australian tax officials, the group that assembled in the Australian Tax Office building included senior officers from the U.S. Internal Revenue Service, the British Inland Revenue, and the Canadian tax authority. The Australian tax commissioner, Michael Carmody, had called the meeting, under the umbrella of tax agreements that linked the four countries, to discuss a way to investigate News Corp's tax structures. He believed that the finances of modern multinational companies had become too complex and crossed too many borders for one national tax authority to be able to regulate them.

The Australian Tax Office (ATO) had been investigating News Corp for at least two years as part of its Large Audit program. According to an internal memo dated May 1996, an ATO team had examined Australian companies that were "thought to represent significant FSI [foreign-sourced-income] risks . . . The analysis that was done resulted in News Limited being classified as high-risk."[34]

News Corp dismissed reports of the international tax inquiry. "News is subject to the normal rotational audits that all large corporations face and the company pays its taxes according to the laws around the world."

The tax officers meeting in Sydney operated in a world that to most taxpayers is bewildering. Even the terminology they used to describe what they were looking for sounded like another language. The May 1996 memo concluded: "The risk assessment in respect of News Limited shows substantial funds movements from unlisted CFCs [controlled foreign companies] to listed CFCs and the audit team is presently identifying the transactions and structures responsible for these movements. The other CFC areas to be examined include the control rule, the active income test, and the attribution percentages escalation."

Other issues studied by the ATO included "implications of offshore structures, residency and PERs [permanent establishment requirements], Royalties (transfer pricing), FIF [foreign investment funds], cross-border finance, losses on redemption of shares [and] increase in share premium account."

To outsiders, the News Corp accounts were the next best thing to magic. By a strange alchemy, each year hundreds of millions of dollars of News Corp earnings bounced around some of the most exotic parts of the world, touring the archipelagos of offshore tax havens. Huge money streams flowed through more than seventy-five News Corp companies in the British Virgin Islands, the Cayman Islands, the Netherlands, the Netherland Antilles, Hong Kong, and Bermuda. By the time News Corp's profits made it to the balance sheet to be reported to shareholders, they had accumulated more frequent flyer points than most accountants could dream of. In the course of this alchemy, most of News Corp's tax bill disappeared. At the heart of the News Corp accounts, the company's accountants had produced a wonderful piece of virtual reality.

It was 1986 when News Corp stopped paying tax in any meaningful way. In

1984 it had paid in tax a respectable 30 cents on each dollar of its reported earnings. A year later this figure had dipped to 23 cents on the dollar. In 1986 it fell to
9 cents on the dollar. The move coincided with Murdoch's big expansion into the
United States with his purchase of 20th Century–Fox and the Metromedia television stations. Murdoch had structured his U.S. operations through holding companies in the Cayman Islands. The structure also allowed him to claim interest
payments on the debt that he had raised against News International in Britain,
which was producing most of his profits. The tax rate blipped up to 15 percent in
1989, then stayed below 10 percent for the next decade. Australian corporate tax
rates during this period moved between 36 percent and 38 percent. By 1997 the
tax savings that the News Corp accountants had produced in the previous decade
were worth a total of A$2.4 billion in extra profits for News.

The architect of the first tax structures was an accountant named Richard
Sarazen, who had advised Murdoch on one of his first U.S. deals in 1983. He
joined News America as vice president of finance, took a two-year sabbatical in
1980 to run a failing manufacturer called Xcor International, then rejoined News
Corp to serve as finance director until being moved sideways just as the company's
1990 debt crisis took hold. His successor, David DeVoe, was a retiring figure, with
a reticence that almost approached mystery. His News Corp company biography
in the 1990s was seven lines long. Besides giving his present titles, the biography
said only two things about DeVoe: that from 1985 to 1990 he had been deputy finance director of News Corp, and that prior to 1985 he had been CEO of Xcor.
Press reports in the early 1990s described DeVoe as joining News Corp as an au-
ditor after an acquisition. Xcor was controlled by Louis J. Nicastro, a controversial
Chicago wheeler-dealer who had made his fortune out of slot machines, casino interests, and video games.[35]

Richard Sarazen was always more comfortable with numbers than with people.
"I can remember a number for years," he would say, waving a cigarette in the air. "A
name, I'll never get straight."[36] And what amazing figures Sarazen produced.
Apart from his tax skill, he racked up several hundred million dollars in both profits and losses from foreign exchange trading. But perhaps his most amazing achievement was a line item in the News Corp annual accounts each year. Sarazen could
make Magic Numbers.

It began in 1987. The profit after tax on News Corp's operating earnings (a
figure described in Australia as profit before extraordinary items) came in at
A$364.364 million. It was a cute little entry. The first three digits were the same as
the last three digits. There was nothing terribly unusual about this: Australian ac-

counting protocols offered four key profit figures that showed how a company was traveling; The odds that one of them should repeat the first three numbers after the decimal place were about one in 250.

But it happened again the next year. On the same profit line, this time the result was A$464.464 million. The 1989 result was A$496.496 million. In 1990 the figure was A$282.282 million. (An Australian accounting change meant the line was now described as profit before abnormal items.) At this stage the chance that one profit figure would repeat itself like that four times in a row was one in one trillion (1,000,000,000,000). There were two ways to interpret this pattern. One was that it was truly a remarkable coincidence. The second view was that it was a piece of pure machismo. It was Sarazen's signature on the accounts, his way of saying, "These numbers will do whatever I want them to do." His signature was discreet, of course, and it worked only in Australian dollars. As soon as U.S. and British investors looked at the result in U.S. dollars or pounds sterling, the effect disappeared.

A company account is a snapshot of that company at one moment in time, which in News Corp's case is midnight on June 30. For multinational companies that snapshot is based not just on the company's earnings but on where exchange rates are at that same moment. Once June 30 is past, the numbers are sacrosanct. A company may have an idea of what its results will be, but it does not know what the exchange rates to convert its foreign earnings will be. So if Sarazen was producing these Magic Numbers, he had to be doing it after the balance date. Any large corporation has arguments back and forth with its auditors about what is and is not profit. It appeared that Sarazen had taken this one step further: He had used these discussions to manufacture the News Corp result to the nearest $1,000.

The 1991 accounts were critical to the future of News Corp. After surviving the debt crisis by the barest of margins, David DeVoe as the new finance director had to produce a solid result that would rally the company's stock price for a stock offering. DeVoe also needed to show that whatever financial hubris News Corp had suffered from in the past, News Corp accountants were now on the straight and narrow path.

DeVoe celebrated News Corp's escape from its debt crisis with the accounting equivalent of a barrel roll. Sarazen had produced his party trick once in the News Corp accounts each year. DeVoe did it three times in the same set of accounts. Profit before abnormal items came in at A$391.391 million. Minority interests of A$70.070 million were subtracted, to give a profit of A$321.321. The odds against three numbers repeating themselves like this were more than 100 million to one.

The Magic Numbers appeared to have become an obsession with the News Corp bean counters. They did it again in more restrained style in 1992 (profit before abnormal items $530.530 million); thereafter News Corp abruptly began reporting its profits only in millions of dollars, dropping the decimal places.

There is nothing actually wrong with such results. Auditors take the view that when a result comes to hundreds of millions of dollars, the minor numbers in the result are not significant. But these results suggest a unique accounting culture at News Corp. The uneasy question that this cheap party trick raises is: If this accounting team is so confident that they can make the minor numbers in a profit report say anything they want, then what does this say about the big numbers the company was reporting? Why should the number technicians stop there?

DeVoe was running a virtual reality machine in the News Corp accounts. In effect there were three separate News Corps, each of which was quite real. Or rather, it was as if News Corp existed in three parallel universes. The simplest way of seeing this was to ask the most basic question about News Corp, which was: How much did it earn? In the shareholders' universe, the answer to this question appeared in the News Corp annual report each year. In the six years from fiscal 1992 to fiscal 1997, for example, excluding tax News Corp reported profits totaling A$5.8 billion. The accounts broke up the profits by divisions and by country and showed strong earnings flowing from the group's operations in the United States, Britain, and to a lesser extent Australia. That was version one. Several months later News Corp filed an alternative reality with the Securities and Exchange Commission in Washington, and the results were not so rosy. The earnings News Corp announced to its shareholders were based on Australian accounting standards, but the results that it filed with the SEC were based on U.S. accounting rules. As News Corp invested heavily in satellite and cable channel start-ups, the American and Australian views of the company began to diverge. Under U.S. rules, almost half of its reported earnings disappeared and its net profits totaled a more modest A$3 billion. This was version two. By 1997 there was a A$1 billion gap between what News Corp reported that it earned each year and the result it reported to the SEC. The gap was produced largely by huge losses in the start-up businesses. In Australia News Corp treated the losses as an asset and capitalized them; in the United States it wrote them off as a cost.[37]

The U.S. earnings were still fabulous compared with the third version of News Corp, which is what the tax officers meeting in Sydney in December 1997 were focusing on. In the same six years News Corp companies paid A$351 million tax, which was the equivalent of six cents on every dollar of profit it reported to shareholders. The tax authorities of the world were not giving News Corp a special break here: It paid the same rate of tax on its taxable income as every other company. What made the difference was the ingenuity with which the News Corp accountants were able to reduce the amount of the company's income that was actually taxable. Working backward from the $351 million tax paid in those six years and assuming an average tax rate levied of 35 percent, we find that in the eyes of tax authorities, News Corp's taxable income during the six years from 1992 to 1997 was only A$1 billion. In those six years alone the News Corp accountants had moved A$4.8 billion of income past the tax authorities in Britain, the United States, and Australia.

There had been no suggestion that News Corp had acted illegally, or that the result was anything other than smart tax planning. The only such suggestion had come from the Israeli tax authority, but on April 3, 1998, even that suggestion was lifted. Even as debate continued in the House of Commons over how much help Tony Blair had offered Rupert Murdoch with the Italian prime minister, News Corp announced a $3 million settlement with the Israel Income Tax Commission. News Corp did not make any admission of wrongdoing but agreed to change its method for calculating tax payable since 1992. The full extent of the settlement was not clear. For example, the prospectus for the NDS IPO in 1999 referred to commitments made to the Israeli tax authority during the investigation period, to invest unstated amounts of money in its Israeli operations.

A News Corp spokesman said the company welcomed the settlement: "NDS has agreed to settle this matter in order to terminate the uncertainties and the exaggerated rumours that have been affecting the company for over a year, as well as to avoid incurring further legal costs."

Again the issue was: To which country was Murdoch responsible? It is not just tax men whom Murdoch could threaten in different parts of the world. News Corp as the ultimate transnational corporation moves markets and routinely transforms industries in one country to provide a benefit in another. Beyond the United States the Murdoch effect has rippled from country to country around the globe. He calls Tony Blair in London so that Blair can phone the Italian prime minister about a Murdoch deal in Rome. Murdoch causes a sensation in Britain by having his HarperCollins London company drop the Chris Patten book about Hong Kong in order to win favor in Beijing. News Corp as an entity had long since outgrown its Australian roots, its British past, and its American heart. It had taken up permanent offshore residence. It existed stateless somewhere beyond the archipelagos.

18

RUPERT'S ROCKET

London, 1998

O N SUNDAY, April 19, 1998, just as the controversy over Tony Blair's telephone conversation with the Italian prime minister Romano Prodi was dying down, Rupert Murdoch faced a more personal crisis: Anna moved out of the Murdochs' house on Angelo Drive. It was a week before the Murdochs' thirty-first wedding anniversary and six weeks after Murdoch's sixty-seventh birthday. Anna flew to London to stay with Elisabeth, whose marriage to Elkin Pianim had fallen apart several months before. The split took members of the Murdoch family by surprise. Even in telephone calls on the Saturday, there had been no hint of what would follow.

In October 1999 Murdoch described for *Vanity Fair* the process whereby he and Anna "drifted apart to the point where things became unhappy." It is the only time he has ever talked about the personal toll that his 1997 battles exacted: "So I was travelling a lot and was very obsessed with the business and perhaps more than normally inconsiderate, at a time when our children were grown up and home was suddenly an empty nest."[1]

The Murdochs' marriage had been one of the few stable points in News Corporation. Its stability had provided Rupert Murdoch not just with a personal centre but with the moral vantage point from which his empire could pour scorn on the emotional foibles and infidelities of others. There had been the odd report of friction between Rupert and Anna, particularly over where they lived. Andrew Neil, in his biography *Full Disclosure,* described the disagreement over Rupert's desire to move back to New York. "You're a perpetual motion machine," Anna snapped. "I've had enough of keeping pace with you. I'm staying in LA."[2] Otherwise, however, they remained the model couple. When parliamentarian-turned-journalist Woodrow Wyatt died, the Murdochs attended the funeral in early April

1998 and Rupert read the scripture passage, again with no obvious sign of tension between them.

At the time of the split, Anna was at the height of her social power in Los Angeles. In 1996 she had been appointed chairwoman of the board of the regents of Children's Hospital of Los Angeles. The regents were a high-powered group founded in 1993 for a $25 million fund-raising drive. She had become a major donor and advocate, regularly lobbying with politicians in Sacramento and Washington for government assistance for at-risk children. Anna was also an influential member of the Colleagues, a group that had supported the Children's Institute International in Los Angeles since the 1950s. Its members included Nancy Reagan and socialite Betsy Bloomingdale. On July 19, 1997, as Murdoch was tying up the details of his Fox Sports deal with Charles Dolan in New York, Anna was named president of the board of trustees for the Children's Institute International in Los Angeles. Five days later she was honored "for her many efforts on behalf of vulnerable youngsters" at the opening of the Anna M. Murdoch Education and Training Center at the institute. She had been honored by the B'nai B'rith Anti-Defamation League, by a home for babies addicted to drugs called Hale House, and by others. The positions carried extensive commitments to social engagements. She had even gone on Fox News to talk about Rupert Murdoch's lobbying on behalf of children.

In early 1998 Anna had clearly been concerned about Rupert's health, with her insistence that he stick to white meat, white wine, and carrot snacks. As he approached sixty-seven, the age at which his father had died, Anna Murdoch was creating a potent series of symbols, all of which pointed toward reducing or ending Rupert's frenetic schedule at the helm of News Corp. They had to do with according recognition to Rupert Murdoch for what he had achieved in nearly half a century of empire building. Her clear hope was that such symbols of recognition would allow her husband an opportunity to walk away, his place in history secure; to retire gracefully, or more likely just to slow down a little.

First there was the fingerprint. In late 1997 Anna arranged for a California artist to make an eleven-meter, ten-panel tin and wood mural for the lobby of a new building at 20th Century–Fox, based on a massive enlargement of the whorls on Murdoch's right index finger.[3] It was undoubtedly a unique tribute, a none-too-subtle statement that Murdoch had left his fingerprints across the world. By a happy stroke of timing the Humanitarian of the Year award came in May 1997. And a papal knighthood came soon after: On January 11, 1998 at St. Francis de

Sales church in Los Angeles, Cardinal Roger M. Mahony invested Rupert and Anna as knight commander and dame in the Pontifical Order of St. Gregory the Great. The Murdochs were no strangers to Mahony—they had contributed $10 million to the building fund for a new cathedral. The spokesman for the L.A. Catholic diocese, the Reverend Gregory Coiro, told reporters that the pope bestowed the titles on people of "unblemished character," including non-Catholics, who had "promoted the interests of society, the Catholic Church and the Holy See Vatican."[4]

In April 1998, after a lifetime of striving and achievement, and after a year of honors, Anna appears to have made her husband an ultimatum: He had to slow down and make room for her in his life. When he refused, she packed her bags.

The next day, Monday, April 20, 1998, Murdoch briefed Liz Smith at the *New York Post* about the split. Smith announced the separation in her gossip column on Tuesday:

> It is with some personal sadness that I announce the amicable separation of Rupert Murdoch and his beautiful wife Anna after thirty-one years of marriage and three children. The Murdochs say their situation is very painful and leaves them torn but they are attempting to work out their differences. Mrs. Murdoch, a novelist and philanthropist, will remain on the board and continue in the Murdoch businesses.[5]

Anna Murdoch clearly expected an eventual reconciliation, but Rupert Murdoch had spent a lifetime leaving people behind. It wasn't just that he never mended broken relationships—he had built his life around a driving ambition to build a worldwide media empire. Former executives claimed that he had no friends. He had the business and his family, in that order. In demanding that he slow down, Anna had been asking him to give up the greater part of his life. As Murdoch would put it a year later, stepping down as head of News Corp was a pretty dismal prospect. What would he do? "Die pretty quickly," he told a British documentary maker. He and Anna continued to talk. According to court papers, the final break came on Friday, June 26. "I don't feel I belong anywhere anymore," Anna told friends.[6]

"You're in such a state of shock," she said later. "I mean, in a way you're sort of mentally ill because you're not absorbing everything. . . . I think I even began to lose my ability with words, which is amazing for me because I am usually quite good with words."[7]

The breakup was sparked in part by Anna's unease about the pressures Rupert was putting on their children. The same concerns she had written about on that summer afternoon in the 1980s on their farm at Old Chatham had resurfaced. The children she had watched run barefoot across the meadow were now adults, but they were more in thrall to their father than ever. But this was not a Greek tragedy—the family was descending into soap opera.

The empire's future now depended upon the succession struggle that was shaping up between Lachlan, aged twenty-six, Elisabeth, twenty-nine, and James, twenty-five: the dutiful son, the ambitious daughter, and the scruffy young man. There was also Prudence MacLeod, thirty-eight, the child of Rupert's marriage to Patricia Booker, whose importance was often underestimated. Part of what gives News Corp its ferociously competitive culture is Rupert Murdoch's habit of putting two people in the same job and leaving them to battle it out. Even with the best of intentions, Murdoch's even-handed insistence that any of his children might succeed him at the helm of News Corp inevitably gave family relations a competitive edge. The pressure was stoked by continual media speculation. "I think they are all so good that they could do whatever they wanted, really," Anna said. "But I think there's going to be a lot of heartbreak and hardship with this. There's been such a lot of pressure that they needn't have had at their age."

The Murdoch succession arguably represented the largest transfer of wealth and global power of the late twentieth century. For four years the four heirs to this fortune had been feted across the world, revered like Indian moonstones, possessed of fabulous wealth and power, in whose tracks lay the professional corpses of those who fought to control them. Murdoch had lost senior executives wherever his children worked in the News Corp empire. Just after Christmas 1996 Murdoch's longtime Australian lieutenant, Ken Cowley, had sent his deputy, Lachlan Murdoch, home to get a more conservative haircut after he appeared at work with a radical Mohawk. Cowley would be shuffled into retirement by April, sparking some wry lines about ruffling the hair apparent.[8]

When he was asked in 1993 whether his children would succeed him at News Corp, Rupert Murdoch said, "The board will have to make their judgment in time. . . . I will certainly engage in sufficient nepotism to see that my kids get a good opportunity."[9] In 1988 Murdoch had told News International director Bruce Hundertmark, "In the longer term I am very much in favour of a bit of nepotism but in the shorter term somehow we must get by."

There seemed little doubt whom Rupert Murdoch was grooming as successor. This close family nevertheless had maintained a pecking order, a routine that extended to which family members were served first at the dinner table. With Lachlan the elder son, Murdoch set out to replicate his own history, to create another version of himself. The clearest sign of the intense pressures that this produced on Lachlan was his intense sensitivity to media criticism.

At Geelong Grammar Murdoch had produced a school magazine called *Isis Revived*. Lachlan at sixteen at his Trinity School in New York helped to found the Trinity Conservative Society. It was open to all who have a "clear conservative conscience," he wrote in his 1987 high school yearbook. His summer jobs ranged from working as a reporter on the *San Antonio Express-News* in Texas, to working in the press room for the News Limited papers in Sydney. Like Rupert, Lachlan left home for a distant university. At Princeton his thesis on Kant and Hegel suggested he had studied a little harder than his father had. From there Lachlan spent several months on the subeditor's desk at the *Sun* in London—the equivalent of his father's 1953 stint with the *Daily Express*. At twenty-two, Rupert Murdoch had been publisher of the Adelaide *News*. Lachlan at the same age in August 1994 became general manager of Queensland Press, the family inheritance sold by Sir Keith's executors. John Cowley—Ken Cowley's brother, who was manager at Wapping during the riots—was entrusted with Lachlan's early education in Brisbane. The *New York Times* described Australia as Murdoch's "social laboratory" where his son could learn his trade away from serious scrutiny.

By late 1996 Lachlan was back in Sydney, buying a sailboat with right-wing News Corp columnist Piers Ackerman and learning to sail. He was appointed managing director of News in Australia in September 1996 and executive chairman seven months later, aged twenty-five. He drove a silver BMW to work and kept a Ducati Monster and Harley-Davidson in the garage. In August 1997 he and his father spent a week at Hamilton Island on the Great Barrier Reef, where Lachlan competed with his luxurious Swan 51 cruising yacht *Karakoram* (named for its owner's love of mountain climbing) in Racing Week. Back in Britain Murdoch told writer Mathew Horsman that his children had agreed that Lachlan was the "first among equals" in the succession. That Christmas Lachlan sailed *Karakoram* in the Sydney-to-Hobart. His father flew to Hobart and at four A.M. accompanied *Karakoram* in a rubber dinghy on the last stretch of the race, up the Derwent River. Murdoch, who had finally been on a winner in the Sydney-to-Hobart in 1995 when he crewed on Larry Ellison's *Sayonara*, wanted Lachlan to buy a faster boat. Instead the following year Lachlan joined the crew on *Sayonara*, which battled through huge seas to win.

From the start Lachlan gave the impression of being a nicer man than his position allowed him to be. He was unusually kind and attentive to the people who worked for him. While he could be highly aggressive in business dealings, he did not always give the impression that his heart was in it. Nevertheless he racked up a high body count of sacked executives, particularly senior executives who were older than he was. He wore his youth like a badge, rolling up his sleeves on formal occasions to show his two tattoos. On the upper arm he had a gecko lizard. The second tattoo, a band around his wrist, was done in 1997, the day after his father flew back to the United States after a visit. In the same period he shaved his head and bought a Rhodesian Ridgeback called Grace. To head up the News Limited digital strategy, he brought a school friend across from the United States. Zeb Rice, the son of a former head of Fox, Gordon Van Sauter, would be best man at Lachlan's wedding. He stayed with Lachlan in his waterfront home on Sydney Harbour. "One morning Zeb and Lachlan came to work with exactly the same crew cuts, and you realized just how young the generals at News really were," former News IT editor Tony Sarno said.[10]

Lachlan gave few interviews and on occasion appeared distraught at adverse press stories about himself. In Brisbane he had confided his belief that he should get married, though his engagement to American merchant banker Kate Harbin foundered. He was throughout the dutiful son. "From a child he said he always remembered everyone who had ever said anything critical about his father," said Australian journalist Ali Cromie, who befriended Lachlan in his early twenties. "He would always remember their name, he said. For always."[11] When he was asked on the Hobart docks if there was anything as challenging as the Sydney-to-Hobart race, he said, "Yes. Getting up each morning, going to work and running News Limited."[12] Lachlan went on to be linked with a string of glamorous girlfriends. The tattoos, the hair, and the striking looks also made him an icon for Sydney's gay scene. At one point the rumor mill reached such a pitch that Murdoch family members asked Australian journalist Ali Cromie if there was any truth to the stories, which Lachlan and his spokesmen denied, that Lachlan was gay. There was no evidence that he was. In a business where appearances matter so much, this intrusive speculation reflected the intense pressures faced by any child of Rupert Murdoch's.

Lachlan was loyal to his small circle of friends. The month he was appointed chief executive of News Limited in Sydney, a new column in the *Sunday Telegraph* announced that Dr. Moose, "a renowned book lover, cultural critic, gourmet and committed sports fan," would be making reading suggestions each week. The recommended books could be bought by ringing the Mooseline, a twenty-four-hour telephone hotline that was run by the Moose Corporation, a play on the News Corporation. Dr. Moose appears to have been Lachlan himself. Moose Corp was a private company owned by Lachlan and his friends Zeb Rice and lawyer Jeremy Philips. In the four months the Moose column appeared, one of the most frequent recommendations was a book cowritten by Philips. When questioned, a News Corp spokesman in New York said arrangements between News Corp and Moose Corp were conducted on an arm's-length basis.[13]

In March 1997, the month Lachlan was appointed executive chairman of News Limited, the National Rugby League (NRL), now controlled by News, dumped Young & Rubicam from its $10 million advertising account. In its place the NRL appointed boutique Sydney agency VCD, which was founded and run by Lachlan's close friend, artistic director George Betsis. In the messy politics of advertising, it wasn't clear what had caused the switch. Betsis said the appointment had nothing to do with his links to Lachlan. In March 1999, the month Lachlan married model Sarah O'Hare, Queensland Press (where Lachlan was now chairman) invested $10 million for control of a futures trading operation run by Joe Cross, thirty-three, who was one of Lachlan's groomsmen. A News Corp spokesman said the deal was conducted on an arm's-length basis.

Before Ken Cowley resigned, he surrounded Lachlan with a kitchen cabinet of advisers who would essentially run News in Australia. Lachlan's track record was tainted by the A$550 million Super League disaster, but it would be unfair to blame Lachlan for Super League. He was twenty-three at the time, with just seven months of executive experience. The mistakes were made by older heads. At the same time this lack of experience did not prevent him from being appointed chief executive of News Limited in Australia eighteen months later. He and James Packer had some success negotiating peace treaties between their warring fathers. Lachlan racked up a A$62 million profit from an investment in a racing satellite channel with the Packer family, but by agreeing to sell half of News Corp's holding in the Foxtel cable company to the Packers at cost, News Corp lost more than it gained. Lachlan played the Australian political scene clumsily. He invested $290 million in a telephone company, One.Tel, that had grand plans to build an Australian cell phone network, but he had overlooked the fact that One.Tel had nowhere near enough spectrum. It was a glaring error that cost One.Tel $300 million to fix. In early 2001, as One.Tel spiraled towards oblivion, Lachlan was one of only four directors left on the board, but he stayed in North America and Europe, apparently oblivious, engrossed in his father's struggle for DirecTV.

Overall, the results on his watch have been poor. Given his level of experience, it would be hard to expect otherwise. In Australia he was working in a mature market where the growth areas were controlled by the Packer family, who had better political connections, and a government that saw him as an American doing an apprenticeship. He faced huge pressure from within News Corp and a stream of daily advice from his father. In February 1999 he was made a senior vice president at News Corp, with responsibility for U.S. newspapers and the inserts business in the United States. In January 2002, Murdoch appointed Lachlan to run News Corp's most important division, the Fox television stations.

*   *   *

Elisabeth Murdoch, three years Lachlan's senior, attended the Brearley School in Manhattan, then went on to Vassar. In October 1990 she began work at Kerry Packer's Channel Nine studio in Sydney. Sam Chisholm had left Nine for Sky in London five weeks before. She went on to work in Salt Lake City, then in programming for Fox television in Los Angeles. In 1992 she was agonizing over her relationship with Elkin Pianim, the son of a well-known Ghanaian political prisoner, whom she had met at Vassar. She gave him until Christmas to propose. "He proposed on Christmas Eve," she said later.[14]

They were married in September 1993 and settled in Los Angeles. In February 1995 they borrowed $35 million with a bank loan guaranteed by Elisabeth's father to buy two television stations in California, near the Murdochs' Carmel Valley ranch. Their first child, Cornelia, was born two weeks after the purchase. Elisabeth was back at work two weeks later. After a torrid and sometimes brutal year reorganizing the television stations, the Pianims sold them for a $12 million profit. They moved shortly afterward to London, where Elisabeth joined BSkyB as general manager (for broadcasting) and later director of programming. Meanwhile Pianim launched *New Nation,* a newspaper aimed at London's Afro-Caribbean community, and a venture capital company called Idaho Partners. Soon after their second child, Anna, was born, their marriage was reported to be on the rocks. They had separated by the end of 1997.

Elisabeth made it clear that she continued to strive for the top job. Lachlan's promotions in Australia were a reminder to her that "I have to get a hurry on," she said. In 1999 she told Channel Four, "I have always and will always strive to be qualified and considered for that position."[15]

In June 1997 Elisabeth's thorny relationship with Sam Chisholm at BSkyB culminated in his departure. Rupert Murdoch complained that Elisabeth had expected Chisholm would "teach her everything, but he didn't. He tried to cut her out. She has some things to work out," he said. "She has to decide how many kids she is going to have, where she wants to live."[16]

Of all the Murdoch children, Elisabeth was the one in 1998 who could most clearly be said to have had a real job. That is to say, she worked in a high-profile position as head of programming for BSkyB, where her success or failure really mattered to the future of the News Corp empire. Lachlan and James were in executive positions where, surrounded by advisers and with a constant stream of advice from the daily telephone conversations with their father, it could be difficult to judge their individual performance. The huge investment decisions they initiated were peripheral to the daily running of the empire and could take years to show up as profit or loss. While Elisabeth had no shortage of advisers, BSkyB programming required creative decisions from her, and their success or failure could be measured in weekly viewer numbers. Her critics claimed that while she was clearly ambitious and had the technical experience in television for the job, she did not have the creative flair that programming required. BSkyB's digital launch, which she headed, initially was unimpressive. On the other hand, several of the programs she commissioned went on to become much more successful when copied elsewhere. *Castaway*, for example, became the huge ratings winner *Survivor* in America.

*   *   *

James arguably cuts the most appealing figure among the Murdoch children, with his black glasses, laid-back appearance, and manic energy. Even in a suit, James Murdoch gives the impression that unless he has done something magical with Velcro, it is only a matter of time before his shirt comes out. As a child he was regarded as the brightest of the Murdoch brood. In 1999, when Michael Eisner was asked who he could see as his successor running Disney, he said either his own son or James Murdoch.[17]

When James married model Kathryn Hufschmid in June 2000, the best man's speech by his longtime friend Jesse Angelo (who is Eisner's godson) shed some light on his and James's shared history: "A best friend would stop you from getting a tattoo," said Angelo. "A best friend would stop you from starting a hip-hop label. A best friend would stop you from getting a second tattoo. A best friend would stop you from getting kicked out of Harvard." James interjected to deny strenuously that he was ever at risk of being kicked out of Harvard. Angelo responded: "You don't have to live that lie tonight."[18]

At Harvard James helped edit *The Harvard Lampoon,* a post that his father suggested had "more to do with drinking," but dropped out in 1994 to start Rawkus Records, a hip-hop label, with friends in New York. In November 1996 his father brought him back into News Corp by buying his company. He headed the small music division at News Corp and was named vice president for new media. Periodically News was said to be considering a bid for EMI, but Mushroom Records in Australia was his only music purchase. In early 1997 James was a key figure in his father's $450 million offer to buy PointCast, a hot Internet company promoting "push" technology. In a lucky escape, PointCast management turned the deal down. Two years later the company was sold for $7 million. In November 1997 James was named president of News America Digital Publishing, a new division that encompassed News Corp's American online business, reporting to Anthea Disney. Its biggest asset was Kesmai, the most popular gaming site on the Web. Within weeks of James's appointment, Steve Case's America Online dumped Kesmai from its homepage and replacing it with its own gaming site. Overnight 90 percent of Kesmai's business disappeared.

It was the perfect time to move into what at the time was a nothing job. The Internet boom, and James's investments in TheStreet.com, Juno.com, PlanetTx, sixdegrees, and Jim Clark's Healtheon put him suddenly on News Corp's star track. In November 1999 he would become executive vice president for News Digital Media. In June 2000 he was named executive chairman for Star TV. He met Kathryn Hufschmid when she was handling public relations for Bob Guccione Jr.'s *Gear* magazine. Among other things, James describes himself as a professional cartoonist. At Harvard he began a politically incorrect cartoon strip called Albrecht the Hun. Hufschmid arranged for his cartoon strips to run in *Gear.*

*   *   *

Prudence is the only Murdoch child to stay outside of the family business, looking after her three children in a house in Notting Hill, near Elisabeth. She said she was horrified when she learned that her second husband, Alasdair MacLeod, was joining News Corp.

In 1997, in an attempt to settle media speculation about who would succeed him at the head of the empire, Murdoch told journalist Mathew Horsman that the shares in Cruden had already been divided between the children. News Corp spokesman Howard Rubinstein was reported to have said the major stakes went to Lachlan, Elisabeth, and James. Accounts differ as to whether this is accurate, but the whole thrust of the family's succession planning—who would guide News Corp after Rupert—has been based on Anna's *uterini.* At the October 1997 News Corp annual meeting, Murdoch was asked a question about the succession. He later said that when he referred to his three children, he had been misquoted—he had actually referred to his three children in the company.

Prudence was furious at being overlooked, at least in the press reports of the conversation. She said later in an interview:

> I didn't speak to him. It was the biggest row I've ever had with my father. I rang up, I screamed at him, I hung up. He was very upset. He then sent the biggest bunch of flowers—it was bigger than that sofa—and two clementine trees. The flowers kept coming, and he felt awful.[19]

After two weeks she made peace again with her father. In an interview she said it still "caused a huge amount of hurt" and indicated she would like to take a non-executive position on the News Corp board when her three children are older. She said she had grown used to the way the media overlooked her in the constant speculation about Murdoch's successor. "I used to get very upset by it, but there's no point," she said. "Dad has always made it very plain that there are four of us, and that's the way it goes."

Prudence's carefully planned remarks—she made it clear in the interview that she expected her father to read the resulting article—were a reminder that, no matter how well advanced the professional careers of the young Murdochs might have been in 1998, they paid a personal price for being who they were. How does anyone cope with the pressure of growing up as the child of one of the most powerful media barons in the world?

*   *   *

In the 1980s, when Anna Murdoch took her children to live in Aspen after reports of behavior problems at school, they spent their summer vacations working in various arms of News Corp around the world. When he was fifteen, James spent a summer working at the old *Mirror* in Sydney. It was the afternoon tabloid where Murdoch had learned his craft. James's best-known exploit was at a momentous press conference, when the Fairfax newspaper group announced it was selling its Seven television network to a young entrepreneur named Christopher Skase. It was a deal that only a few years before Rupert Murdoch would have killed for. Halfway through the press conference James was found and duly photographed at the back of the room, curled up asleep on a couch. The Fairfax *Sydney Morning Herald* ran James's picture alongside its story. James refused to work any more summers in the family business. "Everybody knew who I was," he said later. "I wouldn't do it again." He would never again work under what he called "the long shadow of my father."[20]

This is not a family that values introspection. "We're not a family that believes in looking back," Lachlan told the *New York Times* in August 1998.[21] His sister Elisabeth expressed similar views that same month, when she offered British broadcasters at the Edinburgh International Television Festival "a little self-help, Murdoch style—no couches, no Freud." She had appeared in jeans and boots for the address. The British press tried hard not to like her. The worst thing *The Economist* could say was that she had California hair. Her comment about self-help Murdoch style, as well as being the Murdoch family credo, was a little in-joke. It was a tacit reference to her blossoming romance with Matthew Freud, the grandson of the great psychoanalyst.

It must be one of history's great encounters—Sigmund meets Rupert; the father of psychoanalysis runs up against the Sun King. Sigmund's grandson works in public relations. Rupert's daughter is in television programming. It is a particularly interesting pairing because of what Freud wrote about the difficulties faced by children with overachieving fathers. One of his case studies was based on a man who dreamed of shouting at the sun—which Freud interpreted as the symbol for a father figure. The dream, Freud said, was about a son faced with an overwhelmingly powerful father, struggling to meet him on his own terms, a healthy attempt to cast his own shadow.

Five generations of Murdochs have struggled with the problem of living up to their fathers. The question for Rupert's children would be: How would they assert their own autonomy in the court of the Sun King? It became quickly clear that the flirtation with the left that their father had enjoyed at Oxford was not an option for his children. Their political views have been closely allied with his. The children's statements of autonomy have been more subtle affairs.

Any left-wing views that Rupert Murdoch espoused at Oxford were burned away in the two decades of torrid struggle that followed his father's death. By the late 1960s, as we have seen, News Limited's unofficial employment policy in Australia had become an informal mantra: "No blacks, no poofters [gays], no suede shoes." At least this was the popularly held view on the News Limited papers, though it never spilled overseas to Fleet Street. Rupert Murdoch's children grew up with these and other entrenched maxims. They have challenged most of them.

From his daughter Elisabeth, Rupert has two black grandchildren, Cornelia and Anna. When Elisabeth left BSkyB and News Corp in 2000, it was to have a child with Freud, a relationship of which her father reportedly did not approve. Freud vacationed with Elisabeth and the family in Australia over Christmas 1998, but he was conspicuous by his absence at subsequent family occasions. James dropped out of Harvard to start a fringe record group whose first album was called *Whoregasm.* Lachlan's relations with his father have seemed less conflicted. He has great personal regard for his father and shares his social views, ideologies, and business style. If there has been another side to Lachlan's public filial adherence, it is expressed covertly in his private life.

*   *   *

Their parents' divorce would prove as painful for the Murdoch children as it is for most families. By July 1998 Anna had hired a high-profile L.A. divorce lawyer, Daniel J. Jaffe. She signed a divorce petition on July 5. Jaffe signed a certificate of assessment three days later, then filed the petition in Los Angeles Superior Court on July 21. Anna's petition asked for "spousal support" while the divorce was being finalized. She said she did not know what her husband's assets were. Rupert's lawyer, Robert Kaufman, responded two days after receiving the summons. Rupert said he didn't know what his assets were either.[22]

The divorce petition froze Murdoch's assets. So it was just as well that, four days after the final break with Anna on June 26 but before she signed the divorce petition on July 5, the National Australia Bank took security over a parcel of the News Corp shares held by the family holding company, Cruden Investments. A Murdoch lawyer said at the time that this move on June 30, Anna's birthday, reflected a change in the security held on an already-existing loan facility rather than any predivorce money-shuffling. Part of this loan would be the A$373 million borrowed in February 1996 for the family buyout. Murdoch was due to pay another A$314 million to his sisters' families in March 1999. The divorce proceedings cast some uncertainty on that. Any payout might be subject to Anna's approval. Rupert Murdoch's position was that although he was a director of Cruden, the company was ultimately owned and controlled by the A.E. Harris Trust and other interlocking trusts throughout the Cruden corporate structure, which had been set up to avoid paying death duties. Murdoch had the power to appoint trustees to the trust but not to direct the trustees. Therefore the huge wealth locked up in Cruden didn't belong to him.

Under California's community property laws, however, divorce courts do not always accept trust structures set up to shelter assets. At this point, it still looked like a low-key and relatively amicable divorce. According to News Corp executives, Anna was prepared to accept $100 million and the Murdoch homes in Los Angeles and London as a property settlement. She was also insisting on a guarantee about the future of their three children within News Corp. Murdoch's advisers urged him to settle the divorce quickly.

The early court filings referred to a five-day hearing, but the case was unlikely to come to trial. That would change ten weeks later.

*   *   *

On Sunday, October 4, 1998, the *New York Times* published a brief by Geraldine Fabrikant that stated what had become an open secret in Manhattan media circles: Rupert Murdoch had moved into the Mercer Hotel in SoHo with a young Chinese executive from Star TV, Wendi Deng. The four sentences in Fabrikant's story were picked up and speculated upon in newspapers around the world. Within days the paparazzi had struck.[23]

"The *Mirror* had a picture on a boat taken with a very long lens," Murdoch later told *Vanity Fair*.[24] "I was testing a new sailboat which Lachlan was thinking of buying." The picture, which was reprinted widely, showed Murdoch, Lachlan, Silvio Berlusconi, and a tall slim woman identified as Wendi Deng, otherwise known as Deng Wen Di.

Deng Wen Di was born in the eastern Chinese city of Xuzhou. Her family later moved to Guangzhou, capital of the prosperous southern province of Guangdong, where her father ended up as the director of a machinery factory. Reportedly he was also well connected politically. Bruce Dover, the News Corp executive in Beijing who introduced Deng to Murdoch, believed she was married briefly to a young American businessman in Beijing, David Wolf. She had come to America in 1991 to study at California State University, before completing an M.B.A. at Yale. "She was a fun person to talk to, always happy and eager about her work," said her economics lecturer, Ken Chapman. "But it was always kind of hard to figure her out."[25] Another lecturer, Dan Blake, rated Deng as one of the best students he had taught: "I've been teaching here for about thirty years and I haven't seen many students who were that brilliant. She was really sharp. She didn't speak much English when she got here but she picked it up really quickly."

In November 2000 the *Wall Street Journal* gave a slightly different history for Deng.[26] It quoted divorce records with the Los Angeles Superior Court that showed that she had been married for two years and seven months to an Ameri-

can named Jake Cherry who was in Guangzhou in 1987 working on the construc-
tion of a manufacturing plant. Deng, who was eighteen, received English lessons
from Cherry's then wife, Joyce, who later helped Deng enroll at California State
University.

Joyce and Jake separated in 1988 over Jake Cherry's infatuation with Deng,
who stayed briefly in the couple's home in Los Angeles. After his divorce Jake
Cherry married Deng in February 1990. He was fifty-three. According to the *Wall
Street Journal*, the marriage broke up after four months over Deng's relationship
with a man in his twenties, David Wolf. A later reconciliation with Cherry failed,
and Deng spent several years living with Wolf.

The two-year M.B.A. course at Yale requires a student to work as an intern during the summer. In 1996 Deng booked herself a first-class ticket to Hong Kong.
On the flight over she reportedly made such an impression on the businessman sitting next to her that he offered her the internship she needed. The businessman
was Bruce Churchill, a longtime executive with Star TV. During her stint at the
Star offices at One Harbourfront, in Hunghom, and in Beijing, Deng impressed
executives with her intelligence, tremendous drive, and remarkable ability to
network. In conversation she was street smart, focused, and surprisingly un-
American.

Deng met Rupert Murdoch in autumn 1996 at a cocktail party at tycoon Li Ka
Shing's Harbourfront Plaza hotel, which stands next to the Star offices. The then
chief executive of Star, Gary Davey, had flown the team working on the Phoenix
Television project down from Beijing to meet Murdoch. Star executives later
spoke with some awe of the purpose and speed with which Deng approached
News Corp's chief executive. "We need more people like that in the office,"
Murdoch later told Star executives. Among those present who recalled the meet-
ing, the most memorable aspect was the number of times that Deng said, "Oh
Lupert."[27] Murdoch himself says the story that he met Deng in 1996 is "complete
nonsense. I never met Wendi then."[28]

Whatever Murdoch's recollection, Deng returned to Star in a full-time capacity
in the autumn of 1997, armed with her Yale M.B.A. She moved into a three-
bedroom, thousand-square-foot apartment in Crescent Heights, Tung Shan Terrace, in Hong Kong's Happy Valley, valued at about HK$5 million. She reportedly
acted as interpreter for Murdoch on several trips he made to Beijing that year. According to *Punch*, in the autumn of 1997 drivers in the Star carpool began talking
about Murdoch and Deng holding hands.[29] *Asiaweek* quoted a friend of Deng's
saying that the two had been romantically involved since the northern spring of

1998. Murdoch denies both of these accounts.[30] He says he began seeing Deng in June 1998, about seven weeks after he and Anna separated.

He told *Vanity Fair:*

> I met her casually once or twice at meetings of Star TV in Hong Kong. But I first took her out in June [1998] in London when she came over with a group from Star in Hong Kong and Beijing. I was a recently separated, lonely man, and I said, "Let's go out to dinner one night," and I talked her into staying in London a couple of extra days—and that was the start of it.[31]

Anna Murdoch clearly doesn't accept this account. "I think that Rupert's affair with Wendi Deng—it's not an original plot—was the end of the marriage," she said. "His determination to continue with that. I thought we had a wonderful, happy marriage. Obviously we didn't."

By June 1998, Anna had reestablished a base in rental accommodation in Beverly Hills. The June 26 separation date cited in the divorce papers suggest that the final act in the breakdown of the Murdochs' marriage took place after the London tryst with Deng—though presumably by this point it must have been clear that the marriage was indeed over. After the final break with Anna, Murdoch flew to Beijing, where President Clinton was making a historic state visit. There Murdoch and Deng attended a cocktail party for News Corp executives at the home of James Pringle, the *Times* correspondent. Deng, who came dressed in tight cream-colored jeans and a close-fitting top, described herself as Murdoch's translator for the Beijing visit but gave little detail of the role when queried and left early.[32]

"He behaved badly," said Anna in 2001. "However, for my children's sake, I have said nothing. . . . I've waited all this time for him to make it right again, but he never took the opportunity." Anna's account, as she says, is not original: an older man infatuated by a younger woman. Indeed, Anna and Rupert had been an item for several years before he divorced his first wife, Patricia. But Murdoch's early biographer, Thomas Kiernan, paints a much cooler relationship between Rupert and Anna, with growing friction in the 1970s and 1980s resolved by an entente cordiale, where each maintained an emotional distance. In the late 1980s, when the demands of the empire meant Murdoch was spending more time than ever away from home, a tight circle of senior News Corp staff in Britain were remarking on Murdoch's friendship with a young Chinese executive based in London. "He seemed absolutely fascinated by her," a former News International director said. "You've got to remember that he spent much of his life alone."[33] Whatever was gossiped about, it was never clear whether the relationship went beyond friendship. In any case several years later the friendship ended, though Murdoch's romance with the Orient was only beginning.

The most likely explanation for the breakdown of Murdoch's marriage is not that he fell in love with Wendi but that before that he became alienated from Anna. When Anna made her ultimatum that Rupert slow down, the entente cordiale failed. Once she jumped ship, all she could do was watch the boat sail inexorably into the distance. This is a critical point, because while Rupert would exhibit every symptom of the lovestruck elderly lover, the shrewd calculating business mind would grind on regardless.

The breakdown of his parents' marriage was "a blow to everyone," Lachlan told the *Financial Times*. "For a long time, people in this company looked up to them because here was a couple who obviously sacrificed a lot yet had a wonderful marriage. So when it breaks up, they are obviously disillusioned."[34]

Of the Murdoch children, Prudence has been the one most accustomed to living at a distance from her father. Prudence described her relationship with Anna Murdoch as civilized and warm, though they had contrasting personal styles. "I completely wear my heart on my sleeve, I'm oversensitive and just different," she said. When Rupert and Anna separated, Prudence was the most obviously accepting of her father's new romance, saying, "Who knows what goes on in a marriage. It's very sad. I think it's very sad for anyone to put that much time into a marriage then wake up and think, 'Oh, maybe it's not so great any more.' But I also think it is important that if you are unhappy you've got to get on and if there's a chance for happiness somewhere else, you have to go for it."[35]

Court filings showed a dramatic change in Anna's legal strategy. Initially her lawyer, Daniel Jaffe, had been seeking a five-day hearing. By late 1998 this had become a nine-week hearing, and Anna's demands from the settlement had grown far higher.

Rupert Murdoch was playing hardball. When the News Corp annual report was released in mid-September, it said Anna was resigning from the board. "I wasn't given a choice," she said. "I was told." Anna made an emotional parting speech to the board. On September 17, 1998, Liz Smith announced that Misty Mountain, the house on Angelo Drive so cherished by Anna, was for sale for $19.5 million. Murdoch's position was that, although he controlled one of the world's major fortunes, the huge wealth in Cruden did not belong to him. To satisfy Anna's demand for spouse support, the couple needed to sell some of the few assets held in their names, beginning with the Angelo Drive house, which had been the base for Anna's social power in Los Angeles. The asking price was high, however, and the house attracted no satisfactory offers. In October the Murdochs sold part of their Carmel ranch to a neighbor instead. "I don't want to get too personal about this," said Anna, ". . . but [he] was extremely hard, ruthless, and determined that he was going to go through with this no matter what I wanted or what I was trying to do to save the marriage. He had no interest in that whatsoever."

Rupert Murdoch's lawyer, Robert Kaufman, put enormous pressure on Anna's lawyers. Two days before the Christmas break, Kaufman applied for the court to set a date for the hearing. By insisting on a tight schedule, Anna's lawyers would have limited time to wade through the mountain of paperwork detailing one of the world's most convoluted fortunes, which had been served on them as part of discovery procedures. In January Anna's lawyers applied to have the trial-setting conference on March 11, Rupert Murdoch's birthday. The date was later postponed, but News Corp insiders were comparing the bitter Murdoch family relations with the warring Ewing dynasty on the long-running evening soap *Dallas*.

"I began to think the Rupert Murdoch that I loved died a long time ago," Anna said. "Perhaps I was in love with the idea of still being in love with him. But the Rupert I fell in love with could not have behaved that way."

*   *   *

Running concurrently with the private passions of the Murdoch divorce were the much more public battles over Murdoch's bid to buy Britain's best-known soccer club, Manchester United. On July 1, 1998, the Manchester United chairman, Martin Edwards, had what he expected to be a routine lunch appointment with the chief executive of BSkyB, Mark Booth. Instead Booth dropped the small talk and asked him what he would think about BSkyB making a bid to buy the club.[36] On September 7, BSkyB and Manchester United both issued statements to confirm that they were having takeover talks. A day later the bid was announced at £623 million.

The news unleashed a storm of protest. "Red Devils" was the *Mirror* headline, as the non-Murdoch press set out to do justice to a mood of national indignation. Ominously, the protests did not die down. As with Wapping a decade before, the longer the dispute lasted, the more community opposition grew. By October 27, however, BSkyB had acquired 47 percent of Manchester United shares and appeared to be days away from wrapping up the takeover.

On Monday evening, October 26, 1998, the secretary for Wales, Ron Davies, took a walk on Clapham Common. He was mugged in circumstances that led him the next day to tender his resignation as a minister to Tony Blair at Downing Street. He denied it was a gay liaison. The incident led to widespread media comment, and late on Tuesday night Matthew Parris, a former Tory politician and columnist for the *Sun* and the *Times*, prompted a storm of controversy on a BBC discussion program by outing two members of Cabinet, including the trade minister, Peter Mandelson. Parris, who is gay himself, described Mandelson as "certainly gay." The comment prompted a furious response from Mandelson, which resulted in a BBC directive to make no further reference to the incident. On Wednesday morning, however, the editor of the *Sun*, David Yelland, planned to run the story on page one. After frantic telephone calls from Mandelson and from Tony Blair's chief press officer Alastair Campbell, Yelland reluctantly agreed not to run the story. But he did run an editorial urging Mandelson to come out. The next day Mandelson as trade minister announced that the government had decided to refer the Manchester United takeover to the Mergers and Monopolies Commission.

It is tempting to think the two sets of events were connected. But Manchester United was not a spur-of-the-moment decision. The rising swell of protest over the bid had alarmed the government. The Prodi controversy had put Blair on notice that he was no longer untouchable. Reluctantly the government came to the view that it would have to refer the deal. From that point BSkyB's bid would be doomed.

The hardest part would be breaking the news to Rupert Murdoch. Clearly he had to be told in advance of the public announcement on Thursday. That meant that Mandelson had to tell Murdoch the bad news just as the *Sun* was gunning for him. It was a bizarre subtext. Murdoch wasn't happy about the Manchester United decision, as he made clear at the BSkyB annual meeting on Friday, when he said, "I think it's very hard for the small shareholders of Sky, that they should be punished for the fact that we supported the government in the last election."[37]

A week later the *Sun* used its front page to ask whether Britain was being run by a gay mafia. It urged all gay politicians and public servants to reveal themselves and offered a telephone hotline to assist them. And then, abruptly, the *Sun* changed tack again, promising that it would no longer out gays unless it was in the public interest. Was this Rupert Murdoch's way of getting even with the government? It seems unlikely. Most of the British press seemed to be going through an episode of homophobia. And it wasn't as if gay-bashing was a new discovery by the *Sun*. What was new was that this time it held back. The reputation of the *Sun* was such that it could influence politicians as much by what it did not say as by what it did.

One bright spot for News Corp that autumn was that on November 17 Justice Lindsay handed down his judgment in the News Datacom fraud case—and Michael Clinger was duly crunched. Clinger had promised that Rupert Murdoch and other senior News Corp figures would be called to testify, but when the trial began in the Old Bailey in June 1998, Murdoch was out of the country and unavailable. The legal expression was "over the seas." Siskind was also over the seas, as was News Corp's star witness, Leo Krieger. The hearing received no media coverage.

Michael Clinger testified via video link from a television studio in Israel. He said enough to convince Justice Lindsay that he was a "highly intelligent man, astute and experienced . . . and well equipped to make a fortune in business." Unhappily though, Lindsay went on to comment, "Mr. Clinger has not been content to receive only that reward to which his undoubted experience, ability and intelligence might properly have entitled him." He was also "a skilful liar on whose evidence no reliance can be put."[38] Lindsay found that Clinger had defrauded News Datacom and News International, and he awarded damages of £30 million. He rejected Clinger's counterclaim that News Corp had underpaid him for his 20 percent stake in the News Datacom companies (now NDS Group). Lindsay considered $5 million an excellent return on a $2,000 investment. In one of the many ironies of the case, Lindsay handed down his judgment on what was a fair return just as American investments kicked off an Internet stock boom that fifteen months later would value NDS Group at $5 billion. Extracting the damages it had won out of Clinger would be another story, but Lindsay's judgment finally gave News Corp clear title to the technology on which its future depended.

Cavan March 1999

The day was cold and wet. A small fortune had been spent on flowers, a freshly landscaped rose garden, a marquee draped with red and green and a hand-painted dance floor, a white-frame outdoor chapel built on the riverbank for the occasion, an army of security guards, and an air exclusion zone to keep out the pesky media helicopters. And still it rained. The Murdochs had been gathering over the last week. Two weeks before, Rupert Murdoch had paid A$314 million to complete the buyout of his sisters' families from the holding companies that held the Murdochs' News Corp shares. Now, on Saturday, March 27, 1999, the Murdochs had gathered at their Cavan property near Canberra to celebrate Lachlan Murdoch's marriage to Australian Wonderbra model Sarah O'Hare. His friend

Zeb Rice was best man. Wendi Deng was staying with Rupert in the hotel nearby, but at Anna's request she did not appear at the wedding. Feelings between the groom's parents were still running high. The March 11 trial setting date in the Los Angeles Superior Court had been put back to early June to give the two sides time to negotiate a settlement. Now it was the turn of Lachlan's mother to make a speech. She rose to her feet and began dryly, "Now I have the microphone, and one man in the room must be rather nervous."[39]

"My wife will not do anything that hurts the children," Rupert Murdoch had told the Los Angeles Times two months before, as reports of the divorce infighting spread. What he meant was that any attempt to break up the Cruden trusts or to launch a messy and expensive court case would only hurt the Murdoch heirs. In addition, the more he had to pay Anna, the less money there would be to buy more News Corp voting stock to ensure that his children stayed at the company's helm.

According to a source close to the family, in 1998 Murdoch changed arrangements to ensure that Prudence received an equal share as a natural heir. If this story is true, the move would have changed the dynamics of family decision-making. It also appeared to open the door for other natural heirs, if Rupert and Wendi had children. Media reports had been saying since October 1998 that Murdoch planned to marry Deng. Chinese newspapers had been quoting friends of Deng saying that she was planning to start a family as soon as possible. This was a claim that Murdoch himself denied—but then he also denied planning to marry Deng.

"That was really what I was most anxious about—that my children and their inheritance would be protected," Anna said. "And that's what took so long— between the separation and the divorce—to get that right."

On Tuesday, June 1, Murdoch made Anna an offer she didn't refuse. The next day Cruden raised A$214 million selling some of its News Corp stock. Under the settlement regime at Australian stock exchanges, Cruden would have received the sale proceeds on Monday, June 7. The Murdochs' divorce was finalized by mutual consent the next day. In addition Anna was reported to have received two of the houses, for a total payout of around $200 million.

Anna insisted that Rupert Murdoch's name replace hers on the final divorce papers. "It was important to me, for no other reason except that I believe when you take a vow to be loyal to someone and look after someone all your life, that you try and stick to that," Anna said. "You don't hurt other people for your own happiness. So on the papers, you would see that he was a petitioner for the divorce, not me." By then she had moved to New York and in October would marry William

Mann, a New York businessman five years senior to Rupert. Anna's ex-husband described him as "a nice old guy."[40]

What clinched the divorce settlement was a commitment Anna extracted that the four children would be the exclusive heirs to the bulk of the shares in Cruden. According to sources close to the family, the only remaining block of Cruden shares is the 10 percent stake still held by Dame Elisabeth that will pass to Rupert on her death and that he is free to settle upon his new daughter, Grace Helen, and any further children. But it is locked up until Grace is thirty.

Within days the four children had begun appointing representatives to the boards of Cruden, Kayarem, and other companies in the group. Prudence appointed British merchant banker Richard Oldfield, the oldest at forty-four; Elisabeth selected television producer Henrietta Conrad, thirty-six; Lachlan's appointee was Sydney ad man George Betsis, forty; and James called in his longtime friend Jesse Angelo, twenty-six, a reporter at the *New York Post*.

Late in the afternoon of Friday, June 25, seventeen days after the Murdochs' marriage was dissolved, a fifty-meter yacht slipped away from Chelsea Piers in New York. Through the evening it plied back and forth across the Hudson River, past Ellis Island and the Statue of Liberty. Somewhere near the old immigration processing halls on Ellis Island, Rupert Murdoch married Wendi Deng. The eighty-one guests on board included his four children and their partners, Michael Milken, and Boris Berezovsky. Any tactless question about prenuptial agreements appeared to have been resolved by the choice of celebrant: The twilight wedding ceremony, which began as Murdoch's yacht cruised past the Statue of Liberty, was conducted by New York's senior divorce judge, Jacqueline Silberman, who heads the matrimonial division of the New York Supreme Court. The photographs of the event reflect some of the awkwardness among the Murdoch children. All four of them—Elisabeth, thirty, Lachlan, twenty-seven, James, twenty-six, and Prudence, forty—were there on the huge yacht. In the festive scenes caught by photographers on the dock, in picture after picture it is Prudence, the one most used to living with her father at a distance, who is at her father's elbow.

Murdoch settled the inevitable rash of questions about who his successor would be by announcing that if he fell under a bus tomorrow, News Corp's chief operating officer, Peter Chernin, would run News Corp, perhaps with Lachlan as chairman. Chernin took the comment without flinching. He was merely the latest in a long line of News Corp executives who had been designated Murdoch's successor. In the court of King Rupert, such an honor generally meant that the executive in question was nearing the end of his shelf life. A year later Murdoch was saying that Chernin, "my very good friend," might share the top job with one of his sons.

Could Wendi Deng or any of her children become Murdoch's successor? "Not at all, not at all," Anna repeats. But that will depend upon the four children staying united. Within a year Elisabeth had stormed out of the family business. On paper at least, if two of the four children disagreed over the succession after their father's death, the 10 percent of Cruden stock reserved for Wendi's daughter Grace (and any further children) could hold the deciding vote. The 10 percent block of shares is locked up in a trust until Grace turns thirty. The Murdochs control trusts by the power to appoint trustees. In this case, presumably the trustees would be appointed by Grace's guardian. That would be Wendi.

Cape Canaveral August 1999

As the East Coast of the United States braced itself for Hurricane Floyd, insurance underwriters were already reaching for their ulcer tablets in anticipation of the damage toll. In the first week of August 1999 weather forecasters were describing Floyd as one of the worst storms ever to hit the American coastline. As it bore down on Florida, three rockets sat exposed on the launch pad at Cape Canaveral, too massive to be moved under cover. The rockets' gantries were strong enough to handle winds of up to 110 miles per hour. At Floyd's center, the winds were touching 140 miles per hour. The rockets' survival would depend upon how close the center of the hurricane came to them. Perched atop one of the launch vehicles was a $250 million communications satellite due to be fired into the 110WL orbital slot above North America—the satellite television slot that had caused Rupert Murdoch and Charlie Ergen at EchoStar so much grief. Satellites are covered by insurance policies during their construction and their storage and ground transportation. Separate insurance policies cover the launch and any loss of the satellite in orbit. It wasn't clear who bore the cost if a satellite were damaged while it was on the launch pad. Was it still covered? Media executives held anguished conversations as Hurricane Floyd headed toward Rupert's rocket.

Floyd never lived up to the prepublicity—it swerved away from the coast and petered out. Murdoch's predicament, exposed on the pointy end of a Titan booster, was the product of fifteen months of disastrous reverses. In the same period that his marriage had collapsed and he had been wrong-footed in his bid to buy Manchester United, Murdoch's American satellite dreams had come crashing down again.

On May 12, 1998, the Justice Department filed a suit in federal court to block

Murdoch's sale of the ASkyB satellites and orbital license to Primestar. The writ argued that allowing cable operators to gain the key 110WL orbital license "would be like hiring the wolf to guard the sheep."[41] The Justice Department would not allow the deal through in its existing form, and the peace agreement that Murdoch and Malone had worked so hard to forge the year before would be thrown out. From June through August the two men tossed around possible compromises that might satisfy the concerns of the Justice Department. One alternative was to bring new investors into Primestar that would buy the cable operators out. The plan would incidentally leave Murdoch in control, once again using someone else's money. That would satisfy the government, but Time Warner and the other cable operators were never going to allow this.

There was more bad news for Murdoch on the corporate front. In October 1998 he had spun his American television assets off in a $3 billion initial public offering for Fox Entertainment, but it failed to set Wall Street on fire. On October 14 News Corp released a one-paragraph statement that said ASkyB had terminated its relationship with Primestar. Five months of trying to find a compromise that would satisfy both the Justice Department and the cable partners in Primestar had failed. Now News Corp had its satellite slot and its two satellites back on its hands, and the only way forward was to do a deal with the angry Charlie Ergen at EchoStar.

Back on June 11, 1997, when the cable operators had announced their Primestar deal with Murdoch, Ergen had been on stage in Denver at the Global DBS Summit. Reporters noticed that Ergen was speaking a little strangely. On closer inspection it became apparent he had braces on his teeth. Stephen Keating in his book *Cutthroat* tells the story that one of Ergen's daughters had been advised to get braces. When she said she was frightened, her father told her he would get braces put on as well. When the day came, he had second thoughts about going through with it. His daughter played hardball. "Daddy, that's just like what Mr. Murdoch did," she said.[42]

When Murdoch came calling again in 1998, Ergen was taking no prisoners. He knew Murdoch had no other buyer for his satellite assets. He knew he could take his time and do the deal on his own terms. "Rupert had no choice but to come back and deal with Charlie . . . and he held his hands to the hotplate," one analyst said.[43] Ergen insisted that in exchange for the ASkyB assets, News Corp and MCI would end up with 37 percent of EchoStar stock but only 9 percent of the votes. The terms were such that whether EchoStar's share price went up or down by the settlement date, the deal could only get better for Ergen and worse for Murdoch.

Ergen would pick up ASkyB's satellite uplink station in Phoenix, but News Corp would have to rip out all the electronics and the News Datacom technology. As well, Ergen would be given lucrative contracts to manufacture News Datacom set-top boxes for News Corp clients. News would also have to pay for the two satellites it was providing and insure them for their first year in orbit. If Murdoch agreed to all this, Ergen would take his satellite assets and call off his $5 billion lawsuit from the previous year. News Corp wrote off a A$616 million loss on the deal. Murdoch left no doubt who he blamed for this disastrous outcome: It was the fault of the Clinton administration. Murdoch had always been a virulent critic of Bill Clinton. Five days before he signed the deal with Ergen on November 30, the *New York Post* broke the unofficial media bar on writing about the president's family, with a front-page story about Chelsea Clinton's distraught visit to a university clinic after a failed romance.

The original Sky deal in February 1997 had been for News and MCI to get 45 percent of EchoStar's stock and voting rights—equal to Ergen's holding. When Ergen agreed to the new deal with Murdoch on November 30, 1999, he was in no mood to be generous. This time News and MCI would receive 240 million EchoStar shares valued at just under $1.2 billion.[44] They would end up with 37 percent of EchoStar stock but would have only 9 percent of the voting rights and no board representation. That was bad enough. But the final deal would be based upon the price of EchoStar stock on the settlement date. In his 1996 deal with Ron Perelman, Murdoch had used this device to win an advantage. With EchoStar, Ergen would win and Murdoch would lose whether the stock price went up or down. If it went down, then News Corp and MCI would receive stock that was worth less than the sale price, and that was just their bad luck. If EchoStar stock went up, then it was bad luck for News Corp and MCI again, because they would receive less EchoStar stock, so that they would never get more than their $1.2 billion sale price.

The only way Murdoch would have agreed to this condition was if he didn't believe EchoStar had much of a future. Unfortunately, the market loved the news that Charlie Ergen had swung this deal with Murdoch, and EchoStar stock went through the roof. The stock was at $4.85 when the sale contract was signed in November 1998.[45] By the time the deal closed on June 24, 1999, EchoStar stock had hit $17.13. Nine months later it hit $81. Instead of getting 240 million shares the day before Murdoch's wedding, News Corp and MCI received just 68.8 million shares and 1.7 percent of the voting rights. Put another way: Doing the deal with Murdoch had transformed Ergen's company, but Ergen cleverly structured it so that Murdoch could not benefit from it. If News Corp and MCI had picked up 240 million EchoStar shares as the November 1998 contract stipulated, at the peak in March 2000 that $1.2 billion investment would have been worth $19.5 billion. But because of the way the contract was written, News Corp and MCI ended up with less than a quarter of the 240 million shares originally contracted—and within months they had sold nearly half of the stock they did pick up. Charlie Ergen's revenge on Rupert Murdoch was a mountain of lost opportunity. The opportunity cost to News Corp and MCI at the peak of the market was more than $8.5 billion.[46] And Murdoch still had to sweat it out through Hurricane Floyd.

19

THE MANHATTAN WINDOW

AFTER HALF A CENTURY working in the industry, the media business still had the ability to take Rupert Murdoch by surprise—and never more so than in New York. When his marriage collapsed, like an old crocodile Murdoch headed for the place in the world that he loved most and understood best. New York was his lucky city, where politicians were still for the moment Republican, where the *New York Post* was outrageous, and where fortune smiled on the brave. After a stint at the Mercer Hotel in SoHo, in 1999 Murdoch bought a three-story loft apartment on Prince Street with his new wife. The lifestyle change provided Murdoch's critics with endless delight. "Media Mogul in SoHo Love Nest" was the line taken by the non-Murdoch British press. The headline writers did their best, but you knew that the more ingenious minds at the *Sun* or the *Post* would have come up with something a little more colorful. British columnists were obliged to take matters into their own hands to demonstrate their wonderful sense of irony.

The Murdochs had moved into SoHo in force. Lachlan and Sarah O'Hare had bought half the penthouse floor in an apartment building on Lafayette Street. James and Kathryn Hufschmid had a four-story terrace in the West Village. At sixty-nine, surrounded by his sons, Rupert Murdoch was looking pretty chipper. He was off the Pritikin diet that his ex-wife Anna had kept him on for years, and had bulked up a little. "There's no doubt she's put a spring in the old man's step," one of his executives said of Wendi.[1]

At the turn of the millennium great things were afoot. The rolling series of technological and financial advances and crises loosely called the information revolution was sweeping through the world's capital markets, transforming national economies, making whole swathes of industry obsolete, changing the way the world did business. In two years it had also created more individual wealth than anyone had ever seen. It was changing how we communicate, how we interact with other people, how and what we watch, what entertains us, how we read books, what we value, and who we believe ourselves to be.

So it was hard to figure out what Rupert Murdoch was doing at the end of 1999, hunkered down in New York. His life was the same hectic schedule of deal-making: a billion dollars here, a few hundred million there. All he needed to run his empire was a telephone. The quiet voice would still reach out over thousands of miles of telephone line to whichever part of the company needed his attention. It was a voice that haunted News Corp executives. Some of them dreamed about it. The voice was alternately seductive, endlessly persuasive, or frigidly dismissive. Murdoch was the master of the little politeness, the long silence, the questioning pause, the icy rage. He could inspire remarkable loyalty as well as enormous bitterness. Like the British Empire before it, News Corp at the end of the twentieth century was an undertaking on which the sun never set. What that really meant was that somewhere around the world there was always a News Corp executive whom Murdoch could get out of bed.

There was no shortage of action for Murdoch in 1999. Yet oddly for someone who lived at such breakneck speed, Murdoch for the first time in his life gave the impression that he was a spectator. After a lifetime of striving and despite the huge potential influence that this global empire offered him, in some senses he was reduced to peering through his Manhattan window at the big moves on Wall Street, watching the madness of the Internet boom transform stock markets around the world. He was condemned to wait until the bubble had finished its course, run out of puff, and slid back to earth—to observe with resignation other people's spectacular good fortune.

Even in hindsight it is difficult to say when the information revolution stopped being a load of hocus-pocus and became a part of everyday life. Through the 1980s and most of the 1990s, the most memorable feature of the revolution was its miserable record of broken promises. In the 1980s there was the paperless office. Then in 1992 there were the five hundred cable channels. Fortunes were lost on wild schemes for interactive television and online services—multimedia programming, video telephones—that never met their product description. The information revolution that was going to transform the world's living rooms never quite got there. By early 1997 the information superhighway that Bill Gates liked to talk about looked more like a parking lot. For all the hype, the tidal wave of digital data hadn't arrived. The revolution, it turned out, was all about getting there. It was about distribution.

Appearance is everything. What changed the appearance of the superhighway was money. In September 1998 Wall Street embarked on as wild a ride as capital markets had ever seen. Within six months a small group of Internet companies that had modest revenues, no profits, and limited cash reserves were worth $600 billion. Those months changed the whole perception of the information revolution. Suddenly the information superhighway was the place where everyone wanted to be. This was the shape of the future, and the future would make us rich. The superhighway was still a parking lot, full of people who weren't making any money, whose revenues were still only a tiny fraction of the old-media companies that they were ready to replace. But now it was a parking lot with a checkbook.

In *Cinema Paradiso*, Giuseppe Tornatore's moving 1989 film about a child's love affair with a small-town movie theater in Sicily in the 1940s, there is a poignant scene where the building catches fire. The projector keeps turning, faithfully projecting the image of the film as it bubbles, curls, and goes up in smoke. I have spoken to media executives and bankers who find this scene too painful to watch, evoking as it does so many unhappy memories of their own experiences in film and television investment. It's the nature of the industry. Half a century after Tornatore's childhood cinema closed, the media business remained highly flammable and the metaphorical aroma of singed celluloid was all too pervasive. The medium might have changed, but the risks of total annihilation were higher than ever.

By contrast the quality that distinguished the leaders of the new media was their total indifference to the risks of conflagration. They burned through money like there was no tomorrow. Indeed, the market expected them to burn through the funds that investors were throwing at them. These were dizzy days. The wealth created by rising stock prices had triggered in investors a global suspension of disbelief. All the old yardsticks used to measure the value of a stock or a startup company—profits, cash reserves, previous history—were discarded. All that anyone wanted was a piece of the future. On the wild edge of the wave, investors would believe anything.

But they wouldn't believe Rupert Murdoch. He was on record as an Internet skeptic. He had invested in online businesses like Delphi before anyone else had, but he didn't like the business model. The Internet, he said in February 1999, would destroy more value than it created. Five months later he interrupted his honeymoon to clarify that what he had meant to say was that the Internet was "the most important development in business since the invention of the telephone. . . . Whenever a major change of this order takes place, traditional business models are challenged and sometimes destroyed," he said. "That is what is happening now."[2]

The suspicion remained that he was not a true believer. So his empire sat heavy on the beach as the wild tide came in. Even visionaries have their moments of self-doubt. In December 1999 Murdoch's biggest problem was that he didn't believe in himself quite enough. His senior executives—most notably News Corp finance director David DeVoe—had been selling their News Corp stock. Murdoch himself had been selling call options on his News Corp shares to raise money. At least for the moment he and his lieutenants clearly believed the company was becalmed. And then, incongruously in this dark moment, opportunity beckoned.

*   *   *

In the first weeks of the new millennium, two events inaugurated a new era. The first event began on January 10, 2000, with a press conference in the Time Warner offices at the Equitable Center on Fifty-second Street in New York. Gerry Levin was there, the head of Time Warner, the largest media company in the world. It was immediately apparent that he had news of great import, because he had elaborately removed his tie and shed his moustache. The new look was the marker for a twenty-first-century kind of guy. Next to him was Steve Case, chairman and CEO of America Online, the world's largest Internet company. Steve Case is to Hawaiian shirts what Nureyev was to ballet tights: a true artist for whom expense is no object. Sometimes it looks like Case has paid as much as twenty dollars for some of his brighter combinations. But not that day. You could tell someone was really working on the corporate symbolism here because they had crammed Steve Case into a business suit. Case and Levin were there to announce the end of the world as we knew it.

The AOL–Time Warner liaison they proceeded to announced was the biggest corporate merger or takeover—however you want to put it—in history. It would leave Levin as CEO but Steve Case as chairman and his cybercowboys from America Online in the box seat running Time Warner. The *New York Times* valued the deal at $165 billion and the *Financial Times* put it at $230 billion, but in the confused hours following the announcement you could stick any number you liked on it.

At the climax of the media conference, Levin and Case went into a full-body clinch. It was quite a moment: the heads of the largest and toughest media organizations in the world hugging as if their lives depended on it. Ted Turner, Time Warner's deputy chairman and biggest individual stockholder, was up on the stage beside Levin and Case. Turner, who had separated from his wife Jane Fonda two weeks before, assured all and sundry that the night before he had signed over his stock for the merger with all the excitement of the first time he made love. Judging by his appearance that morning, that would have been, oh, say four hundred years before.

In 1996 Rupert Murdoch had been on the point of buying AOL when he made the mistake of asking advice from Bill Gates, who told him AOL wouldn't be around long enough to be worth the trouble. Murdoch said later that Gates "didn't believe in it at all. He thought there wasn't a real business model there, and you know, none of us quite know yet . . . the jury is still out on AOL. But naturally we had an opportunity to come in when it was worth $4 billion or $5 billion and it went up to being worth $150 billion. So it was a pretty serious opportunity that we missed there."[3]

The AOL-Gates episode makes a funny story at Rupert Murdoch's expense, and as he sat there on the stage at the January 10 press conference, you could almost sense that Ted Turner was dying to retell it. Murdoch had been chasing Time Warner—and before that Time Inc. and Warner Bros.—in one shape or another for almost three decades. The new entity that would emerge from the AOL–Time Warner deal was a superheavyweight that was ludicrously beyond the reach of any of its competitors. Quite apart from everything else, on a personal note it was Ted Turner's final victory over his ancient enemy.

The American media tackled the story with a full court press. The *New York Times* spelled out the numbers on the deal, told the background story of how Steve Case had wooed Gerry Levin, and agonized over the way media outlets were consolidating into fewer and fewer hands. The *Wall Street Journal* spelled out different numbers on the deal, speculated on the synergies of the alliance, and began identifying suspects for the next megamerger. Michael Wolff at *New York* magazine suggested that as both Time Warner and AOL were richer and more powerful than most medium-size countries, newspapers should assign the story to the corporate-state desk. *Vanity Fair* immediately picked up on the hugging thing and asked what this meant for the future of social intercourse. Everyone agreed that this was the most significant deal in the history of media. It was a little harder to say what in particular it signified.

The AOL–Time Warner deal's status as the biggest merger in history lasted for all of one week. Then British mobile phone group Vodafone–AirTouch won a hostile takeover battle for German telco Mannesmann for 181 billion euros, with a little help from Jean-Marie Messier, the little-known head of French media group

Vivendi. This was the second event that would bring in a new era. Its significance went largely unnoticed at the time, but it was a warning signal to the American communications industry that the Europeans were coming.

Wall Street thought about the AOL–Time Warner deal for a bit; then after an initial burst of enthusiasm it decided it didn't like it. When the news first broke, Time Warner's stock price jumped from $64.75 to $90, but by March 6 it had crashed back down to $57. At that level Ted Turner's Time Warner stock was worth $885 million less than it had been before the deal was announced. This was all the more painful because everyone else with media stock was hauling in money with a bucket. The tech boom on Wall Street had established a cycle whereby the market would take off in September or October and run like a mad thing until March or April; then the Federal Reserve would clamp down on money supply, the mutual funds would lose their nerve, the day traders would knock off for the summer, and the market would slide down. In October 1999 a fourth wave of investment in Internet and tech stocks had swept in. The world's central bankers were worried about the millennium bug—the fear that when clocks ticked over into the new century computer chaos would break out—so they had deliberately pumped liquidity into the world's banking system. The millennium bug turned out to be a dud, but the extra money in the system had put the Nasdaq index of tech stocks into turbodrive.

All of these technical issues worked together to ensure that in the middle of January 2000 the telecommunications-media-technology stock wave finally picked up News Corp and carried it along. In seven weeks the News Corp stock price doubled. Rupert Murdoch's personal fortune jumped $6.7 billion. He made almost as much money in those seven weeks as he had in the previous forty-eight years. He owed it all to Ted, of course. His old adversary's support for the AOL deal had changed once again the way media stocks were valued. Was Murdoch thinking of merging with an Internet stock too? the market wanted to know. "Hell no," he told one of his journalists insensitive enough to ask.

It took a little time to work out what had happened. First, everyone agreed that the AOL–Time Warner deal was a turning point. It validated the new economy, proving that the huge surge in Internet stocks was no fly-by-night phenomenon but was a change in value that was here to stay. Gerry Levin had been making bets on technology all his life. His track record showed he had been right about half the time. But even if he had got it wrong this time and the AOL–Time Warner combination proved a fizzler, it had still changed the world. The next point was that if Levin's rivals in conventional old-media companies wanted to keep up with

AOL–Time Warner, they would have to make some sort of alliance of their own with the new media operators. They had to get bigger. What would come after that was a little harder to say.

It's important to keep in mind just what the information revolution was all about. The sharp edge of the revolution had lain not with the digital technology and interactive services that it offered but rather with finding a way of getting that technology into people's homes and then convincing them to use it. Technology was not an end in itself. The fax machine was developed in the 1970s, but it did not become indispensable to the modern office for another decade. Steve Case was pursuing Time Warner not for its cable channels, or for its Warner Bros. studio and film library or for its music division or its magazines, or indeed for any of its content. Rather, AOL wanted to get hold of Time Warner's network of hybrid coaxial-fiber-optic cable, a great fat delivery pipe that Steve Case wanted to use to pump data, information, interactive television, and everything else that the information revolution had been promising, right to the customer in 12 million American households.

The high-speed Internet access provided by Time Warner's cable changed the whole picture of what the Internet could deliver. Broadband had been around for several years, but the telephone and cable companies that operated it had been dismally unsuccessful at convincing people to use it. But in the whole world of media, no one has ever been as successful about convincing customers to take a new product as AOL. In new media, AOL was the master salesman. Its whole future was based on its belief that it could persuade its 19 million customers to take up broadband. It was a given. Its $157 billion stock valuation was based on that belief. And if anyone could make it work, it was Steve Case.

That didn't mean that the merger would be a success. What the AOL–Time Warner deal did was to establish that, one way or another, we were now in a broadband universe. *Click.* It was another change in perception. In ten years' time everyone would have broadband. The question now was: What was the best way for broadband to get to people's homes? Would it be through Time Warner's cable? Would it be through wireless application protocol over mobile phones? Would it be through the telephone companies' ADSL lines? Or by satellite? Broadband all came down to the distribution question. Overnight anything that could deliver broadband was worth a lot of money. This was where Rupert Murdoch saw his big chance.

It took Murdoch five weeks to go from a standing start to announcing a $50 billion deal. He owned the best distribution system on the planet. The BSkyB satellite pay-television service in Britain was a model he had copied around the world. He had brought in partners, but he retained management rights. In Asia there was Star TV, whose footprint reached from Israel across India and China to California. In Japan Murdoch owned 10 percent of Sky PerfecTV! In Latin America he had 36 percent of Sky Brazil; 30 percent of Sky Mexico; and 30 percent of Sky Multi-Country Partners, which broadcast into Colombia and Chile and was moving into Argentina. In Australia he had 25 percent of the leading cable operator, Foxtel. In Europe he was moving to 50 percent of Stream SpA, an Italian pay-television service, and BSkyB owned 24 percent of Germany's digital pay-television platform, Premiere World.

North America was the only significant gap in Murdoch's worldwide satellite reach. There his conventional media interests in the Fox television network, television program production, 20th Century–Fox and cable channels for Fox News, Fox Sports, and Fox Kids made him one of the biggest content producers in the United States. It was content that he could reuse in his satellite systems around the world. This mix of content and distribution made News Corp unique. Holding the system together he had *TV Guide,* which he was folding into Gemstar, which produced an electronic television guide for Internet users and pay-television subscribers; he had just floated the NDS Group, which provided the conditional-access technology for more than half the world's digital television users; and the Open system for interactive television that he was using for BSkyB. Only weeks before no one had been valuing this combination. AOL–Time Warner changed all that.

America's most high-profile media analyst, Merrill Lynch's Jessica Reif-Cohen, was enthusiastic about News Corp's place in this brave new world, saying, "The combination of News Corp's satellite investments into one seamless distribution platform, in our opinion, will launch News Corp into an unparalleled global position as the only company truly capable of providing a video and data infrastructure to the rest of the world."[4]

When News floated 20 percent of NDS in October 1999, the company was worth $900 million. By March the stock market valued NDS at $5 billion. News Corp's own stock price doubled. But BSkyB was the bellwether of Murdoch's fortunes: On September 24, 1999, its shares were selling at £5.20. On March 7, five months later, they hit £22.64. News Corp's 37.6 percent holding in BSkyB jumped from £3.5 billion to £15.5 billion in value. This had a leveraging effect. If BSkyB's value had gone up that much, so had the value of the eight other major pay-television operations that Murdoch operated around the globe.

On February 14 News Corp announced it was examining proposals to float its international delivery platforms, a project that was code-named Platformco, or Platco. Lachlan Murdoch told analysts that the new company would be a vehicle for strategic alliances with companies like Yahoo!, Microsoft, and Vivendi in France. News Corp would remain the controlling shareholder. Jessica Reif-Cohen described the Platco project as the "dream beam" and valued the company at $30 to $50 billion and upward. On Wall Street merchant bankers were floating around plans to raise $18 billion in cash by spinning off 20 to 30 percent of Platco. With the cash from the initial public offering and investments from the new partners, Platco could be worth as much as $90 billion.

To recap: On Friday, January 7, Rupert Murdoch's worldwide empire was worth $35 billion, and Murdoch himself looked like he was spinning his wheels. Five weeks later the Platco IPO, together with Fox Entertainment in the United States and his newspapers plus the various ventures around the world that he managed with minority stakes, meant that he controlled an empire that would be valued at more than $120 billion. His millennium gamble had been to reinvent himself.

In late March 2000 the first sign of how long Murdoch's arm had grown came when reports swept Wall Street that he was about to buy General Motors. Twenty years before Murdoch had bought an airline to get hold of a television station. The same principle seemed to be involved here. Murdoch would buy GM and immediately recover all of the purchase price by selling all those old-economy car plants. But he would hold on to GM's subsidiary Hughes Electronics, which owned America's largest satellite television operator, DirecTV. The reality, not factored into the GM stock price, was that DirecTV was now worth more than GM itself. Had the deal gone through, Murdoch would have filled the North American gap in Platco for, in effect, nothing.

"Well look it, we talk to everybody in the industry, and I can't single Rupert out as having any particular talks," Hughes CEO Michael Smith told Fox News. "We know what Rupert's doing with his Platco company. . . . If you talk to Rupert any given day, Rupert is a satellite bull. He loves satellite."[5]

But in mid-March 2000 the world's love affair with telecommunications-media-technology stocks faltered. The Nasdaq index dived from 5000 to touch 3300. Overnight many of the valuations on which the Platco plan depended were overturned. Platco, which would be renamed Sky Global, was still viable, but now its value—and the value of the partners that Murdoch was trying to bring on board—

was uncertain. Murdoch needed to proceed with the Sky Global IPO that summer before the Nasdaq fell over completely. But the tech crash had triggered a more profound realignment in the media industry. Murdoch found a natural ally in someone who was even more threatened by the new AOL–Time Warner colossus than he himself was.

Bill Gates had been stalking Murdoch since early 1999. Gates had invested $3.7 billion in Murdoch's cable rivals in Britain and encouraged them to merge so that they could challenge BSkyB. Gates also tried to poach BSkyB managing director Mark Booth, then reportedly offered $1.5 billion to a U.K. cable company, NTL, to help pry the broadcast rights for Premier League away from BSkyB. "I think Bill's going at everybody. Bill wants to take over the world," Murdoch told *Vanity Fair* in October 1999. "I don't say it nastily about Bill."[6] Gates responded to the jibe in a BBC interview later that month. How could a software company possibly exert power? he asked expansively. It was Murdoch, he said, who wanted to take over the world: "He's hiding behind me, he's your man."[7]

Gates had declared war because when Murdoch launched BSkyB's interactive television service in October 1998, he made the conscious decision to exclude Microsoft's Windows CE from the digital set-top box. "We don't want Bill Gates to get control of our pictures," Murdoch told the *Financial Times* in July 1997. "That's the real thing."

Instead, BSkyB's system used software from OpenTV, developed in part by Microsoft's rival, Sun Microsystems. BSkyB was the dominant pay-television delivery system in Britain, and Gates was locked out of it. The danger was that, just as Murdoch had used BSkyB as the model to build his satellite empire around the world, he would use this non-Microsoft operating system for South America, Germany, Italy, India, China, and Australia.

On May 5, 1999, BSkyB announced that it would provide its digital set-top boxes to customers free of charge, along with free Internet access and a 40 percent reduction in their telephone bill. To cover this offer, BSkyB would make a straight-off $675 million charge against its earnings. And to protect its position of market dominance, it would keep shelling out whatever it cost. Pay-television operators around the world had offered subsidized prices to customers before, but the sheer scale of this handout was like none other. Overnight it turned BSkyB into the world's leading operator of interactive digital television. Murdoch blew the cable operators away. Then on June 14, 2000, he outmaneuvered them to win the major package of Premier League broadcasting rights again for BSkyB. They cost $1.67 billion. Murdoch had beaten Gates off. Now the two men needed to become partners.

* * *

Jean-Marie Messier, the man the French press called Jean 2M, was a different kind of headache. A former French public servant, he had turned France's oldest water-treatment group, Générale des Eaux, into one of Europe's biggest media groups, renamed Vivendi. Among his other accomplishments, Messier had a remarkable ability to press Rupert Murdoch's button. In February 1999 Murdoch had met with Messier and Pierre Lescure, the chief executive of Canal Plus, Europe's largest pay-television operator, which Messier controlled. They had talked about merging Canal Plus with BSkyB, but fell out over who would end up with control. "We will have the leadership or there will be no agreement," Lescure told French newspaper *Liberation*.[8]

Once the merger was scuttled, the real point of the meeting—at least as Italian politicians came to believe—was that Messier and Lescure wanted Murdoch to stay out of Italy. His investment in the Italian pay-television operator Stream SpA and his moves to buy up broadcast rights for Italian soccer would hurt Telepiu, the leading Italian pay-television operator controlled by Canal Plus. If Murdoch backed off, Messier undertook not to buy any more shares in BSkyB. In the spirit of the meeting, Lescure and Messier agreed to let Murdoch have Germany. They would not oppose his plans to link up with Bertelsmann or Kirch Group there. Senior Italian politicians were hugely indignant that Murdoch and Messier had genially carved up Europe between them. While the prospect that Rupert Murdoch would take over Italy's media and its national sports terrified them, it was outrageous for Murdoch to back away from doing so just because of what someone in Paris told him.

If there was an agreement between Messier and Murdoch, it didn't last. In July Messier bought the British media groups Granada and Pearson out of a joint holding in BSkyB stock. Messier now owned 24.5 percent of BSkyB. Whether by accident or by design, he discovered that the most annoying way to inform Rupert Murdoch of this development was to telephone him in New York in the middle of the night and get him out of bed. Murdoch told his new shareholder, "I don't like waking up in the morning thinking I have to look over my shoulder," Messier recalled later. The two men did not speak for months afterward.[9]

In April 2000, after a routine health checkup in Los Angeles, Murdoch was diagnosed with prostate cancer. His cancer was described as low grade, but his family history offered little comfort. Doctors had operated on Murdoch's father three times for prostate cancer. If Sir Keith had not died of a heart attack, it seemed only a matter of time before he was hit by a further wave of secondary cancers. This was not a condition to trifle with, but the diagnosis came at a critical period for Murdoch in the negotiations for Sky Global. "He has no intention of changing his work schedule," a News Corp spokesman announced quickly. Murdoch put the radiation therapy on hold for a month.

His family was showing signs of the stress. On May 2 his daughter Elisabeth resigned from her position as head of programming at BSkyB. She said at first that she was resigning to start up her own production company. A day later she revealed that she was having a baby with her companion, Matthew Freud. The pair would split for several months at the end of the year. Elisabeth's exit from the family business coincided with her father's decision to include his two sons, Lachlan and James, on the board of Sky Global. Elisabeth, who at BSkyB had been program manager for Sky Global's core operation, had been overlooked. The struggle to determine which of Rupert's children would succeed him seemed to have claimed another casualty.

On Saturday, June 17, the Murdochs gathered on a riverbank in Connecticut to watch James marry Kathryn Hufschmid. Two weeks before, James had had a wild bachelor party in Las Vegas with his friends, his brother, and his father. A weekend of card-playing and drinking climaxed in a visit to a shooting range, where James toted a Magnum. His father's weapon of choice was a machine gun. The following Monday, James was appointed executive chairman of Star TV. As the younger brother, he had little to lose. If he could turn Star TV into a money-spinner, he would have far stronger claims on the succession than Lachlan. The prospectus for Murdoch's Sky Global Networks initial public offering was filed with the Securities and Exchange Commission on Tuesday, June 24. It helped upstage Jean-Marie Messier's announcement that Vivendi and Canal Plus were coming to Hollywood with a $34 billion bid for Seagrams.

In hindsight, Murdoch should have kept running. In the first three weeks of April, the Nasdaq composite index of high-tech stocks, which was the surest guide to the state of the tech economy, had dropped 34 percent down to 3200. But by mid-July it had clawed its way back above 4,100. That is when Murdoch *should* have floated Sky Global. But sources close to Murdoch said that after finally beginning nine weeks of radiotherapy, the treatment had left him for the moment too weak to begin another frenzied round of deal-making. Still, it didn't keep him from pulling off a snap deal at the start of August, snatching Chris-Craft Industries (the television station chain that had blocked Murdoch's run at Warner Bros. seventeen years before) for $5.3 billion from under the nose of Sumner Redstone, who had been negotiating to buy Chris-Craft for months. Murdoch's move set off a new scramble among U.S. broadcasters to keep up with him. A week later Murdoch was at the News Corp annual profit announcement to assure analysts that he was back in charge. The cancer treatments were over, he said, and the whole experience had only "convinced me of my own immortality." But the chance to float Sky Global in a still-buoyant market had slipped away.

The hoped-for October 2000 rally on Wall Street, on which so much of Murdoch's plans depended, never eventuated. By the start of 2001 it was clear that the unthinkable had happened: The wave of technological euphoria that had dominated the last years of the twentieth century was in full retreat. Propelled by the new mood of disenchantment, the price of technology stocks fell like a stone. Among the scenes of carnage that unfolded on stock markets across the globe, the biggest losses were in New York, where the Nasdaq composite index of technology stocks dropped 46 percent in the three months before January 2, 2001. In nine months American technology investors lost more than $3 trillion.[10] The pain was felt across the board. In early 2001 a good technology investment was one that had fallen less than 90 percent from its 2000 high.

The shock waves that this disaster set off reflected more than just a mountain of missing money. After all, there would be stock market rallies—and the chairman of the Federal Reserve, Alan Greenspan, was cutting interest rates doggedly to achieve them. In any case, the process of technological change would go on. The real casualty had been the belief, the credo fostered by a decade of huge tech stock rises, that information technology had ushered in a new economic order. The premise for the tech stock boom was that the path of the information revolution led ever upward, somehow invulnerable to economic cycles. This belief did not survive the first signs in late 2000 that the American economy was turning down.

It is difficult to describe how damaging this disenchantment proved. In many ways belief in technology had become the dominant social paradigm after the end of the cold war. Technology's fall from grace threw the world into paradigm crisis. If, contrary to appearances, technology turned out to be mortal, what did the future hold? As media companies slashed back their ambitious plans for the Internet, the information superhighway was once more characterized by a rush back to the parking lot.

POSTSCRIPT: THE OTHER SIDE OF TUESDAY

About suffering they were never wrong,
The Old Masters

W.H. Auden, "Musée des Beaux Arts"

I N THE GRIM DAYS that followed the events of Tuesday, September 11, 2001, poetry returned to newspaper opinion pages. People reached for words that could explain and give voice to a horrifying new reality. Often their poet of choice was W.H. Auden, a man whose words evoked a society wrestling with its darkest fears.

The unmentionable odor of death
Offends the September night.

Lines from "September 1, 1939" gained new meaning for a country preparing to go to war. Yet in a sense Auden was part of a world that had passed away, changed forever on the day New York's World Trade Center towers fell. Auden saw tragedy as a personal, localized experience. It happens when someone else is opening a window or eating, or "just walking dully along." In "Musée des Beaux Arts," he remarks on Brueghel's painting of Icarus falling into the sea. No one else was really interested . The plowman, the sailing ship went on their way regardless. Tragedy is something that strikes individuals, which cannot be shared, and which most of the world ignores. Life goes on. While this remains generally true— suffering is always personal—in one particular sense September 11 belonged to a different chain of consequence. The events of that day had such impact across the world precisely because none of Auden's strictures applied.

For everyone outside New York and Washington, September 11 was a media
event, one that they knew about only through the electronic images that they saw.
The tragedy unfolded live in front of a worldwide audience. To look at the pictures
of the burning towers, to see the Pentagon enveloped in smoke, to wonder how
many other hijacked planes were still in the air—what would happen next?—was
to be part of a wider, uncharted journey. It was an experience of tragedy that was
shaped by technology, where the restraints of geography and isolation did not
apply. You saw it in the ubiquitous cell phones. The anti–World Trade Organization demonstrations in Seattle in late 1999 had already shown that mobile phones
are an essential accessory when organizing a riot. Now cell phones were used to
direct rescues, to locate people, to say good-bye. Hijackers used cell phones and
emails to coordinate their movements. The passengers on the last plane, informed
by their families by phone of what had happened to the other planes and of their
own likely fate, decided to attack the hijackers. All of these were isolated acts that
in Auden's world nobody would have known about. But we live in a wired society.
We may be no less isolated, but the effect of technology has been to break down
the barriers of separateness. Or maybe not to break them down so much as to
move their boundaries. We are all interactive. We live in a network of networks.

In the summer of 2001 the media had been functioning in its customary role as
a giant transistor, amplifying small specific events: shark attacks, the disappearance of a congressman's aide, a publicist who drove her SUV into a crowd of people outside a Hamptons nightclub. An entire system designed to magnify events
was faced with a catastrophe more shocking in affect, in magnitude, and most important in proximity than it had ever faced. The result was numbing. This breakdown of the boundaries of geography did not make reality clearer. It seemed to
distort reality even further.

One of the great engines of the now-defunct technology stock boom was the
rise of day traders. Their rise was driven by a feedback loop between the business
cable channels that hyped the latest tech stock offering, and the Internet chat
rooms that talked the stocks up. The interaction between cable and Internet produced powerful changes in public sentiment. After September 11 the focus of the
cable channels and the chat rooms switched from the markets to the coming war.
And here the most significant factor was that by the summer of 2001 Murdoch's
Fox News was overtaking CNN in ratings, wherever they went head to head. The
threat that Fox News posed, with its brand of raucous conservatism, forced CNN
to revamp its lineup and to poach Fox anchors, like Paula Zahn. CNN wasn't the
only media outlet rethinking its line. The imperative to keep up with Fox was

pulling the rest of the liberal American news media to the right. As a consequence of Murdoch's battles to launch Fox News in New York five years before, the United States went into the war in Afghanistan with more conservative media than it had had in decades. Across the world the war saw a return to hard news, away from "entertainment" stories.

The continuing rise of Fox, with its no-holds-barred view of the Taliban, terrorists, and all things un-American, underscored a new dynamic in American public opinion. Any war in the end degenerates to a bunch of talking heads discussing what might be happening. The heads on Fox News were the loudest and the most trenchant.

"We say we are absolutely balanced," Murdoch told Charlie Rose in December 2001. But there was no doubt whose side Fox was on and what Fox thought was good and what it thought was evil, Murdoch said. "When it comes to war and our country is at war, we are not neutral."

September 11 also spelled the end of Murdoch's hopes to win Hughes Electronics and DirecTV from General Motors. Owning satellite platforms around the world suddenly seemed much less appealing than owning a home-grown operation in America. In the crisis atmosphere that enfolded Washington, winning antitrust approval to merge with EchoStar now seemed attainable. In a sense Murdoch was also a victim of the game theory that his Oxford friend Robin Farquharson had expounded. A lifetime of opportunistic moves, of pushing the limits of the law, of coming out of any deal better than his rivals—and often better than his partners—had created a climate of automatic distrust of any deal that Rupert Murdoch was prepared to put his name to. General Motors pondered: Where was the hidden catch?

Murdoch's defeat in the race to win DirecTV sparked general celebration among U.S. media executives. Ergen was a tough competitor, but settling the deal with General Motors would leave him strapped for cash. He was less likely to indulge in the reckless price competition for which Murdoch was renowned. The strong growth that Hughes and EchoStar were both experiencing suggested that, by the time they merged, their 17.3 million subscribers in November 2001 would soon be nudging 20 million. Murdoch had based his bid for DirecTV on the belief that he could build subscriber numbers to 30 million—and that was with EchoStar as a competitor. The combined EchoStar-Hughes combination should easily top that number, heading toward 40 percent of the U.S. pay-television market.

Cable companies seized upon the emergence of one unified satellite broadcaster to justify new cable mergers. The larger that satellite grew, the more justification there was for bigger cable companies. Because cable companies operate in discrete territories, mergers don't reduce competition in any geographical area. Four weeks after General Motors sold Hughes to EchoStar, the AT&T board sold AT&T Broadband, the cable operation based on John Malone's former TCI and MediaOne, to the Roberts family's Comcast Corporation for $69 billion in stock and debt. The new cable giant would serve 21 million subscribers.

In early 2002 it looked like the major battle of the future would be between Microsoft and AOL Time Warner. Bill Gates had funded Murdoch's bid for Hughes as a means of challenging AOL Time Warner. Gates now offered $3 billion that had previously been earmarked for Murdoch's Hughes deal as a funding package for Comcast's bid for AT&T Broadband. Gates wanted to ensure that the network did not fall into the hands of rival bidder AOL Time Warner. A remorseless momentum was pushing these mergers. The bigger the mergers became, the more need there was for the remaining players to stage their own megamergers to be able to compete. And the more megamergers there were, the more likely they were to be approved by the FCC and the Justice Department. If the process did not run foul of antitrust reviews, it appeared likely that within five years, the bulk of the American pay-television market would be evenly split among three players— EchoStar, AOL Time Warner, and Comcast—each with about 30 million subscribers.

Ted Turner told the cable industry's western show in November 2001 that he expected the consolidation into just two cable players would take only a year or two, "It's sad we're losing so much diversity of thought."[1]

These mergers posed major threats to Disney, Viacom, and News Corp. When Murdoch launched Fox News in 1996, he believed he needed at least 25 million subscribers to start a new pay-television channel. So each of the three biggest pay-television operators that are emerging will be able to launch new channels and know that they will be commercially viable from day one. This represents a fundamental shift in the power balance of the media industry, between content producers and distribution networks. In the five-hundred-plus cable channel packages of the future, the rise and fall of content providers like Disney and Viacom will be determined by where their channels are placed on the channel dial and on the electronic program guide.

Murdoch had a chilling warning of what this could mean in 1996, when he owned Kesmai, the most popular online electronic gaming site on the Internet. For years it had run as the gaming site on the AOL home page. But in 1996 AOL quietly dropped Kesmai from its homepage and instead linked to its own new gaming site. Overnight customer traffic at Kesmai dropped 94 percent. The Internet offered infinite diversity, but unless you had a brand name like Amazon.com or you were linked with a high-profile portal, commercially you were consigned to the void. This became even more true after the tech crash, when surveys of Internet users showed that surfing was down. The novelty factor was over. People knew the sites they wanted. That's where they hung out.

Thus from two directions—from the Internet and from the pay-television networks—the range of media choices was narrowing. On December 14, three weeks after winning Hughes, Charlie Ergen did his first cash-for-carriage deal when Jean-Marie Messier at Vivendi agreed to invest $1.5 billion for 10 percent of EchoStar. In return, EchoStar would carry five Vivendi channels and use interactive technology from Vivendi's French cable operation, Canal Plus. Up to this point cash for carriage had been the exclusive privilege of the "greedy gatekeepers" of cable. But the world was changing. After the great venting of the tech stock crash, with only the biggest and toughest media operators surviving, the airlock door was closing. With the EchoStar deal, and an $11 billion deal Vivendi did days later to secure control of USA Networks' cable channels, Messier was rushing to make sure he was inside before the door closed.

So whatever happened to the information revolution? Gerry Levin's bold move to merger Time Warner with AOL, which set off the whole rush, had been a gamble on broadband Internet. In the early 1980s computers talked to one another over telephone lines at 300 bits per second. By the late 1990s cable modems were pumping out two megabits of data per second—which worked out at more than six thousand times faster than the modems of a decade and a half before. It takes about three megabits of data per second to carry a television picture. The advent of broadband suddenly made television on the Internet seem terrifyingly close, even with the crash of technology stocks. There were still huge technical and legal problems that would take some years to resolve. But one way or another they would be resolved, either with cable, or with the 3G generation of mobile phone, or with the next generation of low-orbit two-way satellite.

When the problems with broadband were resolved, the casualty toll would surely be enormous. In North American winters, why would consumers venture out in the snow to be mugged on the way to the corner video store, when they could download a wider selection of videos online? That meant conventional video chains were living on borrowed time. Why would pay-television viewers subscribe to a cable company that gave them a bundle of channels, most of which they didn't want, when they could order Discovery Channel directly online? That would be the end of cable companies. If today there are three thousand radio stations on the Net, what would life be like with three thousand television stations? What will that do to local free-to-air television? "When does the concept of prime-time scheduling no longer exist?" said one Internet consultant.[2]

And yet it didn't work out that way. After the tech crash, cable companies were no longer the victims; they were now the great survivors. Americans didn't really want to spend their time in the study leaning forward over the computer, Wall Street decided. They wanted to be twenty feet down the corridor in the living room, leaning back on the sofa with their feet up, watching television. In the middle of the worst advertising recession in a generation, the only winners in television were cable and satellite pay television. After going digital, cable over time would become interactive and offer email, video on demand, and cheap telephone calls. Inch by inch cable and satellite customers would shuffle into the brave new world of the future. They had no serious competitors. The tech crash had seen to that. When cable and television delivery became more interactive and eventually switched to Internet broadband through the cable wire and set-top box, the change would be so smooth that most subscribers probably would not even be aware it had happened. The gatekeepers would suffer no changing of the guard.

This change was five to ten years away. It means two things. First, while it is easy to dismiss the overfueled hype of the technology boom, the process of change has not stopped. Eventually the world's communication will run on broadband or ultrabroadband. At some point in the future, the constraints of geography and isolation will no longer apply to media. It will be as if the whole world is talking in one room. This will not be good news for minorities. The future will not favor those who speak softly. The second thing is that anyone who says this will happen next year, or the year after, is a charlatan or a lobbyist who wants the law changed for an opportunistic client. We can understand the future only with a dollop of credulousness and a bucket of skepticism. Which in the end sums up Rupert Murdoch's view of the information revolution. He never believed in media convergence, that the computer would morph into a television set.

"I'm sorry to break the bad news, but there's been a divorce," Elisabeth Murdoch announced at the Edinburgh International Television Festival in August 1998, two months before BSkyB launched its digital service. It was a little inside joke about the family's marriage problems as well as a comment on convergence. But it underlined that at the heart of Murdoch's strategy was a profound skepticism about where the information superhighway was going. BSkyB and Sky Global were a gamble that the Internet was a dud, that the future lay in pay television, two years before the rest of the world reached the same conclusion.

The media industry's need for secrecy—or at least to restrict information, sounds, and images to the paying customers—continues unabated. The furor over copyright, and programs like Napster that allowed Internet users to swap bootleg copies of music and films, loom as the biggest threat that mainstream media has faced. The fight against hackers and programs that break the encryption on DVDs and other products is likely to turn ugly.

By December 2001 Murdoch had turned his gaze to Europe. The deals that his efforts with General Motors triggered—the EchoStar sale, AT&T Broadband, and Vivendi's acrobatic antics—totaled $107 billion in four weeks. By May 2002, Hughes shares were still trading 20 percent under the EchoStar merger price. The gap represented a $5 billion credibility gap for General Motors: The market's initial reaction was that it didn't believe the Hughes deal would pass the antitrust review in late 2002. Hope flared again that Murdoch might still be able to snatch victory back, to perform yet another implausible reverse ferret. But Sky Global had been such a juggling act with Bill Gates and John Malone that, even if the EchoStar deal failed, it is far from certain whether Murdoch could put his complicated package for Hughes back together again. Meanwhile he had to live with the fallout.

Murdoch had been so desperate to get the Sky Global deal up that in September 2000 he did an asset swap with John Malone that left Malone's Liberty Media with 18 percent of News Corp, the largest stockholder. Murdoch held just 16 percent, but 29 percent of the voting stock. Murdoch took pains to stress that Malone held nonvoting stock. But it represented too much money, and Malone was far too clever, to dismiss. Any chance that Lachlan or James Murdoch had to head News Corp after Rupert's death would depend upon John Malone.

News Corp's share structure made it surprisingly vulnerable to hostile raiders. Two-thirds of its stock had no voting rights—and no reporting requirements either, which meant there was little regulation of shareholdings. News Corp voting stock, which was valued at only $15 billion, was the key to a string of associated media companies around the world that were worth $75 billion. In 2001 Eisner at Disney bought Fox Family for $5.2 billion, after Haim Saban exercized his option to sell out. If Eisner instead had bought a 20 percent stake in News Corp's voting stock for $3 billion, he probably would have had Murdoch on toast. Murdoch would still control News, but his position would be precarious.

Elsewhere the scorecard was mixed. In June 2000 after the animated movie *Titan* flopped, Fox closed the studios in Phoenix that had triggered the animation boom of the 1990s. Results at Fox Sports were up, and Fox News finally broke even. In December 2001 the Chinese government agreed to allow Star TV to broadcast a channel into Guangdong Province. Murdoch's Phoenix television also gained carriage rights in Guangdong. Seven months before, NDS won approval to help China set up a high-speed digital cable network. With 80 million subscribers in 2001, it would be the biggest cable network in the world—larger than all the other cable networks put together. It was Murdoch's speech in 1993 about technology as the great threat to totalitarian regimes that had prompted the Chinese government to pull the plug on satellite television. It was fear of Murdoch that persuaded the Chinese that their future lay with cable rather than satellite. "They feel comfortable that at the end of the day someone with a pair of wire-cutters can always cut a cable," a News Corp executive said. The decision to let NDS provide encryption, set-top boxes, software, and restricted access to Internet sites suggested that Murdoch was in line to become gatekeeper to the market after he himself had locked the door.

In early 2002, Murdoch managed to throw most of Europe's pay-television industry into shambles. It took just three weeks. Admittedly he had quite a lot of help doing this, from an advertising slump, a share market collapse, and disastrous management by his rivals. But a lesser mogul would have struggled to figure in quite so much corporate misfortune.

On March 27, ITV Digital, a struggling British pay-television broadcaster, appointed an administrator (a British insolvency process similar in some regards to Chapter 11) as its shareholders acknowledged that they could not compete with Murdoch's BSkyB colossus. Murdoch's cable rivals, NTL and Telewest, were hanging on by their fingernails as bankers struggled to restructure $15 billion in debt. Meanwhile, the government broadcasting regulator was still deliberating on the appropriate penalty to impose on BSkyB after an earlier finding that it had engaged in anti-competitive behavior.

On April 8, twelve days after ITV hit the wall, Germany's second largest media group, Leo Kirch's Kirch Media, also went the way of all flesh. The group had been fending off its Bavarian bankers since October, when an unnamed News Corp executive told the *Financial Times* that Murdoch was planning to take over the Kirch group as it struggled with its debt problems. The spotlight that this report (later denied by News) threw on Kirch's finances helped trigger a crisis among Kirch's bankers which was fueled by Murdoch's regular announcements that he would use put-option agreements to demand repayment of all the $1.8 billion that BSkyB and News Corp had invested in Kirch. The specter of Murdoch taking over German media had politicians in a funk. It was another nationality thing. In a perfect world Murdoch's task would have been easier, because he would have been born Bavarian. It would be months before it was clear whether Murdoch had orchestrated a brilliant campaign that turned him into Germany's new master media player, or whether he had just lost his shirt.

In Italy, Murdoch's Stream pay-TV operation and its rival Telepiu, owned by Jean-Marie Messier's Vivendi Universal, were losing more than $500 million a year. In April 2002 these losses triggered a management crisis in Vivendi. Jean-Marie Messier was battling to retain his position, in the face of a backlash by investors and French politicians to news that Messier had sacked the head of Canal Plus, Pierre Lescure, over the poor results.

The big losers in these developments were Europe's soccer clubs, with more than 100 clubs in Britain and Germany forecast to close after ITV and Kirch defaulted on their big sports rights contracts. Murdoch had triggered a worldwide surge in broadcast rights for sports with his 1992 deal with BSkyB and the Premier League, then by bidding up the NFL rights in 1994. The tidal wave of money into sport had flowed mainly to the players—so much so that in many sports all but the leading teams were under financial pressure. The clubs were locked into high-salary contracts to keep their players, but now the money from pay-television rights to pay these salaries was gone. In the long term, U.S. broadcasters like NBC were signaling that the great sports boom was over. In the media industry, sports rights are pure content deals, but in the new media economy content is no longer king.

Then in the spring of 2002 came the most sensational report of all from Murdoch's archipelago. The secret side of News Corp once more grabbed the spotlight with the most bizarre tale of Murdoch's career. On March 12, 2002, Canal Plus filed a lawsuit in the California District claiming triple damages for losses of more than $1 billion from what it described as an illegal piracy campaign run by Murdoch's encryption operation, NDS Group.[3] NDS, formerly News Datacom in Israel, has always been the most colorful arm of Murdoch's empire, from the time it was run by a U.S. fugitive to the Israeli tax raid in 1996 and to the 1997 Israeli police investigation into wiretapping tapes discovered in the office of the chief executive, Abe Peled. In fact, the roots of the new controversy went back to those wild days in 1996 when the worldwide investigation into Clinger was at its height—and News Corp had learned the advantages of covert intelligence. The problem was that pirates had cracked the NDS code.

The NDS Videoguard system was based on an encryption algorithm developed by Professor Adi Shamir. However, according to a former employee, for cost reasons the early cards that News Datacom made for Sky and later BSkyB did not carry the entire algorithm. This oversight allowed British video pirates to break the code and produce a wave of counterfeit smartcards. These allowed people to watch the encrpyted BSkyB programs without paying. By 1994 there was a thriving piracy trade in counterfeit BSkyB smartcards, which was costing BSkyB millions of dollars.

In 1996, in between sleuthing after Michael Clinger and negotiating with Israeli tax officers, NDS quietly set up its own covert operation aimed at the pay-television pirates. Reuven Hazak, the former deputy head of Shin Bet, the Israeli internal security service, who was interrogated along with Peled over the wiretapping tapes found in Peled's office, became the NDS security chief in Israel. In the United States, NDS hired Chris Morris, a former army counterintelligence officer who had run sting operations in North America for General Instruments to jail cable-television pirates, as U.S. director of special projects. In the U.K., NDS later hired former Scotland Yard commander Ray Adams as director of security for NDS in Britain, after he was cleared by two inquiries into his links with criminal figures whom he had used as informants.

There was a second, secret arm to the NDS strategy. It was to put a group of hackers on the NDS payroll. It was known as the Swiss Cheese Group. Apparently NDS believed in this way it could keep abreast of developments in the hacking world. It also tapped the hackers' expertise to test their own products, and those of their rivals. Germany was the most fruitful recruiting ground, among hackers associated with the Chaos Computer Club. NDS tried for two years to recruit its most famous member, Boris Floricic, a brilliant Berlin hacker known as Tron.

In October 1998, Floricic's body was found hanging from a tree in a Berlin park, with both feet on the ground. "We're always looking for excellent engineers, and we contacted him with a view to employing him as a consultant," NDS spokesperson Margot Field told the London *Guardian* in December 1998. Floricic's father found among his son's papers an NDS invoice dated July 12, 1998, which read, "Hello Boris, here are the analog devices, good luck." Police say many companies tried to recruit Floricic. They concluded he committed suicide.

Floricic had published a paper about hacking, or reverse-engineering, smart-cards with Marcus Kuhn, a student at the University of Erlangen in Germany (now at Cambridge), who ran a user group called TV-Crypt. In 1999 Kuhn cowrote with another young hacker, Oliver Kömmerling, what became one of the standard texts on how to reverse-engineer a state-of-the-art smartcard, a piece titled "Design Principles for Tamper-Resistant Smartcards," using acid treatments, microscopic probes, laser cutting, ion beam manipulation, and other techniques. In an affidavit filed with the California District Court, Kömmerling says he has worked as a consultant for NDS since mid-1996, helping set up the NDS Matam Centre research facility in Haifa by early 1997, and recruiting and training all the Matam engineers. By 2001, NDS owned a 40 percent stake in Kömmerling's consulting group.

Another NDS recruit in April 1996 was a young hacker living in Germany named Christopher Tarnovsky. I located two 1995 postings to a U.K. Internet bulletin board that are signed Christopher Tarnovsky, with an e-mail address from a U.S. army base in Germany, in which he asks for help hacking a D2Mac encryption chip: "I own a copy of the Black Book and have disassembled the code for dual & single chip but still am a little confused. . . ." Several hours later he repeated the appeal: "Can anybody out there explain the EuroCrypt M/S packet's structure a little bit to me!??! I have the source to single/dual chip version but the packet's structure, etc. is still UNKNOWN! . . . I have the 'Black Book.' That's not enough though."

Another hacker who knew Tarnovsky through Kuhn's TV-Crypt user group and ended up doing consulting work was Jan Saggiori, in Geneva. In 1996 Saggiori introduced Tarnovsky to a Canadian, Allen Menard, who ran a piracy website from British Columbia called DR7.com, and later to another Swiss-based hacker, Vesselin Ivanon Nedeltchev, known as Vesco. Saggiori says in an affidavit in the Canal Plus case that he believed that in 2001 Vesco was working directly for Reuven Hazak at NDS in Israel.

NDS found its biggest problem was in North America, where it provided smartcards for DirecTV, the satellite broadcaster owned by General Motors. NDS went hard after pay-television pirates based in Canada. Simultaneous raids by the Royal Canadian Mounted Police, U.S. Customs, and the FBI in November 1996 saw sixty people arrested for video piracy, but convictions were hard to come by. Canadian courts found it was not illegal for Canadians to pirate the U.S. DirecTV signal, which by law could not be sold in Canada.

By 1998, DirecTV's problems with piracy were so severe that it issued a formal notification to NDS that it was reconsidering its encryption system, and examining its rival, NagraStar, owned by the Swiss Kudelski group, used by EchoStar. At that time Nagra was also hit by a wave of piracy. The hacking community is full of finger pointing, and Nagra was told by some dealers that NDS had released Nagra's source code, which was published on DR7.com.

Tarnovsky, who now lived in California, and his friend Al Menard fell under suspicion. In May 2001, EchoStar security officers used an associate of Menard's to meet Menard in a hotel room in Vancouver, where they urged him to become a witness against NDS and Tarnovsky. However, Menard vigorously denied that Tarnovsky had provided him with Nagra code and said the accusation was nonsense. No further action was taken.

Friction also arose in Britain, with Internet speculation that NDS was linked to a piracy site, hoic.com, also known as the House of Ill Compute, which helped hackers make counterfeit smart cards for ITV Digital, a rival of BSkyB that uses the Canal Plus system. NDS later confirmed that U.K. security chief Adams paid several thousand pounds into the personal bank account of the man who ran the site. Adams says he was not aware the Canal Plus software codes were on the site.

Meanwhile Canal Plus Technologies was also investigating how pirates had been able to flood the market in Italy in late 1999 with counterfeit smartcards that had devastated its Telepiu pay-television operation. By mid-2001 Canal Plus head of security Gilles Kaehlin believed he had tracked the leak down to a file posted on DR7 on March 26, 1999. Earlier that month, Rupert Murdoch had met Jean-Marie Messier of Vivendi Universal, the controlling shareholder in Canal Plus, but talks to merge BSkyB with Canal Plus had broken down. News had been planning to invest in the Italian pay-television operation Stream SpA. Vivendi had been anxious that News Corp stay out of Italy, to avoid competition with the Canal Plus pay-television arm, Telepiu.

Three weeks later, Lachlan Murdoch married Sarah O'Hare on March 27. In Australia, all eyes in the media were focused on the Murdoch family property, Cavan, near Canberra, where Rupert and Anna Murdoch suspended divorce proceedings briefly to stand uneasily together on this happiest of days. What no one at Cavan knew was that, on the other side of the world, where it was still March 26, Allen Menard in British Columbia was posting a computer file on his website, DR7.com. Three years later that file, titled Secarom.zip, would become a $3 billion headache for the Murdochs. The multibillion-dollar question is, where did Menard get the file?

In an affidavit filed in the Canal Plus court case, Kömmerling, who now runs a security consultancy called ADSR that is 40 percent owned by NDS, said in early 1999 he was given a copy of a written summary of the Canal Plus code that had been extracted from a Canal Plus smartcard by the NDS laboratory in Haifa. He later recognised the code file posted on the DR7 site as the same file. NDS employees told him that the code file had been supplied to DR7. The file was posted on DR7 with a Readme text file which said in part, "This file has been downloaded from www.DR7.com. . . . We ask for nothing in return but a simple acknowledgment and thanks and those who redistribute as their own without reference to the source are true losers."

In a second affidavit, Jan Saggiori said when he downloaded the code from DR7 that weekend, part of the code was lost in the transfer. He asked Tarnovsky if he could obtain the missing file from Menard at DR7. Saggiori's affidavit includes a printout of an e-mail he says Tarnovsky sent him with the missing binary file on March 28 as an attachment, which read: "Good news from up north here. Enjoy, keep for you please . . . extremely top secret!"

Gilles Kaehlin says that by mid-2001, while he had narrowed the source of its pirated smartcards to the DR7 file, he didn't know how the file got to DR7, when he met Tarnovsky in London on August 15–16. On October 5 Kaehlin flew to California to meet Tarnovsky at his home in Carlsbad, California. In his affidavit filed in the California District Court, Kaehlin said that Tarnovsky spoke of leaving NDS, but said it would be "extremely difficult for him to leave NDS because he was afraid of certain NDS employees."

However, in what Kaehlin says was a "nonverbal method of communication," Tarnovsky said that NDS was responsible for the publication of the Canal Plus code and that the code had been sent to him by Reuven Hazak via John Norris. Kaehlin says in his affidavit he met Tarnovsky again in Santa Monica on December 16, when Tarnovsky told him "he would tell the truth to the court if he were called to testify but that he would not be the 'whistleblower' on NDS's illegal activities, because he feared too much for his life and that of his family."

In early January 2002, Tarnovsky sent Kaehlin a brief e-mail saying he did not want to talk to him anymore.

Norris in his affidavit says he has never had possession of a file titled Secarom.zip, and denies all of the Canal Plus claims. He says Tarnovsky also denied to him that he had supplied the file to DR7. The NDS chief executive, Abe Peled, also denies the claims, linking the lawsuit to an attempt to extort a higher price in talks to merge Canal Plus Technologies and NDS.

"This is not the suit of a cheated business seeking protection from piracy," NDS said in a motion to dismiss the claim. "It is an attempt by an inept competitor to shift the blame for its incompetence, to damage its skilled competitor behind the shield of litigation privilege and to extract an unfair price in merger negotiations." The colorful claims by Canal Plus were not tested in court by cross-examination by the NDS lawyers. Even if Tarnovsky did supply code to DR7, which was not proven, the Canal Plus case must prove that he was instructed to do so by NDS management. Otherwise he would be just another rogue employee.

Nevertheless the controversy was widening. In Britain, ITV Digital said it was considering suing NDS for £100 million on similar claims of piracy. The *Observer* newspaper in London reported that the industrial espionage division of the French secret service was investigating the case. Kaehlin was listed on a Canal Plus website as a former French Interior Minister and Canal Plus is believed to have close links with the French intelligence community. The U.S. trade publication *Satellite News* described NDS senior executives as former agents of the Israeli intelligence agency, Mossad. A former NDS employee I contacted confirmed the Mossad links. He also said NDS routinely provided British MI5 with "shortcuts" which allowed it to decrypt BSkyB programming, as a security measure. This raises interesting questions about NDS contracts in China to provide encryption technology to the country's huge cable networks. Then in June 2002, Rupert Murdoch announced that his Stream SpA would buy Telepiu from Vivendi for 1.5 billion euros. A condition of the deal was that Canal Plus drop its lawsuit against NDS. Whatever happened to the Canal Plus smart card may never be known.

Where did all this leave Keith Rupert Murdoch? Faced with reverses on all fronts in early 2002, could he still pull off some sort of unlikely reverse ferret, and grab back the momentum he had lost when DirecTV slipped from his grasp, and the entire Sky Global vision faded away?

For Murdoch, Sky Global offered some sort of final redemption. It represented a chance to redefine himself, to stamp his own version of reality across the world: his legacy determined by one throw of the dice. Murdoch has never had an infallible gift for seeing into the future. For much of his life he has got it wrong with the crystal ball as often as not. He is more businessman than wild-eyed visionary. He has made his empire betting against technology rather than for it. When he moved his British newspapers to Wapping in 1986, the move was so focused on secrecy and overturning the power of the printers' unions that he installed antiquated presses that had to be replaced within a couple of years. With Sky Television in Britain, he bet the company that existing, off-the-shelf PAL television would outsell the latest technology. By defeating the government-approved BSB satellite service, Murdoch put high-definition television in Britain—and arguably Europe—on hold for a decade. His great Sky gamble in 1997 was about derailing the move toward a technological future based upon fiber-optic cable. Murdoch's Sky Global platforms in 2000 were based upon putting limits on the Internet, replacing e-commerce with a simpler t-commerce based on television. What Murdoch lacks in crystal-ball abilities or in commitment to technology he makes up for with his remarkable capacity to spot a commercial opportunity and seize upon it. More than that, his genius lies in the survival skills he shows when his latest venture goes wrong. His ability to change the rules, to produce his own versions of reality, to produce the grand illusions that dreamers need, is unparalleled. In an interview with James Harding of the *Financial Times* on June 12, 2002, Murdoch confirmed the new power balance in media, "the issue of people who are going to deliver your programmes. . . . Cable is consolidating. . . . Instead of having twenty gatekeepers, you are going to have three or four," he said. "For content providers, that is very bad news. So, you try to protect yourself in having some distribution power." He talked for the first time of his younger son, James, sharing the succession at News with Lachlan. Murdoch also said he was considering converting to Catholicism. "I believe in the spirituality of human beings, I believe in a God," Murdoch said. "I was brought up as a Protestant . . . I was married for a long time to a Catholic wife [Anna, whom he left for Wendi], which gave me a great insight into the real strength of the Catholic Church."

Murdoch had some barbs about his competitors, starting with "mad" Ted Turner and Gerry Levin, "the chairman of the company which made the biggest blunder" of the tech boom. The Time Warner directors who agreed to the merger must now look back, Murdoch said, and wonder, "What the hell were we smoking that weekend?" And Bill Gates: "I don't dislike Bill," he said, "but Warren Buffett says that Bill Gates is the kind of man who, if he saw a competitor drowning, would push a hose down his throat to make sure." Buffett flatly denied any such comment. And poor Jean-Marie Messier, who suffered from "never having met a journalist he didn't give an interview to." And Michael Eisner? Earlier, Murdoch told Michael Wolff that he had to get Peter Chernin to negotiate the $5.3 billion sale of Fox Family to Eisner because "I couldn't keep a straight face."

He is happy to talk about the people around him, but who is the real Rupert Murdoch?

Decades of Murdoch media interviews suggest that the last person to whom you could address that question is Murdoch himself. And yet no one else would begin to have the answer. In interview after interview Murdoch repeats the same lines, which are no more convincing for the repetition. When Charlie Rose asked him in December 2001 if he was ruthless, Murdoch told him that his reputation was "probably because I've been too close to a lot of executives," and that when newspaper editors were failing, after he had lived with it for a long time, he had had to let them go. It was "very hurtful," but he had a responsbility to look after the tens of thousands of other people who work for News Corp.

This is a formulaic answer he has been making for decades. Neither Murdoch's critics nor his admirers would really suggest, as he does, that his empire building has been motivated chiefly by public-spiritedness. Anna Murdoch, breaking her silence for the first time after the divorce in July 2001, said Rupert had become someone whom she did not know. Were the people who criticized her husband right, Australian journalist David Leser asked her. "Yes," she whispered.[4]

Embittered ex-wives make poor character references. In a world full of people trying to be Rupert Murdoch, where Charlie Ergen, Sumner Redstone, Michael Eisner, Jean-Marie Messier, and so many others have all measured themselves against the Murdoch model, the most important question is not, Who is Rupert Murdoch? In a a sense they are all Murdoch. At any moment in time he is defined most clearly in contrast to the person he is standing next to. He is a superb opportunist, and like many opportunists he is too ordinary to classify. Murdoch is an unprepossessing man, drab to the point of colorlessness, who has built a worldwide empire that has immeasurably changed the way we communicate. He is both a product and a catalyst for a broader wave of social and economic changes that are reshaping the world. To lionize Murdoch, or to demonize him, is to suggest that when he dies, this process that he rides so well will somehow stop. As if there were no other riders.

What of Murdoch's corporate personality? Is the empire he has built any less ambiguous than he is himself? The Israeli-based NDS Group's adventures are a recurring leitmotif in his empire building—this from an operation whose business is all about being indecipherable. It is all very well for Murdoch to maintain that News Corp reflects "my values, my character." But which News Corp are we talking about? Is it the successful worldwide enterprise that reports substantial profits each year? Or the more modest earner portrayed by U.S. accounting standards? Is it the offshore entity that pays minimal tax, or the one that hires private investigators to mount an international manhunt through the tax havens of the world? Or the one that told the FCC year after year that Americans controlled the Fox television stations, while at the same time it told the SEC that control of the stations lay with News Corp? When lawyers for the Australian Rugby League referred in court to an ethical void in News Corp's corporate culture, it was an emotional judgment. It is easier to say that the heart of News Corp's corporate culture is a mystery. It is a place that is held together by magic. It is hard to say how long News Corp will be able to stay together when the master magician departs.

Appearance is everything. At the heart of the postmodern view of the world is the notion that we continue. We survive. Impermanent life goes on, no matter how exhilarated, bleak, or mundane is the mood of the day. The gossamer thread that weaves our world from a thousand unresolved moments continues to unravel unmindfully ahead of us. If there is no final bright morning or dark sunset, if reality is instead a succession of jerky frames that stretch before and behind us, like a silent film played upon an ancient, flickering projector—then what are we to make of Rupert Murdoch? This figure who endlessly reinvents himself, who can be known only as a disconnected sequence of strobe photographs, remains at the end of the day as Medusa-like, as fickle and unknowable as the realities he creates. He is, in the full sense of the phrase, the man of the moment.

CHRONOLOGY

April 9, 1929	Helen Handbury born.
March 11, 1931	Keith Rupert Murdoch born.
September 20, 1935	Anne Kantor born.
January 21, 1939	Janet Calvert-Jones born.
October 4, 1952	Sir Keith Murdoch dies.
October 1953	Rupert Murdoch joins News Ltd. as publisher.
March 1, 1956	Rupert marries Patricia Booker.
August 12, 1958	Prudence Murdoch born to Rupert and Patricia Murdoch.
January 19, 1960	Criminal libel charges filed against News Ltd.; hung jury.
May 21	Murdoch buys *Daily Mirror* in Sydney.
December 1, 1961	Murdoch meets President Kennedy.
April 28, 1967	Rupert Murdoch marries Anna Torv.
August 22, 1968	Elisabeth Murdoch born.
January 2, 1969	Murdoch wins control of *News of the World* in London.
October	Murdoch buys London *Sun*.
September 8, 1971	Lachlan Murdoch born.
December 13, 1972	James Murdoch born.
October 25, 1973	Murdoch buys *San Antonio Express and News*. Murdochs move to New York.
February 4, 1974	Murdoch launches *National Star*.
1975	Bill Gates and Paul Allen found Microsoft.
September 30, 1975	Gerry Levin hires satellite to transmit Frazier-Ali "Thriller in Manila" fight over HBO.
November 19, 1976	Murdoch buys *New York Post*, and later *New York* magazine.
July 13, 1977	New York blackout. Post headline: "24 Hours of Terror: A City Ravaged."
July-Sept	"Son of Sam" stories boost *New York Post* sales.
August, 1979	Anna Murdoch's article "Motherhood and Mythology" is published.
1980	Charles Ergen moves to Denver to sell satellite dishes.
January, 1981	Murdoch buys London *Times* and *Sunday Times*.
April 23, 1983	Times runs Hitler diaries.
December 1	News Corporation buys 6.7 percent of Warner Brothers.
December 29	*Nirvana* runs Ted Turner on *Condor* aground off Hobart. Warner Brothers buy Chris-Craft TV stations. Wedtech directors in secret illegal side deal.
1984	Daniel Garner's Advanced Communications wins 110WL DBS orbital license in United States.
February 10, 1985	Murdoch's British editors plan in secret New York meeting plan move to Wapping.
March 21	News announces it is buying half of Twentieth Century–Fox for $250 million.

March 24	Murdoch discusses TV deal at cocktail party with Barry Diller and John Kluge of Metromedia.
April 18	Ted Turner launches unsuccessful bid for CBS.
May 2	News announces deal to buy Metromedia TV stations for net $1.55 billion.
July 26	Murdoch reveals plan to launch Fox network.
August 7	Turner to buy MGM for $US1.6 billion.
September 15	Rupert Murdoch takes U.S. citizenship.
September 23	News buys other half of Twentieth Century–Fox for $325 million.
January 24, 1986	Wapping newspaper dispute begins in London.
March 6	Michael Milken raises junk preferred stock for Metromedia deal.
March 26	Milken raises $1.2 billion junk bonds for Turner's acquisition of MGM.
December 3	Murdoch bids for father's old company, *Herald and Weekly Times*.
March 1987	Cable companies bail out Ted Turner from MGM mess.
July	SEC in settlement with Michael Clinger over stock fraud claims.
October 13	Murdoch attends Malcolm Forbes' cocktail party, skips News Corporation annual meeting.
October 20	Australian stock market crashes after Wall Street.
October 21	Murdochs' bank takes security on New York penthouse.
October 23	Queensland Press buys News Corp stock from Cruden above market price. Rupert and Anna sign further bank security in New York.
December 8	Queensland Press closes deal with three-year bank loan.
December 22	Late-night amendment by Senator Ernest Hollings forces Murdoch to sell *New York Post*.
February, 1988	News Corp sets up News Datacom in Israel.
March 7	Peter Kalikow buys *New York Post*.
Jun-08	Murdoch announces plan to launch Sky Television.
October 31	News buys Triangle Publications including *TV Guide* for $3 billion.
February 1989	Sky begins broadcasting.
October 4, 1990	David Devoe in debt crisis talks with seven bankers.
November 2	Friday Sky and BSB Holdings merge to form BSkyB.
November 8	New York grand jury issues arrest warrant for Clinger.
December 6	Pittsburgh National refuses to roll $A10 million from 1987 Queensland Press deal.
February 1, 1991	4.15 A.M.: Citicorp calls DeVoe to say last bank has signed override Agreement.
March	Australian Securities Commission launches investigation into *Queensland Press*.
October	News Corp stock offering.
November 6	Israeli shareholders agree to sell out of News Datacom for $12 million.
March 9, 1992	BSkyB operations reach break-even point.
April 13	Clinger meets News representatives in London.
June 29	BSkyB agrees to large price rise for smartcards.
July 1	News Datacom sale settles with Clinger and Israelis.
July-August	Murdochs finalise Cruden buyout while on Alaskan cruise.
January 24, 1993	Peter Kalikow announces Steve Hoffenberg will save *New York Post*.
March 23	Pat Robertson's bodyguard knifed at Kinshasa Intercontinental Hotel.

March 29	Murdoch arrives at *New York Post* newsroom.
September 2	Murdoch's banqueting hall speech in London. Technology is unambiguous threat to totalitarian regimes everywhere.
September	Fox Children's Network gambles on oddball show called *Power Rangers*.
January 1994	Fox wins NFL rights from CBS.
March	Fox to set up animation studio in Phoenix.
March 4	FCC asks Fox for details of alien ownership of Fox television stations.
April	Murdoch drops BBC from Star TV.
	Fox launches f/X cable channel.
May 22	News invests $500 million in Ron Perelman's New World television chain.
May 23	Fox tells FCC it is 99 percent owned by News Corp.
June	Newt Gingrich meets literary agent Lynn Chu to discuss book.
September	*Vanity Fair* runs its first New Establishment issue.
September	John Malone at TCI agrees to buy DBS license at 110WL from Dan Garner for $45 million.
October 20	Murdoch makes "Century of Networking" speech in Melbourne.
November 28	Murdoch meets with Gingrich after Republicans' congressional landslide.
December 1	Lynn Chu formally appointed Gingrich's agent.
December 7	FCC announces Fox inquiry.
December 9	HarperCollins executive prematurely announces Gingrich book contract for $2 million.
December 20	HarperCollins wins Gingrich book option with $4.5 million two-book bid.
March 30, 1995	Super League football war begins with secret Sydney meeting.
March 31	News execs briefed on Clinger fraud in London hotel by Abraham Nantel.
April 19	FCC staff recommends forced divestiture of Fox.
April 26	FCC revokes Daniel Garner's 110WL license.
May-04	FCC commisioners clear Fox of deceptive conduct allegation 5–0.
May-10	MCI announces $2 billion investment in News.
July 31	Disney in $19 billion stock deal to buy Capital Cities/ABC.
August 2	News pulls down first $1 billion from MCI.
August 10	Malone and Murdoch meeting recorded by Ken Auletta; Fox Sports born.
August	Time Warner buys Turner Broadcasting for $7.5 billion.
September 15	Michael Clinger signs cooperation agreement with Israeli tax office.
January 24, 1996	MCI wins FCC auction of 110 WL DBS orbital license for $672.5 million.
January	Murdoch approaches Pat Robertson about buying into Family Channel.
February	Communications Act proclaimed by President Clinton.
February 10	News International sues Michael Clinger in British High Court.
February 23	Australian judge finds News, Super League "corrupted individuals."
March 3	Ergen launches EchoStar's Dish network.
April 26	Murdoch borrows $A373million to pay out family.
June	BSkyB retain Premier League rights for £674 million.
	Murdoch announces launch of JSkyB in Japan.
July 11	Murdoch and Perelman haggle over New World at Herb Allen's conference.

July 16	MSNBC cable channel launches. Murdoch believes Time Warner will run Fox News.
September 12	Federal Trade Commission approves Time Warner-Turner merger.
September 17	Gerry Levin tells Murdoch that Time Warner won't run Fox News in New York.
September 26	Fox secures cable rights for Dodgers from Tele-TV, announces launch of Fox Sports West 2.
September 27	Ted Turner compares Murdoch to Hitler. *Post* says, 'Is Ted Nuts? You Decide.'
October 1	News/Time Warner meeting with deputy mayor. Cocktail party for Fox News launch.
October 4	Australian appeals court overturns Super League finding: Finds a promise is not binding.
October 7	Fox News begins broadcasting.
October 10	Time Warner–Turner merger completes. Fox sues Time Warner for breach of promise.
October 15	News Corp annual meeting in Adelaide, Murdoch announces News Datacom IPO.
October 20	Israelis raid News Datacom offices.
January 7, 1997	Peter O'Malley announces he is selling Dodgers.
January 12	Michael Clinger hears wiretapping tapes at National Serious Crime Unit in Jerusalem.
January 30	Michael Clinger claims to see fax of tapes transcript. In New York, UJA names Murdoch Humanitarian of the Year.
February 4	Disney's Mighty Ducks sue Fox Sports West 2.
February 7	Pat Robertson backs out of News Corp/TCI deal to buy IFE, later calls Murdoch for new talks.
February 7	Murdoch flies to Denver for exploratory meeting with Charlie Ergen at EchoStar.
February 10	Justice Lindsay suspends further hearing on Israeli bugging allegations.
February 13	Murdoch flies to Denver for formal merger talks with EchoStar. Mid-February Murdoch meets Malone to discuss new IFE deal, tells Malone of EchoStar plans.
February 24	News Corp and EchoStar announce Sky merger.
February 24	Fox sues Disney for inciting cable companies not to run Fox Sports West 2.
March 2	News Datacom's Abe Peled interviewed by Israeli police.
March 10	Malone has angry meeting with Murdoch over Sky, IFE and Fox Sports.
March 17	Murdoch buys Heritage Media for $1.4 billion.
March 18	London *Sun* backs Labour party's Tony Blair in British election.
March 24	*Weekly Standard* calls Newt Gingrich "roadkill on highway of American politics."
April 8	Murdoch presents buyout plan to IFE board in New York, talks to Malone about Primestar.
April 10	Murdoch addresses Senate Commerce Committee in Washington.
April 14	Labour Party spokesman Dr Lewis Moonie says Labour will relax U.K. cross media rules.
April 27	*Virginian Pilot* story of Operation Blessing planes used for diamond mining.
April 28	Murdochs' thirtieth wedding anniversary in Bahamas.

May 1	Blair wins British election.
May 2	Pat Robertson offers to take $150 million cut in stock payout from Murdoch.
May 6	Chase Carey flies to Denver, tells Ergen he must resign.
May 8	Fox execs begin final negotiations for Dodgers.
May 9	News Corp tells EchoStar the alliance is over. Ergen sues for $5 billion.
May 12	O'Malley announces Murdoch buying Dodgers.
May 16	After press criticism, IFE says all stockholders to receive same price in takeover.
May 21-28	Murdochs cruising on Great Barrier Reef.
May 29	Murdoch feted at UJA Humanitarian of the Year dinner.
June 2	Fox Kids misses IFE bid deadline, Disney makes higher offer.
June 9	Microsoft buys 11.5 percent of Comcast Corp for $1 billion.
June 9	Malone in $1.1 billion with Cablevision Systems.
June 11	News-Primestar deal announced. IFE board accepts Fox Kids bid.
June 22	Fox Sports pays $850 million for half of Cablevision's MSG network.
July 1	HarperCollins in U.K. signs book contract with Chris Patten's agent.
July 3	Murdoch meets Vice Premier Zhu Rongji in Beijing.
July 23	Time Warner agrees to run Fox News.
December	Inter-government task force meets in Sydney to investigate News Corp's tax structures.
January 15, 1998	NFL finalizes eight-year rights contracts worth $17.6 billion.
February 5	HarperCollins decides to drop Patten book; lawyers gag its editor, Stuart Profitt.
March 6	HarperCollins settles Patten suit after media storm.
March 11	Murdoch turns 67, the age at which his father died of a heart attack.
March 17	Tony Blair discusses Murdoch with Italian PM, setting off new controversy.
March 23	*Titanic* dominates Oscars, Murdochs' last major public appearance.
April 3	News announces tax settlement in Israel.
April 21	Liz Smith at *New York Post* announces Murdochs have split.
April 28	Murdochs' thirty-first wedding anniversary.
May 12	Blair announces government will vote down anti-Murdoch amendment to competition bill.
May 12	Justice Department files antitrust suit to block sale of ASkyB to Primestar.
June 24	AT&T announces deal to buy John Malone's TCI for $68 billion. With January 1999 bid for MediaOne, AT&T outlays $110 billion for cable groups.
June 26	Final separation date that appears on Murdoch divorce papers.
September	Internet stocks on Wall Street, bubbling since June, now take off.
September 7	Manchester United and BSkyB confirm £623 million takeover talks.
October 1	BSkyB launches digital channels.
October 4	*New York Times* reports Murdoch living at Mercer Hotel in Soho with Wendi Deng.
October 14	ASkyB pulls out of Primestar deal.
October 29	U.K. Trade Secretary Peter Mandelson refers the Manchester November30 ASkyB signs deal with EchoStar.
March 1999	Talks between Messier and Murdoch over merging BSkyB and Canal Plusbreak down.

March 26	Al Menard posts Canal Plus Tecnologies smartcard code on DR7.com site.
March 27	Lachlan Murdoch marries Sarah O'Hare.
May 5	BSkyB announces its digital boxes will be free.
June 8	Murdochs' divorce finalized.
June 25	Rupert marries Wendi Deng on *Morning Glory*.
January 10, 2000	AOL–Time Warner merger announced.
February 14	News announces Sky Global proposal.
April 15	SkyNews reports Rupert Murdoch has been diagnosed with prostate cancer.
June 14	BSkyB wins Premier League auction.
June 17	James Murdoch marries Kathryn Hufschmid.
June 20	Sky Global IPO filed with SEC.
June 20	Vivendi, Canal Plus announce $34 billion Seagrams takeover.
August 5	News buys Chris-Craft television stations for $5.3 billion.
February 6, 2001	GM approves due diligence for Sky Global-Hughes deal.
February 20	Hughes chairman Michael Smith walks out of meeting with Murdoch.
April 23	Murdoch flies to Detroit for GM talks; Col Allan appointed to *New York Post*.
May 24	EchoStar files 8-K, stating GM willing to discuss Hughes deal.
May 25	Michael Smith resigns.
July 19	EchoStar says Hughes has suspended talks.
August 5	Ergen announces bear hug for Hughes.
August 12	EchoStar meets with GM execs in LA.
September 11	Murdoch stranded in Washington. Ergen due to meet GM in New York, flight cancelled.
September 16	EchoStar and GM executives meet in DirecTV offices in LA.
September 17	GM's Ronald L Zarella decides on % car financing offer. Murdoch cuts cash offer for Hughes by $1 billion.
October 15	S&P downgrades GM credit rating.
October 17	UBS announces EchoStar has $5.5 billion funding, during Hughes analysts' briefing.
October 26	UBS bails out of EchoStar bid over loan clause.
October 27	Daylong GM board meeting postpones decision on Hughes, Murdoch walks away.
October 29	GM announces Hughes-EchoStar deal, agreed to on previous night.
December 19	Comcast bids $72 billion for AT&T Broadband.
March 12, 2002	Canal Plus Technologies sues NDS for $1 billion in video piracy suit.
June 8, 2002	Embattled Jean-Marie Messier sells Telepiu in Italy to Murdochs' Stream SpA, agrees to drop lawsuit against NDS.

NOTES

Introduction

1. Howard Anderson, "The Man Who Would Be Media King," *Upside* 9, no. 8 (Sept. 1997), pp.110–16.

Chapter 1: A Business of Ferrets

1. Even after the circulation gain, the discounted cover price was costing the *Post* at least $25 million a year, on top of preexisting losses estimated at $20 million. This is before the $250 million cost of the color printing plant in the South Bronx.
2. Rupert Murdoch, interview by *The Economist,* March 4, 1996.
3. Andrew Sullivan, "A Press Lord Without a Rosebud," *New York Times,* Jan. 17, 1993.
4. Peter Chippindale and Chris Horrie, *Stick It Up Your Punter!* (New York: Pocket Books, 1999).
5. Greg Sargent, "Radio Rudy vs. Ferret Man," *New York Observer,* Feb. 8, 1999, p. 2.
6. Greg Sargent and Josh Benson, "Murdoch's *New York Post* Gleefully Roasts Hillary," *New York Observer,* Dec. 6, 1999, p. 1.
7. As the *Post* made clear with the mayor, radiation therapy, besides commonly causing short-term impotence, can have drastic effects on the production of both sperm and semen. When sperm production resumes, there is an additional prospect of radiation-induced abnormalities. For this reason doctors treating prostate cancer with radiation routinely recommend that patients produce sperm samples for storage before treatment begins. This is the medically advisable course for a seventy-year-old prospective father, whose child would be a joint heir to a fortune worth more than $5 billion.

Chapter 2: A Muddle of Moguls

1. "Who's Afraid of Rupert Murdoch," *Frontline,* PBS, Jan. 1, 1995.
2. General Motors–EchoStar press conference, New York, Oct. 29, 2001.
3. "Hughes CEO, Chairman Quits As Takeover Moves Continue," *Wall Street Journal,* May 25, 2001.
4. Rupert Murdoch, interview by Charlie Rose, *Charlie Rose Show,* Dec. 9, 2001.
5. EchoStar press conference, New York, Aug. 5, 2001.
6. Murdoch interview.
7. Ibid.
8. Judianne Atencio, telephone conversation with the author, Oct. 28, 2001.

Chapter 3: Voltaire's Undergraduate

1. Rupert Murdoch, in *Six Australians: Profiles of Power,* Australian Broadcasting Corporation, Jan. 1, 1966.
2. Sir Keith's quote is related in correspondence by a family friend who asked not to be named.
3. Thomas Kiernan, *Citizen Murdoch* (New York: Dodd Mead, 1986), p. 18.
4. Research papers of Australian journalist Dimity Torbett. In 1983–84, while researching the life of Robin Farquharson in London, Torbett conducted a series of interviews with Farquharson's contemporaries at Oxford, many of whom also were contemporaries of Rupert Murdoch. Several of the Australians at Oxford had come from Geelong Grammar. Unless otherwise indicated, the Oxford quotes in this chapter are taken from Torbett's interview notes, contemporaneous records, manuscript, and current recollections.
5. Sir Keith Murdoch, comment made in 1952, recorded in correspondence by Murdoch family friend.
6. John Monks, *Elisabeth Murdoch: Two Lives* (Sydney: Macmillan, 1994), p. 174.
7. Quotes by Michael Weigall, James Mitchell, Patrick Seale, a former contemporary, another fellow undergraduate, Frank Cioffi, and Robert Shackleton are from Torbett interviews, 1983–84.
8. Quotes by J. R. Sargent and Michael Weigall are from Torbett interviews, 1983–84.
9. *Cherwell,* Jun. 11, 1952, and May 28, 1952.
10. Robin Farquharson, *Theory of Voting* (New Haven: Yale University Press, 1969).
11. Robin Farquharson, *Drop Out!* (London: Blond, 1968), pp. 74, 79, Introduction.
12. George Munster, *A Paper Prince* (Melbourne: Penguin, 1987), p. 36.
13. The jackhammer story was related by *Herald and Weekly Times* journalist Peter Thompson, deputy editor of the *Daily Mirror* and editor of the *Sunday Mirror* in London.
14. Torbett interview, September 5, 1983; "The King of Fleet Street," *Times on Sunday* [Sydney] Jun. 7, 1987, p. 26.
15. Various accounts of Sir Keith's newspaper holdings are given by Desmond Zwar, *In Search of Sir Keith Murdoch* (Melbourne: Macmillan, 1980), C. E. Sayers (whose biography of Sir Keith commissioned by the Murdochs was never published), Cecil Edwards, *The Editor Regrets* (Melbourne: Hill of Content, 1972) and historian Michael Cannon (*The Age,* Nov. 21, 1979).
16. Written comment, but made with request for anonymity, after the publication of Simon Regan's *Rupert Murdoch: A Business Biography* (London: Angus & Robertson, 1976).
17. Monks, *Elisabeth Murdoch,* p. 177.

Chapter 4: The Drunken Sailor

1. Maxwell Newton, in Rupert Murdoch, *Six Australians: Profiles of Power,* Australian Broadcasting Corporation, Jan. 1, 1966.
2. In the years after the divorce Patricia Booker had a series of unhappy relationships. Rupert Murdoch is believed to have provided support for her, significantly beyond the requirements of the divorce settlement, until her death in 1998.
3. Anthony Blond, interview by Dimity Torbett, 1982.
4. "Crews Set for Rumpus Rum Round," *Daily Telegraph* [Sydney], Dec. 31, 1983; Bruce Montgomery, "The Romance and the Sadness," *Australian,* Jan. 7, 1984, p. 11.

5. Philip Cornford, "Mouth from South Is Drunk as Skunk," *Daily Telegraph,* Sept. 20, 1977; "Skipper Ted's Cup Runneth Over . . . and Over," *Australian,* Sept. 20, 1977. Both are Murdoch papers.

6. On the origins of the Turner-Murdoch feud, see Paul Farhi, "Mogul Wrestling; In the War Between Murdoch and Turner, Similarity Breeds Contempt," *Washington Post,* Nov. 18, 1996, p. C1.

7. *Warner Communications v. Murdoch et. al,* No. 84-13 CMW, Delaware District Court, Mar. 16, 1984.

8. Glenda Korporaal, "The King of Cable Television," *Australian Financial Review,* Jan. 27, 1984.

9. Ted Turner, National Press Club luncheon, Sept. 27, 1994.

10. Despite reports that Murdoch was planning a Supreme Court appeal against new assessments issued by the tax office based on his ABT testimony, the matter never reached the courts and appears to have been resolved between the two parties. See Richard McGregor, "Tax Office Queries Murdoch's Returns," *Sydney Morning Herald,* Sept. 21, 1985.

11. D. M. Osborne, "Murdoch's Secret Weapon," *American Lawyer,* Dec. 1993, p. 45.

12. *News Group Newspapers et al. v. SOGAT 82 et. al* [1987] ICR 181, [1986] IRLR 337. Queen's Bench Division, Jul. 31, 1986.

13. Andrew Neil, *Full Disclosure* (London: Macmillan, 1996), p. 97; on the MI5 mistake, see p. 102; on Murdoch railing at Adams, see p.125.

14. Geoffrey Richards, letter to Bruce Matthews, Dec. 20, 1985, quoted in Richard Belfield, Christopher Hird, and Sharon Kelly, *Murdoch: The Decline of an Empire* (London: Macdonald, 1991), pp. 93–94.

Chapter 5: The Party Line

1. "Best-heeled Revealed by Forbes," *Advertising Age,* Oct. 19, 1987, p. 104.

2. Nadine Brozan, "The Evening Hours," *New York Times,* Oct. 16, 1987, sec. A, p. 26.

3. P. G. Chegwyn, letter to R. J. Wyatt, Sept. 28, 1987, with attached duplicate copy terms sheet, referred to in Australian Securities Commission, *Report About an Investigation into the Affairs of Queensland Press Limited & Ors Pursuant to Section 17 of ASC Law,* 2nd draft, Jan. 1993, para. 3.04. The ASC report, while never released, is quoted at length in the official response and comment to the report from Allen Allen & Hemsley, representing Queensland Press, News Limited, Cruden Investments, and Queensland Press directors, addressed to Greg Tanzer, Queensland regional general counsel, Australian Securities Commission, Mar. 3, 1993, p. 8. John Atanascovic, formerly of Blake Dawson Waldron, is believed to have been the principal author of the Allen Allen & Hemsley letter.

4. Record of security in favor of Commonwealth Bank of Australia given by Rupert and Anna Murdoch, New York City UCC Filings, Oct. 21, 1987, filing number 87PN61099, discharged Dec. 24, 1990.

5. Details of the deal are contained in the Allen Allen & Hemsley letter response of Mar. 3, 1993, to the ASC report (note 3). Further details appear in *Commissioner of Stamps v. Telegraph Investment Company & Anor.,* FC 95/050, High Court of Australia, Dec. 21, 1995. The case arose after officers of the South Australian Stamp Duties Office raided News Corp's offices in Adelaide, and the commissioner sought to impose $4 million in stamp duties on the Queensland Press transaction.

6. John D'Arcy, conversation with the author, Mar. 1996.

7. Record of security in favor of Commonwealth Bank of Australia given by Rupert

and Anna Murdoch, New York Department of State, Uniform Commercial Code Record, Oct. 23, 1987, filing number 318155, discharged Jan. 25, 1991.

8. Deborah Light and John Lyons, "Murdoch Feels the Strain," *Sydney Morning Herald*, Feb. 2, 1991, p. 33.

9. Rupert Murdoch, correspondence reproduced in Richard Belfield, Christopher Hird, and Sharon Kelly, *Murdoch: The Decline of an Empire* (London: Macdonald, 1991), p. 302.

10. Allen Allen & Hemsley, letter of March 3, 1993, p. 11.

11. U.S. and Australian corporate filings show that News Corp had A$633 million on its books as the holding value of its 44 percent of Queensland Press. It had loaned Queensland Press $170 million directly, and of the joint A$1 billion debt facility with the Commonwealth Bank, A$500 million went to Queensland Press. In addition News Corp had loaned A$230 million to Dexenne, for a total of A$1.53 billion.

12. Of the other A$500 million, News Corp promptly reloaned another A$170 million to Queensland Press for the stock purchase (using another loophole in the restriction on a company financing its own shares) and later loaned a further A$222 million to Dexenne, a company half owned by Queensland Press, to buy the News Corp convertible notes held by Advertiser Newspapers.

13. DM800 million.

14. William Shawcross, *Murdoch: The Making of a Media Empire* (New York: Touchstone, 1993, 1997), p. 363.

15. Geraldine Brooks, "Murdoch," *New York Times*, Jul. 19, 1998, sec. 6, p. 20.

16. Karen Maley, interview by the author, Feb. 2000.

17. Shawcross, *Murdoch*, actually alternates between the two dates, p. 15.

18. Only half of the A$1 billion loan was for Queensland Press. News Corp used the other half to take over Advertiser Newspapers, but both loan facilities shared the same lenders. See Ida Picker, "Bummer Dude! Inside the Murdoch Workout," *Institutional Investor*, March 1991, p. 36.

19. Interviewed by Karen Maley, Mar. 2000.

20. I attended the ASC briefing at the request of Robin Chapman, seeking further details of the 1987 Queensland Press transaction. In July 1990 I had consulted Chapman, who was then a partner in a Brisbane legal firm, about the Queensland Press deal, in the course of researching a looming debt problem in the Murdoch family's private companies for an article for *Australian Business*. While the article was never published, as a courtesy gesture I later supplied a copy to Chapman. This prompted her to launch the ASC inquiry. Adams's question at the ASC briefing about the effects of reversing the Queensland Press transaction was directed at me.

21. The ASC investigator made the Skase comparison in conversation with me. The "routine matter" comment was made by ASC spokesperson Janet O' Connor in conversation with me.

22. Letter to the author, April 2001.

Chapter 6: The Fugitive

1. Hundertmark's history with Murdoch is detailed in an affidavit filed in his witness statement in *News International et al. v. Clinger et al.*, CH 1996 N 4257 & 5450, No. 104, High Court, London.

2. Don Osur, email to the author, Nov. 2001.

3. Hundertmark began legal action against Clinger in Israel in 1995, claiming that he

and Clinger were to have equal shares in Independent Development Group (IDG), but that Clinger had defrauded him. News Corp subsequently claimed that Hundertmark had abused his position as an adviser to take a secret shareholding in NDSP through the IDG holding, so that any money retrieved from IDG should be paid to News Corp. Hundertmark produced detailed diary notes that recorded a conversation in which he cleared his IDG holding with Rupert Murdoch. Hundertmark settled his dispute with News Corp on undisclosed grounds but continued to press his action against Clinger in Israel.

4. *Times* [London], Jun. 9, 1998.

5. "News Datacom Sues Former Employees," *Cable & Satellite Express*, Feb. 1996, p. 4.

6. James Mann, telephone conversation with the author, Jun. 19, 1996. Details of Clinger's SEC settlement in SEC Litigation Release No. 11503/Jul. 27, 1987, Accounting and Auditing Enforcement Release no. 142, *Securities and Exchange Commission v. Clinger et al.*, Civil Action no. 87-2070, U.S. District Court, District of Columbia.

7. Michael Clinger, letter to the author, Apr. 1997. Hundertmark's claim was made in conversation with the author, Nov. 1996. The lawyer to whom Hundertmark says he sent his letter detailing Clinger's history declined to comment upon the allegation.

8. Michael Eisner, *Work in Progress* (London, Penguin: 1998), p. 347.

9. Peter Chippindale and Suzanne Franks, *Dished!* (London: Simon & Schuster, 1991), p. 276.

10. Ibid., p. 279.

11. *Re BSB Holdings Ltd. (No. 2)* [1996] 1 BCLC 155, Chancery Division, High Court, London, Jul. 28, 1995.

12. Ibid.

13. James Mann, telephone conversation with the author, Jun. 19, 1996.

14. Frank Barlow is quoted in Mathew Horsman, *Sky High* (London: Orion, 1997), p. 130.

15. *News International v. Clinger*, Nov. 17, 1998. The account in this chapter is drawn from Justice Lindsay's detailed chronology of the development of the News Datacom business.

16. Ibid.

17. Meir Matatyahu and Clinger are quoted in the transcript of tapes cited in affidavit by Arthur Siskind, signed Feb. 16, 1996, filed in *News International v. Clinger*.

18. Telephone interviews with the author. Of Hundertmark's claim that he informed a British lawyer about Clinger's history in 1989, Arthur Siskind told me in a telephone conversation on Nov. 12, 1996, "It's not a matter that made its way to the top of News management."

19. *News International & Others*, Nov. 17, 1998.

Chapter 7: The Pretenders

1. Anna Maria Murdoch, "Motherhood and Mythology: Summer Thoughts on Sex and Creativity," *Commonweal* (Aug. 31, 1979), pp. 466–69. Niobe's seven sons and seven daughters were killed by Apollo and Artemis after she boasted that her children's beauty rivaled theirs.

2. Thomas Kiernan, *Citizen Murdoch* (New York: Dodd, Mead, 1986), p. 225.

3. Murdoch, "Motherhood and Mythology," pp.467, 469.

4. Philip Townshend, *Just Rupert*, serialized in "Murdoch by His Butler," *Punch* 58–59, Jul. 4–17, 1998, Jul. 18–31, 1998.

5. Louise McElvogue, ". . . And the other Front-runners in the Family," *Guardian*, Apr. 22, 1996, p. T17.

6. *Washington Post*, Oct. 23, 1985.

7. Kiernan, *Citizen Murdoch*, p. 284.

8. Bruce Hundertmark, interview by the author, Nov. 1996.

9. Neil Chenoweth, "The Man from Uncle," *Bulletin* (Sydney), May 11, 1993, p. 79.

10. John Monks, *Elisabeth Murdoch: Two Lives* (Sydney: Macmillan, 1994), p. 308. Monks also details the round robin of £50,000 in checks in Giddy's office on p. 170. I have derived the details of the Cruden shareholdings from an analysis of public filings by the Murdoch companies over the last fifty years. Cruden's annual revenues since 1970 were calculated from dividend and shareholding information in News Limited and News Corp annual reports.

11. In 1978 Kayarem was issued 392,000 B shares and 108,000 A shares in Cruden. The $2 shares were at an $8 premium, giving a total issue price of $5 million. Corporate filings show only $500,000 of this figure had been paid when they were absorbed in a share reconstruction. There is no record in the Corporate Affairs Commission filing that the final $4.5 million was paid up on these shares, though the record may be incomplete.

12. Conversation with the author, Oct. 1993. See Neil Chenoweth, "The Story Behind News' Super Shares," *Australian Financial Review*, Nov. 3, 1993, p. 1.

13. Ibid.

14. Matt Handbury, conversation with the author, Mar. 1993.

15. Townshend, "Murdoch by His Butler," *Punch* no. 58, Jul. 4–17, 1998.

Chapter 8: Lost in Space

1. Rupert Murdoch, interview by Charlie Rose, *Charlie Rose Show*, Dec. 9, 2001.

2. Diane Mermigas, "What's Murdoch Want? Programming," *Electronic Media* Oct. 7, 1996, p. 8.

3. Ken Auletta, "The Pirate," *New Yorker*, Nov. 13, 1995; reprinted in Ken Auletta, *The Highwaymen* (New York: Random House, 1997).

4. In correspondence with the SEC from 1986 to 1985, News Corp's lawyers and accountants had argued that no separate reporting was warranted for 20th Holdings, as News Corp held economic control over it. This was in effect the reverse of the case they argued to the FCC.

5. Edmund L. Andrews, "Mr. Murdoch Goes to Washington," *New York Times*, Jul. 23, 1995, sec. 3, p. 1.

6. *Advertising Age*, April 24, 1995, p. 41.

7. Jube Shiver Jr., "FCC Staff Urge That Murdoch Be Ordered to Restructure Fox," *Los Angeles Times*, April 21, 1995, p. D1.

8. Jube Shiver Jr., "FCC Offers Murdoch a Way Out of Broadcast Ownership Rule," *Los Angeles Times*, May 5, 1995, p. 1.

9. Stephen Keating, *Cutthroat* (Boulder, Colo.: Johnson, 1999), p. 143.

10. *United States v. Primestar, et al.*, Civil no. 1:98CV01193 (JLG), U.S. District Court, District of Columbia, May 12, 1998.

11. Keating, *Cutthroat*, p. 153.

12. Greg Critser, "Heir to the Future," *Washington Post Magazine*, Jun. 16, 1996.

13. Conversation with Mark Furness of the *Australian Financial Review*, who spoke to Malone shortly after the announcement, November 1999.

14. Quoted in Justice Department statement of claim, *U.S. v. Primestar Inc and*

Others, Civil No.: 1:98CV01193 (JLG), District Court, District of Columbia, May 12, 1998, paragraph 54.

15. Michael Eisner, letter to shareholders, Disney proxy statement, 1997.

Chapter 9: Herb Allen's Porch

1. Peter Bart, "The Back Lot; Rupe Group Theory Explains Multiple Murdochs," *Daily Variety,* Jul. 29, 1996.

2. Elise O'Shaughnessy, "The New Establishment," *Vanity Fair,* Oct. 1994, p. 222.

3. Alan Citron, "When Herb Allen Talks, Star Makers Listen," *Los Angeles Times,* Jul. 2, 1993, part D, p. 4; David Lieberman and Tom Lowry, "Media Titans Meet Again, Allen & Co. Conference Draws Big Players; What Will They Cook Up This Time?" *USA Today,* Jul. 9, 1996, p. 1B.

4. Jane Martinson, "Cyber Stars Corralled at the Ranch," *Guardian,* Jul. 10, 1999, p. 27.

5. Howard Anderson, "The Man Who Would Be Media King," *Upside* 9, no. 8, Sept. 1997, pp. 110–16.

6. O'Shaughnessy, "The New Establishment," p. 227.

7. Tom Lowry, "Chats, Rafts But No Word on Deals," *USA Today,* Jul. 11, 1996, p. 10B.

8. Lieberman and Lowry, "Media Titans Meet Again," p. 1B.

9. Mark Warbis, "Playground of the Rich Unphased by Gathering of Media, Computer Moguls," Associated Press, Jul. 9, 1999.

10. Julian Borger, "Disney Admits Defeat in $580 Million Suit; Settlement Ends Long-running Dispute with Little Midget," *Guardian,* Jul. 8, 1999, p. 23.

11. Porter Bibb, *It Ain't As Easy As It Looks* (Boulder, Colo.: Johnson, 1993).

12. Rupert Murdoch, interview by Larry King, *Larry King Live,* CNN, Sept. 12, 1994.

13. Lowry, "Chats, Rafts But No Word on Deals," p. 10B.

14. An alternative version of this story puts this incident in Alaska.

15. Michael Eisner with Jack Schwartz, *Work in Progress* (London: Penguin, 1998), p. 361.

16. O'Shaughnessy, "The New Establishment," p. 222.

17. Anita M. Busch, "Sun Valley Ends in Cyberspace Serenade," *Hollywood Reporter,* Jul. 12, 1999.

18. "Letter from Camp Allen," *Vanity Fair,* Oct. 1996, p. 109.

19. Kevin Maney, "Paul Allen's Eclectic Empire," *USA Today,* Mar. 21, 1995, p. 1B.

20. Eisner, *Work in Progress,* pp. 363–65. Warren Buffett's letter to Berkshire Hathaway shareholders is reproduced in "This Year, Buffett's Letter Highlights Geico; Letter Quotes JFK, Woody Allen, Gilbert & Sullivan," *USA Today,* Mar. 18, 1996, p. 4B.

21. Graydon Carter, interview by Larry King, *Larry King Live,* CNN, Sept. 12, 1994.

22. Bill Gates, interview, *Playboy,* Jul. 1994, p. 55.

23. Charles Dubow, "Getting On Line with Herb Allen," *Forbes,* Apr. 30, 1999.

24. Claudia Eller and Sallie Hofmeister, "Ovitz Smoothing Feathers Around Town," *Los Angeles Times,* Sept. 20, 1996, part D, p. 4.

25. "Letter from Camp Allen," p. 109.

26. Geraldine Fabrikant, "Murdoch Bets Heavily on a Global Vision," *New York Times,* Jul. 29, 1996, sec. D, p. 1.

27. William Neuman and Bill Sanderson, "Mind Games in Revlon Divorce," *New York Post,* Dec. 7, 1998.

28. *Electronic Media,* Jan. 2, 1995, p. 12.

29. Ted Turner, National Press Club luncheon, Sept. 27, 1994.

30. Rupert Murdoch, address to shareholders, News Corp annual general meeting, Oct. 18, 1994.

31. Fabrikant, "Murdoch Bets Heavily on a Global Vision."

32. Jenny Hontz, "Rupert Rules New World," *Daily Variety,* July 18, 1996, p. 1.

33. Fabrikant, "Murdoch Bets Heavily on a Global Vision."

Chapter 10: The Apple Fumble

1. Kevin Shinkle and Michael Stroud, "Media's Quiet Achiever: Bloomberg," *Melbourne Age,* Jul. 21, 1997, p. 2.

2. Kim Masters and Bryan Burrough, "Cable Guys," *Vanity Fair,* Jan. 1997, pp. 64, 125.

3. A November 17, 1983, memo from Philip Altman and Howard Topez (Squadron Ellenoff Plesent & Lehrer associates) addressed to Arthur Siskind, introduced in court, said that Siskind told Altman that Tony Mariotta's ownership of Wedtech stock was to be "for a limited period of time." The Squadron Ellenoff lawyers said the memo was an outline of possibilities that were never put into practice.

4. "On the Record," *Manhattan Lawyer,* Jul. 19–25, 1998, p. 16. See also Howard W. French, "Lawyer Admits Default Scheme Was Discussed," *New York Times,* Jul. 13, 1988, sec. B, p. 3; Howard W. French, "Prosecutors Suggest Wedtech Lawyers Violated Ethics Code," *New York Times,* Jul. 9, 1988, sec. 1, p. 31; Paul Moses, "Squadron Accused in Wedtech Trial; Ex-Exec: Lawyer Knew Contract Was a Fraud," *Newsday,* Mar. 24, 1988, city edition, p. 4; Michele Galen, "Too Close for Comfort," *National Law Journal,* Jul. 6, 1987, p. 1; Ira Lee Sorkin, "Squadron Ellenoff Replies on Wedtech Role," *National Law Journal,* Jul. 13, 1987, letters section, p. 12.

5. Arthur Siskind, telephone interview with the author, Nov. 12, 1996.

6. Arthur Siskind, testimony in the trial of Wedtech executives, Jul. 12–13, 1988, reported in Edward Frost and Rifka Rosenwein, "Wedtech Defense Witness Says He Helped Prosecutors," *Manhattan Lawyer,* Jul. 19–25, 1988, p. 6.

7. Associated Press, Jun. 29, 1992.

8. Greg Sargent and Josh Benson, "Murdoch's *New York Post* Gleefully Roasts Hillary," *New York Observer,* Dec. 6, 1999, p. 1.

9. David Henry and Scott Ladd, *"Post's* Fiscal Physical," *Newsday,* Feb. 24, 1993, city edition, p. 28.

10. Martin Peers, "Three Cheers for Murdoch," *Australian Financial Review,* Mar. 31, 1993, p. 19.

11. Richard Karz, "Ailes Talks Tough on Fox Launch," *Multichannel News,* Sept. 23, 1996, p. 3.

12. "Poised for the Home Run—Ted Turner, Founder of Cable Network News," *Financial Times,* Sept. 20, 1993.

13. Matt Roush, "Ratings, Rivals and Ted Turner," *USA Today,* Jul. 12, 1994, p. 3D.

14. Liz Smith, "Diamonds for NYC," *Newsday,* Apr. 10, 1994, p. A11.

15. Rupert Murdoch, news conference, Feb. 26, 1996.

16. Karz, "Ailes Talks Tough on Fox Launch."

17. The deals are too labyrinthine to uncover. This was the same month that TCI and

News Corp closed the deal to set up the Fox Sports venture, and TCI ended up with a small stake in Murdoch's Star TV in Hong Kong. In this deal TCI reported that it received $100 million more than News Corp reported that it had paid.

18. Masters and Burrough, "Cable Guys," p. 65.

19. Diane Mermigas, "Murdoch Vows Action Against Time Warner," *Electronic Media* Sept. 23, 1996, p. 1.

20. David Lieberman, "Ailes Tackles Toughest Assignment," *USA Today,* Sept. 23, 1996, p. 9B.

21. Masters and Burrough, "Cable Guys," p. 125.

22. David Lieberman, "Time Warner Picks MSNBC over Fox News," *USA Today* Sept. 20, 1996, p. 1B.

23. David Lieberman, "Fox TV Chief Says Time Lied," *USA Today,* Sept. 23, 1996, p. 9B; Bill Carter, "Fox Reacts Angrily to Move by Time Warner on Cable," *New York Times,* Sept. 21, 1996, sec. 1, p. 32.

24. Mermigas, "Murdoch Vows Action Against Time Warner."

25. *Fox News Network v. Time Warner et al.,* 96-CV-4963 U.S. District Court, Eastern District of New York, May 16, 1997.

26. Mermigas, "Murdoch Vows Action Against Time Warner."

27. Details of these events are drawn from *Warner Cable of New York City et al. v. City of New York, Bloomberg LP,* 96 CIV. 7736 (DLC), U.S. District Court, Southern District of New York, 943 F.Supp. 1357; Nov. 6, 1996.

28. Martin Peers et al., "Will Clash of Titans Leave Bruises Across the Biz?", *Variety,* Sept. 30, 1996, p. 11; Arthur Spielgelman, "Ted Turner and Rupert Murdoch Are at War," Reuters, Sept. 27, 1996.

29. David Osborne, "Murdoch Meets His Match," *Independent* (London), Nov. 24 1996, p. 15.

30. Details of Fran Reiter's meeting and comments made are drawn from *Warner Cable of New York City and Others v. City of New York, Bloomberg LP;* also described in Masters and Burrough, "Cable Guys."

31. *Warner Cable of New York City and Others v. City of New York, Bloomberg LP.*

32. Ibid.

33. Judge Jack B. Weinstein's ruling in *Fox News Network v. Time Warner Inc. et al.,* April 10, 1997.

34. Gary Levin, "Fox Sues TW over NY Cable," *Daily Variety,* Oct. 10, 1996, p. 3.

35. Kent Gibbons, "See You in Court, Rudy," *Multichannel News,* Oct. 14, 1996, p. 1.

36. Arthur Siskind, telephone interview with the author, November 12, 1996. Siskind said of the 1988 testimony that he was aware of the Wedtech fraud: "[It came from] two individuals negotiating for leniency with the U.S. Attorney's office. They implicated a whole range of people. The chairman and the president [of Wedtech] both denied I had any knowledge.... I will put my reputation against anybody's reputation and I will put my ability against anybody's ability."

Chapter 11: Wired

1. The Mar. 31, 1995, meeting and its aftermath are described in an affidavit by Arthur Siskind, Feb. 16, 1996, filed in the High Court action against Clinger, paragraph 59, p.18, and in an accompanying affidavit by Greg Clark from February 1996.

2. An extensive description of the fraud is contained in Justice Lindsay's Nov. 17, 1998,

judgment in *News International et al. v. Clinger et al.*, CH 1996 N4257 & 5450, No. 104, High Court, London, paras. 26–139.

3. Clark affidavit, Feb. 1996.

4. Robert Lindsay, "A&O Fails to Get Injunction After Faxed Evidence Blunder," *Lawyer* [London], June 2, 1998, p. 48.

5. Siskind affadavit, para. 73.

6. Johnnie L. Roberts with Mark Dennis, "Villain or Victim?" *Newsweek*, Nov. 4, 1996, p. 40.

7. Neil Chenoweth, "Secret Empire," *Australian Financial Review*, Nov. 15, 1996, Weekend Review section, p. 1; based on Siskind interview, Nov. 12, 1996.

8. Clay Harris, telephone interview with the author, Jun. 27, 1996. See Chenoweth, "Secret Empire." In a telephone conversation with the author on June 25, 1996, Siskind said, "During the course of the investigation it came to our attention that Mr. Clinger had made many phone calls to Mr. Lewis, including calls to his home."

9. Siskind interview, Nov. 12, 1996, reported in Chenoweth, "Secret Empire."

10. Bruce Hundertmark, interview with the author, November 1996.

11. Siskind interview, Nov. 12, 1996.

12. *News International v. Clinger*, interim judgment, Nov. 11, 1996.

13. Siskind interview, Nov. 12, 1996.

14. *News International v. Clinger.*

15. Details of Sheppard's call and his allegations are drawn from a judgment by Justice Lindsay on Feb. 10, 1997, in *News International v. Clinger.*

16. Fax letter from Gavenchak to the author, Mar. 4, 1997. Clinger described the News Datacom building as a high-security installation, with continuous video monitoring and with access controlled by keys, smartcards, and a code, with guards on call, and with Peled's office situated in a section of the office with even more security. By fax to the author on March 11, 1997, Gavenchak denied that access to the News Datacom building was via keys, smartcards, and a code and said that Peled's office was used as a conference room. She declined to give more details. Clinger repeated his claim and said that Peled's office had not been used as a conference room since the early 1990s, while only three people knew the combination for Peled's office safe. He said the security precautions were necessary because the very nature of News Datacom business was encryption and the need for secrecy.

17. Wendy Goldman Rohm, *The Murdoch Mission* (New York: John Wiley & Sons, 2001), p. 95.

18. Audley Sheppard, conversation with the author, Mar. 1997.

19. A week after Sheppard's call to Evans-Lombe, Clifford Chance stopped acting for Clinger. News Corp drew an adverse inference from this action. In correspondence with the author, Clinger said Clifford Chance was too expensive for him in what was becoming a very costly court case. Certainly it is not clear that Clinger showed any more enthusiasm for paying his lawyers than he showed for paying anybody to whom he owed money. Sheppard did not comment upon the reason for the switch but said Clifford Chance continued to be concerned about the possibility that some telephone conversations had been recorded.

Chapter 12: The Poker Player

1. William Shawcross, "Murdoch's New Life," *Vanity Fair*, Oct. 1999, p. 186.

2. Rebecca Cantwell and John Accola, "EchoStar's Charles Ergen's Gambling Savvy

Serves Him Well in the Satellite TV Game," *Rocky Mountain News* [Denver], Dec. 29, 1996, p. 2B.

3. Jim Carrier, "Dish Was Doorway to Dream; Satellite TV Pioneer Sets Industry Agenda," *Denver Post*, Sept. 22, 1996, p. I-01.

4. Cantwell and Accola, "EchoStar's Charles Ergen's Gambling Savvy."

5. Ibid. 2B.

6. Details of the bidding are drawn from FCC filings.

7. Stephen Keating, "TCI Quits Satellite TV Bidding; EchoStar, MCI in Hot Competition," *Denver Post*, Jan. 25, 1997, p. C-01. Bidding details are from FCC filings.

8. "MCI's $450 Million Bid Leads Contest for Full Con-U.S. DBS Slot," *Communications Today*, January 25, 1996.

9. Cantwell and Accola, "EchoStar's Charles Ergen's Gambling Savvy."

10. Keating, "TCI Quits Satellite TV Bidding."

11. Ostensibly MCI had committed to invest only $2 billion in News Corp convertible stock, but if News Corp used this to fund its half share of ASkyB, MCI would have to outlay another $2 billion to match it, on top of the $672 million license fee, which as a foreign company News Corp could not hold or pay for.

12. Martin Peers, "News Corp Satellite TV Plan Stumbles," *Business Review Weekly* [Australia], Dec. 2, 1996, p. 26.

13. Martin Peers, "Murdoch Gets the Cold Shoulder from MCI," *Business Review Weekly*, Dec. 2, 1996, p. 26; see also *Business Review Weekly*, Dec. 16, 1996, p. 48, and *Broadcasting & Cable*, Dec. 9, 1996, p. 64.

14. *News International et al. v. Clinger et al.*, CH 1996 N4257 & 5450, No. 104, High Court, London, Feb. 10, 1997. Things were looking up in Israel as well. Two weeks after Murdoch's UJA dinner with the tribute from Prime Minister Netanyahu, the Israeli finance minister resigned in a party power struggle. He was replaced by former Justice Minister Ja'kov Ne'eman (newly vindicated after charges of witness tampering). Outside politics Ne'eman headed the corporate division at Herzog Fuchs & Ne'eman, which was the News Datacom law firm raided eight months before. This did not affect the impartiality of the Israeli tax authority, but for News Corp shareholders the prospect that its former lawyer now headed the department that was investigating the company for tax fraud was strangely warming.

15. Neil Chenoweth, "Murdoch and the $1 Billion Gap," *Australian Financial Review*, Mar. 21, 1998, p. 1.

16. Stephen Keating, *Cutthroat* (Boulder, Colo.: Johnson, 1999), p. 24.

17. Charles Ergen, unpublished interview by Eric Ellis, Mar. 1997.

18. Jack Egan, "For Satellite Television, the Limit Is the Sky," *U.S. News & World Report*, Mar. 3, 1997, p. 54.

19. Ergen, interview by Ellis.

20. First amended complaint, *EchoStar Communications v. News Corporation*, 96-960, Colorado District Court, paras. 27–28.

21. Eugenie Gavenchak, deputy general counsel of News America Publishing, stated in correspondence with the author in March 1997: "Mr. Peled had scheduled appointments one month and two weeks in advance of his meetings with the Tax Authority and the National Serious Crime Unit for the purpose of assisting in their investigations and presenting News's evidence as to the facts. He was not met at the airport, escorted anywhere or detained by any government authority." Peled later described a grueling 16-hour interview when Israeli interrogators attempted to persuade him to confess to serious crimes. See Wendy Goldman Rohm, *The Murdoch Mission* (New York: John Wiley & Sons, 2001), p. 95.

22. Tom Skotnicki, "News Corp reaches for the Sky," *Advertiser* [Adelaide], Feb. 26, 1997, p. 42.

23. John Accola, "EchoStar, Murdoch Merge," *Rocky Mountain News*, Feb. 25, 1997, p. 1B.

24. "Why Investors in News Are Smiling," *Sydney Morning Herald*, May 28, 1997, p. 30.

25. Terry McCrann, "Murdoch's American Appetites," *Australian*, Mar. 1, 1997, p. 25.

26. Keating, *Cutthroat*, p. 30.

27. Ibid., p. 26.

28. Ibid., p. 206

29. Ibid., p. 207.

30. "Cable Sees Clouds in Sky," *Broadcasting & Cable*, Mar. 24, 1997, p. 53.

31. "Heard at last week's National Cable Television Association Convention," *Hollywood Reporter*, Mar. 25, 1997.

32. *United States v. Primestar et al.*, Civil no. 1:98CV01193 (JLG), U.S. District Court, District of Columbia, May 12, 1998.

Chapter 13: Divided Royalties

1. Matt Pottinger, "Murdoch Calls on Congress to Remove Legislative Hurdles," State News Service, Apr. 10, 1997.

2. Arianna Huffington, "Newt Returns a Changed Man," *Chicago Sun-Times*, Apr. 13, 1997, p. 35.

3. Maureen Dowd, "Genghis Newt," *New York Times*, Apr. 9, 1997, p. 21.

4. Edmund L. Andrews, "Mr. Murdoch Goes to Washington," *New York Times*, Jul. 23, 1995, sec. 3, p. 1.

5. Ken Silverstein, "His Biggest Takeover: How Murdoch Bought Washington," *Nation*, Jun. 8, 1998, p. 18.

6. Quoted in Paul Starubin, "Word Warriors," *Washingtonian*, July 1999, p. 48.

7. Edited version of speech, *The Times* [London], Sept. 3, 1993.

8. Michael Gill, "Satellite Celebration of Brave News World," *Australian Financial Review*, Sept. 3, 1993, p. 5.

9. Rupert Murdoch, "The Century of Networking," Eleventh Annual John Bonython Lecture, Centre for Independent Studies, Melbourne, Australia, Oct. 20, 1994.

10. "Huber's Orwellian Act," *Information Law Alert: A Voorhees Report*, Nov. 30, 1994.

11. *The Progress Report with Newt Gingrich*, Aug. 15, 1995. Transcript accessed by Lexis Nexis, June 1996.

12. David Bicknell, "Only in America," *Computer Weekly*, Oct. 19, 1995, p. 42.

13. Benjamin Wittes, "Telecom Bill Empowers Agency," *Legal Times*, Jun. 5, 1995. p. 1.

14. Peter Huber, *Law and Disorder in Cyberspace: Abolish the FCC and Let Common Law Rule the Telecosm* (Oxford: Oxford University Press, 1997).

15. Press Clips, *Village Voice*, Dec. 13, 1994, p. 8.

16. Karen Tumulty, "When Rupert Met Newt," *Time*, Jan. 23, 1995, p. 34.

17. Jill Lawrence and Jessica Lee, "Gingrich's Triumph and Debacle: GOPAC," *USA Today*, Jan. 16, 1997, p. 8A.

18. Newt Gingrich, press conference, Dec. 30, 1994.

19. Tumulty, "When Rupert Met Newt."

20. Ken Auletta, *The Highwaymen* (New York: Random House, 1997), p. 283.

21. Tumulty, "When Rupert Met Newt."

22. "Mass Media," *Communications Daily,* Jan. 18, 1995, p. 9.

23. Katharine Q. Seelye, "Murdoch, Joined by Lobbyist, Talked of Regulatory Problem at Meeting with Gingrich," *New York Times,* Jan. 15, 1997, p. 18.

24. Auletta, *Highwaymen,* p. 287.

25. House minority whip David Bonior, news conference, Dec. 22, 1994. Bonior's reference to $4 million apparently meant the Penguin USA bid.

26. Timothy J. Burger and Jennifer Bradley, "It's D-Day on Hill (As in Disclosure): Gingrich Book Nets Less Than $500K," *Roll Call,* June 17, 1996; David Eisenstadt, "Newt Opens Books on Literary Front," *Daily News,* Jun. 15, 1996, p. 9.

27. Christopher Stern, "Piqued Pols Left Holding Phone," *Variety,* Mar. 17, 1997.

28. Matt Pottinger, "Murdoch Calls on Congress to Remove Legislative Hurdles," State News Service, Apr. 10, 1997.

29. Ibid.

30. Ibid.

31. David Lieberman, "Murdoch No Longer Reaching for Sky? Media Giant May Shift Focus to Primestar," *USA Today,* Apr. 11, 1997.

32. Ted Turner, interview by Larry King, NCTA 1997, edited transcript; "Turner Speaks Up (As Usual)," *Electronic Media,* Mar. 24, 1997, p. 36.

33. Michael Burgi and Richard Katz, "What Business Are We In Anyway?" *Media Week,* Mar. 24, 1997.

34. Fred Dawson and John M. Higgins, "Cable Puts on Brave Face Amid Worries," *Multichannel News,* Mar. 24, 1997, p. 1.

35. Burgi and Katz, "What Business Are We In Anyway?"

36. Sally Hofmeister, "Murdoch Outfoxing Himself with New Satellite Venture?" *Los Angeles Times,* Mar. 12, 1997, part D, p. 1.

37. Justice Department statement of claim, *United States v. Primestar et al.,* Civil no. 1:98CV01193 (JLG), U.S. District Court, District of Columbia, May 12, 1998, para. 54.

38. Dawson and Higgins, "Cable Puts on Brave Face Amid Worries."

39. Malone's memo and O'Brien's comment are in statement of claim, *United States v. Primestar,* May 12, 1998, paras. 53, 101.

40. Hindery, Malone, and Murdoch are quoted in statement of claim, *United States v. Primestar,* paras. 54, 58.

41. Ibid., para. 53.

42. Lieberman, "Murdoch No Longer Reaching for Sky?"

43. Keating, *Cutthroat,* p. 211.

44. Kent Gibbons and John M. Higgins, "Murdoch Notion Dashed; Primestar Roll-up Rolls Along," *Multichannel News* Apr. 21, 1997.

45. *United States v. Primestar,* para. 56.

46. Ken Western, "Rupert Murdoch Hastens Building of Arizona TV Broadcast Facility," *Arizona Republic,* Feb. 20, 1997.

47. First amended complaint, *EchoStar Communications v. News Corporation,* 96-960, Colorado District Court, para. 51.

48. Keating, *Cutthroat,* p. 213.

49. "Preston Padden Quits Top Post at ASkyB," *Electronic Media,* May 5, 1997, p. 1A.

50. "Digital Jam," CNN, May 2, 1997.

51. First amended complaint, *EchoStar Communications v. News Corporation,* paras. 60–61.

52. Keating, *Cutthroat,* p. 214.

53. The $3.5 billion figure represents opportunity cost, due to the unusual terms that Ergen built into the settlement agreement. News Corp wrote off only $375 million, much of which it would have recovered when it sold its rising EchoStar stock. See Neil Chenoweth, "The Man Who Outfoxed Rupert Murdoch," *Australian Financial Review,* Jun. 24, 1999, p. 1.

Chapter 14: The Testing of Pat

1. Andrew Neil, *Full Disclosure* (London: Macmillan, 1996), p. 166.

2. Richard N. Ostling, "Power, Glory and Politics," *Time,* Feb. 17, 1986, p. 62.

3. Fidelma Cook, "I Love Gays and Lesbians But I Hate Their Sins and Wicked Ways," *Mail on Sunday,* May 2, 1999, pp. 18–19.

4. Gregory Palast, "Inside Corporate America," *Observer* [London], May 23, 1999, Business section, p. 4.

5. Cook, "I Love Gays and Lesbians," p. 18.

6. Prigmore and Bredesen are quoted in Mark O'Keefe, "Pat Robertson's ever-growing business kingdom," *Virginian-Pilot,* Jun. 19, 1994, p. D1.

7. Mark A. Perigard, "Family Matters," *Boston Herald,* Apr. 27, 1997, p. 6.

8. Jim Forkan, "Family Bumps '700 Club' For Crime Time," *Multichannel News,* May 12, 1997, p. 19.

9. Pat Robertson, letter to the author, Nov. 10, 2000.

10. The description of the attack on Naghiu is drawn from *Naghiu and Naghiu v. Intercontinental Hotels,* Delaware District Court, 94-437. 165 F R D 413; 1996 U.S. Dist., Feb. 23, 1996, judgment Judge Murray M. Schwartz.

11. Robertson letter.

12. Cook, "I Love Gays and Lesbians," p. 19.

13. Lynne Heffley, "Low-Tech Equals High Ratings," *Los Angeles Times,* Nov. 25, 1993.

14. Tim Carvell and Joe McGowan, "Showdown in Toontown," *Fortune,* Oct. 28, 1996, p. 100.

15. Fox Kids Worldwide Inc., preliminary prospectus, Securities and Exchange Commission, filed Sept. 27, 1996.

16. Michael Weisskopf and Charles R. Babcock, "Donors Pay and Stay at White House," *Washington Post,* Dec. 15, 1996, p. A1; David Finnigan, *Hollywood Reporter,* Sept. 8, 1999.

17. Details of Robertson's negotiations in this chapter are drawn from International Family Entertainment, Inc., proxy statement, Securities and Exchange Commission, filed June 25, 1997, pp. 5–14.

18. Michael Burgi, "Murdoch and Malone Pursue Joint Bid for IFE," *Media Week,* Feb. 10, 1997, p. 8.

19. Andrew Collier, "Robertson Snag in Sale of IFE." *Hollywood Reporter,* Feb. 18, 1997.

20. *Advertising Age,* Sept. 29, 1997.

21. "News Corp./Family Talks on Track," *Broadcasting & Cable,* Apr. 14, 1997, p. 10.

22. Hindery and Murdoch are quoted in statement of claim, *United States v. Primestar Inc. et al.,* paras. 54, 58.

23. International Family Entertainment, Inc., proxy statement.

24. Robertson letter.

25. Bill Sizemore, "Operation Blessing Planes Were Used Mostly for Diamond Mining, 2 Pilots Say; Pat Robertson's Spokesman Says Planes Were Used, But as a Benevolent Gesture and Robertson Reimbursed the Relief Group," *Virginian-Pilot* [Norfolk, Va.] Apr. 27, 1997, p. A1.

26. Bill Sizemore, "Inquiry Faults Operation Blessing; But Diamond-Mine Questions Won't Lead to Action Against Charity," *Virginian-Pilot,* Jun. 18, 1999, p. A1.

27. Liz Szabo, "Robertson: *Pilot's* report on inquiry is wrong; Operation Blessing Solicitations Were Focus of Investigation," *Virginian-Pilot,* Jul. 22, 1999, p. A1.

28. Robertson letter.

Chapter 15: Man for All Seasons

1. Robert A. Jones, "Hearts of the City: H2 O'Malley, With Regret," *Los Angeles Times,* Jan. 8, 1997, part B, p. 2.

2. Ibid.

3. Eric Ellis, "Murdoch Hesitating About Buying the Dodgers," *Australian Financial Review,* Jan. 20, 1997, p. 10.

4. James Bates, "Watch the Money; Like It or Not, Rupert Murdoch Is Touching the Lives of Everyone in Southern California. How Can Anyone Predict Where He'll Strike Next?" *Los Angeles Times Magazine,* Jan. 31, 1999, p. 10.

5. Connie Bruck, "The Big Hitter," *New Yorker,* Dec. 8, 1997, p. 82.

6. Bates, "Watch the Money," p. 10.

7. Bruck, "Big Hitter," p. 82.

8. "Launch of a Network," *Guardian* (London), Feb. 1, 1999, p. 2.

9. Bruck, "The Big Hitter," p. 86.

10. Larry Stewart, "Anne Meyers—Still Breaking Ground," *Los Angeles Times,* Feb. 21, 1997, p. C6.

11. Lachlan Murdoch, unpublished interview by Ali Cromie, Nov. 1999.

12. Jennie Curtin, "Players' Word Preferred over Anderson, Ribot," *Sydney Morning Herald,* Dec. 22, 1995, p. 34; Jennie Curtin, "Players Were Preyed Upon: Four Bulldogs Released from Contracts," *Sydney Morning Herald,* Dec. 22, 1995, p. 34; AAP, "Super Slipshod, Claims Judge: Ribot, Anderson Charged with Unconscionable Dealing as Contracts Declared Void," *Australian,* Dec. 22, 1995, p. 18; AAP, "Super League Canterbury Contracts Declared Void," *Australian Financial Review,* Dec. 22, 1995, p. 4.

13. *News Limited v. Australian Rugby Football League et al.,* 96000870, Federal Court of Appeal, Australia, Feb. 23, 1996.

14. Roy Masters and Steve Mascord, "Super Under-19s to Tackle the Rest," *Sydney Morning Herald,* Mar. 15, 1996, p. 38.

15. Bruck, "Big Hitter," p. 87.

16. *News Limited v. Australian Rugby Football League et al.,* Feb. 23, 1996.

17. Kathryn Bice, "Attack on Judge Shows News Has Ethical Void: QC," *Australian Financial Review,* May 31, 1996, p. 14.

18. *News Limited et al. v. Australian Rugby Football League et al.,* Oct. 4, 1996.

19. *Fox News Network v. Time Warner et al.,* 96-CV-4963 U.S. District Court, Eastern District of New York, May 16, 1997.

20. John Geddes, "Super Deal Shattering Blow to ARL," *Courier-Mail* [Brisbane] Jan. 17, 1997, p. 60.

21. Michael Freeman, "TV Sports Fox Readies Super Bid II," *Media Week,* Jan. 21, 1997.

Chapter 16: The Mouse Wars

1. *Re The Walt Disney Company Derivative Litigation Consolidated,* C.A. no. 15452 Court of Chancery of Delaware, New Castle 731 A.2d 342; Oct. 7, 1998.
2. Mike Bygrave, "Daggers Drawn in the Magic Kingdom," *Sunday Telegraph Magazine* [London], May 18, 1997, p. 40.
3. Michael Eisner with Tony Schwartz, *Work in Progress* (London: Penguin, 1998), p. 350.
4. Ian Hyland, "Superstar Wars," *Sunday Mirror,* Jan. 19, 1997, p. 27.
5. Frank Rose, "There's No Business like Show Business," *Fortune,* June 22, 1998, p. 86.
6. Jennifer Oldham, "Diminishing Returns," *Los Angeles Times,* July 23, 1996, part D, p. 1.
7. Merrill Lynch report on News Corp analysts' briefing, Mar. 19, 1997.
8. Marc Gunther, "The Rules According to Rupert," *Fortune,* Oct. 26, 1998, p. 92.
9. John M. Higgins and Stephen McClellan, "When Media Moguls Collide," *Broadcasting & Cable,* Jul. 7, 1997.
10. Sallie Hofmeister, "Fox-ESPN Fight over Sports Rights Raising Cable Rates," *Los Angeles Times,* Aug. 29, 1997, part D, p. 1.
11. Higgins and McClellan, "When Media Moguls Collide."
12. This included refinancing some existing debt. Dolan paid $168.75 million to ITT on February 18, 1997, to bring his holding to 50 percent, $500 million on June 19 for a further 38.5 percent, and $150 million for options to buy the remaining 11.5 percent in two years.
13. Leonard Shapiro, "Sports Giants Battle for Air-traffic Control," *Washington Post,* Aug. 15, 1999.
14. Mary Lou Loper, "RSVP/The Social City," *Los Angeles Times,* May 25, 1997, p. E3.
15. Murdoch was to be issued nonvoting stock in Primestar, which would become ordinary voting stock the moment that he sold it to a company not controlled by him. In June 1998 Murdoch sold *TV Guide* into a company called United Satellite Technology, which also held convertible stock in Primestar. Malone and Murdoch ended up each holding 49 percent of the voting rights of United Satellite, which was renamed TV Guide Inc. As neither man controlled TV Guide Inc., it appears that it would have been the perfect vehicle for Murdoch and Malone to hold their Primestar stock (now with full voting rights), which eventually would give them close to half of Primestar's voting shares.
16. Justice Department statement of claim, *United States v. Primestar Inc. et al.,* Civil no. 1:98CV01193 (JLG), U.S. District Court, District of Columbia, May 12, 1998.
17. Colleen Ryan, "Murdoch's Satellite Plan Comes Crashing to Earth," *Australian Financial Review,* May 27, 1997, p. 1.
18. Rose, "There's No Business like Show Business."
19. Ibid.
20. Higgins and McClellan, "When Media Moguls Collide."
21. Ibid.
22. Hofmeister, "Fox-ESPN Fight Over Sports Rights."
23. Ibid.
24. Rupert Murdoch, comment at News Corporation annual meeting, Apr. 7, 1997.
25. From extensive analysis of stock prices by the author. See Neil Chenoweth, "The Mighty Have Fallen: The Future of Internet Stock," *Australian Financial Review,* Aug. 14, 1999, p. 22.

Chapter 17: The Trouble with Tony

1. Robert Preston, "Blair's Press Chief Faces Murdoch probe," *Financial Times,* Mar. 28, 1998, p. 4; Select Committee on Public Administration, minutes of Evidence, examination of witnesses, Jun. 23, 1998.

2. Robert Preston and Liam Halligan, "Government Pressed on Newspaper Market," *Financial Times,* Mar. 25, 1998, p. 12; George Jones, Robert Shrimsley, and Bruce Johnston, "No Special Help for Murdoch," *Daily Telegraph,* Mar. 25, 1998.

3. Michael White and Ewen Macaskill, "Murdoch Boast Amazed Staff," *Guardian,* Mar. 26, 1998, p. 11; Philip Webster, "Blair: No BSkyB Favours," *Times,* Mar. 26, 1998.

4. *Hansard* (House of Commons Debates, London), Apr. 24, 1988, col. 1155.

5. Llewellyn King, *White House Weekly,* Sept. 28, 1998,

6. Matthew Norman, "Diary," *Guardian,* Jul. 16, 1998, p. 20.

7. Hundertmark affidavit in *News International plc and others v. Michael Clinger and others* CH 1996 N No. 4257 High Court, London.

8. Irwin M. Stelzer, "Creating the City of the Future," *New York Post,* May 6, 1998.

9. Andrew Neil, *Full Disclosure* (London: Macmillan, 1996), p. 25.

10. Jason Deparle, "Are Poor People Just More Stupid Than Rich People?" *Sydney Morning Herald,* Oct. 29, 1994, Spectrum section, p. 6.

11. Irwin Stelzer, "Just an Illusion," *Sunday Times,* Sept. 1, 1996.

12. Neil, *Full Disclosure,* p. 131.

13. Norman.

14. Olga Craig, "How Labour Rewards Its Friends: When Business and Number 10 Get Too Close," *Sunday Telegraph,* Mar. 29, 1998, p. 24.

15. Francis Wheen, "A Partisan Briefing from the MD," *Guardian,* May 28, 1997, p. 28.

16. Irwin M. Stelzer, "Christian Socialism in Britain," *Public Interest* 124 (Summer 1996), pp. 3–11.

17. Daniel Colson, "The Cost of the Newspaper Price War," *Daily Telegraph,* May 11, 1998.

18. "We Would Only Say 'Enemies of Success,' " *Times* [London], Feb. 10, 1998.

19. Ken Auletta, *The Highwaymen* (New York: Random House, 1998), p. 268.

20. Neil, *Full Disclosure,* p. 169.

21. News Corp executive, interview by author, June 2000.

22. Masahiko Sasjima, "Murdoch Eyes Chinese Broadcasting Market," *Daily Yomiuri,* July 31, 1997, p. 3.

23. Ibid.

24. Andrew Neil, "Murdoch Diminished by Bowing to China," *Manchester Guardian Weekly,* Mar. 8, 1998, p. 12.

25. Eddie Bell, position paper, quoted Stuart Proffitt, "They Have Tried to Make Me a Scapegoat But They Have Chosen the Wrong Man," *Guardian,* Feb. 28, 1998, p. 2.

26. Proffitt, "They Have Tried to Make Me a Scapegoat."

27. Barbie Dutter, "We Blundered, Says *Times* Media Editor," *Daily Telegraph,* Mar. 2, 1998, p. 7; "Murdoch's Chinese Walls," *Daily Telegraph,* Mar. 3, 1998; Philip Johnston, "*Times* Man Hits at Censor Murdoch: Cut in China Coverage to Protect Business," *Daily Telegraph,* Mar. 4, 1998, p. 1.

28. Nigel Morris, "PM Faces Revolt over His Ties with Murdoch," *Mirror* [London], Mar. 3, 1998, p. 14.

29. George Jones, "Labour MPs Are Uneasy over Chris Patten Book Row," *Daily Telegraph,* Mar. 2, 1998, p. 7.

30. Raymond Snoddy, "Our People Screwed Up in Patten Row, Says Murdoch," *Times,* Mar. 4, 1998.

31. Raymond Snoddy, "Patten Wins Apology from HarperCollins over Book," *Times,* Mar. 7, 1998.

32. Michael Sissons, "The Patten Saga Chapter and Verse," *Guardian,* Mar. 7, 1998, p. 5.

33. Tony Blair, *Hansard* (House of Commons Debates, London), April 1, 1998, col. 1253.

34. Australian Tax Office internal memo, May 1996; cited in Neil Chenoweth and Fiona Buffini, "News Corp Tax Inquiry Goes Global," *Australian Financial Review,* Feb. 5, 1998, p. 1.

35. Patrick Reilly and JoEllen Goodman, *Crain's New York Business,* Dec. 15, 1986, p. 3.

36. Nancy A. Nichols, "The Man Who Stirs the Pot," *Boston Business Journal,* May 25, 1987, p. 1.

37. Neil Chenoweth, "The $1 Billion Gap," *Australian Financial Review,* Feb. 5, 1998, p. 1.

Chapter 18: Rupert's Rocket

1. William Shawcross, "Murdoch's New Life," *Vanity Fair,* Oct. 1999, p. 21.

2. Andrew Neil, *Full Disclosure* (London: Macmillan, 1996), p. 586.

3. "Talk of the Town," *New Yorker,* February 1990.

4. "Pope Cites Bob Hope, Murdoch and Disney," *New York Post,* Jan. 3, 1998, p. 13.

5. Liz Smith, *New York Post,* Apr. 21, 1998, p. 6.

6. Neil Chenoweth, "Three Weddings and a Magnate," July 3, 1999, p. 26.

7. David Leser, "Anna and Her King," *Australian Women's Weekly,* Aug. 2001, pp. 12–22.

8. Paul Kelly, then the editor in chief of *The Australian,* had been with staff at an exotic Sydney restaurant in early 1997 when he saw Lachlan sporting the new haircut. He swore all staff to secrecy.

9. Ali Cromie, "Just Who Is the Chosen One?" *Business Review Weekly,* Nov. 26, 1999, p. 84.

10. Paul Sheahan, "Inside the New Lair," *Sydney Morning Herald,* Apr. 19, 1997, p. 35.

11. Ali Cromie, interview by author, Dec. 2, 2001.

12. Amanda Lulham, "Lachlan Flies the Family Flag," *Sydney Morning Herald,* Sydney, Jan. 1, 1998, p. 57.

13. Neil Chenoweth, "Lachlan the Heir Apparent," *Australian Financial Review,* Feb. 10, 1999, p. 1; Ali Cromie, "Dr. Moose on the Loose at News," *Business Review Weekly,* Sydney, Nov. 26, 1999, p. 86.

14. Richard Kelly Heft, additional reporting by Emilya Mychasuk, "Child's Play," *Sydney Morning Herald,* Dec. 30, 1995, p. 3.

15. Richard Kelly Heft, "Dynasty Daughter," *Scotsman,* Feb. 28, 1996, p. 17.

16. Mathew Horsman, *Sky High* (London: Orion, 1997).

17. Geraldine Brooks, "The Unlikely Murdoch," *GQ,* October 1999, p. 137.

18. Annette Sharp, "Diary," *Sun-Herald,* June 25, 2000, p. 24.

19. Penelope Debelle, "First Among Equals," *Sunday Age,* Mar. 21, 1999, Agenda section, p. 15.

20. Philip Delver Broughton, "Murdoch's Children Ruled Out As He Names Successor," *Daily Telegraph*, London, July 7, 1999, p. 4.

21. Geraldine Brooks, "Murdoch," *New York Times*, Jul. 19, 1998, sec. 6, p. 20.

22. Response filed by Robert S. Kaufman, July 23, 1998, *Anna Murdoch v. Keith Rupert Murdoch*, California Superior Court, BD2823955.

23. Geraldine Fabrikant, "Go East, Not So Young Man," *New York Times*, Oct. 4, 1998, sec. 3, p. 2.

24. Shawcross, "Murdoch's New Life," p. 183.

25. David Lague, Mark Riley, and Penelope Debelle, "The Mistress and Her Mogul," *Sydney Morning Herald*, Apr. 30, 1999, p. 11.

26. John Lippman, Leslie Chang, and Robert Frank, "Meet Wendi Deng: The Boss' Wife Wields Influence at News Corp," *Wall Street Journal*, Nov. 1, 2000.

27. News Corp executive, interview by the author.

28. Shawcross, "Murdoch's New Life."

29. "Rupert's Dragon Lady," *Punch*, Feb. 27–Mar. 6, 1999.

30. Alexandra A. Seno, "People," *Asiaweek*, Oct. 23, 1998, and Dec. 25, 1998.

31. Shawcross, "Murdoch's New Life." p. 135.

32. Lague, Riley, and Debelle, "The Mistress and Her Mogul."

33. Interviews by the author.

34. John Gapper, "A Chip Off the Old Block," *Financial Times*, Oct. 4, 1998.

35. Penelope Debelle, "The Day I Screamed at My Dad Rupert," *Sun Herald* [Sydney], Mar. 21, 1999, p. 58.

36. Emily Bell, Denis Campbell, and Mark Honigsbaum, "How Murdoch Was Caught Offside in United Takeover," *Sunday Telegraph*, Apr. 11, 1999.

37. Reuter's report, "Murdoch Waiting Game On Europe," *Australian Financial Review*, Nov. 2, 1998, p. 30.

38. *News International et al. v. Clinger et al.*, CH 1996 N4257 & 5450, No. 104, High Court, London, Nov. 17, 1998.

39. "Observer," *Financial Times*, April 1, 1999, p. 27.

40. Rupert Murdoch, comment at press conference after News Corp annual meeting, Oct. 1999.

41. Justice Department statement of claim, *United States v. Primestar et al.*, Civil no. 1:98CV01193 (JLG), U.S. District Court, District of Columbia, May 12, 1998.

42. Stephen Keating, *Cutthroat* (Boulder, CO: Johnson, 1999), p. 222.

43. Brian Hale, "EchoStar Snares News's US Satellite Assets for $A1.8 Billion," *Sydney Morning Herald*, Dec. 2, 1998, p. 28.

44. This figure is after allowing for eight-to-one stock splits. The allocation at the time was to be 30 million A shares.

45. This price is after allowing for stock splits. The actual price was $38.81.

46. When EchoStar stock hit $81 in March 2000, its total market value was $38 billion. News Corp and MCI picked up 14.6 percent of EchoStar rather than 37 percent. The 22.4 percent difference in March 2000 was worth $8.5 billion in opportunity cost. News Corp wrote off only $375 million in realized losses, much of which it would have recovered when it sold its rising EchoStar stock.

Chapter 19: The Manhattan Window

1. Mark Honigsbaum, "Astrologer Adds to Fears Sweeping Media Empire as Rupert and Wendy Wed," *Observer* [London], June 27, 1999.

2. "Media Mogul Ties the Knot with the Internet," *Nation,* Jul. 9, 1999.

3. Rupert Murdoch, interview by Willow Bay, *CNN Moneyline,* Sept. 20, 1999.

4. Merrill Lynch, research report on News Corporation, Apr. 10, 2000.

5. *Your World with Neil Cavuto,* Fox News Network, May 29, 2000.

6. William Shawcross, "Murdoch's New Life," *Vanity Fair,* Oct. 1999, p. 183.

7. Simon Mann, "Powerful? Rupert's Your Man, Says Gates," *Sydney Morning Herald,* Oct. 18, 1998, p. 3.

8. Shane Danielson, "Soccer Wars," *Australian,* Jun. 24, 2000, p. 24.

9. "Wake Up Call," *Financial Times,* Observer column, Apr. 7, 2000.

10. This was the total fall in value of just fifty-one high-tech stocks from their 2000 highs. Eleven stocks accounted for $2 trillion of the total. See Neil Chenoweth, "Technology's Mortal Limitations," *Australian Financial Review,* Jan. 20, 2001, p. 25.

Postscript: The Other Side of Tuesday

1. Sallie Hofmeister, "Ted Turner Says Only Two Cable Firms May Survive," *Los Angeles Times,* Nov. 29, 2001.

2. Jim Barthold, "Web on TV No Easy Recipe," *Cable World,* April 10, 2000, p. 20A.

3. Details of NDS section based on court filings in *Groupe Canal Plus and others v. NDS Group and others,* District Court of Northern California, C02-01178.

4. David Leser, "Anna and Her King," *Australian Women's Weekly,* Aug. 2001, pp. 12–22.

BIBLIOGRAPHY

Auletta, Ken. *The Highwaymen: Warriors of the Information Superhighway.* New York: Random House, 1997.

Barry, Paul. *The Rise and Rise of Kerry Packer.* Sydney: Bantam, 1993.

Belfield, Richard, Christopher Hird, and Sharon Kelly. *Murdoch: The Decline of an Empire.* London: Macdonald, 1991.

Bibb, Porter. *Ted Turner: It Ain't As Easy As It Looks.* Boulder, Colo.: Johnson Books, 1993.

Block, Alex Ben. *Outfoxed: Marvin Davis, Barry Diller, Rupert Murdoch, Joan Rivers, and the Inside Story of America's Fourth Television Network.* New York: St. Martin's Press, 1990.

Bruck, Connie. *Master of the Game: Steve Ross and the Creation of Time Warner.* New York: Penguin, 1994.

Bruck, Connie. *The Predators' Ball: The Junk-Bond Raiders and the Man Who Staked Them.* New York: American Lawyer, 1988.

Cashmore, Ellis. *Making Sense of Sports.* London: Routledge, 3rd ed. 2000

Chippindale, Peter, Suzanne Franks. *Dished! The Rise and Fall of British Satellite Broadcasting.* London: Simon & Schuster, 1991.

Chippindale, Peter, and Chris Horrie. *Stick It Up Your Punter.* London: Heinemann, 1990.

Coleridge, Nicholas. *Paper Tigers: The Latest, Greatest Newspaper Tycoons and How They Won the World.* London: Mandarin. 1993, 1994 ed.

Crainer, Stuart. *Business the Rupert Murdoch Way: 10 Secrets of the World's Greatest Deal-Maker.* New York: Amacom, 1999.

Davis, L. J. *The Billionaire Shell Game: How Cable Baron John Malone and Assorted Corporate Titans Invented a Future Nobody Wanted.* New York: Doubleday, 1998.

Eisner, Michael D., with Tony Schwartz. *Work in Progress.* London: Penguin, 1999.

Ellul, Jacques. *The Technological Bluff.* Geoffrey W. Bromiley, trans. Grand Rapids, Mich.: William B. Eerdmans Publishing Company, 1990.

Evans, Harold. *Good Times, Bad Times.* London: Coronet Books, 1984.

Farquharson, Robin. *Theory of Voting.* New Haven: Yale University Press, 1969.

———. *Drop Out!* London: Blond, 1968.

Frow, John. *What Was Post-Modernism.* Sydney: Local Consumption Publications, 1991.

Greenwall, Harry J. *Northcliffe: Napoleon of Fleet Street.* London: Allan Wingate, 1957.

Horsman, Mathew. *Sky High.* London: Orion, 1997.

Inglis, K. S. *The Stuart Case.* Melbourne: Melbourne University Press, 1961.

Jackson, Tim. *Inside Intel.* London: HarperCollins, 1997.

Keating, Stephen. *Cutthroat: High Stakes and Killer Moves on the Electronic Frontier.* Boulder, Colo.: Johnson Books, 1999.

Kiernan, Thomas. *Citizen Murdoch.* New York: Dodd, Mead & Co. 1986.

Kornbluth, Jesse. *Highly Confident: The Crime and Punishment of Michael Milken.* Melbourne: Bookman, 1992 ed.

Leapman, Michael. *Barefaced Cheek: The Apotheosis of Rupert Murdoch.* London: Hodder & Stoughton, 1983.

Lewis, Michael. *The New New Thing: How Some Man You've Never Heard of Just Changed Your Life.* London: Hodder & Stoughton, 1999.

McCracken, Jarrod, with Daniel Lane. *A Family Betrayal.* Sydney: Ironbark Pan Macmillan Australia, 1996.

Mair, George. *The Barry Diller Story: The Life and Times of America's Greatest Entertainment Mogul.* New York: John Wiley & Sons, 1997.

Marjoribanks, Timothy. *News Corporation, Technology and the Workplace: Global Strategies, Local Change.* Cambridge: Cambridge University Press, 2000.

Monks, John. *Elisabeth Murdoch: Two Lives.* Sydney: Macmillan, 1994.

Munster, George. *Rupert Murdoch: A Paper Prince.* Melbourne: Penguin, 1987.

Murdoch, Patrick. *Sidelights to the Shorter Catechism.* Melbourne: Harcliffe, Waddell and Falconer, 1908.

Neil, Andrew. *Full Disclosure.* London: Macmillan, 1996.

Ramsay, Douglas K. *The Corporate Warriors: The Battle of the Boardrooms.* London: Grafton. 1987.

Regan, Simon. *Rupert Murdoch: A Business Biography.* London: Angus & Robertson, 1976.

Shawcross, William. *Rupert Murdoch: Ringmaster of the Information Circus.* London: Pan, 1993. First published 1992, Chatto & Windus Ltd. Also as

Murdoch: The Making of a Media Empire. New York: Touchstone, 1992, 1997 rev.

Stewart, James B. *Den of Thieves.* New York: Simon & Schuster, 1991.

Sykes, Trevor. *Operation Dynasty: How Warwick Took John Fairfax Ltd.* Melbourne: Greenhouse, 1989.

Thompson, Marilyn W. *Feeding the Beast: How Wedtech Became the Most Corrupt Little Company in America.* New York: Charles Scribner's Son, 1990.

Traub, James, *Too Good to Be True: The Outlandish Story of Wedtech.* New York: Doubleday, 1990.

Tucille, Jerome. *Murdoch: A Biography.* London: Piatkus, 1990.

Wasserstein, Bruce. *Big Deal: The Battle for America's Leading Corporations.* New York: Warner Books, 1998.

Wolff, Michael. *Burn Rate: How I Survived the Gold Rush Years on the Internet.* London: Orion, 1998, 1999 edit.

Zwar, Desmond. *In Search of Keith Murdoch.* Melbourne: Macmillan, 1980.

ACKNOWLEDGMENTS

I am deeply indebted to my agent, John F. Thornton, who trudged through five years of turgid correspondence from me while retaining his sense of humor, as the structure of *Rupert Murdoch* evolved through a series of implausible gymnastic positions to reach its present form. I'm also indebted to his partner, Joe Spieler; to my London agent, Abner Stein, and his staff; my editor John Mahaney; and my British editor Geoffrey Mulligan.

This book could not have been written without the generous support and encouragement of my editor at the *Australian Financial Review*, Colleen Ryan. I am particularly grateful for assistance from my colleague Dimity Torbett, from associate professor Deirdre Coleman, Richard Coleman, Ali Cromie, John Davidson, Alan Deans, Valentina Hazell, Dr. Sylvia Haworth, Deborah Light, Karen Maley, Malcolm Schmidtke and Trevor Sykes.

Rupert Murdoch draws heavily from my published work with the *Australian Financial Review* over the last nine years. However, the forensic process is a wide one. By its nature it builds upon the previous efforts of many other journalists and writers, not all of whose contributions can be acknowledged. To those writers whose work, whether for reasons of space, time, or my own lapses I have not been able to properly recognize, please accept my apologies. The failure is entirely mine.

For time out of mind while this book has spluttered into existence, Joëlle Chenoweth has argued with me, laughed with me, and most often covered for me. Despite all this, she still seems to like me.

INDEX

ABC network, 56, 144, 247, 258, 262, 263–64, 270
Adams, Barrie, 85
Adams, James, 65
Adams, Ray, 352, 354
Adleman, Leonard, 89
Adler, Ed, 165
Advanced Communications, 125
Advertiser Newspapers, 4
Advertising, 310
A.E. Harris Trust, 114, 316
Ailes, Roger, 21, 162, 165–67
Ali-Frazier fight (Thrilla in Manila), 52, 134
Allan, Col, 3, 6, 7, 8, 12
Allen, Herb, 133, 135–41
Allen, Paul, 134, 139
Allen & Co., 133, 137, 232
Alpert, Michael, 188
America Online (AOL), 333, 334, 346
    See also AOL Time Warner
America's Talking cable channel, 160, 162
Anaheim Angels, 259, 265, 266
Anaheim Mighty Ducks, 265–66, 270
Anastasia (movie), 263
Anderson, Chris, 251, 252, 254
Angelo, Jesse, 312, 325
Animated films, 260, 263, 350
Annenberg, Walter, 77
Anstrom, Decker, 215, 216
Antunes, Xana, 3, 6, 12
AOL Time Warner, 9, 10, 333–37, 339, 346, 347
Arden, Justice, 97
Arffa, Alan, 168, 170
Argen Limited, 174
Armstrong, Ben, 224
Armstrong, Michael, 15
Arthurson, Ken, 254, 257
ASkyB, 188–90, 192, 193, 196, 217–19, 221, 236, 271, 327–28
AT&T, 276, 346
AT&T Broadband, 9, 15, 346, 349
Atanaskovic, John, 86
Atencio, Judianne, 20, 23, 24, 28, 220
Atex (co.), 59
Auden, W.H., 343
Auletta, Ken, 122, 130, 210–11
Aurelio, Dick, 168
Australia, 5, 60–61, 250, 298–99
Australian, 48, 49, 292
Australian Rugby League, 250–57, 359
Australian Securities Commission, 85–86
Auto industry, 22

Baby Bells, 206, 207, 214, 275, 276
Baen, Jim, 209, 210

Baird, Rick, 137
Baker, Norman, 282
Bakker, Jim and Tammy, 224
Barlow, Frank, 99
Barraclough, Stephen, 103, 104
Barrett, Andrew, 124
Barton, Peter, 197
Baseball, 242–43, 245–46, 248
BBC network, 203, 207, 247, 290
Beddow, David, 187
Beggs, James M., 125
Bell, Eddie, 292–94, 296
Bell Curve, The (Murray and Herrnstein), 284–85
Bennett, Bill, 210
Berg, Jeff, 139
Berlusconi, Silvio, 281, 288, 297
Betsis, George, 310, 325
Bevins, Bill, 143
Bharat Kumar Marya (BK), 102
Binzell, Peggy, 209
Black, Conrad, 298
Black Monday (1987), 70, 73, 77
Blacks, 50, 168, 285
Blair, Tony, 21, 66, 94, 135, 216, 281–83, 285–87, 289, 297, 303, 322
Bliley, Thomas, 208, 210, 213
Blockbuster video stores, 134
Blond, Anthony, 50–51
Bloomberg business news, 170
Bluth, Don, 263
Boies, David, 20
Bonior, David, 211
Booker, Patricia, 11, 48, 49, 307
Booth, Mark, 321, 339
Bornstein, Steve, 267
Boston Herald, 51, 60
Bourne, Adrian, 292, 293–94, 296
Brademas, John, 41
Breindel, Eric, 183
Briggs, Asa, 40, 41
British journalism, 5, 7
British labor unions, 59, 60, 63–67, 77
British Satellite Broadcasting (BSB), 77, 92–94, 96–97
Broadband, 347–48
Broadcasting licenses, 127–29, 184, 185
Bronfman, Edgar Jr., 21, 135, 139, 164
Brown, David, 72
Brown, Steven, 105
Brown's Guide to Growing Gray, 72
Bruck, Connie, 246
BSB. See British Satellite Broadcasting
BSkyB, 9, 97–105, 120, 126, 131, 162, 246–48, 257, 282, 287, 311–12, 321–22, 336–37, 339–41, 348, 350–52, 354

Buffett, Warren, 56, 72, 140, 262, 357
Burchett, James, 250–52, 254–56

Cable Act, 160, 162, 168, 169
Cable television, 247, 269, 273
  antitrust action, 126
  in China, 350
  competition from satellite systems, 196–97, 217–18,
    274–75, 339
  and Congress, 214–15
  and Gates, 274, 276
  innovation by Fox News, 163, 233
  and Internet, 344
  Malone's role, 119, 121, 133–34
  mergers, 345–46
  Murdoch on, 357
  "must carry" provisions, 160
  National Cable Television Association convention,
    216–17
  old analog, 194
  pay-television platforms, 161–62
  pioneers, 185
  Primestar, 127, 128–29, 327
  Prime Ticket, 130–31
  Robertson's first launch, 224
  "Thrilla in Manila," 52–53
  See also specific stations and networks
Cablevision, 131, 266–67, 272, 273, 276
Cameron, James, 140, 263, 281
Campbell, Alastair, 281–82, 322
Canada, 353
Canal Plus, 340, 341, 347, 351, 354–56
Capital Cities/ABC, 56, 129, 134, 140, 262
Carey, Chase, 165, 166, 192, 219, 221, 267, 271, 272
Carmody, Michael, 298
Carr, Sir William, 49
Carr family, 49
Carter, Graydon, 140–41
Case, Steve, 333–34, 336
Castle Rock Entertainment, 139
Cato Institute, 213
CBN. *See* Christian Broadcasting Network
CBS network, 56–57, 143, 144, 247, 257, 278
Cell phones, 344
Chandler, Ken, 3, 6, 12, 160
Chandler, William B. III, 259
Chapman, Robin, 85
Chernin, Peter, 12, 245, 263, 264, 325–26, 357
Cherwell (student magazine), 42
Children's programming, 230–31
Chimbu tribe, 90–91
China, 203–4, 290–92, 295, 296, 298, 303, 350, 356
Chisholm, Sam, 93, 97–98, 101–2, 203, 246–47, 250,
    311–12
Chong, Rachelle, 124
Chris-Craft Industries, 54–55, 156, 341–42
Christian Broadcasting Network (CBN), 225–27, 233,
    234, 236–41
Christian Coalition, 225, 229, 287
Christianity, 286–87
Chrysler Corporation, 22
Chu, Lynn, 209, 210, 212
Churchill, Bruce, 318
Citibank, 79, 81, 87, 96
Citicorp, 84
Clark, Greg, 172, 173
Clifford Chance law firm, 78, 178, 180
Clinger, Michael, 89–90, 94–96, 98–104, 171, 173–82,
    184, 191, 251, 323

Clinton, Bill, 22, 125, 200, 328
CNBC cable channel, 160
CNN (Cable Network News), 55–56, 58, 130, 161, 164,
    167, 215, 344
Coiro, Reverend Gregory, 306
Collins, Joe, 164
Colson, Dan, 289
Comcast Corporation, 268, 274, 276, 346
Commonwealth Bank of Australia, 74–77, 84, 99
Communications Act of 1934, 55
Computers, 4, 59, 64, 141, 347
Conrad, Henrietta, 325
CONUS slots, 126, 193
Copyright, 92, 199, 214, 349
Cote, Denise, 169, 170
Cousins, Geoff, 253–54
Cowley, John, 308
Cowley, Ken, 216, 251, 254, 255, 307, 310
Cox Communications, 268, 271, 276
Crawford, Gordon, 196
Cromie, Ali, 309
Cross, Joe, 310
Crotty, Paul, 167
Cruden Farm, 34–35, 111
Cruden Investments, 45, 47, 68, 69, 74–77, 85, 99,
    111–15, 151, 313, 316, 324–26
Cruthers, Sir James, 89
Cudlipp, Hugh, 44
Cuomo, Mario, 13, 158, 160

Daily News (N.Y.), 5
Daily Telegraph (Great Britain), 288–89
Daily Telegraph (Sydney), 6
Daley, Robert, 164
D'Amato, Alfonse, 160, 169
D'Arcy, John, 76
Davey, Gary, 318
Davies, Quentin, 297
Davies, Ron, 321
Davis, Marvin, 56, 57
Davis, Peter, 96
DBS. *See* Direct Broadcast Satellite
DeConcini, Dennis, 214
DeFranco, James, 186, 187, 188
Deng, Wendi, 10, 14, 21, 138, 317–20, 324, 326,
    330
Deng Rong, 290
Deng Xiaoping, 290
Denks, David, 113
Deutsche Bank, 24
Devine, John, 20, 24, 26, 27
DeVoe, David, 79, 80, 82, 96, 300, 301, 333
Dexenne (co.), 77
Diller, Barry, 14, 28, 56, 61, 90, 115, 123, 133, 134, 142,
    244, 260
Direct Broadcast Satellite (DBS), 125–27, 129, 185,
    186, 188, 190, 194, 198, 268, 275
DirecTV, 9, 11, 15–16, 19, 23, 26, 27, 127, 188, 198,
    338, 345, 353–54
Disney. *See* Walt Disney Company
Disney, Anthea, 292–94, 313
Disney/ABC, 140
Dolan, Charles, 131, 266–67, 270, 272–73
Dole, Bob, 208
Dolphin Memorandum, 83
Dover, Bruce, 317
DreamWorks SKG, 134, 139, 140, 261, 263
Dressler, Fred, 165
Drexel Burnham Lambert, 56, 66, 136, 142

Dunleavy, Steve, 13
Dux, John, 89, 288

East and West (Patten), 292–96
EchoStar Communications, 17, 19–20, 22–28, 126,
   187–88, 191–93, 195–96, 198, 217–22, 235–36,
   267–68, 326–29, 345–47, 349, 354
Edwards, Jonathon, 174
Edwards, Martin, 321
Effros, Stephen, 215
Eisenach, Jeff, 209
Eisner, Michael, 134, 135, 139, 259, 278
   buying of Fox Family, 349, 357
   and Disney/ABC, 140
   and Dolan, 273
   downslide, 262–63
   and ESPN, 129–30, 131, 258
   and Hughes Electronics deal, 28
   and IFE, 272
   and Katzenberg, 138, 142, 260, 261–62
   leveraging of Disney, 260, 262
   and Malone, 122
   Mighty Ducks, 265, 269–70
   proposed venture with Murdoch, 92, 96
   and Robertson, 241, 270
   on successor, 312
   as threat to Fox, 240
   See also Walt Disney Company
Ellen (TV show), 270
Ellicott, Bob, 255, 256
Ellison, Larry, 53
Encryption, 89, 94, 96–98, 172, 194–95, 220, 351–56
Endo-Lase (co.), 95
English, Sir David, 289
Ergen, Cantey, 186
Ergen, Charlie, 17, 218–22, 237, 267
   background, 186
   Direct Broadcast Satellite, 185–88
   and Garner, 126
   Hughes Electronics deal, 18–28, 345
   money problems, 190–91
   and Murdoch, 191–96, 220, 245, 268, 273, 326–29
   personal characteristics, 185–86
   Vivendi deal, 347
   See also EchoStar Communications
ESPN sports channel, 129–30, 258, 262, 266, 267, 273
European Broadcasting Union, 248
European Monetary Union, 284, 287
Evans-Lombe, Justice, 179, 182

Fabrikant, Geraldine, 317
Family Channel, 226–27, 233–36, 267, 270, 273
Farquharson, Robin, 40–44, 51, 345
Farrer & Co., 66, 95
FCC. *See* Federal Communications Commission
FCN. *See* Fox Children's Network
Federal Communications Commission (FCC), 60, 61,
   91, 122–25, 127–30, 154, 160, 185, 189, 207–8,
   210, 358
Federal Trade Commission (FTC), 150, 154, 163–64,
   166
Felker, Clay, 51, 55, 106
Fiber-optic cable, 190, 275, 277, 336
Field, Margot, 352
Fields, Jack, 124, 208, 210
Films. *See* Animated films; Movies; *specific movies*
Financial Times (London), 175, 176
Fischer, Gus, 94, 102, 103, 173–74, 286, 288
Flextech, 133

Flint, Joe, 149
Floricic, Boris, 352–53
Forbes, Malcolm, 72
Forbes magazine, 71–72
Ford Motor Company, 22
Fox Broadcasting Company. *See* Fox television
   networks
Fox Children's Network (FCN), 231–32
Fox Entertainment, 11
Fox Family, 349
Fox Kids, 230, 232–34, 236, 237, 239–40, 270, 272, 273,
   337
Fox News, 8, 155, 161–71, 183–84, 197, 215, 216, 230,
   233, 256, 273, 274, 337, 344–46, 350
Fox Sports, 131, 162, 197, 235, 248, 264–67, 270, 273,
   337, 350
Fox Sports West (FSW), 265–66
Fox Sports West 2 (FSW2), 265–67, 271
Foxtel, 251, 253, 257, 310, 337
Fox television networks, 52, 57, 59, 66, 90, 120,
   122–24, 143–46, 207–8, 210, 311, 337
Freedom of speech, 205–6
Free-to-air stations, 160, 162, 194
Freud, Matthew, 11, 315, 316, 341
FTC. *See* Federal Trade Commission
Full Disclosure (Neil), 304
f/X cable channel, 130, 160–61, 162, 197

Gabelli, Mario, 240
Game theory, 42–43, 345
Garner, Daniel, 125–27, 129, 185, 197
Gates, Bill, 11, 18, 120, 133, 135, 136, 140, 141, 274,
   276, 331, 334, 339–40, 346, 349, 357
Gavenchak, Eugenie, 175, 181
Geffen, David, 134, 139, 140, 261
Gem Plus, 96, 102
General Instruments, 120
General Motors, 9–12, 15–29, 198, 338, 345, 349, 353
Germany, 340, 351
Giddy, Harry, 45, 46, 111, 112
Gingrich, Newt, 199–201, 205–13
Giuliani, Rudolph, 7–9, 10, 156–58, 166–69, 171
Globo Organization, 131
Goldberg, Gary David, 271
Goldman, Gary, 263
Goldman Sachs, 233
Good Society, The (Galbraith), 285
Goodwill Games, 164, 167
Gorbachev, Mikhail, 211–12
Gore, Al, 134
Gray, Jim, 219
Graziano, Bob, 245
Great Britain, 135, 179, 216, 285–89, 294–95, 298, 322
Greene, Martin, 54
Greene, Rupert, 34
Grove, Andy, 141
Grupo Televisa, 131

Hacking, 353, 354
Hadden, Jeffrey, 224
Hamill, Pete, 159
Hamilton, Alexander, 5
Hammond, Eric, 59
Handbury, Geoff, 111
Handbury, Helen, 34, 35, 37, 111, 112, 115
Handbury, Matt, 109–10, 115
Hanover, Donna, 8
HarperCollins, 52, 78, 91, 209–12, 290, 292–94,
   296–97, 303

Harris, Clay, 175
Harris, Scott Blake, 127–28
Hartigan, John, 12
Hatch, Orrin, 214, 215
Hawke, Bob, 60, 61, 88
Hazak, Reuven, 180, 352, 353, 355
Hell Week, 166
Herald and Weekly Times (HWT) group, 34, 45, 46,
    67–68, 74, 77
Heritage Media, 235, 245
Heseltine, Michael, 60
Hill, Brian, 252, 253
Hill, David, 264
Hindery, Leo, 198, 217, 219, 235, 268–69, 271
Hinkle, Robert, 238
Hirschfeld, Abe, 159
Hoffenberg, Steve, 158–59
Hollings, Ernest, 91
Holmes à Court, Robert, 68
Homosexuality, 43–44, 50, 225, 322
Hong Kong, 290, 292, 295, 303
Hontz, Jenny, 149
Horn, Alan, 139
Horsman, Mathew, 99, 313
Howard, John, 21, 216
Huber, Peter, 204–7, 284
Hufschmid, Kathryn, 312, 313, 330, 341
Hughes Electronics, 9, 10, 12, 15–29, 127, 198, 338,
    345, 346, 349
Hundertmark, Bruce, 88–90, 93–95, 110, 176, 211,
    283, 307
Hundt, Reed, 124, 128, 129, 185
Hurricane Floyd, 326
HWT. *See* Herald and Weekly Times (HWT) group
Hygiene, 4

Icahn, Carl, 143
IFE. *See* International Family Entertainment
Independence Day (movie), 140, 263
Independent (Great Britain), 288, 289
Independent Television (ITV), 246
Information revolution, 330–32, 336, 347, 348
Intelligence, 285
International Family Entertainment (IFE), 226,
    233–37, 239–41, 267, 270, 272, 273
International Tennis Federation, 248
Internet, 206, 276–77, 331–32, 335, 336, 344, 347–49,
    357
Irvine, Ian, 96
Israel, 176–80, 182, 183, 191, 195, 272, 303, 351, 356
Italy, 281, 288, 297, 340, 351, 354
ITT hotel group, 267
ITV Digital, 350, 351, 354, 356

Jacobs, Robert, 168
Jaffe, Daniel J., 316, 320
Jerrard Electronics, 120
Jews, 167, 183–84, 225, 272
Jiang Zemin, 290, 291, 292
Johnson, Derek, 168
Jones, Glenn, 217
Jones, William, 112
J.P. Morgan, 18

Kaehlin, Gilles, 354–56
Kalikow, Peter, 158
Katzenberg, Jeffrey, 134, 138, 139, 142, 260–63
Kaufman, Gerald, 44, 295
Kaufman, Robert, 316, 321

Kayarem (co.), 74, 112, 114, 325
Keating, Charles H., 214
Keating, Stephen, 197, 219
Kennedy, Teddy, 91
Kerkorian, Kirk, 57–58, 150
Kesmai (gaming site), 313, 346–47
Kiernan, Thomas, 37, 107, 109, 319
King, Cecil, 45, 50
King David Society, 183
King World Productions, 145, 148, 150
Kinnock, Neil, 216
Kirch Media, 340, 350–51
Kirsch, Michael, 179, 180, 181, 182
Kluge, John, 56, 57, 72
Koch, Ed, 51, 158
Kömmerling, Oliver, 353, 355
Kornizky, Ben Zion, 172–73
Koszniak, Daphna, 174
Krieger, Leo, 100, 173–76, 323
Kristol, Irving, 286
Kristol, William, 200–201, 213
Ku-band broadcast frequencies, 125, 186
Kuhn, Marcus, 353
Kundun (movie), 290

Laing, Adrian, 296
Langan's Bar and Restaurant (N.Y.), 5, 6
Lawson, Nigel, 40
Lescure, Pierre, 340, 351
Lessons Learned the Hard Way (Gingrich), 212, 213
Levin, Gerald, 21, 28, 52–53, 131, 134–35, 138–40,
    153–55, 163–65, 167–70, 190, 217–19, 221, 256,
    268–69, 274, 333–35, 347, 357
Levy, Doron, 177
Lewis, William, 175
Leys, Colin, 41
Liberty Media, 11, 18, 133, 197, 235, 349
Licenses. *See* Broadcasting licenses
Lieberman, David, 219
Liebovitz, Annie, 138
Lindsay, Justice, 100, 104, 105, 181, 182, 191, 323
Lion King, The (movie), 260, 262, 263
Loesch, Margaret, 231, 232
London Post, 64–65
Lord, Shirley, 72
Los Angeles Dodgers, 235, 242–46, 259, 264–65,
    267–70
Losing Ground (Murray), 284
Luppov, Eugene, 211
Lustgarden, Marc, 267
Lutz, Robert, 22

Mackinley, Andrew, 295
MacLeod, Alasdair, 313
MacLeod, Prudence, 48, 49, 107, 307, 313–14, 320,
    324
Madison Square Garden (N.Y.), 267, 272
Mafia, 157–58
Magness, Bob, 119, 197, 274
Mahoney, David, 72
Mahony, Cardinal Roger M., 306
Major, John, 216, 287, 297
Malara, Tony, 143
Maley, Karen, 83–84
Malone, John, 12, 21, 28, 213, 245, 275, 277
    on Direct Broadcast Satellite, 186
    and Dolan, 266–67, 273
    and fiber-optic cable, 190
    and Fox News, 163, 197

Malone, John (*cont'd*)
  and f/X, 160, 162, 197
  and Gates, 274
  at Herb Allen's retreat, 133–36, 138
  and Murdoch, 119–22, 125, 130–31, 136, 163, 168,
    217–19, 235–36, 269
  as possible successor to Murdoch, 12
  and Primestar, 127, 185, 217–19, 268–69, 327
  and Robertson, 233, 234, 272
  satellite license, 127–29, 185
  and Sky Global, 18, 197, 220, 349
  and Time Warner, 155, 164
  and Turner, 58, 164, 168
  See also Tele-Communications Inc.
Malone, Leslie, 119
Manchester United, 321, 322
Mandel, Jon, 227
Mandelson, Peter, 322
Mann, James, 95, 98
Mann, William, 324–25
Marcus, Jeff, 217
Marcus Cable, 217
Mariotta, Tony, 156
Marvel Comics, 143
Masterman, George, 40
Matatyahu, Meir, 100
Maxwell, H.W.H., 213
Maxwell, Robert, 49
Mayer, Peter, 210
Mayne, Stephen, 6
Maynes, Charles William, 202
McCain, John, 9, 213–15
McDonald, Keith, 75, 84
MCI, 126, 128–30, 185, 187–89, 192, 195, 221, 268,
  328–29
McKenzie, Kelvin, 7
McKeown, Jack, 210
Mechanic, Bill, 263
Media, 56, 132–33, 135–36, 141–42, 203, 273–74, 332,
  344, 357
MediaOne, 268, 271, 276
Mediaset, 281, 297
Menard, Allen, 353, 354, 355
Mergers, 345–46
Messier, Jean-Marie, 21, 28, 334, 340, 341, 347, 351,
  354
Metromedia, 52, 56, 57, 59–63, 66, 77, 123
MGM/UA studio, 57, 150
Microsoft Corporation, 11, 18, 25, 141, 274, 276–77,
  339, 346
Mighty Ducks. *See* Anaheim Mighty Ducks
Mighty Morphin' Power Rangers, The (TV show), 231
Milken, Michael, 56, 57, 62, 63, 66–69, 128, 136,
  142–44
Mills, Wilbur, 125
Mirsky, Jonathan, 295
Misty Mountain (Los Angeles), 244–45, 320–21
Mitchell, James, 39, 40
Mobutu Sese Seko, 227
Moonie, Lewis, 287
Moore, Peter, 254–55
Morgenstern, Oskar, 42
Morgenthau, Robert, 157
Morning Glory (yacht), 138, 288
Morris, Chris, 352
Moskowitz, David, 19, 23–25, 27, 28, 192, 195, 221
Movies, 56–57, 92–93, 96, 153, 332
MSNBC, 162, 163–64, 215
Murdoch (Shawcross), 52

Murdoch, Anna (wife), 11, 49, 50, 75, 76, 106–9, 124,
  138, 157, 245, 268, 304–7, 314, 316–17, 319–21,
  324–26, 358
Murdoch, Anne (sister), 35, 37, 111, 112
Murdoch, Dame Elisabeth (mother), 33–38, 45, 46,
  111–14, 325
Murdoch, Elisabeth (daughter), 11, 49, 108, 109, 124,
  285, 304, 307, 311–12, 313, 315, 316, 325, 326,
  341, 348
Murdoch, Grace Helen, 325, 326
Murdoch, Helen. *See* Handbury, Helen
Murdoch, James, 11, 50, 108–9, 307, 312–16, 325, 330,
  341, 349, 357
Murdoch, Janet, 35, 111, 112
Murdoch, Lachlan, 4, 11–12, 14, 21, 50, 53, 82, 109,
  245, 251–52, 255, 256, 307–13, 315, 316, 320, 323,
  325, 330, 338, 341, 349, 354, 357
Murdoch, Prudence. *See* MacLeod, Prudence
Murdoch, Rupert:
  business style as "reverse ferret," 7
  buying of New York Post, 159–60
  challenge to British trade unions, 59, 63–67, 77
  childhood, 35–38
  chronology, 360–65
  close call with bankruptcy, 78–86
  and Ergen, 192–96, 220, 245, 268, 326–29
  family problems, 10–11
  family succession, 110–12, 151, 307, 314, 324–26,
    357
  father's death, 45–47
  and FCC, 207, 210
  finances, 74–76
  at Forbes's party (1987), 72–73
  and Gingrich, 208, 209–12
  handling of crises, 14, 82–83, 183
  and Jews, 183–84, 272
  and Levin, 154–55, 163, 165
  loss of Hughes Electronics deal, 15–29
  loss of *New York Post,* 91
  and Malone, 119–22, 130–31, 136, 163, 218–19, 235
  media empire, 10, 144, 274, 295, 338, 358
  move to West Coast, 157
  at Oxford, 38–44, 51
  and Packer, 249–50, 256–57
  and Perelman, 142–52
  personal charm, 145–46
  Pittsburgh bank incident, 52, 78–86
  political speech, 202–3
  prostate cancer, 340–41
  publication of books by political leaders, 211
  and Roberts, 128–29, 189
  and Robertson, 229–30, 234, 236–37, 239
  satellite empire, 9, 11
  and Turner, 52, 53, 55–56, 155, 161, 167–68, 171,
    183–84, 196, 216–17, 221, 277
  See also specific companies and publications
Murdoch, Sir Keith, 33, 34, 36–38, 40, 44–47, 110–12,
  114, 341
Murdoch Magazines, 110
Murdoch Research Institute, 113
Murray, Charles, 284–85
"Must carry" provisions (Cable Act), 160, 162

Naghiu, Leslie, 227–29
NagraStar, 354
Nantel, Abraham, 172–73, 174, 251
Nash, John F., 42
Nathan, Judith, 8
National Economic Research Associates, 283

National Enquirer, 51
National Football League (NFL), 143–44, 247–48, 257–58, 278, 351
National Hockey League, 248
National Nine Network, 254, 257, 311
National Star, 51
NBC network, 143, 160, 162, 163, 207–8, 210, 247, 248, 258
NDR. *See* News Datacom Research
NDS Group, 323, 337, 350, 351–56, 358
NDSP. *See* News Data Security Products
Nedeltchev, Vesselin Ivanon (Vesco), 353
Neil, Andrew, 65, 93, 283–86, 290, 293, 304
Ness, Susan, 124
Netanyahu, Benjamin, 183, 272
News (Adelaide), 50
News (San Antonio), 50
News Corporation:
    accounting methods, 300–303
    after debt crisis, 109
    Americanization of, 60, 61
    annual meeting, 71, 73
    aversion to paying taxes, 87, 90, 177
    bid for Hughes Electronics, 16–29
    and Britain's national interests, 298
    and BSkyB, 96–105, 162
    close call with liquidation, 78–86
    and EchoStar, 220–21
    and FCC, 122–25, 207, 358
    fear of Murdoch at, 331
    finances, 73–74, 298–303, 358
    and Herald and Weekly Times takeover, 68
    and MCI, 128–29, 188–89, 192, 328–29
    and Metromedia, 60–63
    Murdoch family control, 11–12
    and New World Communications, 147–52
    and Queensland Press, 75–77, 84
    secret side of, 175–76, 180–82, 351–52
    stock structure, 349
    Sydney headquarters, 4
    and Time Warner, 155, 163–71
    and 20th Century–Fox, 56
    value of, 9–10, 62, 67, 72, 73, 114, 115, 189–90, 192–93, 335, 337
    voting stock, 151–52
    and Warner Communications, 54–55
News coverage, 161, 344–45
News Datacom, 105, 172–82, 191, 194, 220, 323, 351, 352
News Datacom Research (NDR), 90, 93, 94, 98, 100, 104
News Data Security Products (NDSP), 90, 97, 99–100, 102–5
News Digital Systems, 172, 194–95
News International, 59, 63, 66, 67, 100, 104, 175, 288–89, 300
News Limited, 45, 46, 48, 112, 251–57
News of the World (Great Britain), 49, 59, 63, 65, 90–91, 152
News of the World Organisation Limited, 49
Newspapers:
    compositing, 64
    offices, 3–5
    pricing, 288–89
    unions, 59, 60, 63–67, 285
    See also specific papers
Newsprint, 288
News Publishing, 90, 99
Newton, Maxwell, 48

New World Communications, 142–52
New York City, 153, 160–61, 163, 166–67, 170, 183, 330
New York magazine, 51, 106
New York Magazine Company, 51
New York Post, 60, 106, 120, 157, 160
    Allan as new editor, 3, 6, 13
    alleged Mafia control of, 157–58
    as America's oldest paper, 5
    close calls with demise, 158–59
    coverage of blacks, 285
    and Giuliani, 7–9, 10
    Hoffenberg's move to save, 158–59
    move in 1990s, 5
    Murdoch's buying of, 159–60
    Murdoch's loss of, 91
    old pressroom, 4
    resemblance to English tabloids, 7
    on Time Warner merger, 167
NFL. *See* National Football League
Nicastro, Louis J., 300
1984 (Orwell), 202
Norman, Greg, 248

O'Brien, Dan, 217
O'Brien, Mark, 253, 255
O'Hare, Sarah, 310, 323, 330, 354
Oldfield, Richard, 325
Olympic Games, 248
O'Malley, Peter, 234, 242–46, 259, 267, 268
O'Malley, Walter, 242, 243
O'Neill, Bill, 88–89
One.Tel, 12, 310
OpenTV, 339
Operation Blessing, 227, 238–39
Optimism, 202
Optus Vision, 251, 253–54
O'Reilly, Tony, 288
Orwell, George, 202–4, 207, 284
Orwell's Revenge (Huber), 204
Osur, Don, 89, 95
Ovitz, Michael, 139, 142, 259, 260

Packer, James, 254, 256, 310
Packer, Kerry, 249–51, 253–54, 256–57, 311
Packer family, 311
Padden, Preston, 192, 193, 196, 208–10, 219–21
PAL television format, 93, 97
PanAmSat, 23, 27
Pandolfi, Filippo Maria, 101
Paramount Pictures, 134
Parris, Matthew, 322
Parry & Romani Associates, 214
Parsons, Richard, 153, 155, 164, 168–70, 274
Pataki, George, 167, 169
Patten, Chris, 292–96, 303
Pay-televison systems, 93, 95–97, 339, 346–50
Pearce, Harry, 19, 26
PEG (public, educational, government) channels, 162, 168–70
Peled, Abe, 180–82, 191, 195, 351, 355
Penguin USA, 210, 212
Perelman, Ron, 132, 138, 142–52
Peters, Fonda, 137
Peyser, Andrea, 8
Philip Morris, 213
Philips, Jeremy, 310
Phoenix Channel, 291, 298, 350
Phoenix Micro, 102, 173

Pianim, Elkin, 124, 285, 304, 311
Piracy, 353–54
Pitofsky, Robert, 163, 164
Pitt, Harry, 40
Pittsburgh National Bank, 79, 82
Platco (Platformco), 338
PointCast, 313
Politics, 201, 204
Porter, Bibb, 53
Power Rangers, 231–32
Predator's Ball, 56, 143
Premier League, 104, 246–47, 339, 351
Pressler, Larry, 208, 210, 213
Price, Tom, 94, 173
Prigmore, Robert M., 226
Primestar, 127, 129, 130, 185, 217–19, 236, 268–69,
     271, 273, 274, 276, 327
Prime Ticket, 130, 266
Prisoner's Paradox, 42–43
Prodi, Romano, 281, 322
Profitt, Stuart, 292–94, 296
Programming, 144, 161–62
Progress and Freedom Foundation, 205–7, 214
Public trust, 184

Queensland Newspapers, 4, 45, 46
Queensland Press, 68, 69, 74–77, 84–86, 113, 114
Quello, James, 124

Rainbow Media, 266–67, 270, 272, 273
Rangel, Charles, 7
Reagan, Ronald, 60, 61
Redstone, Sumner, 28, 134, 135, 139, 184, 267, 272,
     342
Reed, Ralph E. Jr., 225
Regal, Bruce, 168
Regent University, 226, 227, 229, 233, 234, 236, 237,
     240
Reif-Cohen, Jessica, 337, 338
Reiss, Elaine, 168
Reiter, Fran, 167, 168, 169–70
Reverse engineering, 353
Reverse ferret, 7
Ribot, John, 251
Rice, Zeb, 309, 310, 324
Richards, Geoffrey, 66, 95, 96, 103–4
Riley, Mike, 210
Rivest, Ronald, 89
Rivett, Rohan, 50
Roberts, Bert, 126, 128–30, 187, 189
Robertson, Pat, 223–30, 233–41, 245, 267, 270–72,
     287
Robertson, Tim, 226, 233, 236, 237, 241
Rogge, Jacques, 248
Rohm, Wendy Goldman, 181
Rosenthal, A. M., 158
Ross, Steve, 54, 55, 134, 153–54, 155
Roth, Joe, 263
Rothfield, Deborah, 95
RSA encryption system, 89
Rubenstein, Howard, 211, 313
Rugby, 248, 250–57

Saban, Haim, 230–33, 237, 349
Saban Entertainment, 232
Saggiori, Jan, 353, 355
Salhany, Lucy, 231
Samuel Montague (bank), 79, 81
San Antonio Express, 50

Sarazen, Richard, 62, 80, 90, 300–301
Sargent, J. R., 40
Sarno, Tony, 309
Sassa, Scott, 139
Satellite systems, 9, 120–21, 131, 161–62, 185–99, 203,
     214–15, 217–22, 275, 326, 337, 345, 350
     See also Direct Broadcast Satellite; *specific systems*
Scherman, Bob, 188, 218, 219
Schiff, Dorothy, 51
Schneider, John, 139
Schwartz, Murray M., 228
Schwartz, Tony, 261
Schwartzman, Andrew, 123
Seale, Patrick, 39
Searby, Richard, 71, 88
Searle, John, 40
SEC. *See* Securities and Exchange Commission
Secrecy, 89, 172
Securities and Exchange Commission (SEC), 95, 98,
     302, 358
September 11 (2001), 21, 343–44, 345
700 Club, The (TV show), 224, 226, 227, 233, 234, 236,
     238, 240, 270, 272
Seventeen magazine, 77
Shackleton, Robert, 40
Shaffron (co.), 180
Shamir, Adi, 89, 94, 101, 103–5, 352
Shaw, Jack, 23, 26
Shawcross, William, 52, 79, 83, 184
Sheehy, Gail, 107
Sheppard, Audley, 178–82, 191
Shuman, Stanley S., 54, 233
Siegel, Herbert J., 54
Simel, Terry, 164
Sinel, Norman, 168, 170
Siskind, Arthur, 18, 23, 26, 55, 62, 99–100, 102,
     156–57, 160, 166–67, 170, 174–78, 181, 192, 195,
     221, 255, 323
Sissons, Michael, 292, 296
Sizemore, Bill, 238
Skadden Arps Slate Meagher & Flom, 18, 26
Skase, Christopher, 85, 314
Sky, 193–99, 214–15, 217, 220, 222, 235, 245, 268,
     273–76, 352, 357
Sky Cable, 127
Sky Global, 9, 11, 16, 18, 26, 338–39, 341–42, 348–49,
     356, 357
Sky Latin, 131, 162
Sky Television, 77, 88, 91–97
Sloan, Allan, 72
Smart, Michael, 41, 45
Smartcards, 94, 96, 101, 104–5, 173, 352–56
Smith, David, 251, 254
Smith, Jack, 9, 11, 15, 17, 25, 26, 28
Smith, Liz, 271, 306, 320
Smith, Michael, 16, 17, 19, 338
Snoddy, Raymond, 176, 295–96
Soccer, 104, 246, 257, 321, 351
Soley, Clive, 295
Space, 121
Spielberg, Steven, 134, 261
Sports programming, 246–49, 257–58, 264–65, 351
Squadron, Howard M., 55, 183
Squadron Ellenoff Plesent & Lehrer, 55, 62, 63,
     156–57, 159, 171
Star magazine, 51
Star TV, 203–4, 318, 337, 341, 350
Stehrenberger, Peter, 102, 172–74, 251, 288
Stelzer, Irwin, 93–94, 135, 283–87

Stevens, Ted, 215
Stock market, 332, 335, 338, 341, 342, 344
Stothard, Peter, 290, 295
Stream SpA, 337, 351, 354, 356
Stuart, Rupert, 50
Sullivan, Andrew, 5–6
Sun (Great Britain), 7, 49–50, 59, 63, 96, 216, 287, 288, 322
Sunday Times (Great Britain), 51, 59, 63, 65, 284
Sun Microsystems, 339
Sun-Times (Chicago), 51
Sun Valley (Idaho), 132–47
Super League, 252–57, 310
Sydney Bulldogs, 251, 252
Sydney-to-Hobart yacht race, 53–54, 155, 308, 309

Tarnovsky, Christopher, 353–56
Taxation, 87, 90, 174, 176–78, 298–300, 302–3
TBS. *See* Turner Broadcasting System
TCI. *See* Tele-Communications Inc.
Technology, 201–6, 335–36, 342, 344
Telecommunications Act of 1996, 144
Tele-Communications Inc. (TCI), 119, 127, 128, 133, 160, 185, 187, 190, 192, 197, 218, 233–36, 268, 273, 274, 276
Telecommunications technology, 203
Telegraph Group, 289
Telephone companies, 206, 207, 214, 275, 276
Telepiu, 351, 356
Tele-TV, 265
Televangelists, 224
Television, 9, 56–58, 161, 264, 291, 332, 339, 357
    See also Cable television; Satellite systems
Telstra, 251
Tennis, 248
Thatcher, Margaret, 60, 61, 286, 287
Thomson Consumer Electronics, 93
Tibbitts, James, 97
Time magazine, 51, 120
Times (Great Britain), 51, 59, 63, 288–89, 294–95
Time Warner, 8, 127, 131, 134–36, 139, 150, 153–55, 160–71, 190, 216, 218–19, 256, 268–69, 274, 276, 327, 333–36
    See also AOL Time Warner
Tisch, Laurence, 57, 247, 278
Titanic (movie), 140, 263, 281
TNT Limited, 65–66
TNT network, 258
Tobacco industry, 213–14
Toffler, Alvin and Heidi, 210
To Renew America (Gingrich), 212
Totalitarian regimes, 203, 204, 290, 350
Towers Financial Corporation, 159
Townsend, Philip, 108
Triangle Publications, 72, 77, 91
Turner, Ted, 135, 136, 138, 139, 154, 357
    alleged drunken speech after yacht race, 53–54
    background, 52–53
    bid for CBS, 56–57
    on cable industry, 346
    and CNN, 55–56, 161, 164
    and Levin, 52–53, 131, 134, 164–65
    and Murdoch, 52, 53, 55–56, 143–44, 155, 161, 167–68, 171, 183–84, 196, 216–17, 221, 277
    personal attacks on, 167–68
    similarities with Robertson, 225

and Time Warner, 154, 164, 167, 170, 219, 333–34, 335
    See also Turner Broadcasting System
Turner Broadcasting System (TBS), 56, 57–58, 134, 140, 150, 154, 163, 166, 167, 169, 170, 274
TV Guide, 52, 77, 91, 337
20th Century–Fox, 51, 56, 57, 59, 62, 77, 263, 337
20th Holdings Corporation, 61, 122–23

UBS Warburg, 18, 20, 23, 24, 27, 28
Unions, 59, 60, 63–67, 77, 285
United Jewish Appeal (UJA), 183–84, 271
U.S. West, 276

Vacco, Dennis, 170
Vanity Fair, 120, 139, 140–41
Van Sauter, Gordon, 309
Vash, Daniel, 177
Vatistas, Paul, 104
VideoCrypt, 94, 97, 99
Videos, 347
Village Voice, The, 51
Virginian-Pilot, 238–39
Virtuous circle, 277
Vivendi Universal, 21, 335, 340, 341, 347, 349, 351, 354, 356
Vlahos, Michael, 205
Vodafone-AirTouch, 334
Vogel, Carl, 192, 196
Voltaire Society, 41–42
Von Neumann, John, 42
Von Weisl, Niva, 90, 174
Vradenburg, George, 247

Wagoner, Rick, 19, 21, 22, 25, 26
Wallace, Kim, 215
Walt Disney Company, 92, 96, 122, 129–30, 134, 258–63, 265–67, 270, 272, 273, 278, 290, 312, 346, 349
Walton, Sam, 71–72
Warner Bros., 156, 263, 334
Warner Communications, 54–55
Wedtech (co.), 156–57, 171
Weekly Standard, The, 200–201
Weigall, Michael, 39, 41, 42, 44
Weinstein, Jack, 166, 171, 256, 269
Weizmann Institute, 89, 101, 103, 105
Welfare system, 284
Wells, Frank, 261
Westerman, Rick, 221, 271
Westpac (bank), 99
Williams, Jack, 45
Wilson, Howard, 157
Wiretapping, 176, 179–81, 191
WLUK-TV, 124
Wright, Greg, 210
Wright, Jim, 208
Wright, Robert, 135, 163, 207
WTCG (Atlanta), 53
Wyamba (co.), 111
Wyatt, Woodrow, 304

Yeda Research and Development Company, 89, 90
Yelland, David, 322

Zackheim, Adrian, 209
Zaire, 227–28, 238–39
Zhu Rongji, 290–91

ABOUT THE AUTHOR

In 1991 Neil Chenoweth triggered an Australian government inquiry into Rupert Murdoch's family companies—an inquiry that threatened to reverse the secret deals that secure Murdoch's control of his media empire. His forensic style as one of Australia's toughest investigative journalists has made him the leading figure charting both the public and the hidden worlds of the Murdoch empire. He is a senior writer with Australia's daily business newspaper, the *Australian Financial Review*. He was born in Thailand, spent the 1980s in the Middle East, and now lives in Sydney with his wife and two children.